Advances in Artificial Intelligence in Education

Volume 5

This book series focuses on using artificial intelligence (AI) in educational contexts, providing the venue to showcase the latest developments in this rapidly moving field. From personalised instruction to adaptive assessments and immersive learning experiences, AI tools and technologies can revolutionise education and empower educators, students, and decision makers.

A wide range of topics surrounding the use of AI in learning and teaching are explored, covering global perspectives from different communities and disciplines. The book series approaches the use of AI in education with caution and addresses ethical considerations such as data privacy, algorithmic bias, and transparency. By examining AI socially responsible and inclusively, AI's full potential shall be unlocked and create a future of education that is personalised, engaging, and equitable for all learners.

The titles in the series cover the use of AI within K-12 through tertiary settings and in other domains such as professional, lifelong, and work-integrated learning. The series accepts monographs and edited volumes that fit the scope mentioned above and covers various topics, including (but not limited to) tutoring systems, adaptive learning, feedback provision, learner modelling, assessment analytics, as well as teaching and learning support. The series also includes titles covering related issues of ethical and responsible use of AI, data privacy, bias and transparency, educational design, institutional adoption, and inclusion.

Please contact Professor Dirk Ifenthaler at dirk@ifenthaler.info if you wish to discuss a book proposal for the series.

Stamatios Papadakis
Editor

AI Applications in Preschool and Primary Education

Teaching with Artificial Intelligence

Springer

Editor
Stamatios Papadakis
Department of Preschool Education
University of Crete
Rethymno, Greece

ISSN 3004-9903 ISSN 3004-9911 (electronic)
Advances in Artificial Intelligence in Education
ISBN 978-3-032-17189-4 ISBN 978-3-032-17190-0 (eBook)
https://doi.org/10.1007/978-3-032-17190-0

This Springer imprint is published by the registered company Springer Nature Switzerland AG
The registered company address is: Gewerbestrasse 11, 6330 Cham, Switzerland

Contents

Chapter 1
Introduction: Navigating the Intelligence Age in Early Childhood and Primary Education

Stamatios Papadakis

The Pedagogical Pivot: From Digitization to Agency

For the better part of three decades, the discourse surrounding Educational Technology (EdTech) has been governed by the logic of the Information Age. The primary aims were digitization, connectivity, and the democratization of access to static content. The educational landscape is currently undergoing a major change that makes these older paradigms insufficient. We are seeing the transition from the "Information Age" where tools store and retrieve data to the "Intelligence Age," characterized by systems that actively synthesize, generate, and interact with information in ways that mimic human conversation.

The change lies not just in what AI generates, but in its new capacity to act independently. Newer systems can set sub-tasks, connect to other tools, and act with limited oversight, rather than simply producing a text or an image and stopping there. For teachers, this marks a clear break from earlier tools and forces a rethink of how much initiative is delegated to software. We are no longer discussing tools that passively await a student's input; we are discussing systems that can proactively nudge, scaffold, and assess the learner, fundamentally altering the pedagogical dynamic (SURF, 2025).

While the integration of these technologies into higher education has dominated recent policy debates, the formative years of Preschool and Primary Education have historically been treated as a peripheral concern. This volume, AI Applications in Preschool and Primary Education—Teaching with Artificial Intelligence, takes the early years as its starting point instead. It brings together international scholars, researchers, and practitioners to argue that the "digital shift" is a cultural and developmental change, rather than just a technical upgrade, which must be understood from a child-centred point of view.

S. Papadakis (✉)
Department of Preschool Education, University of Crete, Rethymno, Greece
e-mail: stpapadakis@uoc.gr

S. Papadakis (ed.), *AI Applications in Preschool and Primary Education*, Advances in Artificial Intelligence in Education 5, https://doi.org/10.1007/978-3-032-17190-0_1

This question can no longer be left for later stages of schooling. As the European Commission (2025a) argues in Shaping Europe's Digital Future, the deployment of AI must be grounded in conditions where schools can use AI safely and effectively to ensure that technology serves the developmental needs of the child rather than reducing the educational experience to data points. This is nowhere more critical than in the early years, where the boundaries between reality and simulation are fluid, and where the child's cognitive faculties are still developing. If we do not define the pedagogical parameters of AI for our youngest learners, we risk ceding the classroom to the commercial logic of the technology sector.

Why Technology Alone Is Not the Answer: The Framework Guiding this Book

A key tension running through the chapters in this book is the conflict between 'techno-solutionism', the belief that AI can easily solve the complex social challenges of education—and the everyday relationships in the classroom. Education International and the OECD (, 2025) forcefully argue that while AI systems are becoming incredibly sophisticated at pattern recognition and content delivery, they lack the essential human qualities of intentionality, care, and moral judgment. The contributors here do not treat AI as a teacher replacement or as an autonomous tutor. Instead, we adopt a sociocultural perspective, viewing AI as a support tool for reasoning or a cultural artifact.

Co-Regulation and the "more knowledgeable other"

Building on Vygotsky's notion of the Zone of Proximal Development (ZPD), we can think of AI tools as elements within the "More Knowledgeable Other" (MKO) environment. In the traditional classroom, the MKO is usually a teacher or a more experienced peer. When AI is introduced, an adaptive system can, for short periods, take part of this role by offering timely feedback and supporting learners through demanding tasks. This interaction is, however, still different from human pedagogy.

It is vital for educators to understand that generative AI tools function as "prediction engines" rather than sources of truth (Department of Education, 2025). They run on probability rather than pedagogy. The theoretical framework of this book emphasizes 'co-regulation'. The teacher stays responsible; the algorithm does not replace them. AI can ease certain cognitive tasks, but the human teacher leads the process, especially where social-emotional learning and critical inquiry are concerned.

Rethinking Literacy in the Age of AI

We also need to rethink what we mean by 'literacy' in this setting. For a long time, the key message in primary education was simply 'learn to code'. Technical coding skills alone are no longer sufficient. In an age where natural language can generate code, the educational imperative shifts toward "AI Literacy"understanding the agency, mechanisms, and limitations of the systems we interact with (Raspberry Pi Foundation, 2025).

In this view, AI literacy is not only about technical skills; it is also part of preparing children to take part in civic life. According to the AI Literacy XE "AI Literacy" Coalition (2025), this involves equipping young learners with the ability to distinguish between human and machine intent, to recognize that AI is a human-designed tool with specific limitations, and to identify the biases inherent in algorithmic decision-making.

The Rights of the Child: A "design for childhood"

One important strand in recent work—and a guiding principle of this book—is the reminder that children are not simply "small adults" when they interact with AI. The 5Rights Foundation (2025) provides a crucial normative framework here, arguing that the design of AI systems often ignores the specific developmental needs and vulnerabilities of children, treating them as standard users in a digital marketplace.

Throughout the book, the authors assume that AI in early education should follow the "Privacy by Design" and "Safety by Design" principles. This "Design for Childhood" approach requires us to scrutinize the tools we bring into the classroom. For example, commercial Large Language Models (LLMs) are trained on the open internet, a dataset rife with bias, adult themes, and misinformation. UNESCO's (2025) revised orientations warn that introducing such tools to children under the age of 13 without strict mediation poses significant risks to their cognitive and emotional development.

Young children may anthropomorphize chatbots, forming para-social relationships that can exploit their trust or manipulate their behavior. This book advocates an approach where children learn to use AI but also to step back and question it. We must teach young children to use AI tools while simultaneously helping them understand the "machiness" of the machine—demystifying the algorithm so they view it as a tool to be commanded rather than a friend to be trusted.

Protecting Autonomy: Data Sovereignty, Ethics, and Human Oversight

The integration of AI also raises profound questions about schools' ability to decide how data about students is collected and used, as well as about the commercialization of public education. As the French Ministry of National Education (2025) highlights, there is a growing danger of schools becoming dependent on a single company's platform, and of public education systems relying on opaque, proprietary models owned by a handful of global technology giants. In the context of primary education, this is not just an economic issue; it is a critical privacy issue. The data generated by a 6-year-old interacting with an adaptive learning platform is sensitive biometric and cognitive data.

The chapters in this book consistently assume that a teacher should always review and confirm AI suggestions, in line with the "human-in-the-loop" ethical standard outlined by the European Commission (2025b). This principle mandates that decisions that affect a child's educational path such as grading, tracking, or disciplinary action must not be made by an AI system without human review. In the early years classroom, this means the teacher is still the gatekeeper. Following Furze (2025), we can think about ethical integration in terms of three linked concerns:

1. Augmentation over Automation: AI should automate administrative drudgery (lesson planning, resource differentiation), thereby freeing up time for the teacher to engage in high-value, face-to-face interactions.
2. Data Sovereignty: Schools must prioritize tools that guarantee data does not leave the educational environment to train commercial models. As UNESCO (2021) implies in their guidance for policymakers, the growing pressure to measure and store everything children do online must be resisted through strict procurement policies that prioritize educational value over data extraction.
3. Bias Mitigation: Algorithms can show significant bias. In a diverse classroom, when an AI system does not recognize a child's face or understand their dialect, this is more than a technical error; it is an equity problem. Teachers need preparation to notice these patterns, report them, and, where appropriate, use them as starting points for discussion about fairness and technology.

From Theory to Practice: Adaptive and Generative Modalities

In the chapters that follow, AI is discussed in relation to two kinds of classroom use.

Adaptive AI refers to systems designed to personalize learning paths. As discussed in Part III, tools like Intelligent Tutoring Systems (ITS) analyze a student's performance in real-time to adjust the difficulty of mathematics problems or reading tasks. In primary education, these tools promise more tailored support for individual pupils than a single teacher can easily provide in a large class. At the same time, educators must remain alert to the risk that such systems narrow the curriculum or isolate pupils behind screens.

Generative AI (GenAI) introduces new possibilities for children's creative work. In the early years classroom, GenAI can act as a tool that helps children create stories, images, or code, generating illustrations for a child's story or coding blocks for a robot. This technology is plagued by the "hallucination" problem, where models present falsehoods as facts. As the European Commission Joint Research Centre (2025) warns, this causes a shift in teaching practice from "instruction" to "curation, "where teachers guide students in evaluating and refining AI outputs.

Structure of the Book

The book moves from core ideas to classroom practice, and finally to the ethical and policy questions that surround AI in early education.

Part I sets out the main ideas that underpin the rest of the book. It moves from linguistic inclusion in Chap. 1, which examines AI's role in bilingual development, to the ethical imperatives discussed in Chap. 2. Chap. 3 completes the section by treating AI as a technology that carries ideas and values from the society in which it was built and using literary translation to explore how meaning travels between systems and languages.

Part II turns to the people who must make AI work in real schools: teachers. We first show in Chap. 4 how co-designing curricula can foster teacher ownership and then explore the transition from anxiety to mastery in Chap. 5. Chap. 6 complements this by offering practical strategies for using ChatGPT to differentiate instruction, directly addressing the workload challenges faced by primary teachers.

Part III focuses on concrete tools and resources and offers a set of practical resources for teachers who want to experiment with AI in their own classrooms. It begins with Chap. 7, which connects AI literacy to playful inquiry, and Chap. 8, which offers a framework for selecting digital narrative platforms. The focus then narrows to mathematics, with Chapters 9, 10, and 11 providing specific guides for resource generation, concept teaching, and automated assessment. These chapters emphasize the "Human-in-the-Loop" model, showing how teachers can curate AI outputs to suit specific learning goals.

Part IV looks at what happens when AI becomes a partner in creative work. It analyzes teachers' perspectives on the challenges of Generative AI in Chap. 12. Chap. 13 then proposes a novel pedagogical approach, using "AI Personas"to ease co-creativity in the classroom. This section challenges the notion of AI as a passive tool, positioning it instead as an interactive partner in the creative process.

Finally, Part V widens the focus from classrooms to systems. It examines national contexts and global challenges through the lens of Irish primary schools (Chap. 14) and sustainability education (Chap. 15). Chap. 16 critically reviews AI-driven assessment tools, while Chap. 17 provides a comprehensive scoping review of the field. These chapters bring us back to questions of policy, equity, and assessment. They ask what happens when the ideas and tools discussed earlier meet real systems of regulation and accountability.

Moving Forward

As new technologies enter early childhood education, this book aims to help educators make deliberate choices about how, when, and whether to use AI in their own settings. The contributors to this volume do not shy away from the complexities of the digital divide, the lack of transparency in how many AI systems work, or the need for robust data protection. They share a collective optimism that with the right frameworks—rooted in pedagogy rather than profit—AI can be a way to help more children take part and create in meaningful ways.

We hope that the combination of conceptual chapters and concrete examples will help educators to make informed decisions about AI use, and to keep children's interests at the centre of those decisions.

References

5Rights Foundation. (2025). *Guidance for the AI code: Designing for children's rights*. https://5rightsfoundation.com/resource/children-ai-design-code/

AI Literacy Coalition. (2025). *The blueprint for action: Comprehensive AI literacy for all*.

Department of Education. (2025). *Guidance on artificial intelligence in schools*. Government of Ireland. https://assets.gov.ie/static/documents/dee23cad/Guidance_on_Artificial_Intelligence_in_Schools_2025.pdf

Education International & OECD. (2025). *AI and the future of pedagogy: Teaching in a world with intelligent machines*.

European Commission. (2025a). *Artificial intelligence: Shaping Europe's digital future*. Publications Office of the European Union. https://digital-strategy.ec.europa.eu/en/policies/european-approach-artificial-intelligence

European Commission. (2025b). *Ethical guidelines on the use of artificial intelligence (AI) and data in teaching and learning for educators*. Publications Office of the European Union. https://op.europa.eu/en/publication-detail/-/publication/d81a0d54-5348-11ec-91ac-01aa75ed71a1

European Commission, Joint Research Centre. (2025). *Generative AI outlook report 2025*. Publications Office of the European Union. doi:https://doi.org/10.2760/1109679.

French Ministry of National Education. (2025). *Guidance on the future of computer science education in an age of AI*.

Furze, L. (2025). *Teaching AI ethics: A guide for educators*. https://leonfurze.com/ai-ethics/

Raspberry Pi Foundation. (2025). *Why kids still need to learn to code in the age of AI* [Position paper]. https://static.raspberrypi.org/files/about/Why-kids-still-need-to-learn-to-code-in-the-age-of-AI-2025-Raspberry-Pi-Foundation-position-paper.pdf

SURF. (2025). *Tech trends 2026: Agentic AI and the future of education*. https://www.surf.nl/files/cocoon_media_files/surf-tech-trends-2026_ttr26.pdf

UNESCO. (2021). *AI and education: Guidance for policy-makers*. UNESCO Publishing. https://unesdoc.unesco.org/ark:/48223/pf0000376709

UNESCO. (2025). *Guidance on generative AI in education and research* (Revised orientations). UNESCO Publishing. https://unesdoc.unesco.org/ark:/48223/pf0000386693

Part I
Conceptual Foundations of AI in Early Childhood

Chapter 2
Exploring AI for Bilingual Language Development in Early Education: Current Applications and Future Directions

Trisha Thomas

Abstract This chapter examines the current applications of AI technologies in supporting bilingual language development in preschool and primary schools. AI-driven tools offer personalized, culturally responsive learning experiences that can promote heritage language acquisition. However, challenges remain, including biases in speech recognition technologies, effectively handling code-switching, and the limitations of ASR systems in accurately recognizing bilingual speech. This chapter will review existing research on the integration of AI in bilingual education and explore future directions for overcoming these technological barriers to create more inclusive and effective learning environments for young multilingual learners.

Keywords Speech recognition · Bilingual development · Conversational agents · Learning tools

Introduction

The present chapter situates bilingual language development within the broader theme of Artificial Intelligence integration in early and primary education. It explores how emerging AI technologies, such as conversational agents and adaptive systems, can complement and enhance developmentally appropriate pedagogy in multilingual classrooms. The chapter examines the practical applications of these tools for fostering language and literacy, aligning them with the unique learning trajectories of young bilingual children. Key design challenges are addressed, including handling child speech and code-switching. to ensure these innovations responsibly serve diverse learners. By drawing on classroom realities, it offers actionable insights for educators and stakeholders looking to develop and integrate AI tools for young learners.

T. Thomas (✉)
Harvard University, Cambridge, MA, USA
e-mail: trisha_thomas@g.harvard.edu

S. Papadakis (ed.), *AI Applications in Preschool and Primary Education*, Advances in Artificial Intelligence in Education 5, https://doi.org/10.1007/978-3-032-17190-0_2

Digital tools and programs that use AI offer new ways to supplement learning opportunities, personalize instruction, and support diverse student needs. Common uses of these tools include adaptive learning platforms, intelligent tutoring systems, and speech recognition technologies. These innovative technologies have substantial potential to transform how children engage with language learning, both in and out of the classroom. With millions of children worldwide being raised in multilingual households and many more learning a second language in school, the demand for effective language support has never been greater.

Although bilingualism in early childhood has been linked to cognitive benefits, such as greater cognitive flexibility, recent research indicates that these advantages may not be as universal or consistent as once thought (see Bailey et al., 2020, for a review). Nevertheless, it is well established that children are fully capable of acquiring multiple languages simultaneously, and bilingualism can provide certain long-term academic and linguistic benefits when supported appropriately. Despite these potential benefits, implementing effective bilingual education remains a challenge, particularly in settings where resources and bilingual educators are limited. AI tools have the potential to bridge these gaps by providing interactive, personalized learning environments. However, these technologies do not come without their risks and challenges. Scientists and developers are still studying whether these tools are effective and accessible across diverse groups of learners. It is also important to consider the pedagogical implications of their widespread use.

This chapter explores the intersection of AI and bilingual language development in early education. It provides a general summary of existing AI applications that support young bilingual learners and some challenges and limitations associated with their use. The chapter concludes with a discussion of future research directions and the evolving role of AI in bilingual education. The chapter is structured as follows: Section Background and Theoretical Framework provides an overview of AI in language education and discusses cognitive and linguistic considerations in bilingual education, particularly the developmental factors that influence how young children engage with AI technologies. Section Current Applications of AI in Bilingual Language Development reviews some current AI applications for early bilingual learners. Section Challenges and Limitations discusses challenges related to equity, accessibility, and pedagogical integration. Finally, Sect. Future Directions and Research Opportunities outlines future research directions and discusses implications for educators. Overall, the chapter aims to provide readers with a deeper understanding of the potential and limitations of AI in early bilingual language development.

Background and Theoretical Framework

An Overview of AI in Language Education

The use of AI in language education has been expanding rapidly, with growing research interest in its ability to analyze learner input, provide personalized feedback, and facilitate meaningful language practice. The core of AI's educational potential lies in its ability to enhance learning outcomes through adaptive and interactive environments. Numerous applications have emerged, each addressing distinct aspects of the language learning process.

To better understand the breadth of AI's role in education, Kukulska-Hulme and Lee (2020) proposed a useful framework that classifies the impact of AI in educational contexts into three categories: learning for AI (developing AI literacy and skills to design or manage AI technologies), learning about AI (understanding how AI works and its implications), and learning with AI (using AI tools to support learning). The current chapter focuses on learning with AI, particularly in the context of early bilingual language development. Within this category, they further identified three types of applications: system-facing tools that support institutional administration, student-facing tools that provide learners with personalized feedback and practice opportunities, and teacher-facing tools that assist educators by automating administrative and pedagogical tasks (Son et al., 2023). These classifications provide a conceptual foundation for examining AI's practical contributions to language education.

In bilingual learning, AI technologies are being used across age groups through multiple channels. AI is used to analyze both textual and spoken input, deliver adaptive feedback, and facilitate interactive learning experiences. Table. 2.1 summarizes the most prominent AI applications and their roles in language learning contexts

As AI technologies continue to advance, their applications in language education hold significant promise for supporting bilingual children. AI can support language acquisition and learner engagement by offering personalized, interactive, and linguistically rich environments. However, to fully realize these benefits, these technologies must be designed with an understanding of the cognitive and linguistic development of young learners. The following sect. (Cognitive and Linguistic Considerations for Bilingual Education) addresses these developmental considerations in the context of bilingual education.

Cognitive and Linguistic Considerations for Bilingual Education

Historically, concerns about bilingualism often centered on the belief that exposure to multiple languages could impede children's acquisition of the dominant societal language. As a result, many families and educators discouraged the use of heritage languages, fearing that bilingualism might result in confusion or delay language

Table. 2.1 Overview of AI Tools for Language Learning

Applications	Description	Impact on language learning
Natural language processing (NLP)	Enables machines to interpret human language for tasks like translation and text analysis	Facilitates learner input analysis and generates adaptive language tasks (Alhawiti, 2014)
Data-driven learning (DDL)	Uses corpora to help learners discover language patterns and grammatical rules	Promotes pattern recognition and authentic language exposure (Boulton & Cobb, 2017)
Automated writing evaluation (AWE)	Provides immediate feedback on grammar, coherence, and structure	Enhances writing accuracy and autonomy (Rahimi et al., 2024; Stevenson & Phakiti, 2019)
Computerized dynamic assessment (CDA)	Offers tailored feedback to assess learners' developmental potential	Supports diagnosis and scaffolded L2 growth (Shabani, 2012)
Intelligent tutoring systems (ITSs)	Adapts instruction to individual learner needs	Provides personalized practice and adaptive feedback (Son et al., 2023)
Automatic speech recognition (ASR)	Transcribes spoken input for fluency and pronunciation assessment	Improves pronunciation and speaking skills in mobile learning apps (Korzekwa et al., 2022; McCrocklin, 2019)
Chatbots and conversational agents	Simulate real-time dialogue with learners	Increase interaction and willingness to communicate (Huang et al., 2022; Jeon, 2024)

This table presents key types of AI tools used in early bilingual education. Examples are illustrative and may not represent an exhaustive list.

development. However, by the early 2000s, this perspective began to shift, giving rise to the concept of a "bilingual advantage"— the idea that bilingualism offers cognitive, academic, and/or social benefits. Some studies have suggested that bilingual children may exhibit enhanced executive functions, such as attentional control, working memory, and cognitive flexibility (Ali & Al-Mahmoud, 2023; Bialystok & Craik, 2015). These findings contributed to growing enthusiasm for bilingual education. Nonetheless, the evidence remains mixed, with some studies questioning the extent and consistency of the cognitive advantages associated with bilingualism (see Klein, 2016).

Despite these ongoing debates, there is now broad consensus that children are capable of acquiring multiple language systems simultaneously. Their cognitive flexibility allows them to navigate different linguistic environments, and young learners are particularly adept at absorbing phonetic inventories and grammatical structures across languages (Kuhl, 2010). Consequently, there is increasing interest in bilingual and heritage language education, particularly for young children, whose language acquisition can benefit from early and sustained exposure to their languages. This growing interest in bilingual education has also sparked new attention to how AI might be used to enhance both language and cognitive development. Emerging

AI technologies such as those incorporating adaptive feedback, turn-taking, and attention-based interactions may help support the development of executive functions, including cognitive flexibility, working memory, and attention control in bilingual learners (see Pergantis et al., 2025, for a review).

However, when integrating AI technologies into bilingual education, it is important to consider the developmental stage of the learners, especially with regard to their cognitive and linguistic abilities. Many young learners who engage with AI tools, such as chatbots and Automatic Speech Recognition (ASR) systems, are still developing foundational reading and writing skills. As a result, these children may rely more heavily on spoken language when interacting with AI technologies. This reliance on spoken input and output presents unique challenges, particularly given the developmental trajectory of children's speech systems.

Children's vocal tracts and articulatory systems are still maturing, which can influence their pronunciation and speech production. For instance, plosives such as [p] and [t] tend to be acquired earlier, whereas liquids like [ɹ] and [l] develop later, often posing greater difficulty for young learners (McLeod & Crowe, 2018). These developmental differences can impact children's ability to engage effectively with ASR systems, which may struggle to accurately recognize and transcribe immature or non-standard speech patterns. Consequently, AI systems designed for young bilingual learners need to account for these developmental factors to ensure more accurate speech recognition and meaningful feedback.

By acknowledging these cognitive and linguistic considerations, AI tools can be better optimized to support young bilingual learners. Designing adaptive technologies that account for phonological development and speech variability can enhance the effectiveness and accessibility of AI applications in bilingual education. The next section explores existing AI applications in this field.

Current Applications of AI in Bilingual Language Development

AI-Driven Learning Tools for Early Bilingual Learners

AI technologies are increasingly being employed to support bilingual language development in early childhood by providing interactive, adaptive, and engaging learning experiences. These tools create opportunities for young learners to develop language skills through dialogue and interactive play, supporting multilingual language acquisition. As AI systems become more sophisticated, they are increasingly being explored as tools for supporting language development during a developmental period that can strongly influence phonetic and syntactic acquisition (Li, 2018; Li, 2024).

One of the most common applications of AI in early education is through intelligent tutoring systems (ITSs). These systems provide young learners with individualized, scaffolded language instruction that adapts to their developing linguistic abilities. They analyze learner input and modify content dynamically, ensuring that children receive targeted support in both languages. In bilingual contexts, ITSs can alternate between languages, model accurate grammar and vocabulary, and offer interactive exercises that aim to promote balanced language acquisition. For early learners, AI-driven systems can incorporate playful and intuitive interfaces that maintain engagement while gradually introducing complexity. Tools like Khan Academy Kids and ABCmouse demonstrate how AI can support young learners by adapting content to their skill levels, though further research is needed on their impact in bilingual learning environments.

Another growing application is AI-powered storytelling and conversational agents, which aim to provide early bilingual learners with immersive and dynamic language experiences. These tools adapt narratives based on a child's input in service of their comprehension and engagement (see Xu et al., 2023; Xu et al., 2024). AI-enhanced storytelling can introduce culturally relevant material, presenting multilingual content in ways that are meaningful and accessible to children. Platforms such as Bookful and Novel Effect integrate AI to personalize the reading experience by adjusting language complexity, vocabulary, and narrative elements in real time. Conversational agents also engage young learners in dialogue, encouraging them to practice speaking in both languages while reinforcing linguistic patterns, including syntactic structures, morphological rules, and core vocabulary.

In addition to voice and computer-based interactions, AI-powered social robots have been used to support early language learning (see van den Berghe et al., 2019, for a review). Social robots, such as NAO, iROBI, and Inky, create interactive and engaging environments where young learners can practice language through play and conversation. These robots can simulate natural dialogue, model language use, and encourage participation through both verbal and nonverbal cues. By adapting their responses to the child's input, these robots create a more personalized and immersive experience. Studies have shown that interacting with humanoid robots can enhance vocabulary acquisition, improve conversational skills, and build children's confidence in using a second language (Alemi et al., 2014; Kennedy et al., 2016). Robots designed for early learners often incorporate games, storytelling, and problem-solving activities that encourage sustained engagement and deeper language learning.

Tools like these demonstrate how AI can support bilingual learning through adaptive practice and interactive dialogue. Many of these applications depend on underlying Automatic Speech Recognition (ASR) technologies to function effectively with young learners. The following section explores the specific role of ASR in supporting bilingual language development.

Speech Recognition and Conversational AI for Language Development

Automatic Speech Recognition (ASR) is a foundational technology that enables young bilingual learners to engage with spoken language and receive immediate feedback on pronunciation and fluency. In early language development, ASR systems play an essential role by allowing learners to practice producing phonemes (speech sounds), lexical items (words), and syntactic structures (sentence patterns) in both languages. Because children's vocal tracts and articulatory patterns are still maturing, ASR tools designed for young learners must account for developmental variability in speech production and phonological patterns. However, ASR accuracy for children particularly younger or bilingual speakers remains a significant challenge, as will be discussed further in Sect. Challenges and Limitations.

Several commercially available apps, such as Speech Blubs and Lingokids, have integrated child-friendly ASR features aimed at promoting playful language exploration and providing feedback on pronunciation. While these tools are increasingly popular, peer-reviewed research on their pedagogical impact remains limited, and further study is needed to evaluate their effectiveness in real-world bilingual learning environments.

Conversational AI systems, such as chatbots and interactive virtual assistants, also aim to provide young learners with opportunities to engage in simulated dialogues that encourage bilingual language use. These AI systems can create low-pressure environments in which children practice conversational skills and experiment with different language structures to develop fluency. Examples of commercially available conversational agents for children include Moxie and Woogie. These systems are designed to foster back-and-forth dialogue, potentially supporting language comprehension and production through interactive conversational engagement. However, independent evaluations of their educational impact remain limited (but see Hurst et al., 2020).

Advancements in conversational AI are enhancing its capacity to support bilingual learners by providing context-rich conversations and culturally relevant interactions that promote balanced language development. To fully realize this potential, continued research is essential to assess their impact on early bilingual outcomes and to ensure equitable access for all learners.

Challenges and Limitations

While this section focuses primarily on technical and developmental challenges related to speech recognition and multilingual input, it is important to acknowledge that broader ethical issues are also critical when considering the integration of AI in bilingual education. These are discussed further in Sect. Addressing Bias and Equity in AI-Based Language Learning.

Biases in AI Speech Recognition for Bilingual Learners

While ASR is an invaluable technology for facilitating access to AI-enhanced learning for young children, it is not without challenges. It is well-documented that machine-learning technologies are susceptible to biases based on age, race, gender, and other demographic factors (Castro, 2019; Chouldechova, 2017; Chouldechova & G'Sell, 2017; Obermeyer et al., 2019). These biases extend to ASR systems, which have been shown to exhibit disparities in transcription accuracy across different linguistic and demographic groups (see Koenecke et al., 2020). Models used to train the systems can struggle to account for the phonological, phonetic, and prosodic characteristics of non-standard dialects.

Similar challenges arise in the context of bilingual learners. Bilingual children often acquire two distinct phonological systems simultaneously, and while research shows that they can differentiate between these systems by the age of two (Meisel, 1989), cross-linguistic transfer the influence of one language on another can result in phonetic and prosodic patterns that diverge from monolingual norms (Barlow, 2003; Fabiano & Goldstein, 2005; Hossein Keshavarz & Ingram, 2002). These interactions between languages may confuse AI models, leading to inaccuracies in transcription and misaligned feedback. Moreover, minority languages and regional dialects are often underrepresented in ASR training data, further contributing to errors when processing the speech of bilingual and heritage language speakers.

Even for monolingual children, ASR systems face limitations. The majority of training data is drawn from adult speech samples (Y. Zhang et al., 2024), whereas children's developing speech systems—marked by age-specific articulation and intonation patterns—can lead to inaccurate transcriptions or misinterpretations of their responses.

Handling Code-Switching and Multilingual Interactions

Code-switching, alternating between two or more languages within a single conversational exchange or utterance, is a common and natural phenomenon among bilingual speakers (Poplack, 2000). Young bilingual learners frequently engage in code-switching as they navigate different linguistic environments, using elements from both their heritage language and the societal language to express themselves. However, many AI models, including ASR systems, often struggle to process mixed-language input accurately. Most AI systems are designed to operate in monolingual contexts, making it difficult for them to recognize, parse, and transcribe code-switched speech effectively (Madhumani et al., 2020).

Even multilingual AI models trained on diverse datasets struggle to capture the fluid and dynamic nature of code-switching (Hsieh et al., 2020). Recognizing when a speaker has switched languages, identifying appropriate linguistic boundaries, and maintaining contextual coherence across languages remain substantial challenges.

These limitations reduce the accuracy and usefulness of AI-driven tools for young bilingual learners, who naturally switch between languages as part of their cognitive and linguistic development (Bhardwaj et al., 2022; Wills et al., 2023).

Preparing Educators to Integrate AI Tools Effectively

The effective integration of AI technologies in bilingual education requires that educators not only understand how to use these tools, but also recognize their pedagogical strengths and limitations. Professional development and ongoing support are essential to ensure that AI applications are implemented meaningfully and responsibly in the classroom (Tan et al., 2025; Walter, 2024; X. Zhang, 2024). However, many educators lack experience with AI tools and may feel unprepared to evaluate or integrate them into bilingual learning environments. Some may overestimate the capabilities of AI, leading to an overreliance on technology without sufficient pedagogical insight, while others may struggle to interpret AI-generated feedback or adapt tools to their students' needs.

Another challenge lies in evaluating the transferability of learning outcomes observed from these tools (Weng et al., 2024). Gains observed in AI-mediated learning environments may not always extend to broader language proficiency or real-world language use. Educators must be equipped with the skills to critically assess the effectiveness of AI tools, adapt them to the specific needs of their learners, and avoid potential pitfalls associated with misuse or overuse. Schools may also benefit from the involvement of technology specialists or instructional designers who can support teachers in aligning AI use with established educational goals, ensuring that these tools complement, rather than replace, traditional language teaching practices. These challenges underscore the need for ongoing research and thoughtful design to ensure that AI tools serve all learners equitably. The next section outlines future directions and practical strategies for improvement.

Future Directions and Research Opportunities

As these challenges demonstrate, addressing the limitations of current AI tools requires not only critical reflection, but also innovation. The following section outlines areas for future development, including the need for more inclusive AI models, ethical and equitable practices, and collaborative efforts to support teachers in meaningfully integrating AI into classroom instruction.

Improving AI Models for Multilingual Learning

One of the most pressing areas for future research is the improvement of AI models to better support young multilingual learners. Although multilingual corpus data is becoming increasingly available for model training, there remains a need to include a broader range of linguistic inputs, including non-standard dialects, heritage languages, and child speech. Recent models trained on more diverse datasets have shown promise in processing code-switching and recognizing accents with greater accuracy, but their performance in real-world bilingual learning contexts remains inconsistent (Ugan et al., 2024). Building comprehensive and inclusive datasets can lead to more accurate and culturally responsive AI applications. Future research should also examine the impact of guided practice facilitated by ASR-powered apps on pronunciation development, particularly for young learners who rely more heavily on spoken input (H. H.-J. Chen, 2011; Dai & Wu, 2023; Dizon, 2017; Evers & Chen, 2022; S. McCrocklin, 2019; S. M. McCrocklin, 2016).

ITSs are expected to become increasingly sophisticated, with advances in NLP enabling these systems to provide highly individualized, targeted feedback on written interactions. Research should explore how ITSs can be optimized for children's learning by evaluating cognitive, emotional, and behavioral states using big data, and by aligning instruction with personalized learning goals (Son et al., 2023).

Similarly, chatbots powered by adaptive algorithms can offer real-time, human-like feedback. Future research may explore how these models can reliably assess learner progress and generate age-appropriate, responsive interactions (Ashfaque et al., 2020; Gutiérrez, 2023; Kerlyl et al., 2007). As models such as ChatGPT and other AI-powered conversational agents continue to advance, they present opportunities for enhancing early bilingual education by supporting engaging, adaptive, and context-rich learning environments.

Addressing Bias and Equity in AI-Based Language Learning

Addressing bias and promoting equity in AI-based language learning is essential to ensure that all learners regardless of socioeconomic status, linguistic background, or geographic location have access to high-quality educational tools and experiences. Research has shown that language-minority learners, such as Spanish heritage speakers in the United States, often face educational disparities, partly due to limited early exposure to academic language in their home language (Irwin et al., 2021). Without careful design and evaluation, AI tools risk reinforcing these disparities by reflecting existing societal and linguistic biases.

Future research must grapple with the ethical implications of AI integration in educational contexts, including concerns around data privacy (e.g., how children's speech is collected, stored, and used), cultural representation (e.g., whether narratives reflect diverse identities), algorithmic accuracy, and environmental impact.

Addressing these issues will require coordinated efforts from researchers, developers, and educators to design inclusive systems that provide equitable access and meaningful learning opportunities across socioeconomic and linguistic backgrounds.

One area where cultural responsiveness is especially important is in the development of AI storytelling applications for bilingual educational settings. These tools should be designed with particular attention to cultural relevance and sensitivity to avoid perpetuating stereotypes or marginalization (G. Chen, 2024). AI models used in multilingual and multicultural contexts should reflect the lived experiences and linguistic realities of the learners they serve. Developing culturally responsive AI systems that promote inclusivity and linguistic diversity will help ensure that these technologies provide empowering learning experiences for all students.

AI and the Classroom: Practical Applications for Educators

As AI technologies become increasingly embedded in educational settings, their successful application in bilingual classrooms depends on thoughtful integration into everyday teaching practices. Beyond training and the needs outlined in Sect. Preparing Educators to Integrate AI Tools Effectively, educators play an integral role in shaping how AI tools are used to meet language learning goals. This involves making pedagogical choices about when and how to incorporate AI-based tools to ensure they complement, rather than replace, human interaction and culturally responsive instruction. Collaboration between educators, policymakers, and technology developers will be key to designing AI tools that are aligned with curriculum standards and sensitive to the linguistic and developmental needs of bilingual learners (G. Chen, 2024). Educators bring valuable insights into classroom dynamics, helping to shape tools that are both instructionally relevant and adaptable to a range of learning contexts.

To support meaningful integration, educators can start by selecting AI tools that offer multilingual content and customizable difficulty levels. They should establish clear pedagogical goals before introducing AI into lessons, such as targeting vocabulary growth or encouraging verbal participation. Teachers can also create structured reflection activities to help students critically evaluate their interactions with AI. Additionally, partnering with technology specialists or researchers can help schools adapt tools to better align with local linguistic and cultural contexts.

Promoting AI literacy among both educators and students is equally essential, not only to ensure these tools are used ethically and supportively, but also to help level the playing field for students from lower socioeconomic backgrounds, who may have less exposure to emerging technologies at home due to cost or access limitations. Indeed, research suggests that improving AI literacy can enhance students' academic well-being and educational outcomes (Xiao et al., 2024). Educators should recognize that AI is quickly becoming a permanent fixture in education. Both children and educators must understand how to use it critically, ethically, and effectively.

AI-enhanced learning environments offer the potential for personalized, adaptive instruction that can supplement classroom-based learning. However, educators must be mindful of the limitations of these systems and consider how best to balance the use of AI with more traditional, interactive language teaching approaches. Importantly, the focus should not be on maximizing AI use but on enhancing the quality of teaching and learning and on identifying how AI can best serve that goal. Looking ahead, the main challenge will be to ensure that AI is integrated in ways that reflect pedagogical best practices and support rich and equitable learning experiences for all bilingual learners. As AI continues to advance, its successful application in early bilingual education will depend on how educators, developers, and policymakers collaborate to ensure these tools promote inclusive, engaging, and culturally affirming learning environments.

Implications for Practice and Ethics

Teachers and school administrators can use AI to extend, rather than replace, rich, interactive language teaching. Prioritize tools that support oral practice, scaffold turn-taking, and honor the heritage language alongside the societal language. Policymakers should fund inclusive datasets (child speech, dialects, minority languages) and require transparent evaluations demonstrating benefits for multilingual learners. Ethical considerations must also include prioritizing the security of children's data, the ability for users to delete their data, and audits for bias in ASR/chatbots. Equity also demands accessible design, culturally responsive content, and ongoing teacher training.

Acknowledgements Part of this text was assisted by language-editing AI software; the author reviewed and verified all content.

References

Alemi, M., Meghdari, A., & Ghazisaedy, M. (2014). Employing humanoid robots for teaching English language in Iranian junior high-schools. *International Journal of HR: Humanoid Robotics, 11*(03), 1450022. https://doi.org/10.1142/s0219843614500224

Alhawiti, K. M. (2014). Natural language processing and its use in education. *International Journal of Advanced Computer Science and Applications, 5*(12), 136–142.

Ali, H., & Al-Mahmoud, A. (2023). Use of bilingualism in business and commerce: A study of multilingual communication strategies in global organizations. *Research Studies in English Language Teaching and Learning, 1*(1), 11–19. https://doi.org/10.62583/rseltl.v1i1.4

Ashfaque, M. W., Tharewal, S., Iqhbal, S., & Kayte, C. N. (2020). A Review on Techniques, Characteristics and approaches of an intelligent tutoring Chatbot system. *2020 International Conference on Smart Innovations in Design, Environment, Management, Planning and Computing* (ICSIDEMPC), 258–262. doi:10.1109/icsidempc49020.2020.9299583.

Bailey, C., Venta, A., & Langley, H. (2020). The bilingual [dis]advantage. *Language and Cognition, 12*(2), 225–281. https://doi.org/10.1017/langcog.2019.43

Barlow, J. (2003). The stop-spirant alternation in Spanish: Converging evidence for a fortition account. *Southwest Journal of Linguistics, 22*(1), 51.

Bhardwaj, V., Ben Othman, M. T., Kukreja, V., Belkhier, Y., Bajaj, M., Goud, B. S., Rehman, A. U., Shafiq, M., & Hamam, H. (2022). Automatic speech recognition (ASR) systems for children: A systematic literature review. *Applied Sciences (Basel, Switzerland), 12*(9), 4419. https://doi.org/10.3390/app12094419

Bialystok, E., & Craik, F. (2015). Cognitive consequences of bilingualism. In J. W. Schwieter (Ed.), *The Cambridge handbook of bilingual processing* (pp. 571–585). Cambridge University Press. https://doi.org/10.1017/cbo9781107447257.025

Boulton, A., & Cobb, T. (2017). Corpus use in language learning: A meta-analysis. *Language Learning, 67*(2), 348–393. https://doi.org/10.1111/lang.12224

Castro, C. (2019). What's wrong with machine bias. *Ergo (Ann Arbor, Mich.), 6*(20201214). https://doi.org/10.3998/ergo.12405314.0006.015

Chen, G. (2024). The impacts of AI-driven storytelling applications on language acquisition and literacy development in early childhood education: A systematic review. *Asian Journal of Advanced Research and Reports, 18*(11), 1–12. https://doi.org/10.9734/ajarr/2024/v18i11770

Chen, H. H.-J. (2011). Developing and evaluating an oral skills training website supported by automatic speech recognition technology. *ReCALL, 23*(1), 59–78. https://doi.org/10.1017/s0958344010000285

Chouldechova, A. (2017). Fair prediction with disparate impact: A study of bias in recidivism prediction instruments. *Big Data, 5*(2), 153–163. https://doi.org/10.1089/big.2016.0047

Chouldechova, A., & G'Sell, M. (2017). Fairer and more accurate, but for whom? In *arXiv* [stat.AP]. arXiv. http://arxiv.org/abs/1707.00046

Dai, Y., & Wu, Z. (2023). Mobile-assisted pronunciation learning with feedback from peers and/or automatic speech recognition: A mixed-methods study. *Computer Assisted Language Learning, 36*(5–6), 861–884. https://doi.org/10.1080/09588221.2021.1952272

Dizon, G. (2017). Using intelligent personal assistants for second language learning: A case study of Alexa. *TESOL Journal, 8*(4), 811–830. https://doi.org/10.1002/tesj.353

Evers, K., & Chen, S. (2022). Effects of an automatic speech recognition system with peer feedback on pronunciation instruction for adults. *Computer Assisted Language Learning, 35*(8), 1869–1889. https://doi.org/10.1080/09588221.2020.1839504

Fabiano, L., & Goldstein, B. (2005). Phonological cross-linguistic effects in bilingual Spanish—English speaking children. *Journal of Multilingual Communication Disorders, 3*(1), 56–63. https://doi.org/10.1080/14769670400027316

Gutiérrez, L. (2023). Artificial intelligence in language education: Navigating the potential and challenges of chatbots and NLP. *Research Studies in English Language Teaching and Learning, 1*(3), 180–191. https://doi.org/10.62583/rseltl.v1i3.44

Hossein Keshavarz, M., & Ingram, D. (2002). The early phonological development of a Farsi-English bilingual child. *The International Journal of Bilingualism: Cross-Disciplinary, Cross-Linguistic Studies of Language Behavior, 6*(3), 255–269. https://doi.org/10.1177/13670069020060030301

Huang, W., Hew, K. F., & Fryer, L. K. (2022). Chatbots for language learning—Are they really useful? A systematic review of chatbot-supported language learning. *Journal of Computer Assisted Learning, 38*(1), 237–257. https://doi.org/10.1111/jcal.12557

Hsieh, I.-T., Wu, C.-H., & Wang, C.-H. (2020). Acoustic and textual data augmentation for code-switching speech recognition in under-resourced language. *2020 Asia-Pacific Signal and Information Processing Association Annual Summit and Conference* (APSIPA ASC), 302–307. https://ieeexplore.ieee.org/abstract/document/9306347/?casa_token=wjhGFMPtNwYAAAAA:U4ad5kcWVcvNGVVQwJkFIYhQA3qUjR3l3s4WBMigl8oB-9Vx9qjKIdaJgGC1ECUT3Gg0gHEBEQ

Hurst, N., Clabaugh, C., Baynes, R., Cohn, J., Mitroff, D., & Scherer, S. (2020). Social and emotional skills training with Embodied Moxie. *In arXiv* [cs.RO]. https://doi.org/10.48550/ARXIV.2004.12962

Irwin, V., Wang, K., Cui, J., Wang, X., Bullock Mann, F., & Dilig, R. (2021). *Report on the condition of education*. National Center for Education Statistics.

Jeon, J. (2024). Exploring AI chatbot affordances in the EFL classroom: Young learners' experiences and perspectives. *Computer Assisted Language Learning, 37*(1–2), 1–26. https://doi.org/10.1080/09588221.2022.2147093

Kennedy, J., Baxter, P., Senft, E., & Belpaeme, T. (2016, March). Social robot tutoring for child second language learning. *2016 11th ACM/IEEE International Conference on Human-Robot Interaction* (HRI), Christchurch, New Zealand. doi:https://doi.org/10.1109/hri.2016.7451757

Kerlyl, A., Hall, P., & Bull, S. (2007). Bringing chatbots into education: Towards natural language negotiation of open learner models. In *Applications and innovations in intelligent systems XIV* (pp. 179–192). Springer. https://doi.org/10.1007/978-1-84628-666-7_14

Klein, R. M. (2016). What cognitive processes are likely to be exercised by bilingualism and does this exercise lead to extra-linguistic cognitive benefits? *Linguistic Approaches to Bilingualism, 6*(5), 549–564. https://doi.org/10.1075/lab.15045.kle

Koenecke, A., Nam, A., Lake, E., Nudell, J., Quartey, M., Mengesha, Z., Toups, C., Rickford, J. R., Jurafsky, D., & Goel, S. (2020). Racial disparities in automated speech recognition. *Proceedings of the National Academy of Sciences of the United States of America, 117*(14), 7684–7689. https://doi.org/10.1073/pnas.1915768117

Korzekwa, D., Lorenzo-Trueba, J., Drugman, T., & Kostek, B. (2022). Computer-assisted pronunciation training—Speech synthesis is almost all you need. *Speech Communication, 142*, 22–33. https://doi.org/10.1016/j.specom.2022.05.001

Kuhl, P. K. (2010). Brain mechanisms in early language acquisition. *Neuron, 67*(5), 713–727.

Kukulska-Hulme, A., & Lee, H. (2020). Intelligent assistants in language learning: an analysis of features and limitations. In *CALL for widening participation: short papers from EUROCALL 2020* (pp. 172–176). Research-publishing.net. https://doi.org/10.14705/rpnet.2020.48.1184

Li, Q. E. (2018). A review of the critical period hypothesis in second language acquisition. *International Journal of Linguistics and Communication, 6*(2). https://doi.org/10.15640/ijlc.v6n2a2

Li, Y. (2024). Can late language learners acquire second language grammar? Evidence from linguistic to neuroscience methods. *Frontiers in Psychology, 15*, 1421072. https://doi.org/10.3389/fpsyg.2024.1421072

Madhumani, G. R., Shah, S., Abraham, B., Joshi, V., & Sitaram, S. (2020). Learning not to discriminate: Task agnostic learning for improving monolingual and code-switched speech recognition. *In arXiv* [eess.AS]. https://doi.org/10.48550/ARXIV.2006.05257

McCrocklin, S. (2019). ASR-based dictation practice for second language pronunciation improvement. *Journal of Second Language Pronunciation, 5*(1), 98–118. https://doi.org/10.1075/jslp.16034.mcc

McCrocklin, S. M. (2016). Pronunciation learner autonomy: The potential of automatic speech recognition. *System, 57*(1), 25–42. https://www.researchgate.net/profile/Shannon-Mccrocklin-2/publication/293801439_Pronunciation_learner_autonomy_The_potential_of_Automatic_Speech_Recognition/links/5c74149fa6fdcc47159be210/Pronunciation-learner-autonomy-The-potential-of-Automatic-Speech-Recognition.pdf

McLeod, S., & Crowe, K. (2018). Children's consonant acquisition in 27 languages: A cross-linguistic review. *American Journal of Speech-Language Pathology, 27*(4), 1546–1571. https://doi.org/10.1044/2018_ajslp-17-0100

Meisel, J. M. (1989). Early differentiation of languages in bilingual children. In K. Hyltenstam & L. K. Obler (Eds.), *Bilingualism across the lifespan* (pp. 13–40). Cambridge University Press. https://doi.org/10.1017/cbo9780511611780.003

Obermeyer, Z., Powers, B., Vogeli, C., & Mullainathan, S. (2019). Dissecting racial bias in an algorithm used to manage the health of populations. *Science (New York, N.Y.), 366*(6464), 447–453. https://doi.org/10.1126/science.aax2342

Pergantis, P., Bamicha, V., Skianis, C., & Drigas, A. (2025). AI Chatbots and cognitive control: Enhancing executive functions through Chatbot interactions: A systematic review. *Brain Sciences, 15*(1), 47. https://doi.org/10.3390/brainsci15010047

Poplack, S. (2000). Toward a typology of code-switching. L. WEI (éd.), The bilingualism reader.: Routeledge, 221–255.

Rahimi, M., Fathi, J., & Zou, D. (2024). Exploring the impact of automated written corrective feedback on the academic writing skills of EFL learners: An activity theory perspective. *Education and Information Technologies*, 1–45. https://doi.org/10.1007/s10639-024-12349-z

Shabani, K. (2012). Dynamic assessment of L2 learners' reading comprehension processes: A Vygotskian perspective. *Procedia—Social and Behavioral Sciences, 32*, 321–328. https://doi.org/10.1016/j.sbspro.2012.01.048

Son, J.-B., Ružić, N. K., & Philpott, A. (2023). Artificial intelligence technologies and applications for language learning and teaching. *Journal of China Computer-Assisted Language Learning*, 1–19. https://doi.org/10.1515/jccall-2023-0015

Stevenson, M., & Phakiti, A. (2019). Automated feedback and second language writing. In K. Hyland & F. Hyland (Eds.), *Feedback in second language writing: Contexts and issues* (pp. 125–142). Cambridge University Press.

Tan, X., Cheng, G., & Ling, M. H. (2025). Artificial intelligence in teaching and teacher professional development: A systematic review. *Computers and Education: Artificial Intelligence, 8*(100355). https://doi.org/10.1016/j.caeai.2024.100355

Ugan, E. Y., Pham, N.-Q., & Waibel, A. (2024). DECM: Evaluating bilingual ASR performance on a code-switching/mixing benchmark. *International Conference on Language Resources and Evaluation*, 4468–4475.

van den Berghe, R., Verhagen, J., Oudgenoeg-Paz, O., van der Ven, S., & Leseman, P. (2019). Social robots for language learning: A review. *Review of Educational Research, 89*(2), 259–295. https://doi.org/10.3102/0034654318821286

Walter, Y. (2024). Embracing the future of artificial intelligence in the classroom: The relevance of AI literacy, prompt engineering, and critical thinking in modern education. *International Journal of Educational Technology in Higher Education, 21*(1). https://doi.org/10.1186/s41239-024-00448-3

Weng, C., Kassaw, K., Astatke, M., & Yang, C. (2024). Online learning environments for transferable skills development: A systematic literature review from 2013–2022. *Interactive Learning Environments, 32*(10), 6894–6914. https://doi.org/10.1080/10494820.2023.2294769

Wills, S., Bai, Y., Tejedor-Garcia, C., Cucchiarini, C., & Strik, H. (2023). Automatic speech recognition of non-native child speech for language learning applications. *arXiv* [cs.CL]. https://doi.org/10.48550/ARXIV.2306.16710

Xiao, J., Alibakhshi, G., Zamanpour, A., Zarei, M., Sherafat, S., & Behzadpoor, S.-F. (2024). How AI literacy affects students' educational attainment in online learning: Testing a structural equation model in higher education context. *The international review of research in open and distributed. Learning, 25*, 179–198. https://doi.org/10.19173/irrodl.v25i3.7720

Xu, Y., He, K., Levine, J., Ritchie, D., Pan, Z., Bustamante, A., & Warschauer, M. (2024). Artificial intelligence enhances children's science learning from television shows. *Journal of Educational Psychology, 116*(7), 1071–1092. https://doi.org/10.1037/edu0000889

Xu, Y., He, K., Vigil, V., Ojeda-Ramirez, S., Liu, X., Levine, J., Cervera, K., & Warschauer, M. (2023, June 19). "Rosita reads with my family": Developing A bilingual conversational agent to support parent-child shared reading. *Proceedings of the 22nd Annual ACM Interaction Design and Children Conference*. IDC'23: Interaction Design and Children, Chicago IL USA. https://doi.org/10.1145/3585088.3589354

Zhang, X. (2024). Leveraging AI tools for discourse analysis in early childhood bilingual education: Enhancing language development. *Journal of Education and Educational Policy Studies, 2*(1), 24–32. https://doi.org/10.54254/3049-7248/2/2024011

Zhang, Y., Yue, Z., Patel, T., & Scharenborg, O. (2024). Improving child speech recognition with augmented child-like speech. In *arXiv* [cs.CL]. arXiv. http://arxiv.org/abs/2406.10284

Chapter 3
Examining Artificial Intelligence Curricula for Ethical Principles—A Bridge to Human Flourishing

Janice Mak, Wen Wen, and Marissa Castellana

Abstract With the ubiquity of artificial intelligence (AI) in society and generative AI (GenAI) tools rapidly infusing K-12 learning environments, there is an urgent need to ensure that students understand and can navigate this digital landscape. The ethical and societal impacts of GenAI tools must be explicitly taught through AI curricula that provide educators with opportunities to facilitate students' understanding of how AI works, along with its possibilities, potential harms, and benefits. This study examines two AI curricula through the lens of AI ethical principles and bridges these principles to the strengths of a virtuous, flourishing life. Findings indicate that the AI ethical principles of transparency, privacy, non-maleficence, responsibility, pedagogical appropriateness, and AI literacy were addressed to some degree in both curricula. However, the AI ethical principles of children's rights, freedom, and autonomy were underexplored. The analysis reveals opportunities to develop AI ethics curricula in alignment with the AI ethical principles and the framework of eight strengths for a flourishing life. This chapter also discusses ways to ensure AI ethics instruction bridges the complex relationship between AI use and students' moral capacities. Through grounding curricula in evidence-based pedagogy, AI ethics instruction should span disciplinary boundaries and center on children's developmental needs.

Keywords Generative artificial intelligence · AI · Curriculum evaluation · Ethics · Primary education · K-12 education · Implications

J. Mak (✉)
Learning Engineering Institute/Mary Lou Fulton College for Teaching and Learning Innovation, Arizona State University, Tempe, AZ, USA
e-mail: janice.mak@asu.edu

W. Wen
Secondary Education and Educational Technology, State University of New York Oneonta, Oneonta, NY, USA
e-mail: wen.wen@oneonta.edu

M. Castellana
Department of Psychology, Arizona State University, Tempe, AZ, USA
e-mail: macaste8@asu.edu

S. Papadakis (ed.), *AI Applications in Preschool and Primary Education*, Advances in Artificial Intelligence in Education 5, https://doi.org/10.1007/978-3-032-17190-0_3

Introduction

A Google Scholar search on AI in K-12 education yields a range of AI in K-12 education frameworks (Gouseti et al., 2024), the integration or use of AI for teaching and learning (Casal-Otero et al., 2023), and contextualizing AI education through culturally responsive approaches (Eguchi et al., 2021). In addition to research on the use of AI in K–12 education, another emerging area of focus is the critical need to teach about the ethics of AI to K–12 learners (Biagini, 2025). Researchers have highlighted the need to address ethical and societal aspects of AI in K-12 settings through a range of pedagogical approaches including curricular ones that recommend the integration of use cases such as biased facial recognition technology or implications of recommendation engines for students to understand impacts of AI (Akgun & Greenhow, 2022; Zhang et al., 2023). Other researchers have utilized project-based learning approaches where students actively explore AI in the world around them through examining SMARTcar technology (Gong et al., 2018), agriculture-sensing (Sakulkueakulsuk et al., 2018), and redesigning YouTube (Fernández-Martínez et al., 2021).

We maintain that teaching AI in K-12 must center on developing students' ability to navigate the world of AI in ethical and moral ways. This vision has implications for both the content and pedagogy of AI curriculum created for K-12 educators. Moreover, as K-12 educators curate, contextualize, and use AI curricula with their students, we posit that it is critical to account for the students' developmental stages as they relate to the integration of AI literacy instruction. To this end, the existing AI literacy curriculum for younger learners is a critical area to explore since these curricula, often developed by large technology companies, have a broad reach and the potential to impact scores of classrooms and students. In this study, we explore the following research question by analyzing two AI curricula using an ethical framework: *In what ways do two curricula designed for learners between the ages of 10–14 address ethical and societal impacts of artificial intelligence?*

In this study, we focus on the ethical component of AI curricula designed for learners as young as 10 years old and use the ethical principles for AI in K-12 education (Adams et al., 2023) to analyze these curricula while grounding our work in the strengths for human flourishing (Davidson et al., 2007, 2014; Peterson & Seligman, 2004). We then consider the implications of this study for younger learners and AI + ethics education in K-12.

Literature Review

We reviewed existing research that examined how AI is taught in K–12 education, including learning content, instructional approaches, and challenges and considerations (e.g., Su et al., 2024; Yue et al., 2022). Learning content specifically refers to the knowledge, concepts, and skills that are discussed in the curriculum. Previous studies have shown that K–12 AI curricula cover a range of topics, including foundational AI knowledge and technical concepts such as machine learning (ML), large language models (LLM), and algorithms (Lee & Kwon, 2024; Michaeli et al., 2023; Sanusi et al., 2023). For example, Sanusi et al. (2023) conducted a literature review that highlights current research on ML education in K–12 education, including teaching strategies, technological tools, and professional development opportunities. Fernández-Martínez et al. (2021) introduced the practical implementation of AI in a Spanish secondary education curriculum, including topics such as the history and evolution of AI, major areas of AI (e.g., robotics, learning algorithms), human versus machine capabilities, and societal implications. Lee and Kwon's (2024) systematic review examined various topics covered in K–12 AI education, including fundamental AI concepts, types of AI, applications, and ethical considerations.

Previous studies have also explored various pedagogical approaches for teaching AI to K–12 learners (Li et al., 2024). Williams et al. (2023) used project-based, active learning to promote students' understanding and critical thinking about AI. Ma et al. (2022) found that incorporating game-based learning into AI courses can help students master AI subject knowledge and improve their computational thinking skills. Similarly, Ali et al. (2021) developed an online, collaborative game to simulate how generative adversarial networks (GANs) function. Students then interacted with four web-based tools that use GANs to generate media content. These studies have indicated that well-designed hands-on activities can effectively increase students' engagement and promote meaningful AI learning (Li et al., 2024).

Other studies have taken a broader perspective, proposing key principles for designing AI curricula, such as "The Five Big Ideas in AI4K12" (Touretzky et al., 2019). Chiu (2021) argued that six key components are essential in designing a K–12 AI curriculum: AI knowledge, AI processes, the impact of AI (both content and product), student relevance, teacher–student communication, and flexibility (in both process and praxis). Su and Zhong (2022) recommended developing AI literacy through three core competencies—knowledge, skills, and attitudes—for building AI curricula in early childhood education.

With teaching AI in K–12 settings becoming increasingly prevalent, a primary challenge centers on how to teach AI ethics to young learners (Akgun & Greenhow, 2022; Li, 2022). Emerging studies have shown that learners' understanding of AI ethics and AI content is the strongest predictor of successful learning outcomes (Sanusi & Olaleye, 2022). A growing body of scholarly work has begun to address this issue. For example, Grover (2024) maintained that AI ethics should be integrated alongside technical knowledge. Eguchi et al. (2021) introduced culturally responsive approaches to raise middle schoolers' awareness and understanding of AI ethics. Michaeli et al. (2023) presented learning objectives for AI in secondary education, including an understanding of AI ethics such as bias, transparency and reliability of AI systems, data protection, to name a few. Emphasizing ethical education in AI remains a critical and complex issue that needs to be prioritized (Berson & Berson, 2024).

It is critical to not only educate young learners about AI knowledge and skills, but also to equip them with a foundation in ethics and moral reasoning to navigate the myriads of moral dilemmas in a complex GenAI landscape. There is the "need to maintain the very analogue capacity of judgment in the face of a digitally mediated world" (Conroy, 2021, p.1), to be able to think through, identify the moral or ethical issues involved in a dilemma, and then arrive at an ethical decision. We define ethics in a multidimensional way based on Starratt's (2014) three ethics: 1) justice, which considers fairness and equity in decision-making, 2) care, which centers the intrinsic worth of human beings, and 3) critique, which interrogates injustice and bias. We also hold to Furman's (2004) ethic of community which postures communal participation that strives to attain common good.

With the rapidly emerging field of AI curriculum research, there is an urgent need to understand how AI ethics is currently presented in curricula with the goal of identifying ways that curriculum developers and educators can further nurture and develop learners' ability to critique and reason about GenAI (Akgun & Greenhow, 2022; Conroy, 2021). In this study, we explore two AI curricula developed for young learners (10+ years old) by examining and interrogating the ways in which each curricula integrates AI ethics.

Methodology

The materials included two open-source AI curricula (Payne, 2019; Raspberry Pi Foundation, n.d.-a, b), developed respectively by Raspberry Pi Foundation (Curriculum A) and Massachusetts Institute for Technology Responsible AI for Social Empowerment and Education (MIT RAISE) (Curriculum B). These curricula, referred to as Curriculum A and Curriculum B, are specifically designed for teaching AI to K–12 learners. Curriculum A includes a range of resources—lesson plans, presentations, videos, simulations, worksheets, and engaging hands-on projects—to support learners aged 10 to 14 to learn AI and safety. Curriculum B also provides a set of activities, teacher guides, assessments, and other materials, to assist educators in teaching about the ethics of AI for middle school students.

We adopted the deductive content analysis (Elo & Kyngäs, 2008) method to analyze two curricula based on an existing research-based framework (Polit & Beck, 2004). Our guiding framework, Ethical Principles for AI in K-12 Education (Adams et al., 2023), synthesizes principles from four international frameworks that provide ethical guidance of AI for children in K-12 education: the World Economic Forum (2019), the Institute for Ethical AI in Education (IEAIED, 2021), UNESCO (2021), and UNICEF (2021) (see Introduction). Using the AI ethical principles outlined in this framework (Adams et al., 2023), we developed a matrix to code, organize the data and guide our analysis (Elo & Kyngäs, 2008): Transparency, Justice & Fairness, Non-maleficence, Responsibility, Privacy, Beneficence, and Freedom & Autonomy. An additional set of principles unique to K-12 education were also identified: Pedagogical Appropriateness, Children's Rights, AI Literacy, and Teacher Well-being (Adams et al., 2023). While Teacher Well-being (acknowledged by IEAIED, 2021) maintains that teachers should be empowered by AI, this principle falls outside the scope of the study and is therefore not discussed.

Firstly, the initial two authors independently reviewed the data and provided a rating of 2 (strong integration and presence across multiple lessons), 1 (presence in one lesson or activity), or 0 (not evident) for each AI ethical dimension (see Table 3.1). During this process, the first two researchers identified evidence from each curriculum that corresponded to an AI ethical principle (see Table 3.1) and cited evidence of this AI ethical principle by including examples from the curriculum itself (Polit & Beck, 2004). After completing their independent analysis, all three researchers met to compare and discuss the data and examples they had categorized. Through following an iterative process to data analysis with the third researcher present as a peer observer to ensure the validity of the coding, the research team developed a shared understanding and agreement of the data used to address the research question through including relevant supporting examples for each AI ethical principle.

Findings

To address our research question (In what ways do two curricula designed for learners between the ages of 10–14 address ethical and societal impacts of artificial intelligence?), we organized our findings based on our coding system and included examples/evidence from each curriculum (see Table 3.1). Our final consensus rating along with an example of evidence for Curriculum A and B is included below.

Transparency: Highlights Concepts, Such as Algorithmic Accountability, Transparency in all Stages of AI Deployment, Interpretability, Explainability for Children

One major component of Curriculum A is AI foundations. For example, the first lesson in the curricular sequence explains the basic concept of AI and how algorithms work using developmentally appropriate language for children. Another example can be found in the lesson that introduces decision trees by explicitly explaining how to measure the interpretability of a model's predictions, informing students that some types of models are more explainable than others. In Curriculum B, students understand supervised machine learning and algorithmic bias through hands-on activities.

Table 3.1 Example of Data Analysis using AI Ethical Principles

AI Ethical Principle	Rating		Example of Evidence of AI Ethical Principle	
	Cu-A	Cu-B	Curriculum A	Curriculum B
Transparency	2	1	Explainability of model cards & transparency to reduce likelihood of harm (e.g. facial recognition technology).	Apply both technical understanding of AI and knowledge of stakeholders to determine a just goal for a socio-technical system; explore algorithms and bias through teachable machine.
Justice and fairness	1	1	Societal bias scenario: Imagine an AI application that predicts the job a person might do. The model has been trained using employment data from 1960. If gender was in the data used to train the model, could this lead to the AI application making biased predictions?	Students watch gender shades facial detection video and discuss unequal user experiences between groups and "technology doesn't work unless it works for everyone."
Non-maleficence	2	1	Are there ways in which machine learning models can be created to **reduce inequalities** in the world?	Students interact with various technologies, such as emotion detection software. They then respond to creative writing prompts about who might be affected by the technology and how the technology might produce harm or benefit in the future.
Responsibility	2	1	Students asked to think about how societal bias could appear in the data.	Speculative futures activity: Students think about the world they want to make when building a new technology and the unintended consequences that can occur when building that technology.
Privacy	2	1	Students asked to create an AI app that lets parents check on their child's online activities without invading their privacy.	Students asked how to find images to better curate a dataset: Which of these (e.g., social media, mug shots, ID cards) would be okay to use? Lead to more bias? Breach privacy?

(continued)

Table 3.1 (continued)

AI Ethical Principle	Rating		Example of Evidence of AI Ethical Principle	
	Cu-A	Cu-B	Curriculum A	Curriculum B
Beneficence	2	1	Focus on: "A user-focused approach aims to avoid harm by focusing on benefitting users over making profit." (e.g., computer vision - who would benefit from this use of AI? How would this impact people's privacy?)	Students reason about secondary and tertiary effects of a technology's existence and the circumstances the technology creates for various users.
Freedom & Autonomy	1	1	Students explore: Would the use of GenAI change your choice of actions? Would you share/double check/ignore output? Would your action change if the content was…interesting? Controversial? Emotional?	Curriculum highlights "humans decide the goals of the socio-technical systems they create" (e.g., humans have agency in curating training datasets).
Pedagogical appropriateness	2	1	Lessons include relevant use of examples; data detective: (e.g., where is your friend's personal data going and who is using it?	Socratic seminar discussing whether technologies like autoplay (YouTube kids app) should exist
Children's rights	1	1	Topics covered, but not explicit (e.g., data protection, privacy, design of AI tools and systems and implications).	Students read and analyze an abridged version of a wall street journal article titled YouTube Weighs Major Changes to Kids Content Amid FTC Probe
AI literacy	1	2	Students learn about machine learning models, how they can make biased predictions, and about data and societal biases.	Understand the effect training data has on the accuracy of a machine learning system; understand how the composition of training data affects the outcome of a supervised machine learning system.

Note: Cu = curriculum

Justice and Fairness: Promotes Equitable, Inclusive, and Ethical AI Use, with a Particular Focus on Children's Rights, Such as Non-discrimination and Fairness

Curriculum A includes lessons that are designed to build students' knowledge about the existence of data bias and societal bias, and ways to reduce bias in the use of AI.

For example, students are prompted with questions regarding whether a dataset from 1960 adequately represents the diversity of today's workforce. They also explore societal bias evident in a facial recognition system that has not been trained with enough data from a range of people from different skin tones.

Non-maleficence: Addresses the Avoidance of Harm and Emphasizes the Need to Ensure Children's Safety, Security, and Integrity

Through providing a simulated social media platform, Curriculum A provides students with the experience of understanding how their data is being used by the social media platform and other key stakeholders. This activity helps students develop a deeper awareness of their online presence, privacy rights, and data privacy issues.

Responsibility: Promotes Clarity and Accountability in AI Tools Used with Children, Aligning with Broader Principles of Ethical Responsibility

Curriculum A contains activities that teach students ways to evaluate the accuracy of different language models and the types of information they might need to help make their decision including answers to questions such as: What data was used? What was the confidence threshold used to measure the accuracy of their model? Through this scenario, students can develop a nuanced understanding of how AI models produce reliable and trustworthy outputs, and that errors or biases are identified. Curriculum B uses an ethical matrix activity that engages students to consider the relationship between algorithmic features and stakeholders.

Privacy: Highlights the Importance of Protecting Children's Data and Privacy, which Ensures Transparency, Auditability, and Traceability in Data Usage, which Extends to both Teachers and Parents

Curriculum A discusses how data is shared with AI tools and how growing AI use might affect students' need to protect their personal information. To this end, Curriculum A includes a hands-on activity to engage students in exploring concepts of privacy and transparency in data collection and usage, and ethical decision-making.

Beneficence: Emphasizes Supporting Students' Well-being, Development, Recognizing the Needs in Policymaking, and Promoting Children's Overall Growth

Curriculum A highlights a user-focused approach to engage students in understanding the stages of the AI project lifecycle through centering empathy in the design process and mitigating the harms associated with AI applications. Moreover, Curriculum A integrates the UN Sustainable Development Goals to teach students about developing a sustainable and equitable future for humanity. Curriculum B includes a series of discussion questions about YouTube and its AI functions, which aims to develop students' understanding of how algorithms work, content is controlled, and profits are made.

Freedom and Autonomy: Focuses on Informed Participation, and Learner-Centered AI Use to Promote Students' Agency. Meanwhile, it Encourages Students to Practice Data Safety and Ensure they Have Agency over their Learning

When Curriculum A discusses machine learning (ML) and AI, it encourages students to think critically about which ML models are appropriate to use to solve problems. It emphasizes students' agency by asking them to examine different example applications and evaluate whether a data-driven approach would be effective or appropriate in each case.

Pedagogical Appropriateness: Emphasizes the Appropriate Use of AI by Aligning Educational Goals with Ethical Principles, Applying Evidence-Based Practices, and Fostering Supportive Learning Environments that Promote Children's Well-being

Both curricula use discussion, project-based learning, and hands-on activities to engage students in exploring AI-related concepts and ethical considerations. Curriculum A includes a science lesson that integrates AI knowledge to engage students in exploring both the benefits and drawbacks of using AI. Curriculum B focuses more on the idea that bias is inherent in Algorithms, primarily as they reflect the interests of certain groups over others. However, the ethical lens is not explicitly addressed in the curriculum itself.

Children's Rights: Emphasizes Using AI to Empower both Children and the Institutions that Support them

Both curricula equip young students with AI knowledge and skills to understand the benefits and potential harms of AI with the goal of helping them to better adapt to an AI-driven world. For instance, Curriculum A uses animations, videos, and real-world examples to explain AI technologies, how they make predictions, and the biases and inaccuracies associated with them. Curriculum B engages students in considering who might be affected by the technology and how the technology might produce harm or benefit by responding to creative writing prompts.

AI Literacy: Conceptualized in Various Ways, Including Public Education, Integrating AI Skills into School Curricula, and Preparing Children for the Future of AI

The two curricula offer a variety of learning activities to help students build their knowledge, skills, and ethical awareness. For instance, Curriculum A introduces media literacy in the AI era, which underscores the importance of evaluating media information. These lessons equip young students who use social media with the essential skills and dispositions to distinguish mis- and dis-information, and build an understanding of fairness, accountability, and transparency around AI content on social platforms.

Our findings indicate that Curriculum A exhibits a more comprehensive and robust presence of the AI ethical principles of responsibility, privacy, beneficence, and pedagogical awareness. Since many ethical principles overlap and intersect, some examples may fit into multiple ethical categories. For example, students' understanding of data privacy is also associated with AI transparency (i.e., how data is collected). While Curriculum B possesses a strong AI literacy presence, with much emphasis on algorithmic knowledge, the activities do not explicitly address the ethical lens. For example, it contains an activity which asks students to identify stakeholders and redesign YouTube to achieve the learning objective of determining a just goal for a socio-technical system. Although the activity provides clear steps and prompts for students (e.g., identifying stakeholders, filling out an ethical matrix), it does not necessarily guide students toward defining a just goal for the socio-technical system. The activity should have had a clear ethical framing, such as prompting students with questions on ethical issues: What does "just" mean in the context of a platform like YouTube? How might power, bias, or inequality be embedded in design choices? Without a clear ethical framing, this activity risks being a design exercise without ethical depth.

Implications for Practice and Ethics

There are three major implications of our study as it relates to learning and teaching about the ethics of AI: 1) AI ethics instruction needs to address the complex relationship between AI and personal moral capacities, 2) AI ethics education should be designed in ways that span boundaries, and 3) AI ethics instruction should be grounded in evidence-based pedagogy. Lastly, we discuss the implications of this study for students in preschool and primary education.

Learning and Teaching about AI Ethics Should Address the Complex Relationship Between Technology and Personal Moral Capacities

The two curricula addressed in this study centered on technical ethics (e.g., algorithms. Data processes) rather than taking the approach of exploring the moral reasoning ability required to navigate deeper and complex social and equity-related issues (Sperling et al., 2024). One key is to connect the AI ethics topics to the body of research on moral education and human flourishing and vice versa. We focus here on the empirically classified Eight Strengths of Character are seen as assets needed for a flourishing life, answering the question of what it means to educate the whole child (Davidson et al., 2007). These assets are: 1) lifelong learner and critical thinker, 2) diligent and capable performer, 3) socially and emotionally skilled person, 4) ethical thinker, 5) respected and responsible moral agent committed to consistent moral action, 6) self-disciplined person who pursues a healthy lifestyle, 7) contributing community member and democratic citizen, and 8) spiritual person crafting a life of noble purpose.

Now more than ever, it is critical to apply these assets to learning and teaching in the age of AI in mutually supportive and reinforcing ways. For example, being an ethical thinker and being able to discern the benefits and harms of AI tools ensures a flourishing life. All other strengths are dependent on being a self-disciplined person who pursues a healthy lifestyle. In the age of GenAI, being healthy means being able to navigate a world with new forms of surveillance, (dis)connectedness, mis- and dis-information in ways that sustain strong and healthy faculties to critique, reason, and sift through evidence (Conroy, 2021).

Learning and teaching AI must address the complex, multiple layers and probe beyond the technical level to consider the societal impacts of AI technology. The AI ethical principles distilled by Adams et al. (2023) overlap and intertwine, just as the assets needed for a flourishing life. When delving into the ethical and societal impacts of AI, it is critical to address moral reasoning, and the cognitive processes that young learners go through as they make decisions in the face of dilemmas (Harding, 2017). This means providing active exploration opportunities for learners to determine the ethical issues present within a given scenario, then scaffolding their ability to reason through the context to ultimately arrive at an ethical decision. Exploring scenarios that confront personal, social, economic, environmental, and ethical consequences of AI technology is essential to fully address the complex and nuanced approach needed to educate young learners in the age of GenAI.

Design AI Ethics Education in Ways that Span Boundaries

Just as AI is ubiquitous, it is essential that AI ethics education be infused into K-12 education in ways that span disciplinary and grade level boundaries in aligned and developmentally appropriate ways. The two curricula in this study included AI literacy components (e.g., how AI works), with much of the content through the technical lens of computer science. The lessons included topics such as how machine learning, algorithms, supervisory models, and large language models work. Adjacent to these computing-centric topics, the curricula included opportunities for students to reflect on AI in society such as YouTube recommendation engines and facial recognition algorithms.

Infusing AI into other subject areas and other disciplines into AI provides a rich opportunity for students to see the AI that is often masked or hidden. For example, in social studies or English class, students can read current headlines and about the ethical and societal impacts of GenAI in everyday life, whether in education, economics, healthcare, traffic, or weather. They can then do additional research into the opportunities and potential challenges of AI in society along with ways to best mitigate harm. Younger children can begin to build a foundation in what algorithms are through picture books and engaging in unplugged (activities without a computer) or simple block coding (e.g., Blockly, Scratch). Students can connect AI, data, sensors, and algorithms to science projects that solve a problem.

There is also the urgent need to infuse the lens of critical media literacy into AI ethics education. In a world where many media outlets have integrated Gen-AI since 2023 and AI continuing to rapidly evolve, it is becoming increasingly challenging to discern high-quality, reliable news from deceptive content such as fake news (created to intentionally mislead), disinformation (fake news that is intentionally disseminated to deceive), and misinformation (dissemination of false information believed to be true by the sender) (Ranieri et al., 2024). GenAI has even been referenced as "digital plastic" (n.p., Roe et al., 2025), analogous to physical plastic, where GenAI presents the opportunity for content creation, accessibility of information, while at the same time contributing pollution that degrades the digital ecosystem.

An example of critical AI literacy can be seen in the Tools and Awareness about (Dis)information, Algorithms, and Media (TADAM) project that aimed to: 1) support a critical understanding of GenAI tools used in media processes, 2) support learners' capacity to generate AI content in deliberate and thoughtful ways, and 3) enable learners to transfer their critical GenAI knowledge to be ethical, informed decision-makers and citizens. Through active, hands-on exploration, TADAM participants became critical prompters to strategically create input intended to elicit certain responses from AI tools. These types of experiences led them to a deeper understanding of GenAI which in turn had the effect of showing students the inherent limitations of AI tools (Ranieri et al., 2024).

AI Ethics Instruction in K-12 Years Should Be Grounded in Evidence-Based Pedagogy

Our findings indicate that both curricula in this study addressed the ethical principle of "pedagogical appropriateness" to some degree through integrating relevant use-cases, Socratic seminars, speculative futures activities, and engaging in tools such as Google Teachable Machine. Ensuring that appropriate pedagogy along with the other AI ethical principles are integrated consistently and throughout AI curricula continues to be an urgent need. Developing innovative, reliable, and valid ways to assess and evaluate learning outcomes is also critical.

Building on prior research that integrates ethics and career future with technical learning to advance AI literacy for middle school students is a promising avenue to explore (Zhang et al., 2023). Bridging this with career-technical education pathways in high school could be another way to extend this connection to students' future careers. It is also essential to include multiple ways for learners to reflect on the social impact of mistakes made by AI models in training datasets in curricula (Lin & Chen, 2022). Ensuring a range of examples and scenarios, particularly in an age where AI can generate a range of media outputs (i.e., text, audio, video) is critical. For example, including examples from the healthcare field where privacy and security are of utmost importance is important. Providing learners with opportunities to analyze the scenarios and dilemmas from a range of perspectives/stakeholders is also critical to develop empathy and discernment when faced with making decisions about which AI to use or not use and in which context.

Complementing project-based learning approaches and firsthand, active exploration of AI with adequate time for learners to reflect on their learning is another way to ensure the pedagogical appropriateness of AI ethics curricula. Rather than random, episodic moments in the classroom, reflection promotes students' ability to link and construct meaning from their experiences of learning (Costa & Kallick, 2008). When reflection is intentionally integrated into classroom practice, students' ability to construct connections in knowledge and socially with peers is enhanced (Chang, 2019). Explicitly teaching students metacognitive strategies and requiring them to reflect in written and oral modalities as they engage with AI will support them on the way to being ethical decision-makers. In the age of rapid digital disruption, it is more urgent than ever to equip students with the agency to apply skills such as analysis, diagnosis, and prognosis (D'Olimpio, 2019). Integrating reflection into AI ethics instruction aligns with the need to support young learners' autonomy and agency in moral reasoning and judgement.

Implications for Students in Preschool and Primary Education

Although AI curricula are typically designed for upper elementary-aged students and beyond (as examined in the current study), their core principles, especially around AI literacy and ethics, can be adapted for preschool and primary education. Current research demonstrates that young children can benefit from interacting with intelligent robotics, conversational agents, and game-based learning environments, which supports their curiosity and computational thinking (see Su & Yang, 2022 for a literature review). However, significant gaps remain in understanding young children's knowledge of ethics (Durrani et al., 2024; Kurian, 2023; Su et al., 2023), which is critical for setting the foundation for responsible AI use and mitigating potential harms (Kurian, 2023).

Considering Vygotsky's sociocultural theory, teaching AI ethics within children's zone of proximal development (i.e., the space between what children can do independently and with support) is crucial (Vygotsky, 1978). This requires not only adapting content to the needs of young learners but also pedagogical approaches that can scaffold children's learning about ethics in AI. While 10- to 14-year-olds can learn well from online instruction compared to younger students (e.g., curricula explored in this study; Wallace, 2009), ensuring knowledge has been retained in younger learners may involve the curricular content being shared by a more knowledgeable individual (e.g., teacher, parent) through developmentally appropriate ways.

Previous research has found that reading aloud storybooks with themes on morality and engaging children in dialogue about ethics during the shared reading activity can support children's knowledge of ethics (Thambu, 2017). Thus, reading activities may be a promising mechanism for sharing the curricular content explored in this study with young learners. Further, role-playing is another pedagogical approach and has been used for late elementary and middle school students to learn about human-computer interaction (Cakici & Bayir, 2012; Henry et al., 2021) and explore gender bias (Melsión et al., 2021). Specifically, integrating situational learning through children's literature into younger ages, such as preschool-aged children, has been found to be developmentally appropriate ways to nurture learners' moral reasoning ability (Gallavan & Fabbi, 2004). Applying this approach to stimulate students' moral reasoning with integrity as they navigate the AI-infused landscape (Su et al., 2023). By embedding creative, play-based learning strategies into AI education, educators can introduce foundational concepts of ethics, equity, and technological responsibility in a way that resonates with young learners.

Conclusions

This chapter explored how two curricula designed for learners aged 10–14 years address ethical and societal considerations of GenAI. Our content analysis, which used the Ethical Principles for AI in K-12 Education (Adams et al., 2023) framework, illustrated that the two curricula discussed ethical principles to different degrees. While they addressed transparency, privacy, non-maleficence, responsibility, pedagogical appropriateness, and AI literacy, the principles of children's rights and autonomy were underexplored. These findings highlight the critical need for future curricula to address the complexities between AI and ethics, grounded in evidence-based pedagogy and presenting developmentally appropriate content. This would allow students to meaningfully understand AI through an ethical and critical lens. Additional research is needed to understand how these curricula may apply to younger learners, such as preschool and elementary-aged children, especially given the increased integration of GenAI into education.

Funding Information The authors declare that no funding was received to support this study.

References

Adams, C., Pente, P., Lemermeyer, G., & Rockwell, G. (2023). Ethical principles for artificial intelligence in K-12 education. *Computers and Education: Artificial Intelligence, 4*, 100131. https://doi.org/10.1016/j.caeai.2023.100131

Akgun, S., & Greenhow, C. (2022). Artificial intelligence in education: Addressing ethical challenges in K-12 settings. *AI and Ethics, 2*, 431–440. https://doi.org/10.1007/s43681-021-00096-7

Ali, S., DiPaola, D., & Breazeal, C. (2021). What are GANs?: Introducing generative adversarial networks to middle school students. *Proceedings of the AAAI Conference on Artificial Intelligence, 35*(17), 15472–15479. https://doi.org/10.1609/aaai.v35i17.17821

Berson, I. R., & Berson, M. J. (2024). AI in K-12 social studies education: A critical examination of ethical and practical challenges. In A. M. Olney, I.-A. Chounta, Z. Liu, O. C. Santos, & I. I. Bittencourt (Eds.), *Artificial intelligence in education. AIED 2024. Communications in Computer and Information Science* (Vol. 2150, pp. 101–112). Springer. https://doi.org/10.1007/978-3-031-64315-6_8

Biagini, G. (2025). Towards an AI-literate future: A systematic literature review exploring education, ethics, and applications. *International Journal of Artificial Intelligence in Education*. https://doi.org/10.1007/s40593-025-00466-w

Cakici, Y., & Bayir, E. (2012). Developing children's views of the nature of science through role play. *International Journal of Science Education, 34*(7), 1075–1091. https://doi.org/10.1080/09500693.2011.647109

Casal-Otero, L., Catala, A., Fernández-Morante, C., Taboada, M., Cebreiro, B., & Barro, S. (2023). AI literacy in K-12: A systematic literature review. *International Journal of STEM Education, 10*, 29. https://doi.org/10.1186/s40594-023-00418-7

Chang, B. (2019). Reflection in learning. Online. *Learning, 23*(1), 95–110.

Chiu, T. K. (2021). A holistic approach to the design of artificial intelligence (AI) education for K-12 schools. *Tech Trends, 65*, 796–807. https://doi.org/10.1007/s11528-021-00637-1

Conroy, J. C. (2021). Chaos or coherence? Future directions for moral education. *Journal of Moral Education, 50*(1), 1–12. https://doi.org/10.1080/03057240.2020.1830578

Costa, A., & Kallick, B. (2008). Learning through reflection. In A. Costa & B. Kallick (Eds.), *Learning and leading with habits of mind: 16 essential characteristics for success* (pp. 221–235). Association for Supervision and Curriculum Development.

D'Olimpio, L. (2019). Moral education within the social contract: Whose contract is it anyway? *Journal of Moral Education, 48*(4), 515–528. https://doi.org/10.1080/03057240.2019.1580565

Davidson, M., Lickona, T., & Khmelkov, V. (2007). *Smart and good schools. Education Week, 66*(2), 24–30.

Davidson, M., Lickona, T., & Khmelkov, V. (2014). Smart and good schools: A new paradigm for high school character education. In L. Nucci, D. Narvaez, & T. Krettenauer (Eds.), *Handbook of moral and character education* (2nd ed., pp. 290–307). Routledge. https://doi.org/10.4324/9780203114896

Durrani, R., Iqbal, A., & Akram, H. (2024). Artificial intelligence (AI) in early childhood education, exploring challenges, opportunities and future directions: A scoping review. *Qlantic Journal of Social Sciences, 5*(2), 411–423. https://doi.org/10.55737/qjss.135537445

Eguchi, A., Okada, H., & Muto, Y. (2021). Contextualizing AI education for K-12 students to enhance their learning of AI literacy through culturally responsive approaches. *KI-Künstliche Intelligenz, 35*, 153–161. https://doi.org/10.1007/s13218-021-00737-3

Elo, S., & Kyngäs, H. (2008). The qualitative content analysis process. *Journal of Advanced Nursing, 62*(1), 107–115. https://doi.org/10.1111/j.1365-2648.2007.04569.x

Fernández-Martínez, C., Hernán-Losada, I., & Fernández, A. (2021). Early introduction of AI in Spanish middle schools. *A motivational study. KI-Künstliche Intelligenz, 35*, 163–170. https://doi.org/10.1007/s13218-021-00735-5

Furman, G. C. (2004). The ethic of community. *Journal of Educational Administration, 42*(2), 215–235. https://doi.org/10.1108/09578230410525612

Gallavan, N. P., & Fabbi, J. L. (2004). Stimulating moral reasoning in children through situational learning and children's literature. *Social Studies and the Young Learner, 16*(3), 17.

Gong, X., Wu, Y., Ye, Z., & Liu, X. (2018). Artificial intelligence course design: iSTREAM-based visual cognitive smart vehicles. In *2018 IEEE intelligent vehicles symposium (IV)* (pp. 1731–1735). IEEE. https://doi.org/10.1109/IVS.2018.8500457

Gouseti, A., James, F., Fallin, L., & Burden, K. (2024). The ethics of using AI in K-12 education: A systematic literature review. *Technology, Pedagogy and Education, 34*(2), 161–182. https://doi.org/10.1080/1475939X.2024.2428601

Grover, S. (2024, March). Teaching AI to K-12 learners: Lessons, issues, and guidance. In *Proceedings of the 55th ACM Technical Symposium on Computer Science Education*. Vol 1. pp. 422–428. doi:https://doi.org/10.1145/3626252.3630937.

Harding, C. (Ed.). (2017). *Moral dilemmas and ethical reasoning*. Routledge.

Henry, J., Hernalesteen, A., & Collard, A. S. (2021). Teaching artificial intelligence to K-12 through a role-playing game questioning the intelligence concept. *KI-Künstliche Intelligenz, 35*, 171–179. https://doi.org/10.1007/s13218-021-00733-7

Institute for Ethical AI in Education (IEAIED). (2021). *The ethical framework for AI in education. University of Buckingham.* https://www.buckingham.ac.uk/wp-content/uploads/2021/03/The-Institute-for-Ethical-AI-in-Education-The-Ethical-Framework-for-AI-in-Education.pdf.

Kurian, N. (2023). AI'S empathy gap: The risks of conversational artificial intelligence for young children's Well-being and key ethical considerations for early childhood education and care. *Contemporary Issues in Early Childhood, 26*(1), 132–139. https://doi.org/10.1177/14639491231206004

Lee, S. J., & Kwon, K. (2024). A systematic review of AI education in K-12 classrooms from 2018 to 2023: Topics, strategies, and learning outcomes. *Computers and Education: Artificial Intelligence, 6*, 100211. https://doi.org/10.1016/j.caeai.2024.100211

Li, L. (2022). A literature review of AI education for K-12. *Canadian Journal for New Scholars in Education/Revue canadienne des jeunes chercheures et chercheurs en éducation, 13*(3).114–121.

Li, L., Yu, F., & Zhang, E. (2024). A systematic review of learning task design for K-12 AI education: Trends, challenges, and opportunities. *Computers and Education: Artificial Intelligence, 6*, 100217. https://doi.org/10.1016/j.caeai.2024.100217

Lin, T. A., & Chen, P. H. C. (2022). Artificial intelligence in a structurally unjust society. *Feminist Philosophy Quarterly, 8*(3/4). https://doi.org/10.5206/fpq/2022.3/4.14191

Ma, J., Zhang, Y., Bin, H., Wang, K., Liu, J., & Gao, H. (2022). The development of students' computational thinking practices in AI course using the game-based learning: A case study. In *2022 international symposium on educational technology (ISET)* (pp. 273–277). IEEE. https://doi.org/10.1109/ISET55194.2022.00065

Melsión, G. I., Torre, I., Vidal, E., & Leite, I. (2021, June). Using explainability to help children understand gender bias in AI. In *Proceedings of the 20th Annual ACM Interaction Design and Children Conference*, pp. 87–99. doi:https://doi.org/10.1145/3459990.3460719.

Michaeli, T., Romeike, R., & Seegerer, S. (2023). What students can learn about artificial intelligence—Recommendations for K-12 computing education. In T. Keane, C. Lewin, T. Brinda, & R. Bottino (Eds.), *Towards a collaborative society through creative learning. WCCE 2022. IFIP advances in information and communication technology* (Vol. 685, pp. 196–208). Springer. https://doi.org/10.1007/978-3-031-43393-1_19

Payne, B. (2019). *AI + ethics curriculum for middle school.* Massachusetts Institute of Technology Media Lab.

Peterson, C., & Seligman, M. E. (2004). *Character strengths and virtues: A handbook and classification* (Vol. 1). Oxford University Press.

Polit, D. F., & Beck, C. T. (2004). *Nursing research: Principles and methods.* Lippincott Williams & Wilkins.

Ranieri, M., Cuomo, S., & Biagini, G. (2024). Co-designing media education strategies: A workshop on ai and information literacy. In *Proceedings of the Second International Workshop on Artificial Intelligence Systems in Education co-located with 23rd International Conference of the Italian Association for Artificial Intelligence* (AIxIA 2024), volume—of CEUR Workshop Proceedings.

Raspberry Pi Foundation. (n.d.-a). *Foundations of AI* [Curriculum]. https://experience-ai.org/en/units/foundations-of-ai

Raspberry Pi Foundation. (n.d.-b). *AI Safety* [Curriculum]. https://experience-ai.org/en/units/ai-safety

Roe, J., Furze, L., & Perkins, M. (2025). *GenAI as digital plastic: Understanding synthetic media through critical AI literacy.* arXiv:2411.14730. https://doi.org/10.48550/arXiv.2502.08249.

Sakulkueakulsuk, B., Witoon, S., Ngarmkajornwiwat, P., Pataranutaporn, P., Surareungchai, W., Pataranutaporn, P., & Subsoontorn, P. (2018). Kids making AI: Integrating machine learning, gamification, and social context in STEM education. In *In 2018 IEEE international conference on teaching, assessment, and learning for engineering (TALE)* (pp. 1005–1010). IEEE. https://doi.org/10.1109/TALE.2018.8615249

Sanusi, I. T., & Olaleye, S. A. (2022). An insight into cultural competence and ethics in K-12 artificial intelligence education. In *2022 IEEE global engineering education conference (EDUCON)* (pp. 790–794). IEEE. https://doi.org/10.1109/EDUCON52537.2022.9766818

Sanusi, I. T., Oyelere, S. S., Vartiainen, H., Suhonen, J., & Tukiainen, M. (2023). A systematic review of teaching and learning machine learning in K-12 education. *Education and Information Technologies, 28*, 5967–5997. https://doi.org/10.1007/s10639-022-11416-7

Sperling, K., Stenberg, C. J., McGrath, C., Åkerfeldt, A., Heintz, F., & Stenliden, L. (2024). In search of artificial intelligence (AI) literacy in teacher education: A scoping review. *Computers and Education Open, 100169*. https://doi.org/10.1016/j.caeo.2024.100169

Starratt, R. J. (2014). The purpose of education. In C. M. Branson (Ed.), *Handbook of ethical educational leadership* (pp. 43–61). Routledge.

Su, J., Guo, K., Chen, X., & Chu, S. K. W. (2024). Teaching artificial intelligence in K–12 classrooms: A scoping review. *Interactive Learning Environments, 32*(9), 5207–5226.

Su, J., Ng, D. T. K., & Chu, S. K. W. (2023). Artificial intelligence (AI) literacy in early childhood education: The challenges and opportunities. *Computers and Education: Artificial Intelligence, 4*, 100124. https://doi.org/10.1016/j.caeai.2023.100124

Su, J., & Yang, W. (2022). Artificial intelligence in early childhood education: A scoping review. *Computers and Education: Artificial Intelligence, 3*, 100049. https://doi.org/10.1016/j.caeai.2022.100049

Su, J., & Zhong, Y. (2022). Artificial intelligence (AI) in early childhood education: Curriculum design and future directions. *Computers and Education: Artificial Intelligence, 3*, 100072. https://doi.org/10.1016/j.caeai.2022.100072

Thambu, N. (2017). Storytelling and story reading: A catalyst for inculcate moral values and ethics among preschoolers. *International Journal of Academic Research in Business and Social Sciences, 7*(6), 1116–1130. https://doi.org/10.6007/IJARBSS/v7-i6/3143

Touretzky, D., Gardner-McCune, C., Martin, F., & Seehorn, D. (2019). Envisioning AI for K-12: What should every child know about AI? *Proceedings of the AAAI Conference on Artificial Intelligence, 33*(1), 9795–9799. https://doi.org/10.1609/aaai.v33i01.33019795

United Nations Children's Fund (UNICEF). (2021). *Policy guidance on AI for children 2.0. UNICEF*. https://www.unicef.org/innocenti/.

United Nations Educational, Scientific and Cultural Organization (UNESCO). (2021). *AI and education: Guidance for policy makers*. https://unesdoc.unesco.org/ark:/48223/pf0000376709.

Vygotsky, L. S. (1978). *Mind in society: The development of higher psychological processes*. Harvard University Press.

Wallace, P. (2009). Distance learning for gifted students: Outcomes for elementary, middle, and high school aged students. *Journal for the Education of the Gifted, 32*(3), 295–320. https://doi.org/10.4219/jeg-2009-855

Williams, R., Ali, S., Devasia, N., DiPaola, D., Hong, J., Kaputsos, S. P., Jordan, B., & Breazeal, C. (2023). AI+ ethics curricula for middle school youth: Lessons learned from three project-based curricula. *International Journal of Artificial Intelligence in Education, 33*, 325–383. https://doi.org/10.1007/s40593-022-00298-y

World Economic Forum. (2019). *Generation AI: Establishing global standards for children and AI*. https://www.weforum.org/reports/generation-ai-establishing-global-standards-for-chi ldre n-and-ai

Yue, M., Jong, M. S. Y., & Dai, Y. (2022). Pedagogical design of K-12 artificial intelligence education: A systematic review. *Sustainability, 14*(23), 15620. https://doi.org/10.3390/su142315620

Zhang, H., Lee, I., Ali, S., DiPaola, D., Cheng, Y., & Breazeal, C. (2023). Integrating ethics and career futures with technical learning to promote AI literacy for middle school students: An exploratory study. *International Journal of Artificial Intelligence in Education, 33*(2), 290–324. https://doi.org/10.1007/s40593-022-00293-3

Chapter 4
Artificial Intelligence as a Way of Entering Culture. A Case Study in the Translation of a Literary Work

Gérard Sensevy, Guy Jodry, Pascale Menez, Fabrice Lesage, Christèle Hamard, Carole Le Hénaff, Vasilisa Livinchik, and Caroline Perraud

Abstract This chapter presents a teaching-learning experiment in grade 6 (11-year-olds) focusing on the understanding of literature and language through the specific use of a software program built on a large language model (MLM) infrastructure, the DeepL translator. We describe how this process unfolded in two classes, through the Cooperative Engineering Collective analysis of study films, which we use to show how this device enables students to construct a practice of translation and a new conception of what a language is. This chapter thus describes, in an exploratory manner, a first way of integrating the DeepL translator into an instructional apparatus intended for young students. This chapter is about students starting secondary education, but it is based on a way of teaching and using AI that is also relevant

G. Sensevy (✉) · G. Jodry · C. Hamard · C. Le Hénaff · V. Livinchik · C. Perraud
University of Western Brittany, Brest, France
e-mail: gerard.sensevy@inspe-bretagne.fr

G. Jodry
e-mail: guy.jodry@club-internet.fr

C. Hamard
e-mail: Christele.Hamard@ac-rennes.fr

C. Le Hénaff
e-mail: carole.le-henaff1@inspe-bretagne.fr

V. Livinchik
e-mail: vasilisa.livinchik@etudiant.univ-brest.fr

C. Perraud
e-mail: caroline.perraud@inspe-bretagne.fr

P. Menez
Collège Mathurin Méheut, Melesse, France
e-mail: Pascale.Menez@ac-rennes.fr

F. Lesage
Collège Louis Guilloux, Montfort-sur-Meu, France
e-mail: Fabrice-Mi.Lesage@ac-rennes.fr

S. Papadakis (ed.), *AI Applications in Preschool and Primary Education*, Advances in Artificial Intelligence in Education 5, https://doi.org/10.1007/978-3-032-17190-0_4

to primary education. The chapter is presented as an initial inquiry, intended to be extended over a long duration, into the didactic use of an MLM translator from a culturalist perspective, in which artificial intelligence should help to better understand and renew culture.

Keywords Culture · Literary work · Translation · Artificial intelligence · Massive language model

Introduction

In this chapter, we present a teaching-learning experiment in grade 6 (11-year-olds) focusing on the understanding of literature and language through the specific use of a software program built on a large language model (MLM) infrastructure, the DeepL translator. We describe how this process unfolded in two classes, through the Cooperative Engineering Collective analysis of study films, which we use to show how this device enables students to construct a practice of translation and a new conception of what a language is. This chapter thus describes, in an exploratory manner, a first way of integrating the DeepL translator into an instructional apparatus intended for young students.

This chapter is about students starting secondary education, but it is based on a way of teaching and using AI that is also relevant to primary education. As we will see below, our approach to teaching is based on Joint Action Theory in Didactics (JATD), *which has been developed primarily through research in primary and kindergarten education*. Thus, our approach to studying literary works is informed by primary and kindergarten education (Sensevy & Le Hénaff, 2025). While the integration of AI obviously modifies the structure of apparatuses constructed whether at kindergarten, primary or secondary school, it does not fundamentally alter their structure, as we will explain throughout the text.

The chapter is presented as an initial inquiry, intended to be extended over a long duration, into the didactic use of an MLM translator from a culturalist perspective, in which artificial intelligence should help to better understand and renew culture.

What Is Cooperative Engineering?

We implemented the learning sequence in a Cooperative Engineering Collective (Sensevy et al., 2013; Sensevy & Bloor, 2020), a collective which brought together teachers and researchers.

In the JATD, Cooperative Engineering (CE, Sensevy & Bloor, 2020) is a specific process of design-based research (Cobb et al., 2003), and design-based implementation research (Penuel et al., 2011). The characteristic features of CE broadly situate it within the learning science paradigm (e.g. Koschmann, 2011), and it shares some of its features with lesson studies (e.g. Elliott, 2012) and educational action research (e.g. Kemmis, 2009). The idea of cooperative engineering is closely related to Cultural Historical Activity Theory (Radford, 2024), and particularly to the work of Yrjö Engeström and his colleagues on Expansive Learning (see Engeström, 2016, 2024; Engeström et al., 2023).

In CE, a collective of teachers and researchers engage in a joint action to codesign, implement and re-implement a teaching sequence on a particular topic. Each stage of the process is based on an analysis and evaluation of the previous stage. Therefore, a critical aspect of building cooperative engineering is its iterative structure, which allows the CE team to incrementally build designs that are rooted in culture as craft.

It is important to note that this cooperative work, which brings together researchers and teachers, is in no way dependent on the academic level of the students. For example, it can be carried out in kindergarten (Le Hénaff & Sensevy, 2023; Sensevy & Le Hénaff, 2025), as well as in primary school (CDpE, Didactique & pour Enseigner (CDpE, 2024). Indeed, it is often undertaken outside the school setting (Perraud, 2022).

In this regard, it should be noted that this text itself is the product of this cooperative approach, since the inquiry was constructed in the following process: the collective development of a classroom sequence by both the researchers and the teachers on the team, whom we will refer to as teacher-researchers; the implementation of a sequence S1 by the teacher-researchers with observation and, in some cases, participation of the researchers from the team; the evaluation of the implemented sequence S1 by the entire research team; its reworking to obtain a sequence S2, which in turn is implemented by the teacher-researchers, etc. Finally, the writing itself was a cooperative effort, with a first draft being collectively rewritten by the research team, each of its members, whether teacher-researcher or researcher, participating in the writing process.

The whole process is thus part of an iterative approach aimed at a progressive refinement of hypotheses (Engle et al., 2007), towards a continuous improvement of the Instructional Design.

Elements of Theory and Method

Elements of Theory

The Joint Action Theory in Didactics (JATD)

The Joint Action Theory in Didactics (JATD) has been developed in many research projects in various disciplines (CDpE, Collectif Didactique pour Enseigner (CDpE), 2019, Collectif Didactique pour enseigner (CDpE), 2020, Didactique & pour

Enseigner (CDpE), 2024[1]), on the basis of the following hypothesis. One cannot understand the didactic system (a system in which someone tries to have somebody learn something) without recognizing the relationships between its three subsystems—teacher (X), student (Y), the piece of knowledge at stake (S)—as a whole.

The JATD institutes a specific unit of analysis that is called an epistemic joint action. It is impossible to describe joint action without describing *at the same time* the teacher's action, the student's action, and the way the knowledge at stake shape and is shaped by these actions.

This assertion is a very general and anthropological one. For example, if a parent holds her hands out to a young child, who is learning to walk, as an incentive to make her walk toward these hands, while the young child tries to take some steps to reach these hands, this is an epistemic joint action.

This clearly illustrates the fact that JATD is not focused on a specific age, academic level or setting, as we stated above. It is this anthropological aspect of JATD that leads us to argue that the work presented in this article can be generalized to other age groups, particularly primary school students.

It is important to note that one cannot understand—and even describe—each behavior (parent/teacher or child/student) without considering the joint process and the knowledge (walking) that gives its form to the enacted meanings and gestures.

For example, in this chapter, we will see how the students' translation work is based on their joint action with their teachers in studying the texts and the different possible translations of the same word of sentence—with the help of the MLM Translator.

Culture and Epistemic Kinship

In the JATD, *Culture is seen as a craf*t, a system of skills (know-how) that a person is able to master. In that way, a general exemplar of culture is that of work in professions. A pianist, a surgeon, a glassblower, a fitter, a gardener, a carpenter, a lawyer, etc. demonstrate directly, in their work of *practical connoisseur*, through their *arts of doing* (CDpE, Didactique & pour Enseigner (CDpE), 2024), what culture is. One needs to study how these crafts must be done to understand what culture is, in practical connoisseurs' achievements.

Seeing Culture as a craft has important consequences on education. In the JATD, we follow Charles Péguy's idea: 'the teacher must ensure the representation of culture' (Péguy, 1902/ Péguy, 1993).

We will return to the meaning of this phrase in this chapter, in the structural analysis of the instructional device, and in the study of student's productions. If we accept this idea (*teaching as representation of culture*), the paradigm of Culture as

[1] Readers might want to read a special issue dedicated to the JATD in the journal *Perspectiva Educational:* https://www.perspectivaeducacional.cl/index.php/peducacional/issue/view/62, which focuses in particular on the issue of cooperative engineering.

a craft shapes in a particular way the educational process. Through that perspective, whoever teaches anything has first to think about the content of her teaching not as knowing *that*, but as a knowing *how* (Ryle, 1949, 2009). It is on this condition, in our view, that teaching can achieve a powerful knowledge, and a sufficient epistemic quality (Gericke et al., 2018; Hudson et al., 2023). In other words, whoever teaches anything has to refer first to a specific practice, not to an abstract piece of knowledge. This reference to a specific practice is a reference to a craft, a system of skills. In that way, it is possible to ensure the representation of culture.

This is not to say that the teacher should imitate how a skilled craftsperson works, let alone that the student should do so. We contend that a teaching design must meet the aim of an *epistemic kinship* (Sensevy, 2025) between the practice of practical connoisseurs and the didactic activities of students and teachers. What do we mean by *epistemic kinship*, in the JATD? First of all, it is necessary that the teacher builds a model of the practical connoisseur's activity. This refers to get the essence of the practical connoisseur's craft, relatively to a given situation of teaching and learning. In this chapter, we refer to the practical connoisseur as a reader who is both a connoisseur of literature and a translator. This person is capable of appreciating a given expression in one language, its translation, and the range of meanings that translation can open up. It should also be a practical connoisseur of MLM. We will return to this point later.

Literature, and Moral Life

We therefore subscribe to a vision of culture as a craft, a culture that teachers must represent. By having students read Mark Twain's Tom Sawyer (Twain, 2012), we subscribe to a vision of literature as a means of increasing our sensible attention to human life, as expressed by Sandra Laugier:

> Literature, through the education of sensibility it offers us, has given rise to a new form of attention to ordinary human life, with an awareness of its details and differences, a sensitivity to meaning, and an appreciation of the importance of its moments. Reading proves to be a true experience, indissolubly intellectual and sensible: an "adventure of the personality" (Martha Nussbaum) that transforms the nature of moral thought.[2] (Laugier, 2006).

Thus, when we work in JATD, we try to find meanings in a literary work that can increase our sensibility and attention to the ordinary lives of the characters, and thus to the people that these characters represent. But this attention must go beyond generalities. From our perspective, which is one of the ascent from the abstract to the concrete, we focus our didactic activity on very concrete passages of the work, passages of a few lines, that seem to us to be emblematic of a dimension of human life that this passage is working on, not in a general, abstract way, but in the materiality of ordinary life. Thus, in this article, we will focus on two moments of this kind in the plot of Mark Twain's Tom Sawyer, in order to carry out this work of attention, in the study and translation, with the help of the MLM translator, of the literary passage.

[2] Our translation.

Representations, Intelligence, Epistemic Solidarity

The JATD, as we have said, attaches great importance to *the ascent from the abstract to the concrete*, in the process of knowledge in general and in the process of education in particular. For us, to educate means, in the words of Charles Péguy, to *ensure the representation of culture*. *Representation* must be understood here in its *concrete, material sense* (Hacking, 1986), not only of works of all kinds in their materiality, but also in the symbolic systems that make it possible to represent them. Thus, for us, to understand something is first and foremost to be able to *represent* it, through words, through a text, through symbolic systems such as a diagram (Brender & Marrinan, Bender & Marrinan, 2010), in the broad sense of the term diagram (tables, graphs, maps, figures, infographics, etc.), as formalisms, but also through pantomime or gestures as found in theatrical representation (Brecht, 1995, 2019).

For this reason, in the empirical part of this text, we will focus our discussion on diagrams, in particular "translation tables", which represent the conceptual activity necessary for a manifold understanding of the literary passages under study. We believe that translation is a way of understanding (Eco, 2001), in the sense of a creative understanding, also a creative imitation. To translate is, in a way, to imitate-understand the other, to develop attention to human life, as we mentioned in the preceding part.

It is therefore understandable that representations construct intelligence about what they represent, providing objective knowledge in the sense that Popper intended (Popper, 1995). But they do more than that. By objectifying knowledge in a material form (oral, graphic, gestural, etc.), representations, if studied in a certain way, enable what we call in JATD "epistemic solidarity". Epistemic solidarity is what happens when each person in a collective has the epistemic and affective real possibilities to work on the same problem. The joint study of representations of knowledge within a collective, up to and including the joint construction of a common representation of that knowledge, is a means, which we believe is essential in this collective, of creating epistemic solidarity.

Elements of Method: A Method of Paradigmatic Analogy

In this paper, we explore a specific method, which we could call the ascent from the abstract to the concrete *method* (on *the ascent from the abstract to the concrete*, see Engeström et al., 2012; Ilyenkov, 1982; Marx, 1993). We want to concretize our theoretical analyses in emblematic examples, potential *exemplars*, in the sense of Kuhn (1977). It is the description of these exemplars, as we will do below, that allows us to work out the problem we described above, that is, the way in which a teacher, working within a cooperative engineering framework, can build an epistemic kinship between the activity of the practical connoisseur (here, the translator) and the didactic activity, in order to ensure the representation of culture. This method can thus be described in an *epistemology of paradigmatic analogy*. Exemplars are thus conceived as paradigms *of* and *in* culture, the concrete study of which constitutes the method described above.

The device has been implemented with grade 6 students, three teachers-researchers (French and English (2)) of the cooperative engineering team in a secondary school. Its implementation has been filmed and partly transcribed, and the documents used by the students working with the MLM translator have been collected.

Instructional Design: An Overview

The students were asked to study Mark Twain's classic, *The Adventures of Tom Sawyer*, in both French and English.[3]

Mark Twain's tom Sawyer

This book was chosen for two main reasons. Firstly, because it is a masterpiece, and a classic work of literature, and we believe it is important to expose students to essential works at an early age. Ernest Hemingway (Hemingway, 1996/ Hemingway, 1996, p. 29) said of Tom Sawyer's companion book, Huckleberry Finn: "It's the best book we've had… All American writing comes from that. There was nothing before. There has been nothing as good since." One might think that Tom Sawyer is not very different from its older brother, especially since it offers many passages that are very dense in both sense and sensibility, in describing human condition.

The Structure of the Instructional Design

The General Structure of the Instructional Design

The general instructional design was as follows.

The student started by working out a general overview of the book, both in French and in English. To do this, they first watched the original 1938 film, without subtitles, directed by Norman Taurog (Taurog, 1938) and entitled *The Adventures of Tom Sawyer*. Although this film is not entirely faithful to Twain's book, it offers many of the basic episodes from the book and therefore allowed the students to

[3] The edition the students worked on was an abridged translation (Twain, 2022), based on the old translation by François de Gaïl (First years of the twentieth century, see below). We also used the translation from the Pléiade library (Twain, 2025) by Thomas Constantinesco, and several editions of Mark Twain's book in the original language, notably Twain (2012)/.

develop a *global vision* of the story. The students then read the book, focusing particularly on certain chapters and drawing on the many original illustrations by Truman Williams, while referring back to the filmed passages as often as necessary. The cooperative engineering teacher-researchers were the teachers of the English (two teachers-researches) and French (one teacher-researcher) classes in which the study was conducted.

As we have begun to see, an essential part of this apparatus was the translation of certain passages of the work. We will describe this part of the apparatus below, but it should be noted that the teachers often worked in co-teaching teams, with one English teacher and one French teacher leading the students' study, and a researcher observing the session and intervening with the students in certain cases.

The Specific Structure of the Translational Design

We will describe the students' activity in translational design in more detail below, but here we will outline the general form of the apparatus.

The students are presented with a specific statement within a passage or scene that the engineering collective has deemed particularly interesting, both from the point of view of language and from the point of view of attention to human life. In this chapter, we will focus on two short statements from the dozen or so that have been studied and translated in classes over two years.

The first statement is "*His gratitude for their gifts had always smote their conscience before. It cut deeper than ever this time.*" The second statement is "*His soul was at peace.*"

This work is done after the students have built up an overall picture of the book and have studied the scene in question. It is done in the following stages

1. The students make a personal translation proposal without any tools. They don't have computers, otherwise they are tempted to use the DeepL MLM Translator directly without searching—some of them being either too afraid to make a mistake or don't dare to express their own idea.
2. They look up the translations proposed by the DeepL translator.
3. They find in the French text how the French translator (François de Gaïl) translated the proposed statement.
4. They propose a new translation, taking into account their overall study.

Two Emblematic Examples of the Study of Mark Twain's tom Sawyer

As we have already mentioned, we document the work carried out by presenting two examples, which we consider emblematic, of how, in our cooperative engineering collective, we have worked in the classes studying Mark Twain's Tom Sawyer, organizing this study around the translation of certain statements.

Muff Potter and the Dilemma of tom Sawyer

The Dilemma of tom Sawyer

The first statement we present in this study comes from Chap. X of Tom Sawyer. Muff Potter, a villager with a drinking problem, is accused of a murder he did not commit. Because he was drunk and knocked out at the time of the crime, he cannot remember that he is innocent. However, Tom and Huckleberry Finn (Huck) witnessed the crime and know that Injun Joe is the real culprit, not Muff Potter, with whom they have been friends for a long time. But the two children are afraid to report the murder. They fear the revenge that Injun Joe would inflict on them if they took responsibility. So they remain silent, while trying to help Muff Potter by showing him friendly attention, especially by offering him small gifts (tobacco) through the bars of the prison where they have come to visit him. The statement "His gratitude for their gifts had always smote their conscience before. It cut deeper than ever this time" must be understood in this context. Muff Potter is moved to tears by Tom and Huck's gifts and expresses his deep gratitude to them, which further reinforces the guilt of the two children, who only need to report the real culprit to have their friend released.

Therefore, one way of paraphrasing and commenting on Mark Twain's statement in order to extract its meaning might be: His gratitude for their gifts (which was unwarranted, since those gifts covered up Potter's "betrayal" by the two children) "had always smote their conscience before" (had already smoted their conscience before, precisely because it was unwarranted and made that betrayal all the more salient). "It cut deeper than ever this time" (because Potter had never expressed this gratitude with such emotion and strength, reflecting the strength and emotion with which the children feel their "betrayal", which is also an inability to take responsibility and have the courage to denounce Injun Joe).

The Translation Table for "The dilemma of Tom Sayer": Presentation and some Comments

Below (Fig. 4.1) we can see the translation table referred to above. (We have translated the original French (on the left) into English (on the right)):

The worksheet

Nom:

Le dilemme de Tom Sawyer : la scène avec Muff Potter devant la prison, exercice de traduction

Objectif de la séance:
Traduire « His gratitude for their gifts had always smote their consciences before, it cut deeper than ever this time. »

Colonne par colonne, suis les étapes du travail : (si tu as de la place dans les cases, tu peux ajouter des remarques sur la traduction)	1.Relie les déterminants possessifs aux personnages de l'image	2. Fais une première proposition de traduction sans outil.	3. Recherche dans DeepL ce qui est proposé par le traducteur	4. Recherche dans le texte français (scène devant la prison avec Muff Potter) comment la phrase est traduite	5. Fais ta deuxième proposition de traduction
	His gratitude				
	for **their** gifts				
	had always smote **their** consciences before				
	it cut deeper than ever this time				

Au cours du travail, tu peux noter des mots intéressants à rechercher sur le wiktionnaire :

Worksheet translation

Name:

Tom Sawyer's dilemma: the scene with Muff Potter outside the prison, translation exercise

Session's objective:
Translate: « His gratitude for their gifts had always smote their consciences before, it cut deeper than ever this time. »

Colonne par colonne, suis les étapes du travail : (si tu as de la place dans les cases, tu peux ajouter des remarques sur la traduction)	1. Link the possessive determiners to the characters in the picture.	2. Make a first translation proposal without a tool	3. Search in Deepl the translator's suggestions	4. Find out in the French text (scene in front of the prison with Muff Potter) how the sentence is translated	5. Make your second translation
	His gratitude				
	for **their** gifts				
	had always smote **their** consciences before				
	it cut deeper than ever this time				

As you work, you can write interesting words to look up on Wiktionary:

Fig. 4.1 "His gratitude for their gifts" translation table. *Source* authors, 2025

The columns of the table (starting with the third above) follow the structure already mentioned: the students make a personal translation proposal *without* the MLM translator (designated column 1); they look up the translations proposed by the DeepL translator (designated column 2); They find in the French text how the French translator (François de Gaïl) translated the proposed statement (designated column 3); they propose a new translation, taking into account their overall study (designated column 4).

This translation table is therefore a *representation*, in the sense explained above. It acts as a tool in several ways: 1) it structures the students' perception and understanding with the titles of each column, which make them consider the possible diversity of translations as "natural"; it thus encourages the students not to accept directly their initial idea, or the translation by the DeepL translator "because it is a machine that cannot make mistakes", or that of the professional translator (François de Gail), even if it is established by a certain tradition; 2) it encourages them, in the incentive provided in the last column ("make your second translation proposal"), to produce a new, more accurate proposal based on the previous ones. We will consider this case in the following example (His soul was at peace).

Muff Potter and the Dilemma of tom Sawyer: In the Classroom

The classroom sessions were filmed and then studied by the engineering collective. Below (Fig. 4.2) is a short example of this work, at the beginning of the process.

We start with a screenshot from one of the films used by the team for analysis.

As a simple illustration, this screenshot can give some indication of how the study (Sensevy et al., 2022; Sensevy & Bloor, 2020) is a tool for engineering work.

In the upper left half, we can see an excerpt from the transcript of the exchange between a pair of students working in the session at the top, and the two students

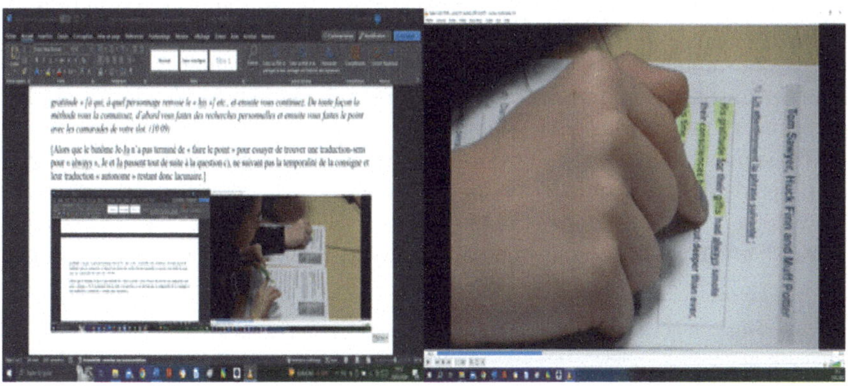

Fig. 4.2 The Cooperative Engineering Collective at work, a screenshot from a study film. *Source* authors, 2025

Table 4.1 Transcript "cut" and "smote" between the E1 et E2 students

A pair of students come up with the words "smote" and "cut". One of the students organizes the "division of labour"
E1: You type in your code and look up "smote" and I'll look up "cut".
E2: (searches on DeepL and finds "frappé" [hit]— El repeats the process after E2, and both conclude that "frappé" is the translationfor "smote) El and E2 look at each other in amazement at the translation they have obtained, and E2 says "hit"?
El: (searches for "cut") "cut"
E2: Try an e El:
E1: (checks on DeepL) mignon (cute)!
E2: It goes from couper (cut)" to mignon (cute)" (to El who starts writing) it's "couper" (cut) (affirmative) El raises her hand to ask the teacher for help
E2: No, don't raise your hand! I want to / I think we can do it ourselves

Source authors, 2025

working together at the bottom left; in the right half, we can see a close-up of a student's hand reading the statement "His gratitude".

The work is not easy for these young pupils and the pair faces many difficulties. Nevertheless, progress can be made. Consider the following example of a first use of the DeepL translator:

This excerpt shows us students using the DeepL translator. When confronted with words they don't know ("smote" in the expression "smote their conscience before" and "cut" in the expression "It cut deeper than ever this time"), they share the task. It is interesting to note their legitimate surprise at the verb "smote" (it should be noted that this verb is always replaced by DeepLWrite when asked to "correct" Mark Twain's text[4]). It is also interesting to note that, given the choice between "cute" and "cut", they chose "cut" without hesitation.

This first example seems to show how these students can maintain a certain clarity when faced with DeepL's proposals and how, on the other hand, this translator leads them to question the language and their knowledge. This is the beginning of their use of the translator and we will see a more in-depth use in the following example.

The rest of the exchange is worth noting.

After almost 30 minutes of work, this pair, who had never been helped on this point, opted for a "wording" ("*sa* (his) gratitude") that seemed to them to be in line with the meaning of the rest of the sentence, but without ever having managed to "translate" the "his" with any certainty, only by "default". They have "found" a

[4] It is interesting to note that in De Gail's translation the word "remorse" (remords) is used in a periphrasis to translate "smote". However, the etymology of the word "remorse" refers to the idea of "couper" ("smote"). This idea was available to the students in their Wiktionary research and had been mentioned in French class. Thus, the specific intelligence of the "human" translation of the word "remords", which does not appear in Mark Twain's text, is clearly evident here and provides an opportunity for an inquiry into the language itself, which allows us to note, for example, that the English word "remorse" comes from the French "remords".

Table. 4.2 The rest of the exchange between the E1 and E2 students

El and E2 now really have to translate. The pronoun "his" is a problem for all pairs of students in the class. El and E12 try to start the translation into French with the determiner "le" (the), but don't continue...
E2 (to E1) in the worst case, put SA Sa gratitude (El writes according to E2's suggestion, who follows suit) Sa.-. Gratitude... (a correct translation)

Source authors, 2025

solution based on the text (and) in order to be consistent with it. This seems important to us because it shows a way of thinking about translation that gives a prominent place to the linguistic situation in which the sentence occurred.

Let us now consider the second emblematic example of this chapter.

His Soul Was at Peace

His Soul Was at Peace

The studied extract from *Tom Sawyer* is to be found in chap. 10.

There is something essential in the brevity of the plot. Sid, Tom's half-brother, told their Aunt Polly after Tom had played truant. In retaliation, he threw clods at him, which hit their target. Describing Tom's final state of mind, Twain said that "his soul was at peace".

This little story interested us for two reasons. To put it in a nutshell, from an ethical point of view, there is a curious contradiction between Tom's state of mind, having committed a (minor) act of violence against his brother, and the phrase "his soul was at peace", which one would expect to be used to characterize an act of peace, describing a form of blissful harmony, rather than, as here, the state following an act of violence. From a novelistic point of view, this is not an insignificant detail: Tom is a complex character, always ready to slip into ethically questionable behaviour (as shown at the end of Huckleberry Finn, where Tom displays quasi-sadistic behaviour towards the slave Jim). From a linguistic point of view, the statement is interesting, especially in the light of what we have just said because François de Gaïl,[5] the French translator of the book used by the students, translated this expression as "Il avait la conscience tranquille" ("He had a clear conscience"), which introduces an interesting nuance with a certain irony (how can one have a "clear conscience" when one has just committed an act of violence?)

[5] François de Gaïl (1874–1947) is the first French Translator of Mark Twain: https://fr.wikisource.org/wiki/Auteur:Fran%C3%A7ois_de_Ga%C3%AFl

The Translation Table for "His soul was at peace": Presentation and some Comments

Below (Fig. 4.1) we can see the translation table relating to the study of this excerpt. (As before, we have translated the original French (on the left) into English (on the right)):

The worksheet

Objectif de la séance : bien traduire «His soul was at peace» (fin du chapitre 2)

La vengeance de Tom contre Sid :
Rappel : Tom vient de se venger de Sid qui l'a dénoncé à Tante Polly.

First and family name: ________________ Date: ________

English words or sentence to translate	1.Fais une première proposition de traduction sans outil.	2. Recherche sur le site de traduction Deepl ce qui est proposé et écris 3 traductions possibles:	3. Recherche dans le texte français (à la fin du chapitre 2 page27) comment la phrase est traduite et recopie cela :	4. Rédige ta propre traduction en français de la phrase en anglais « his soul was at peace » pour bien montrer la manière de penser de Tom par rapport à Sid
Soul		1. ____ 2. ____ 3. ____		
Peace		1. ____ 2. ____ 3. ____		
His soul was at peace		1. ____ 2. ____		

Lorsque tu as trouvé la traduction proposée p.27 du livre, réponds à la question suivante

Qu'est-ce que cela montre du personnage de Tom Sawyer ?

____

Présente ton travail à ton professeur

Puis, rédige ta propre production en réponse à la question 4 ; lorsque tu as terminé, va au bureau et récupère la fiche pour apporter tes commentaires.

Worksheet translation

Session's objective : find a good translation of «His soul was at peace» (end of chapter 2)

Tom's revenge against Sid
Reminder : Tom has just taken revenge on Sid who has denounced him to Aunt Polly.

English words or sentence to translate	1. Make a first suggestion of translation without a tool	2. Search on the Deepl translation site what's on offer and write down three possible translations	3. Search in the French text (end of chapter 2, page 27), how is the sentence translated? Copy this	4. Write your own French translation of this English version "his soul was at peace" to show Tom's way of thinking in relation to Sid
His soul was at peace		1. ____ 2. ____		

When you have found the translation proposed on p.27 of the book, answer the following questionwhat does it tell about Tom Sawyer?

Present your work to your teacher

Then write your own production in question 4. When you have finished, go to the teacher's desk to take the worksheet and make your comments

Fig. 4.3 "His soul was at peace" Translation table. *Source* authors, 2025

It is interesting to compare the two translation tables (The "Potter Table" and the "Peace Table"), a comparison that can illustrate how the iterative refinement process specific to cooperative engineering affects the representations here.

Indeed, we can see that while the first "effective" column of this representation system is the same in both cases ("Make a first translation proposal without a tool"), the others are different. The second column presents a different incentive. In the "Potter table", students are told: "Research DeepL for translator's suggestion"; in the "Peace Table", they are asked "Search on the DeepL translation site for what's on offer and *write 3 possible translations*". Time has passed and the students have practiced using DeepL Translator, and they have practiced the fact that the translator can offer several possible translations. By instituting this fact at the center of the representation (since it is part of the normal work of the class to ask for multiple translations of the same word or phrase), the class makes it a habitual way of working, in *epistemic kinship* with the culture of professional translators, for whom this multiple possibility is at the heart of their profession.

The fourth column also represents an important shift. We move from "Make your second translation proposal" (The "Potter table") to "Write your own translation of the English sentence" to show Tom's way of thinking in relation to Sid" (The "Peace table").

Here we can see how the problem is made more complex in the sense that not only a new translation based on the previous work is required, but also additional commentary on the meaning of the expression. The iterative improvement here concerns the epistemic density of the translation work, i.e., the need to ensure that the work is consistent and resonant with the book's universe, and, in particular, with the relationships between the characters.

His Soul Was at Peace: In the Classroom

To give an idea of the students' work with this translation table, we provide two examples of their work.

Example 1. Student A

In this first example, several elements can be highlighted by focusing on columns 1, 3 and 5:

- The student did not manage to produce a correct initial translation, as he suggested "La musique et la paix" (probably based on "*soul* music"), then "l'âme de la paix"; – the second column shows the "multiple translation" work that becomes a habit with DeepL, as the student manages to come up with several translations for each word, relying on DeepL;
- The third column also shows interesting work, as the student used DeepL to "back-translate" François de Gaïl's French translation ("Il avait la conscience tranquille") into English, coming up with "Tom had a clear conscience". He then added his own translation ("il avait la mémoire libérée" - his memory was liberated), which gives

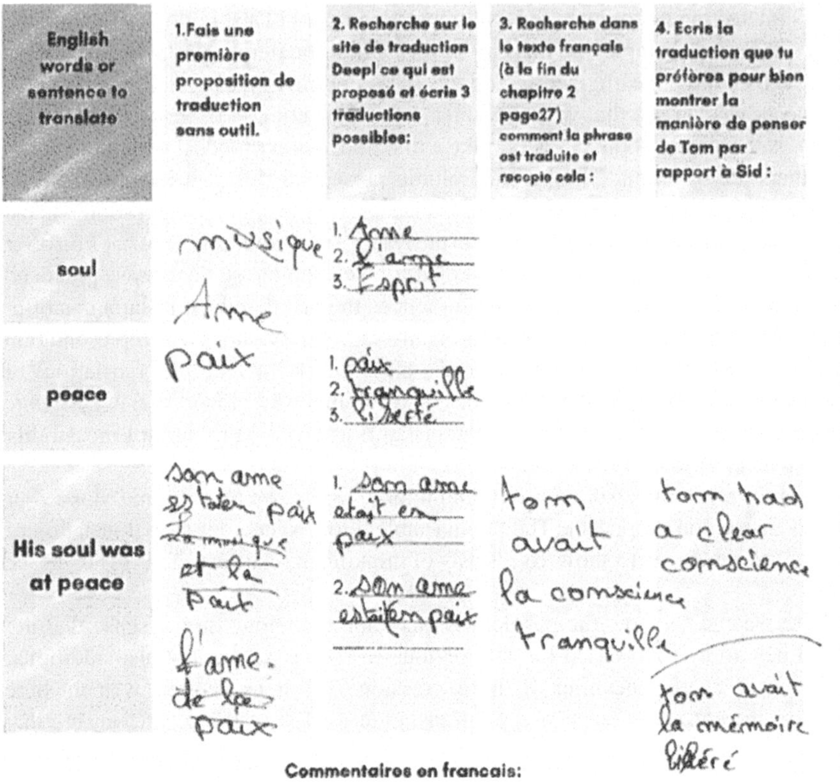

English words or sentence to translate	1.Fais une première proposition de traduction sans outil.	2. Recherche sur le site de traduction Deepl ce qui est proposé et écris 3 traductions possibles:	3. Recherche dans le texte français (à la fin du chapitre 2 page27) comment la phrase est traduite et recopie cela :	4. Ecris la traduction que tu préfères pour bien montrer la manière de penser de Tom par rapport à Sid :
soul	musique Ame	1. Ame 2. l'ame 3. Esprit		
peace	paix	1. paix 2. tranquille 3. liberté		
His soul was at peace	son ame est en paix ~~la musique~~ et la paix l'ame. de ~~la~~ paix	1. son ame était en paix 2. son ame est en paix	tom avait la conscience tranquille	tom had a clear conscience tom avait la mémoire libéré

Commentaires en francais:

Fig. 4.4 Student A ("His soul was at peace"). *Source* authors, 2025

the phrase an interesting "memorial" meaning that is not obvious in Twain's original phrase, and which implies a relationship, to be deepened, between "memory" and "peace".

On this last point, it is worth noting—and we will return to this briefly in the summary of this text—that obtaining a translation table corresponding to a given passage for each student is a substance for future work. Here, for example, the whole class will be able to discuss how the student has back-translated the French professional translator's translation of the work, and they will also be able to discuss the student's own translation. The translation tables therefore constitute the subject of a collective inquiry designed to promote epistemic solidarity, the fact that a common background is gradually built up *as each student works on the same problem* (here, the translation of "His soul was at peace") and *understands as well as possible how each other student* has worked on this very problem.

Example 2. Student B

English words or sentence to translate	soul	peace	His soul was at peace.
1) **Ecris** une première proposition de traduction, sans outil :	Nettoyer	pièce	Tu nettoies cette pièce
2) **Recherche** ce qui est proposé sur le site de traduction **DeepL**, et **écris** 3 traductions possibles :	1. âme 2. esprit 3. cœur	1. paix 2. liberté 3. tranquilité	1. Son âme était en paix 2. Il a l'âme en paix 3. Son esprit est en paix
3) **Recherche** dans le texte français (à la fin du chapitre 2, p 27) comment la phrase est traduite, et **recopie** cela :			Traduction en français (p.27) : Tom avait la conscience tranquille,
4) **Rédige**, en français, ta propre traduction de la phrase en anglais « His soul was at peace. » **Montre** bien la manière de penser de Tom par rapport à Sid :			Ma / Mes proposition(s) : Tom était tranquille parce que la justice était faite.

Fig. 4.5 Student B ("His soul was at peace"). *Source* authors, 2025

This example was produced in another cooperative engineering class (which explains the different presentation of the translation table, where the rows correspond to the columns in the table above).

As in the previous example, several points can be highlighted:

- Line 1, the student did not manage to provide a correct initial translation as he proposed "Tu nettoies cette pièce" (You clean this room), probably because "peace" is phonetically similar to "pièce";
- In line 2, he uses DeepL effectively, first to find three translations for each of the suggested words, and then to suggest three translations for the entire sentence. These translations show his efforts to stick to the source sentence, as each of them contains the word "paix" (peace), which seems to indicate a confident and relevant understanding of this source sentence;
- Line 4, the student produces his own translation. It is worth noting that that he provides a translation ("Tom était tranquille"—"Tom was tranquil") that shows an interesting choice, particularly in that it avoids translating the word soul—which can also be seen as a way of avoiding the difficulty of translation. This avoidance strategy is in a way inherent to translation (the translator can cut the Gordian knot of translating a difficult word or expression by leaving out the more or less direct translation of that word or expression) and would be revisited later

in a class discussion. This avoidance strategy, with its strengths and weaknesses, can then become part of the class's didactic memory as an emblem (or "sub-paradigm") attached to this emblematic example of "His soul was at peace". The student's production also contains an attempt to address the prompt "Show how Tom thinks about Sid", as the student gives a reason for Tom's "peace of mind". If he is at peace, it is because "justice has been done" ("justice était faite"). The idea somehow reverses the responsibility. Tom's violence becomes "legitimate" because it was produced in response to an injustice. It is interesting to note that this interpretation based on justice comes from the French translation by François de Gaïl, reproduced here by the student, and is absent from Mark Twain's original ("His soul was at peace, now that he had settled with Sid"). Thomas Constantinesco, the French translator of the latest French edition (2017), translates the whole sentence much more literally as "Il avait l'âme en paix, maintenant qu'il avait réglé ses comptes avec Sid" (His soul was at peace, now that he had settled his accounts with Sid).

Elements for a Synthesis

We would now like to provide some elements of a synthesis of this text.

A Practice of Translation Including AI

About the Practice of Translation

In our cooperative engineering team, where teacher-researchers and researchers work together, the use of the MLM translator is part of a specific conception of teaching work. This is a conception in which teaching activity, didactic activity, must be produced over a long duration. This didactic time, as we call it in JATD (see in particular Sensevy, 2025), is therefore not that of a curriculum whose elements must be skimmed over one after the other, sequentially. It is a time for inquiry, based on the students' productions, from which the class moves forward. From this perspective, the *translation tables* we gave a few examples of above are not just a product of inquiry, they are the starting point for a new inquiry (the same inquiry continued).

For example, the teacher-researcher (the English teacher-researcher and the French teacher-researcher together, within the cooperative engineering collective) can choose some of the translation tables produced by the students based on the epistemic possibilities they offer. The class collective can then compare them in the light of their translation choices and study them for what they can reveal about each language. The class collective can also use them to explore, as we have indicated above, the moral lives of the characters that the literary work allows us to understand.

The two extracts studied above give us a clear understanding of how Tom's sensibility is touched by Potter's unjustified gratitude (we know that he will end up, with great courage, taking responsibility for denouncing Injun Joe) and how he behaves with a certain violence towards Sid with a good conscience. Far from being a machine that quickly produces a ready-made truth, the MLM translator is therefore part of this process of study and personal (for each student) and collective deliberation. This requires the use of different strategies. Below we describe three that we have begun to explore.

The Student's First Translation as a Starting Point, the Student's New Translation as an End Point

When studying the translation tables, we noticed that students are systematically asked to start the table with their own translation, in order to anchor the work in their own abilities. Often these young students do not have sufficient skills to produce even an approximate translation, but on the one hand this initial effort allows them and their teachers to become aware of their way of translating and thus of their relationship with the language (source and target language), and on the other hand to measure the progress made between their first translation (column 1 of the table) and their (provisional) last translation (column 4 of the table). The MLM Translator is part of this study as a kind of aid to the student's "translation journey", which they can use at the same time as the other kind of analysis of the literary text that is the subject of the inquiry.

This brings us to a second strategy based on the MLM Translator.

Systematic Multitranslation

As we have seen above, this strategy consists of asking students to use DeepL not to obtain the "right answer" for translation, but to understand the diversity of solutions available for translating Twain's book. We have seen that students understand this diversity first at the level of the isolated word, then at the level of the sentence, thanks to the suggestions provided by the MLM Translator. The MLM translator therefore does not act as a "reducer of possibilities", but as a machine for working on the plasticity of language (Culioli, 1995), i.e. the ability of language to adjust to different constraints of utterance. More specifically, in literary translation, the MLM Translator helps students to produce different translations of the same term or phrase, thereby integrating multitranslation as a fundamental category of their relationship with language. This relationship has to do with that of a practical connoisseur in translation (in line with our conception of epistemic kinship). In that way, when we asked the students to explore the alternatives offered by the MLM Translator and choose the three that seemed most relevant, the challenge was to understand and integrate that a translation is not literal. It is also important to note that it was necessary to work on concrete examples of multitranslation before the actual work. With this in mind, we feel it is crucial to make the following point here. This systematic multitranslation is not provided ready-made by the MLM Translator. It requires learning. For example, we had to remind students or explicitly teach them that the alternatives appeared in a "drop-down menu", i.e., that they have to scroll down with their cursor and see "other suggestions", some of which were much more appropriate for the translation.

There is therefore a learning process for using this device (computer plus MLM translator) that is intertwined with the more or less deep exploration/exploitation of DeepL's potential in terms of alternatives.

Reverse Translation and Translation Circle

In one of his books, Umberto Eco (2001) mentions a translation practice that involves taking a text written in language L1, translating it first into language L2 and then translating it back into language L1. The "translation circle" can be extended and the same process can be applied to three, four or more languages. We used a variation of this principle in our cooperative engineering collective, as shown below. This means that the students start with the French translation of their reference work to obtain an English version in several forms (for example, in François de Gail's translation, "*il avait la conscience tranquille*" (literally "the had his conscience tranquil") is translated back by DeepL as "he had a clear conscience" or "he felt clear about his conscience", etc.) and then compare it with Mark Twain's text. Reverse translation, in the example above, therefore incorporates the multitranslation capabilities offered by the MLM Translator.

Towards a New Conception of What a Language Is

Such translation work gradually builds a new conception of what language is, in that language is no longer an exact cutting of reality in an essentialist vision, but a means of grasping very specific realities through adjustments. These adjustments are made possible by the plasticity of language (Culioli, 1995, 2009), which allows us, through language, to deal with the realities of the situations we face and to understand each other. Translation from one language to another, insofar as it allows us to become aware of the different cuts that each language produces from the different situations that people face, is a privileged means of constructing a more precise and accurate anti-essentialist conception of language.

From the perspective of using the MLM translator, we would like to emphasize the following point. The way in which language is conceived through this use seems particularly appropriate for primary school and kindergarten. Translating from one language to another is an effective way to stimulate an interest in languages and develop an understanding of language from an early age (García et al., 2019), in particular at primary school. This approach makes students, particularly young ones, aware that different languages, in order to "say the same thing", actually say *more or less* the same thing, *almost* the same thing (Eco, 2001[6]). This *more or less*, this *almost*, are not a flaw, but a valuable asset in dialogue between people who speak different languages. Using an MLM translator aligns with this way of thinking and acting.

AI and Culture

Artificial Intelligence and the representation of culture

It may be useful to comment on the term "artificial intelligence". In our work, we use the word "intelligence" to refer to the intelligence *of* something (Sensevy, 2025; Sensevy & Le Hénaff, 2025). For example, in this paper, intelligence is not a "general ability", but lies in the way one is able to deeply understand the meaning of a given precise sentence, able to build an intelligence *of* this sentence, within "the ethical adventure of the book"'. We also see knowledge, as we have said, in its material form. So, for us, artificial intelligence through MLMs is above all an instrument that helps to materialize, to amplify, our concrete intelligence of language and culture in a particular sentence. In this sense, an MLM translator is not artificial, but a concrete instrument of human work. Its main task, working on texts, is to *represent* these texts. In this sense, an MLM translator can be an instrument that helps to *ensure the representation of culture*, as Péguy said.

Culture, confidence and critique.

We believe that a key issue in culture is the dialectic between confidence and critique. Our hypothesis is this: in order to progress in culture, in the crafts and skills that it can equip us with, it is essential to develop a strong confidence in the people who transmit this culture to us. But this trust, as necessary as it may be, must not become a form of servitude, especially a form of epistemic servitude. In our view, it requires a form of critique, not of the person who transmits an element of culture to us, but of that element of culture itself. In this text, the use of the MLM translator is a kind of metaphor for this dialectic. Because they represent a part of culture as it can be expressed in texts, the translations of the MLM Translator must be viewed with a certain amount of confidence. But they must also be subjected to critical thinking, particularly, as we have seen, in the use of multitranslation and translation circle techniques. The relationship that the students establish with the MLM Translator can therefore be considered as the relationship with any source of knowledge: confidence, when we know that this source represents human work and culture; criticism, which always encourages, in the spirit of the Enlightenment, not to accept without rigorous examination the proposals of this source of knowledge, be it a teacher, a politician, oneself or an AI.

[6] The original title of Eco's book is *Dire quasi la stessa cosa*, (*To say almost the same thing*)

Artificial Intelligence and co-intelligence of

From this perspective, we can think of AI as a "thinking companion", as Mollick invites us to do when he writes:

> AI can act as a thinking companion to improve our own decision-making, helping us to reflect on our own choices (rather than simply relying on the AI to make choices for us). (Mollick, 2024, p. 49).

In this chapter we have tried to demonstrate in a concrete way how MLM Translator can be a "thinking companion". It should be noted that the use of this translator in the apparatus we have presented makes it possible to build a literary co-intelligence of the sentences and statements studied and, moreover, to enable students to better understand, by comparing different translations, the nature of the moral dilemmas that the characters may face and, more generally, the ethical significance of their behaviour.

Moreover, we must be aware that this co-intelligence of translation problems, which the MLM translator helps to understand, must also be based on a specific intelligence, first on the part of researchers and teachers, and then on the part of students, an intelligence of how such an MLM works (Mollick, 2024; Sundarajan, 2024), in epistemic kinship with the *art of doing* of a practical connoisseur of MLM. In order for the MLM translator to become a "thinking companion", we must learn to think as it "thinks" itself, in order to be able to construct with it a specific joint action that produces the intelligence *of* what is being studied (on this point, see notably Clark, 2004, 2011, 2024).

Artificial intelligence and common good

It is widely acknowledged that the environmental impact of AI is a matter of serious concern.

Bolon-Canedo et al. highlight the following facts:

> Some authors have estimated that training GPT-3 on a database of 500 billion words required 1287 MWh of electricity and 10,000 computer chips, equivalent to the energy needed to power around 121 homes for a year in the USA. Furthermore, this training produced around 550 tons of carbon dioxide, equivalent to flying 33 times from Australia to the UK. Since the subsequent version, GPT-4, was trained on 570 times more parameters than GPT-3, it undoubtedly required even more energy. The environmental cost is not restricted to training, as using these systems also has a cost. As an example, GPT-3 was accessed 590 million times in January 2023, leading to energy consumption equivalent to that of 175,000 persons. Moreover, in inference time, each ChatGPT query consumes energy equivalent to running a 5 W LED bulb for 1hr 20 min, representing 260.42 MWh per day. (Bolon-Canedo et al., Bolón-Canedo et al., 2024, p. 128096).

This raises the general question of how to think about AI from an environmental perspective, which is to say from an inseparable ethical and political perspective (Bolte & van Wynsberghe, 2024).[7] We therefore argue that it is essential to consider AI from a democratic perspective of emancipation within the New Enlightenment,

---

[7] It is important to note that this research complies with the general rules about ethics and data privacy. These rules are set out in French law (RGPD: General Data Protection Regulation). It

as proposed by Hilary Putnam (2001), i.e., from a perspective of *the common good*. We thus agree with what Coeckelberg calls a *republican approach* that combines democracy and the common good in an Aristotelian perspective:

> AI for democracy and AI for the common good, then, requires a recognition of the intrinsic political dimension of AI *and* of the common good:… we may agree *that* AI needs to promote the common good and agree on what the common good means *in general* (for example we may adopt the Aristotelian, republican notion that the common good is about the flourishing and good life of the polis and its citizens and not just the pursuit of private interest). (Coeckelberg, Coeckelbergh, 2024).

For Coeckelberg, this general vision of the common good must be specified for AI, which he begins to do below:

> Making and doing AI should already be democratized *before* it is governed by states or corporations and before we vote. If the republican tradition is right, then making sure that AI contributes to the common good is also a matter of doing our civic duty and exercising civic virtue in concrete AI practices: as software developers, for instance, but also as (end-) users of AI and in education at all levels and all stages of life. If the republican approach to democracy and common good is right, then whether and how much AI contributes to the common good does not only depend on governance by "them" (nation states, international organisations, multinational corporations, unions, consumer organisations, etc.) but also on (all of) us as citizens: on our creativity as tech developers and tech users and on our personal willingness and democratic commitment to publicly engage with others about how AI can contribute to more flourishing and more common good. (Coeckelberg, Coeckelbergh, 2024).

This view of things has, of course, important educational consequences. The modest work we have described in this chapter is part of a long-lasting effort to enable citizen-students to develop a critical, enlightened relationship with the apparatuses in which they work. As we have tried to show above, this enlightened relationship requires the integration of AI into culture—in this case the culture of literature—which AI can in turn help to reinvent.

Funding This research is funded as part of the NEFLE programme run by the French Ministry of Education.

References

Bender, J. B., & Marrinan, M. (2010). *The culture of diagram.* Stanford University Press.

Bolón-Canedo, V., Morán-Fernández, L., Cancela, B., & Alonso-Betanzos, A. (2024). A review of green artificial intelligence: Towards a more sustainable future. *Neurocomputing, 599*, 128096. https://doi.org/10.1016/j.neucom.2024.128096

Bolte, L., & van Wynsberghe, A. (2024). Sustainable AI and the third wave of AI ethics: A structural turn. *AI and Ethics*. https://doi.org/10.1007/s43681-024-00522-6

Brecht, B. (1995). Brecht on theatre: The development of an aesthetic (J. Willett, Trad.; Reprinted)..

should also be noted that the use of MLM Translator was appropriate for the age of the students and, thanks to its speech synthesis features, could be useful in early childhood settings.

Brecht, B. (2019). *Brecht on theatre*. Bloomsbury Academic.
Clark, A. (2004). *Natural-born cyborgs: Minds, technologies, and the future of human intelligence*. Oxford Univ.
Clark, A. (2011). *Supersizing the mind: Embodiment, action, and cognitive extension*. Oxford university press.
Clark, A. (2024). *The experience machine: How our minds predict and shape reality*. Penguin books.
Cobb, P., Confrey, J., diSessa, A., Lehrer, R., & Schauble, L. (2003). Design experiments in Éducational research. *Éducational Researcher, 32*(1), 9–13. https://doi.org/10.3102/0013189X032001009
Coeckelbergh, M. (2024). Artificial intelligence, the common good, and the democratic deficit in AI governance. *AI and Ethics*. https://doi.org/10.1007/s43681-024-00492-9
Collectif Didactique pour Enseigner (CDpE). (2019). *Didactique pour enseigner*. Presses Universitaires de Rennes.
Collectif Didactique pour enseigner (CDpE). (2020). Enseigner, ça s'apprend.. Retz.
Culioli, A. (1995). *Cognition and representation in linguistic theory*. J. Benjamins.
Culioli, A. (2009). *Variations sur la linguistique: Entretiens avec Frédéric Fau*. Klincksieck.
Didactique, C., & pour Enseigner (CDpE). (2024). *Un art de faire ensemble*. Presses Universitaires de Rennes.
Eco, U. (2001). *Experiences in. translation* (A. McEwan, Trad.). University of Toronto Press.
Elliott, J. (2012). Developing a science of teaching through lesson study. *International Journal for Lesson and Learning Studies, 1*(2), 108–125. https://doi.org/10.1108/20468251211224163
Engeström, Y. (2016). *Studies in expansive learning: Learning what is not yet there*. Cambridge University Press.
Engeström, Y. (2024). *Concept formation in the wild*. Cambridge University Press.
Engeström, Y., Nummijoki, J., & Sannino, A. (2012). Embodied germ cell at work: Building an expansive concept of physical mobility in home care. *Mind, Culture, and Activity, 19*(3), 287–309. https://doi.org/10.1080/10749039.2012.688177
Engeström, Y., Rantavuori, P., Ruutu, P., & Tapola-Haapala, M. (2023). Finding life beyond the classroom walls: A change laboratory supporting expansive de-encapsulation of school. *Éducation & Didactique, 17*(2), 125–141. https://doi.org/10.4000/educationdidactique.11773
Engle, R. A., Conant, F. R., & Greeno, J. G. (2007). *Progressive refinement of hypotheses in video-supported research*. In R. Goldman, R. Pea, B. Barron, & S. J. Derry (Éd.), video research in the learning sciences (p. 239–254).
García, O., Laponte, G. Y., & Le, K. (2019). Primary bilingual classrooms. Translations and translanguaging. In S. Laviosa & M. Gonzalez-Davies (Eds.), *The Routledge handbook of translation and education* (pp. 81–94). Routledge.
Gericke, N., Hudson, B., Olin-Scheller, C., & Stolare, M. (2018). Powerful knowledge, transformations and the need for empirical studies across school subjects. *London Review of Éducation, 16*(3) https://doi.org/10.18546/LRE.16.3.06
Hemingway, E. (1996). Green Hills of Africa*: The Hemingway Library Edition*. Scribner.
Hudson, B., Gericke, N., Olin-Scheller, C., & Stolare, M. (2023). Trajectories of powerful knowledge and epistemic quality: Analysing the transformations from disciplines across school subjects. *Journal of Curriculum Studies, 55*(2), 119–137. https://doi.org/10.1080/00220272.2023.2182164
Ilyenkov, E. (1982). *The dialectics of the abstract and the concrete in Marx's capital*. Progress Publishers.
Kemmis, S. (2009). Action research as a practice-based practice. *Éducational Action Research, 17*(3), 463–474. https://doi.org/10.1080/09650790903093284
Koschmann, T. (2011). *Theories of learning and studies of instructional practice*. Springer.
Kuhn, T. (1977). Second thoughts on paradigms. In *F. Suppe, the essential tension: Selected studies in scientific tradition and change* (pp. 293–319). University of Chicago Press.
Laugier, S.(2006). *Ethique, littérature, vie humaine*. PUF.

Le Hénaff, C., & Sensevy, G. (2023). Représenter la culture à l'école: Apprendre à transmettre un geste juste, un énoncé juste: Un exemple avec une recette de cuisine en anglais, en maternelle. *Questions vives recherches en éducation, N°* 39. doi:https://doi.org/10.4000/13b8d.
Marx, K. (1993). *Grundrisse: Foundations of the critique of political economy*. Penguin books.
Mollick, E. (2024). *Co-intelligence: Living and working with AI*. Portfolio/Penguin.
Péguy, C. (1993). De Jean Coste..
Penuel, W. R., Fishman, B. J., Cheng, B. H., & Sabelli, N. (2011). Organizing Research and Development at the intersection of learning, implementation, and design. *Éducational Researcher, 40*(7), 331–337. https://doi.org/10.3102/0013189X11421826
Perraud, C. (2022). *Travail, handicap et coopération en ESAT: Vers un dispositif émancipateur*. Presses universitaires de Rennes.
Popper, K. R. (1995). *Objective knowledge: An evolutionary approach (9. Impr)*. Clarendon Press.
Putnam, H. (2001). *Enlightenment and pragmatism*. Koninklijke Van Gorcum.
Radford, L. (2024). The dialectic between knowledge, knowing, and concept in the theory of objectification. *Éducation & Didactique, 18*(2), 147–159. https://doi.org/10.4000/11xa9
Rüther, M. (2024). Why care about sustainable AI ? Some thoughts from the debate on meaning in life. *Philosophy & Technology, 37*(1), 37. https://doi.org/10.1007/s13347-024-00717-z
Ryle, G. (1949). *The concept of mind*. Hutchinson's University Library.
Ryle, G. (2009). *Collected essays. 1929-1968. Collected papers. Volume 2*. Routledge.
Sensevy, G. (2025). Towards an epistemic kinship between school mathematical practices and the practice of mathematicians: The journal of number. In X. Yan, A. Mamolo, & I. Kontorovich (Éds.), Where is the math in your mathematics education research?: Personal accounts of leading educators (p. 221–248). Research in Mathematics Education Book Series. Springer.
Sensevy, G., Blocher, J.-N., Goujon, C., & Forest, D. (2022). Le film d'étude. In B. Albero & J. Thievenaz (Éds.), Enquêter dans les métiers de l'humain (p. 631–647). Éditions Raison et Passions. doi:https://doi.org/10.3917/rp.alber.2022.02.0631.
Sensevy, G., & Bloor, T. (2020). Cooperative didactic engineering. In S. Lerman (Éd.), Encyclopedia of mathematics Éducation (p. 141–145). Springer International Publishing. doi:https://doi.org/10.1007/978-3-030-15789-0_100037.
Sensevy, G., Forest, D., Quilio, S., & Morales, G. (2013). Cooperative engineering as a specific design-based research. ZDM, The International Journal on Mathematics Éducation. doi:https://doi.org/10.1007/s11858-013-0532-4.
Sensevy, G., & Le Hénaff, C. (2025). A cultural turn in educational action and research. *Journal of Curriculum Studies, 1-25*. https://doi.org/10.1080/00220272.2025.2476953
Sundarajan, M. (2024). Thinking like a large language model: Become an AI manager. Independently published.
Taurog, N. (Réalisateur). (1938). *The Adventures of Tom Sawyer* [Enregistrement vidéo].
Twain, M. (2012). The adventures of tom sawyer. Dover Publications.
Twain, M. (2015). *Œuvres*. Gallimard.
Twain, M. (2022). *Les aventures de Tom Sawyer* (F. de Gaïl, Trad.). Belin éducation.

Part II
Building Teacher Competence and Classroom Practice

Chapter 5
Co-Designing a UDL-based AI-Integrated Robotics Instructional Unit: Integrating Educator Insights to Teach AI Perception in Elementary Classrooms

LaToya Chandler, Nicole Hutchins, Shan Zhang, Yuhan Lin, Jason McKenna, Joanne Barrett, and Maya Israel

Abstract This chapter examines how a co-design approach, underpinned by Universal Design for Learning (UDL), can advance early AI literacy in elementary settings. Centering on AI perception—specifically how computers interpret images and colors—our team collaborated with 20 elementary teachers and instructional coaches to craft lessons that spark curiosity while remaining developmentally appropriate. Teacher insights informed every stage, from identifying socioemotional supports for student frustration when sensors fail, to developing hands-on activities that promote critical thinking. Thematic analysis of co-design discussions, classroom artifacts, and post-implementation reflections highlighted the vital role of contextual knowledge in shaping inclusive and adaptable instruction. We also introduce a holistic model of professional development that provides educators with ongoing support,

---

L. Chandler (✉) · J. Barrett · M. Israel
CSEveryone Center, University of Florida, Gainesville, FL, USA
e-mail: latoya.chandler@ufl.edu

J. Barrett
e-mail: jrbarrett@coe.ufl.edu

M. Israel
e-mail: misrael@coe.ufl.edu

N. Hutchins · S. Zhang
CSEveryone Center, University of Florida, Gainesville, FL, USA
e-mail: nikki@accingo.co

S. Zhang
e-mail: zhangshan@ufl.edu

Y. Lin · J. McKenna
CSEveryone Center, University of Florida, Gainesville, FL, USA
e-mail: jimmy@vex.com

J. McKenna
e-mail: jason@vex.com

S. Papadakis (ed.), *AI Applications in Preschool and Primary Education*, Advances in Artificial Intelligence in Education 5, https://doi.org/10.1007/978-3-032-17190-0_5

on-demand resources, and structured opportunities for reflection. By placing teacher expertise at the heart of curriculum design, this work demonstrates how AI topics can be seamlessly integrated into elementary education, cultivating lifelong learning and future-ready skills.

Keywords AI literacy · K-12 robotics · Computational thinking · Teacher development · Co-design

Introduction

Artificial Intelligence (AI) is rapidly influencing how we live and learn, yet elementary students rarely encounter it in meaningful ways (U.S. Department of Education, 2023; Shah, 2023). To address this gap, we designed an AI literacy curriculum that focuses on how computers "see" the world, grounding it in the principles of Universal Design for Learning (UDL) to ensure accessibility and engagement for all primary education learners (Hutchins et al., 2024).

Early exposure to AI can cultivate critical thinking, creativity, and adaptability (Wagner, 2024). However, effective integration of AI concepts into primary education requires more than simply "downscaling" complex concepts (Saavedra & Opfer, 2012). Teachers—who best understand their students' social-emotional needs, classroom dynamics, and real-world constraints—must be co-designers of these learning experiences (Kim et al., 2022; Lin & Van Brummelen, 2021; Saavedra & Opfer, 2012). By collaborating with educators, we enrich the curriculum with insights on hands-on activities, assessment strategies, and interdisciplinary connections that resonate with elementary-aged children.

This chapter addresses two central research questions:

> **Question.** How does educator input influence the development of UDL-based AI curricula that foster critical thinking and adaptability in young learners?
>
> **Question.** What tools and professional development strategies enable teachers to successfully integrate AI literacy into elementary instruction?We begin by outlining key concepts in AI education and UDL, then describe our co-design process with 20 elementary teachers and instructional coaches. We highlight how their feedback—ranging from practical classroom adaptations to socioemotional supports—shaped the curriculum. We also detail the professional development resources essential for building teacher confidence and competence in teaching AI. Finally, we discuss broader implications, offering recommendations for scaling this collaborative model to other contexts.

Background

The Artificial Intelligence for K-12 (AI4K12) initiative provides guidelines focused on the aspects of AI that K-12 students should learn. The guidelines provide implications for supporting students to use AI effectively and helps them understand the impact of AI on the world around them (AI4K12, 2024). Specifically, AI4K12 introduces Five Big Ideas, which guide educators in teaching AI concepts to young learners (AI4K12, 2024). This initiative promotes the following Five Big Ideas to make AI concepts relevant for young learners lived experience (Touretzky et al., 2019):

1. Perception: How machines interpret the world through sensors such as cameras and drawing in comparison to the human sense of perception.
2. Representation & Meaning: How AI organizes data representations and algorithms to reason and make decisions.
3. Learning: How the computer uses training data to refine decisions.
4. Natural Interaction: How AI uses natural language to communicate factual information.
5. Societal Impact: Biases and ethical decisions that influence AI system design can have an impact on the world.

Although the five big ideas provide the concepts that children should know, they do not provide approaches for how these big ideas should be taught to young learners. There is, however, a growing body of research and interest in understanding how to integrate AI in K-12 education (Park & Kwon, 2023; Kaazemetabar et al. 2012; Sarsa et al., 2022; Lu et al., 2021). Prior work has focused on integrating foundational AI concepts to promote young students' thinking on how AI impacts society and everyday life (Ng et al., 2022; Touretzky et al., 2019). However, limited research has focused on reducing the barriers to learning AI concepts while integrating the relevant competencies, which translate to real-world practice for primary grade students (Aung et al., 2022; Clarke & Whittlestone, 2022; Lee & Kwon, 2024). Even less research focused on how to consider the needs of students with a range of academic needs, including those with disabilities.

Teaching AI Literacy Through Computer Science and Robotics

The integration of emerging technologies has grown rapidly in the K-12 classroom setting with limited understanding of young students' ability to constructively engage in the competencies for learning with AI-driven technologies (Long & Magerko, 2020; Van Mechelen et al., 2023). Specifically, novel technologies such as robotics have been rapidly produced to support K-12 computing with limited information on children's perception of how machines learn and make decisions (Van Mechelen et al., 2023). There is a growing need to develop children's perception of AI technologies that center around the human and societal impacts of their everyday life (Kafai et al., 2019; Tissenbaum et al., 2017; Touretzky et al., 2019). Research suggests that the underlying concepts of computational thinking (CT) are key to becoming a societal practitioner of AI-driven technologies (Iversen et al., 2018; Kafai et al., 2019; Tissenbaum et al., 2017).

CT approaches provide a computational structure to engage in the competencies of programming in addition to integrating ideas about technology into a real-world problem (Kaspersen et al., 2021). CT is a thinking process for analyzing problems and designing solutions (Wing, 2006; Wing, 2010). The core skills of the CT process include abstraction, pattern recognition, decomposition, algorithmic thinking, and debugging (BBC, 2025). Thinking computationally in robotics situates students to think about how the robot will interact within its world and to make decisions on how programming instructions will achieve the robot's task (Lee et al., 2011). From a perspective of computing with robotics, supporting AI literacy may require children to regard the role of the robot in relation to their everyday life while situated into a critical decision-making process (Iversen et al., 2018). However, this raises questions on how the approach to AI literacy is designed to support K-12 students' understanding of machine learning in real-world scenarios.

Universal Design for Learning

Universal Design for Learning (UDL) is a framework for proactively designing learning environments that address the needs of a wide range of learners (CAST, 2024). The framework aims to reduce the barriers to learning through three core principles: multiple means of engagement, representation, and action & expression. These principles have been integrated into K-12 CS education (Israel et al., 2020) and AI learning (Song et al., 2024). Young students often encounter challenges when learning CS, and it can be also challenging for teachers to provide support for complex learning situations (Lechelt et al., 2018). However, when robotics and AI literacy tasks are designed with UDL at the forefront, support can be integrated into the learning context to provide students with a wide range of abilities an opportunity to engage in the curriculum (Israel et al., 2020; Lechelt et al., 2018). The following core principles provide guidelines for teachers to integrate a broad range of learners into CS experiences (Israel et al., 2020). These guidelines include (CAST, 2024):

- Multiple means of engagement: Options to engage in students' interests and sustaining effort
- Multiple means of representation: Using multiple modalities to represent content in varied ways
- Action & Expression: Options for students to demonstrate their understanding in flexible ways

Co-design and Teacher Collaboration

To create an AI literacy curriculum that authentically integrates into classroom instruction, it is critical to engage with educators throughout the curriculum design process. Co-design is a method to generate new ideas and practices in collaboration with those who participate, such as teachers and researchers, through educational partnerships (Xie et al., 2024). Engaging in co-design broadens the access of "who" designs the curriculum to a range of different perspectives (Penuel, 2019). In this case, teachers, researchers, and administrators work together to generate and improve existing education curricula that is used in ongoing practice to address the needs of students in the classroom (Xie et al., 2024).

Implementing co-design has the potential to produce innovative solutions unique to the educational problems which exist in the context of classroom learning (Penuel, 2019). As a team, teachers identify the key problems of their educational context to which the co-design will address. Teachers then collaborate to develop an intervention that is tested in their classrooms and provide feedback for further refinement (Roschelle et al., 2006). The collaboration involves a series of structured idea sharing, discussion, notes, and artifact creation which is recorded and transcribed as a data source so that the participants' dialogue, interaction, and artifacts may be analyzed (Xie et al., 2024). Based on implementation, the process may play a critical role in strengthening the integration of a curriculum that teachers can meaningfully use in their classrooms (Roschelle et al., 2006).

Roschelle et al. (2006) described seven features of co-design as a method in which teachers, researchers, and developers work together in a facilitated process to design a prototype of an educational curriculum:

- An *innovation challenge* that explores an educational problem space or theoretical construct.
- *Taking stock* of current practice to understand the classroom context.
- *Flexible input,* which includes teachers' suggestions for the curriculum.
- *Bootstrapping event* or design workshop to establish a common understanding of the curriculum goals.
- *Timed-to-fit* co-design sessions which *fit* teachers' work schedules.
- Researchers *facilitate* keeping the team connected to the goal and the development process.
- *Shared accountability* amongst the researchers, teachers, and developers for the design system.

As core AI knowledge and skills become more critical to teach in the K-12 classroom, it is important for teachers in schools to pilot a wide range of innovative curriculums which practice real-world scenarios and ethics in AI learning activities (Touretzky et al., 2019; Walsh et al., 2023; Yau et al., 2022). When planning and implementing AI literacy in K-12 education, co-design of curriculum has been suggested as an effective solution because teachers play an important role in determining the content that resonates with the students (Lin & Van Brummelen, 2021; Yau et al., 2022). Our rationale for examining the implementation of co-design focuses on the need for AI related learning activities to be relevant and accessible for K-12 students (Walsh et al., 2023). Thus, through co-design, teachers work together to integrate the technology, AI content, and the appropriate pedagogical approaches to design a rich curriculum for the K-12 educational context (Walsh et al., 2023).

Teacher Development

Teacher professional development (PD) in the context of AI integration is not solely about building technical proficiency; it must also focus on building teachers' confidence, autonomy, and anxiety about AI in education (Penuel, 2019). PD should not impose pre-set definitions or tools but instead empower educators to align AI with their existing pedagogical values and instructional units (Klein & Riordan, 2011; Lin & Van Brummelen, 2021). The co-design model responded to this need by providing activities such as AI tool walkthroughs and ethical scenario simulations, enabling teachers to engage in low-stakes, iterative experimentation (Hutchins & Biswas, 2024; Klein & Riordan, 2011). Educators also valued opportunities for peer discussion and reflection, recognizing that collaborative interpretation of AI concepts helped refine their understanding and classroom implementation strategies (Hutchins & Biswas, 2024).

Informed by these insights, our co-design process extends previous work by engaging elementary school teachers directly in the development and piloting of an AI literacy instructional unit. The use of VEX robotics in our process allowed us to leverage the teachers' current instructional practices as well as provide a hands-on learning experience that supports understanding and retention (Elkin et al., 2014; Swanson & Bianchini, 2015).

Co-design Process

Throughout the co-design process, our team investigated how to implement an AI and CT learning activity for primary school students using VEX 123 and VEX Go robotics. The goal of the co-design sessions was to provide a synergistic learning of AI and to develop a robotics instructional unit by establishing the learning goals of the instructional unit, create an initial framework for teacher-student engagement and test run the intervention to conduct feedback for curriculum refinement (Roschelle et al., 2006).

Participants and Context

Twenty elementary school teachers (K-5) with two years of classroom VEX (VEX 123 and/or VEX Go) robotics experience participated in this co-design process. However, they were all new to AI literacy and had minimal UDL background. Thus, the participants worked through an online introductory module about both AI and UDL prior to the start of co-design. The PD was initiated with a "Bootstrapping Event", a workshop used to activate the teams' effort in designing the UDL-based AI curricular unit. The initial co-design in-person workshop introduced the Big Idea concept of Perception (AI4K12), reviewed the UDL framework, and conducted a walkthrough of a VEX 123 robotics model lesson (As shown in Fig. 5.1). The team members collaborated to establish a shared understanding of the parameters of the VEX curriculum unit and the need to adopt the UDL and Big Idea frameworks (Roschelle et al., 2006).

After the in-person session, they attended a series of remote planning sessions that focused on AI, CT and robotics over a six-week period. The remote PD consisted of 30-minute bi-weekly sessions. In these sessions, teachers, researchers and curriculum designers participated in reflection exercises, group discussions and generated lessons that will be used in ongoing robotics classrooms (Xie et al., 2024).

The teachers provided several unique contributions to the pedagogical vision of the curriculum unit, allowing us all to collectively support and refine our contributions to the curriculum task:

1. Teachers–provided the pedagogical content knowledge, classroom experience, knowledge of classroom factors that impact application of the curriculum and served as the implementers of this curriculum.
2. VEX Curriculum Designers provided the VEX 123 curriculum lesson experience and reasoning for linking practitioner research and pedagogical practice to the lesson activity.
3. Researchers Provided the UDL, Integration of Five Big AI Ideas, and Learning Sciences Theory behind Curricular Approaches and Analysis Methods for Evaluating Implementation (Roschelle et al., 2006)

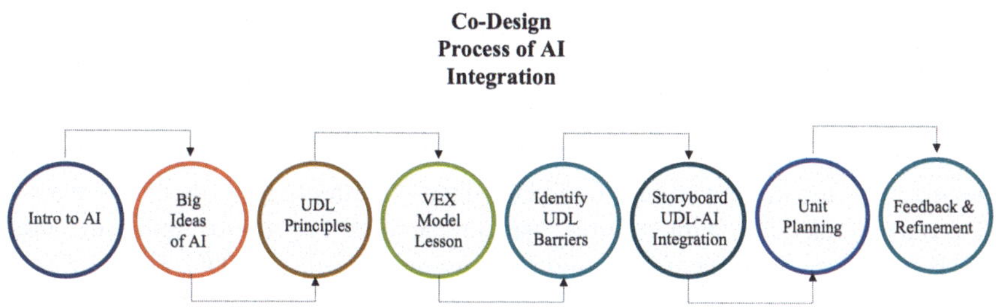

Fig. 5.1 The process of Co-Design *Source* Chandler et al., 2025

Session I: AI Literacy

This session focused on teachers building foundational understanding of AI through a series of tasks to explore examples of how AI is transforming the educational landscape. Teachers explored a hands-on task with Google's "Teachable Machine" explaining how a machine learns to identify a ripe and unripe banana. Session I, continued the exploration of AI by examining the AI4K12 Five Big Ideas of AI. The goal of the session was for teachers to be able to discuss how to integrate lessons on the concept of *perception* in primary CS classrooms. Teachers engaged in tasks to build foundational AI concepts that are key for K-12 students to understand how AI works and how it is currently impacting the world around them. After understanding the five big ideas, the teachers took a deeper exploration into the big idea of perception to consider preliminary approaches for integrating the AI concept into teaching the VEX 123 activity. To explore initial concepts of sensitivity, teachers implemented a color picking tool to explore images, pixels, and Red, Green, Blue (RGB) to understand how machines detect and differentiate colors. The task is related to the sensors on a robot which rely on detecting precise RGB values to interpret colors.

Session II: Model Lesson VEX 123 Mars Rover Activity

The VEX Mars Rover is an activity where the 123 robot drives until it detects an object on the mars planet by using the eye sensor. The project was used as a "model lesson" to guide teachers' exploration of sensing in the Rover activity, which focused on analyzing how the sensor identifies colors and the concept of AI perception.

As teachers explored sensing in the model lesson, researchers guided the implementation of the UDL framework. The framework was used to guide teachers to proactively seek out any potential barriers to learning the big idea of perception before determining how their students might engage in the VEX Mars Rover learning activity (Israel et al., 2020). A card sorting activity guided teachers in categorizing the potential barriers under multiple means of engagement, representation and expression.

Once potential barriers were identified, researchers and teachers collaborated to determine the prospective opportunities of integrating perception into the Mars Rover lesson and determine ways to leverage UDL to support students in learning AI perception (Israel et al., 2020; Touretzky et al., 2019). Teachers were grouped and worked in teams to define the potential AI and computational thinking goals in the lesson. The groups iterated on AI integration based on the VEX 123 robots' ability to sense color hues and the concepts from previous training sessions on UDL.

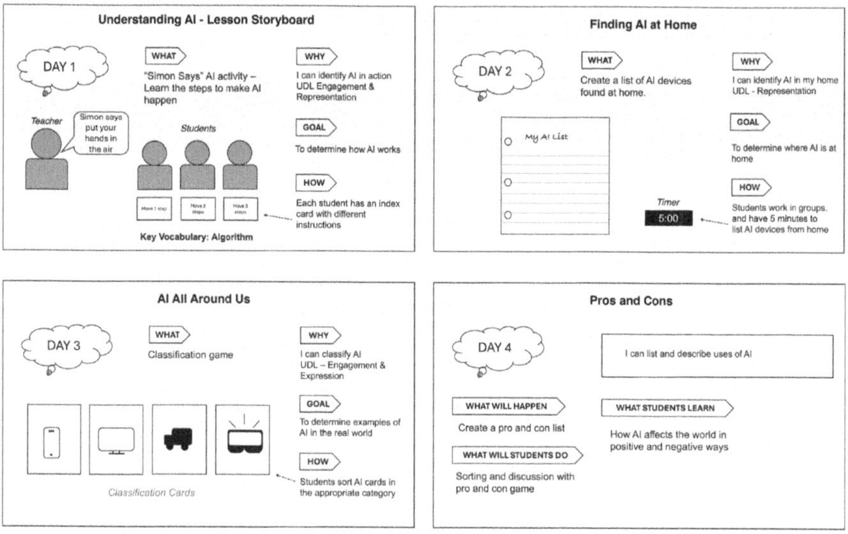

Fig. 5.2 AI Lesson Storyboard Activity *Source*: Chandler et al., 2025

Session III Storyboarding

The group's pedagogical ideas were translated into storyboards. Teachers created a "curriculum storyboard" that illustrated a sequence of "scenes" which represented how students will engage in a new VEX Mars Rover activity integrated for AI perception. As shown in Fig. 5.2, the storyboards illustrated what students needed to do to meet their learning goals and how teachers could integrate UDL practices to support the learners' exploration of the AI concepts.

PD Curriculum Sequence Planning

The initial ideas developed by the teachers' storyboard consisted of a five-day sequence of activities which introduced students to AI through robot sensing. Early on, the teachers focused on conceptual AI knowledge, which minimally integrated the big idea of *perception* where students could use the robot to explore color hues on an unknown planet. As part of this activity, the teachers had to consider the sequence of activities to both introduce AI as well as the use of sensor perception.

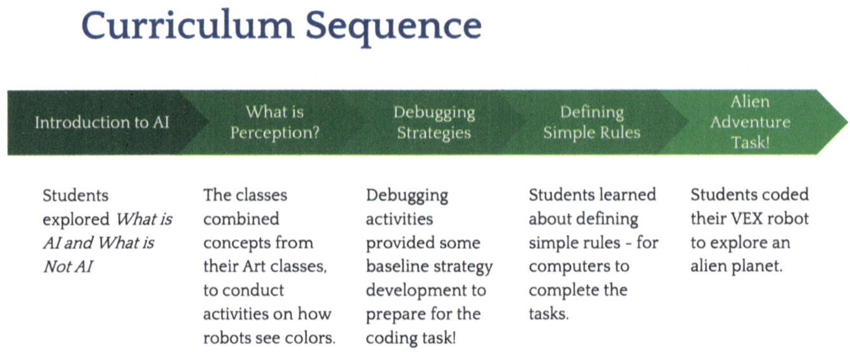

Fig. 5.3 Example of Alien Adventure activity sequence *Source*: Chandler et al., 2025

Instructional Unit Refinement (Called Alien Planet Exploration)

The initial lesson ideas were refined into a more detailed design plan. This session focused on teachers' conceptualizing a "walkthrough" of what the final version of the instructional unit might look like in their classrooms based on grade level and identifying the learning gaps which must be supported for all students to reach the learning goals.

The teachers provided feedback on all materials, which resulted in further segmenting the unit into a 10-day sequence of lesson activities through VEX 123 and VEX Go robots (refer to the instructional unit). The sequence provided hands-on activities for students to build background knowledge and understand what is and engage with relevant concepts of human versus computer learning. The activities build up to the final culminating activity, which is the Alien Planet exploration, as illustrated in Fig. 5.3.

Post-Implementation and Evaluation

The research team conducted semi-structured teacher interviews and questionnaires after the robotics unit was implemented to assess feedback on lesson sequence, self-efficacy, and AI content knowledge implementation. The team also collected unit design artifacts and reflections for processing and analysis.

Co-design Data Collection and Analysis

As part of the co-design process, it was important to understand how the teachers' input and co-design aspects influenced the development of UDL-based AI curricula for primary grade levels. Data for this study were collected across all phases of the co-design process wherein we compiled a rich dataset that included participant dialogue, instructional artifacts, design revisions, and reflective narratives. To systematically analyze the data, we employed a thematic analysis framework (Clarke & Braun, 2017), allowing for an inductive exploration of patterns across multiple forms of teacher contributions.

The following sources comprised our dataset:

- Peer discussions, card sorting activities, and group storyboards were collected during the initial in-person UDL workshop. These artifacts captured early-stage teachers thinking about AI perception, UDL barriers, and curriculum.
- Lesson design walkthrough feedback was documented in shared Google Docs, where teachers provided in-line comments and revisions. This data illustrated how participants refined content collaboratively and highlighted critical points of negotiation regarding instructional choices, pacing, and accessibility.
- Post-implementation reviews and reflections were collected via teacher planning packets and semi-structured interviews conducted by instructional facilitators. These reflections revealed how the designed lessons played out in practice, what adaptations were made during implementation, and how teachers evaluated student engagement and learning outcomes.

Through iterative coding and constant comparison across these sources, we identified emergent themes related to teacher perceptions of AI, anticipated and actual student challenges, and the professional growth trajectories experienced during the co-design process.

Teacher Feedback: What Is AI?

Teachers' feedback pointed to an overarching theme of "navigating a relevant definition of AI for primary students". Teachers determined that concepts such as AI and perception required customizing the material to relate their students' lived experience and integrating the concepts with the tools that use AI in their everyday life. A third-grade teacher expressed the need for a practical purpose for primary students learning AI explaining that "students should understand a practical purpose for AI, so they are not learning this concept in isolation, but rather connecting it to how robotics and AI are used in daily life applications."

Findings

The following themes emerged from the co-design process. Teachers were tasked to consider how they might implement instruction using the VEX + AI materials as part of a learning sequence. Additionally, in co-design sessions, the teachers were given access to instructional materials created in various states of design and were asked to provide critical feedback on these materials. Feedback focused on what the lesson might look like in their classrooms based on grade level and identified learning gaps which needed to be supported for all students to reach the learning goals.

Teacher Feedback: Big Idea of Perception

Other ideas emerged around students making discoveries to explore the big idea of perception. Themes from teachers' feedback on teaching perception, pointed to leveraging the sensors for students to predict and test how the VEX robot can detect color in comparison to the students' own visual detection of color. A teacher described that the VEX robot uses numeric codes to determine color and explained that "the colors having a numeric code would mesh well with this lesson and explain why the sensors did and sometimes did not recognize various shades of color". Ideas emerging around hands-on discovery were focused on students making predictions, testing and discussing the outcomes to recognize a practical distinction between human and computer perception.

Teacher Feedback: Coding and Defining Simple Rules

Teachers developed ideas around coding indicating that their students needed the opportunity to build skills in coding the robot's navigation. A third-grade teacher mentioned that at a specific time in the lesson, coding "skills become a logical segway into the concept of AI." Some prior coding skills may be a support to transition students into exploring how the robot learns to make decisions in comparison to humans. A teacher explained that modeling how to code could be used to demonstrate how robots follow rules by explaining that "rules are instructions that tell the AI in VEX robots what to do in different situations and relate it to human rules". This potentially would lead to the overarching concept explaining that the teachers' students are the conductors of AI because they set the parameters of the VEX robots' intelligence.

Teacher Feedback: Alien Planet Exploration

Themes around student navigation preparation and collaboration emerged from Teachers' reflections on students' ability to code the alien task. Students taking on a role as the robot's "trainer" was an important concept for teachers to help guide them in teaching the robot how to think. For third grade a teacher liked the idea of "exploring physical planets and modeling the idea kinesthetically with students as manipulatives." Students directing their classmates to use their senses prior to exploring robot's sensors was expected to reinforce the role of the student training the robot how to sense like a human via code.

Post Implementation Review

Semi-structured interviews and questionnaires were conducted after the unit was implemented to assess feedback of the lesson sequence and AI content knowledge. Several ideas emerged from teachers' feedback and reflections after the unit implementation are described.

Teacher Feedback Days 1–7 Lesson Implementation

Teachers at both second and third grade levels determined that the AI lesson unit could have been more effective later in the school year when students have built more coding experiences. Because several students struggled with the code, sections Day 5–7 (debugging and defining simple rules) were done in collaboration as a class group to support the coding experience.

Themes emerged around young students having limited knowledge in using coding blocks with sensors and debugging algorithms. Teachers recognized the computational skill of debugging as a critical task and recommended that students understood how to make changes to errors in their code. Because second graders had little experience using the eye sensor a teacher recommended that using the coding software in context of the programming scenario must be modeled "for students to be able to complete the task of using AI".

Teacher Feedback Days 8–10 Lesson Implementation

Feedback on the implementation of the Alien planet task contained varied suggestions noting that the activity concept needed to be introduced to help students better understand the objective of sensing colors. Teachers found that using a single color to explore the lesson worked well, while introducing several colors at once proved to be overwhelming for students. One method that helped mitigate the challenge of sensing was hiding the colors that were not relevant for the robot to recognize. In this situation, the computational process needed some additional support to help students analyze the robot's sensing task into achievable steps (Lee et al., 2011). Hiding the irrelevant colors helped to break the task into smaller parts (e.g., Abstraction, Decomposition). Analyzing a single color, allowed students to verbally guide others through the coding process to understand how the code worked and what the robot was doing when following instructions (Lee et al., 2011). Once students were able to understand how to debug the robots' path, they were then able to progress adding the next color in the planet and build on the existing code.

Co-design Strategies

This section reports on the essential co-design strategies. Overall, our findings reinforce the benefit of co-design on curricular development (Hutchins & Biswas, 2024; Roschelle et al., 2006), as well as strategies such as experiencing content as students (Ke et al., 2023; Klein & Riordan, 2011), peer dialogue and reflection (Iraola et al., 2024) and created opportunity to share knowledge and resources to develop an innovative curriculum unit (Yau et al., 2022). Our approach has also illustrated some key additional aspects of co-design which may be playing a role in a tighter integration of AI and UDL into the robotics activity through teachers' involvement of the PD sessions (Roschelle et al., 2006).

Supporting Teacher Confidence in Robotics and AI

While teachers supported researchers' rationale of using the AI4K12 framework to simplify relevant AI concepts for their students, they did not "feel" like they were teaching AI. This led to a conceptual disconnect between relating the VEX robot sensors to AI perception. Researcher's memo during the AI exploration stated, "they did not "feel" like they were teaching about AI and did not feel prepared to discuss AI." An essential dynamic of providing teacher support in learning AI concepts appears to point beyond identifying AI tools and resources and more emphasized on expanding teachers' AI literacy to improve self-efficacy and professional growth in teaching AI topics.

While building competence in AI perception in the context of programming, CT was implicitly included in the co-design process. However, a CT framework might be useful for thinking and framing how to integrate AI perception into the robotics setting (Iversen et al., 2018). Researchers' memos suggested that teachers may need more experience in practicing the strategies of CT and teaching those strategies to prepare for robotics integrated in AI concepts. In robotics context, CT is one of the sub-goals of the co-design process that is suitable for learning to integrate AI in the K-12 curriculum (Mannila, 2024). Researchers and teachers recognized a need to include a well-defined alignment of CT practice when developing AI literacy activities for students.

Empowering Teachers as Designers

The co-planning task may have provided context for teachers to draw on one another's prior knowledge and robotics classroom experiences (Swanson & Bianchini, 2015). Since teachers had prior experience using VEX 123 Mars Rover lessons in their classrooms, researchers used the lesson to facilitate teachers in recognizing core concepts of AI perception within the existing material. Connecting teachers to the core concept of perception in AI before they begin establishing new learning goals may be a prerequisite of developing an approach for adding UDL-driven ideas into the lesson (Israel et al., 2020; Swanson & Bianchini, 2015).

The co-design process emphasized that teachers take a major role in making UDL-driven curricular choices for their classrooms to foster ownership of the implementation (Tayne et al., 2024). Leveraging the UDL principles emphasized that teachers do not regard the VEX robotics activity as a "one-size-fits-all" lesson unit, to encourage building upon the accessibility of the lesson and improve AI integration into their classrooms (Yau et al., 2022).

Discussion

This project wove together the experiences of the curriculum designers, teachers and researchers in a new and relevant way. The implementation of co-design allows the curriculum designers to learn what is most important and relevant to the reality of the classroom (Lin & Van Brummelen, 2021; Penuel, 2019; Xie et al., 2024; Yau et al., 2022). Co-design, by its nature, is an extension of the UDL framework because it allows for the implementation of both learner voice and choice–both important components for learner agency (Penuel, 2019). Taking the time to think about implementing UDL holistically when developing new lesson plans, such as perception in AI, provides the opportunity to think through a wide range of potential barriers to learning the concept meaningfully, which supports academic and emotional growth through relevant learning experiences.

Conclusion

This chapter demonstrated that when educators co-design AI curricula with researchers, the result is more than just a set of lesson plans—it's a learning ecosystem rooted in practicality, inclusivity, and engagement. By integrating UDL, we ensured that AI concepts became accessible to young learners, regardless of their backgrounds or prior experiences. Our focus on how computers "see" the world generated hands-on, curiosity-driven activities that catalyzed student interest and fostered a sense of agency and resilience in troubleshooting AI-related tasks PRINTDATE * MERGEFORMAT.

In an era where AI shapes personal, professional, and societal landscapes, equipping our youngest learners with foundational AI literacy is no longer optional—it is essential. By partnering with educators in the design and delivery of these lessons, we not only elevate the quality and relevance of AI instruction but also empower teachers to be active shapers of the future of education.

Implications for Practice and Ethics

Insights from the co-design process suggest several implications for integrating AI concepts in primary education. Since, teachers play a major role in shaping the ways that AI learning will be integrated in the primary classroom, we first encourage building upon the accessibility of learning the AI big ideas by making proactive, UDL-driven choices to address a broad range of learners (Yau et al., 2022). Co-designing should facilitate teachers with a professional framework for building foundational knowledge in AI concepts and confidence in mapping the AI big ideas with practical sensor activities rather than theoretical application (Roschelle et al., 2006). Finally, we recommend a field experience that facilitates teachers' pedagogical practice in adapting AI concepts to the context of their existing lesson units. These implications may foster ownership in designing lessons which help young students to learn AI concepts meaningfully (Xie et al., 2024).

Competing Interests Latoya Chandler, Nicole Hutchins, Shan Zhang, Yuhan Lin, Jason McKenna, Joanne Barret and Maya Israel declare that they have no competing interests.

Ethics Approval The study was approved by the institutional review board of the University of Florida (IRB202401103), and informed consent was obtained from all individual participants included in the study.

References

AI4K12. (2024, April 17). *Executive summary: The state of K-12 AI education in your state workshop*. AI4K12. https://ai4k12.org/executive-summarythe-state-of-k-12-ai-education-in-your-state-workshop/

Aung, Z. H., Sanium, S., Songsaksuppachok, C., Kusakunniran, W., Precharattana, M., Chuechote, S., Pongsanon, K., & Ritthipravat, P. (2022). Designing a novel teaching platform for AI: A case study in a Thai school context. *Journal of Computer Assisted Learning, 38*(6), 1714–1729. https://doi.org/10.1111/jcal.12706

BBC (2025) Introduction to computational thinking–KS3 Computer Science Revision. (n.d.). *BBC*. Retrieved June 9, 2025, from https://www.bbc.co.uk/bitesize/guides/zp92mp3/revision/1

CAST, Inc. (n.d.). *The UDL Guidelines*. Cast.org. Retrieved April 3, 2025, from https://udlguidelines.cast.org/

Clarke, S., & Whittlestone, J. (2022). A survey of the potential long-term impacts of AI: How AI could lead to long-term changes in science, cooperation, power, epistemics and values. *Proceedings of the 2022 AAAI/ACM Conference on AI, Ethics, and Society*.

Clarke, V., & Braun, V. (2017). Thematic analysis. *The Journal of Positive Psychology, 12*(3), 297–298. https://doi.org/10.1080/17439760.2016.1262613

Elkin, M., Sullivan, A., & Umashi Bers, M. (2014). Implementing a robotics curriculum in an early childhood Montessori classroom. *Journal of Information Technology Education Innovations in Practice, 13*, 153–169. https://doi.org/10.28945/2094

Engaging Learning. (2024), April 17. *Executive summary: The state of K-12 AI education in your state workshop*. AI4K12. https://ai4k12.org/executive-summarythe-state-of-k-12-ai-education-in-your-state-workshop/

Hutchins, N. M., & Biswas, G. (2024). Co-designing teacher support technology for problem-based learning in middle school science. *British Journal of Educational Technology: Journal of the Council for Educational Technology, 55*(3), 802–822. https://doi.org/10.1111/bjet.13363

Iraola, E. A., Romero, G. R., & Millera, M. J. (2024). Dialogue among educators: Rethinking and recreating scenarios of cooperative and inclusive learning. *International Journal of Educational Research Open, 6*(100322), 100322. https://doi.org/10.1016/j.ijedro.2024.100322

Israel, M., Jeong, G., Ray, M., & Lash, T. (2020). Teaching elementary computer science through universal design for learning. *Proceedings of the 51st ACM Technical Symposium on Computer Science Education*. doi:https://doi.org/10.1145/3328778.336682.

Iversen, O. S., Smith, R. C., & Dindler, C. (2018). From computational thinking to computational empowerment: A 21 st century PD agenda. *Proceedings of the 15th Participatory Design Conference: Full Papers–Volume 1*. doi:https://doi.org/10.1145/3210586.3210592.

Kafai, Y., Proctor, C., & Lui, D. (2019). From theory bias to theory dialogue: Embracing cognitive, situated, and critical framings of computational thinking in K-12 CS education. *Proceedings of the 2019 ACM Conference on International Computing Education Research*. doi:https://doi.org/10.1145/3291279.3339400.

Kaspersen, M. H., Bilstrup, K.-E. K., Van Mechelen, M., Hjorth, A., Bouvin, N. O., & Petersen, M. G. (2021). VotestratesML: A high school learning tool for exploring machine learning and its societal implications. *FabLearn Europe/MakeEd 2021–An International Conference on Computing, Design and Making in Education*. doi:https://doi.org/10.1145/3466725.3466728.

Kazemitabaar, M., Chow, J., Ma, C. K. T., Ericson, B. J., Weintrop, D., & Grossman, T. (2023). Studying the effect of AI code generators on supporting novice learners in introductory programming. *Proceedings of the 2023 CHI Conference on Human Factors in Computing Systems, 37*, 1–23. doi:https://doi.org/10.1145/3544548.3580919

Ke, L., Friedrichsen, P., Rawson, R., & Sadler, T. D. (2023). Teacher learning through collaborative curriculum design in the midst of a pandemic: A cultural historical activity theory investigation. *Teaching and Teacher Education, 122*(103957). https://doi.org/10.1016/j.tate.2022.103957

Kim, J., Lee, H., & Cho, Y. H. (2022). Learning design to support student-AI collaboration: Perspectives of leading teachers for AI in education. *Education and Information Technologies, 27*(5), 6069–6104. https://doi.org/10.1007/s10639-021-10831-6

Klein, E. J., & Riordan, M. (2011). Wearing the "student hat": Experiential professional development in expeditionary learning schools. *The Journal of Experimental Education, 34*(1), 35–54. https://doi.org/10.1177/105382591103400104

Lechelt, Z., Rogers, Y., Yuill, N., Nagl, L., Ragone, G., & Marquardt, N. (2018). Inclusive computing in special needs classrooms: Designing for all. *Proceedings of the 2018 CHI Conference on Human Factors in Computing Systems*. doi:https://doi.org/10.1145/3173574.317409

Lee, I., Martin, F., Denner, J., Coulter, B., Allan, W., Erickson, J., Malyn-Smith, J., & Werner, L. (2011). Computational thinking for youth in practice. *ACM Inroads, 2*(1), 32–37. https://doi.org/10.1145/1929887.1929902

Lee, S. J., & Kwon, K. (2024). A systematic review of AI education in K-12 classrooms from 2018 to 2023: Topics, strategies, and learning outcomes. Computers and Education: Artificial Intelligence, 6(100211), 100211. doi:https://doi.org/10.1016/j.caeai.2024.100211.

Lin, P., & Van Brummelen, J. (2021). Engaging teachers to co-design integrated AI curriculum for K-12 classrooms. *Proceedings of the 2021 CHI Conference on Human Factors in Computing Systems.* doi:https://doi.org/10.1145/3411764.3445377

Long, D., & Magerko, B. (2020). What is AI Literacy? Competencies and Design Considerations. *Proceedings of the 2020 CHI Conference on Human Factors in Computing Systems.* doi:https://doi.org/10.1145/3313831.337672

Lu, S., Guo, D., Ren, S., Huang, J., Svyatkovskiy, A., Blanco, A., Clement, C., Drain, D., Jiang, D., Tang, D., Li, G., Zhou, L., Shou, L., Zhou, L., Tufano, M., Gong, M., Zhou, M., Duan, N., Sundaresan, N., … Liu, S. (2021). CodeXGLUE: A machine learning benchmark dataset for code understanding and generation. In *arXiv [cs.SE].* http://arxiv.org/abs/2102.04664

Mannila, L. (2024). Co-designing AI literacy for K-12 education. Proceedings of the 19th WiPSCE Conference on Primary and Secondary Computing Education Research, 1–3.

Ng, D. T. K., Luo, W., Chan, H. M. Y., & Chu, S. K. W. (2022). Using digital story writing as a pedagogy to develop AI literacy among primary students. *Computers and Education: Artificial Intelligence, 3*(100054). https://doi.org/10.1016/j.caeai.2022.100054

Park, W., & Kwon, H. (2023). Implementing artificial intelligence education for middle school technology education in Republic of Korea. *International Journal of Technology and Design Education, 34*(1), 1–27. https://doi.org/10.1007/s10798-023-09812-2

Penuel, W. R. (2019). Co-design as infrastructuring with attention to power: Building collective capacity for equitable teaching and learning through design-based implementation research. In *Collaborative curriculum Design for Sustainable Innovation and Teacher Learning* (pp. 387–401). Springer International Publishing. https://doi.org/10.1007/978-3-030-20062-6_21

Roschelle, J., Penuel, W., Schectman, N. (2006). Co-design of innovations with teachers: Definition and Dynamics. Retrieved April 3, 2025, from https://repository.isls.org/bitstream/1/3563/1/606-612.pdf

Saavedra, A. R., & Opfer, V. D. (2012). Learning 21st-century skills requires 21st-century teaching. *Phi Delta Kappan, 94*(2), 8–13. https://doi.org/10.1177/003172171209400203

Sarsa, S., Denny, P., Hellas, A., & Leinonen, J. (2022). Automatic generation of programming exercises and code explanations using large language models. *Proceedings of the 2022 ACM Conference on International Computing Education Research–Volume 1.* https://doi.org/10.1145/3501385.3543957

Shah, P. (2023). *AI and the future of education: Teaching in the age of artificial intelligence.* Sybex.

Song, Y., Weisberg, L. R., Zhang, S., Tian, X., Boyer, K. E., & Israel, M. (2024). A framework for inclusive AI learning design for diverse learners. *Computers and Education: Artificial Intelligence, 6*(100212), 100212. https://doi.org/10.1016/j.caeai.2024.100212

Swanson, L. H., & Bianchini, J. A. (2015). Co-planning among science and special education teachers: How do different conceptual lenses help to make sense of the process? *Cultural Studies of Science Education, 10*(4), 1123–1153. https://doi.org/10.1007/s11422-014-9582-3

Tayne, K., Stevenson, K., McCollum, A., DeMattia, E., Janosko, J., Tuttell, F., & Haynes, L. (2024). Co-designing an adaptable curriculum with teachers: Affordances and tensions in flexible partnership and collaboration. *Proceedings of the 18th International Conference of the Learning Sciences–ICLS 2024.* https://doi.org/10.22318/icls2024.111926

Tissenbaum, M., Sheldon, J., Seop, L., Lee, C. H., & Lao, N. (2017). Critical computational empowerment: Engaging youth as shapers of the digital future. *IEEE Global Engineering Education Conference (EDUCON)*, 1705–1708. https://doi.org/10.1109/EDUCON.2017.7943078

Touretzky, D., Gardner-McCune, C., Martin, F., & Seehorn, D. (2019). Envisioning AI for K-12: What should every child know about AI? *Proceedings of the AAAI conference on artificial intelligence*, AAAI conference on artificial intelligence, *33*(01), 9795–9799. https://doi.org/10.1609/aaai.v33i01.33019795

U.S. Department of Education, Office of Educational Technology, Artificial Intelligence and Future of Teaching and Learning: Insights and Recommendations, 2023.

Van Mechelen, M., Smith, R. C., Schaper, M.-M., Tamashiro, M., Bilstrup, K.-E., Lunding, M., Graves Petersen, M., & Sejer Iversen, O. (2023). Emerging technologies in K–12 education: A future HCI research agenda. *ACM Transactions on Computer-Human Interaction: A Publication of the Association for Computing Machinery, 30*(3), 1–40. https://doi.org/10.1145/3569897

Wagner, M. (2024). Adaptive educational strategies for creative fields in the era of generative Ai: A framework for navigating technological uncertainty. *ICERI Proceedings, 1*, 3068–3075. https://doi.org/10.21125/iceri.2024.0799

Walsh, B., Dalton, B., Forsyth, S., & Yeh, T. (2023). Literacy and STEM teachers adapt AI ethics curriculum. *Proceedings of the... AAAI conference on artificial intelligence. AAAI Conference on Artificial Intelligence, 37*(13), 16048–16055. https://doi.org/10.1609/aaai.v37i13.26906

Wing, J. (2010). Computational Thinking: What and Why? Retrieved April 3, 2025, from https://www.cs.cmu.edu/~CompThink/resources/TheLinkWing.pdf

Wing, J. M. (2006). Computational thinking. *Communications of the ACM, 49*(3), 33–35. https://doi.org/10.1145/1118178.1118215

Xie, B., Sarin, P., Wolf, J., Garcia, R. C. C., Delaney, V., Sieh, I., Fuloria, A., Varuvel Dennison, D., Bywater, C., & Lee, V. R. (2024). Co-designing AI education curriculum with cross-disciplinary high school teachers, Proceedings of the AAAI conference on artificial intelligence. AAAI conference on artificial intelligence, *38*(21), 23146–23154. https://doi.org/10.1609/aaai.v38i21.30360

Yau, K. W., Chai, C. S., Chiu, T. K. F., Meng, H., King, I., Wong, S. W.-H., & Yam, Y. (2022). Co-designing artificial intelligence curriculum for secondary schools: A grounded theory of teachers' experience. *International Symposium on Educational Technology (ISET)*, 58–62. https://doi.org/10.1109/ISET55194.2022.00020

Zhang, H., Lee, I., Ali, S., DiPaola, D., Cheng, Y., & Breazeal, C. (2022). Integrating ethics and career futures with technical learning to promote AI literacy for middle school students: An exploratory study. *International Journal of Artificial Intelligence in Education, 33*(2), 1–35. https://doi.org/10.1007/s40593-022-00293-3

Chapter 6
From Concerns to Competence: Empowering K–12 Teachers for Generative AI Integration

Tianchong Wang, Zamzami Zainuddin, Chidozie Alozie, and Trudy Sweeney

Abstract As Generative Artificial Intelligence (GenAI) increasingly permeates educational contexts, K–12 teachers grapple with concerns and uncertainties about effectively integrating these technologies to realise their pedagogical potential. This study investigates the concerns of K–12 teachers regarding GenAI integration in their teaching practices, utilising the Stages of Concern (SoC) framework from the Concerns-Based Adoption Model. We conducted an SoC questionnaire with K–12 teachers (n = 58) from an independent school in Australia to assess their concerns about GenAI adoption. Quantitative analysis shows a distinct pattern dominated by Stage 1 (Informational) and Stage 4 (Consequence) concerns, indicating teachers are simultaneously seeking foundational knowledge while contemplating educational impacts. The qualitative data expand upon the quantitative findings, revealing five key themes: GenAI as a tool for efficiency and workload relief, academic integrity issues, potential loss of the human touch, variable relevance across subjects, and specific professional learning needs. Drawing on these insights, we propose a targeted approach to teacher professional development (TPD) that begins with GenAI literacy and ethical considerations, then moves through pedagogical application, practical implementation, and collaborative learning, ultimately creating space for innovation and transformative practice. This approach allows professional learning to unfold with a developmentally appropriate focus, optimising resources while addressing teachers' varied readiness levels and evolving concerns. In doing so, the study

T. Wang (✉) · Z. Zainuddin · C. Alozie · T. Sweeney
College of Education, Psychology and Social Work, Flinders University, Adelaide, Australia
e-mail: tianchong.wang@flinders.edu.au

Z. Zainuddin
e-mail: zamzami.zainuddin@flinders.edu.au

C. Alozie
e-mail: chidozie.alozie@flinders.edu.au

T. Sweeney
e-mail: trudy.sweeney@flinders.edu.au

S. Papadakis (ed.), *AI Applications in Preschool and Primary Education*, Advances in Artificial Intelligence in Education 5, https://doi.org/10.1007/978-3-032-17190-0_6

contributes both to theoretical understanding of GenAI integration in education and to the design of responsive, teacher-informed professional development strategies.

Keywords Generative AI · GenAI · Stage of concerns · Teacher professional development · K–12 education

Introduction

The emergence of Generative Artificial Intelligence (GenAI) represents one of the most significant disruptive technologies in recent years. Large Language Models (LLMs) like ChatGPT, Claude, Google Gemini and DeepSeek possess unprecedented capabilities to generate novel content, engage in sophisticated dialogues, provide personalised feedback, and support complex tasks across various domains. In education, this technological revolution has ignited critical debates about the future of teaching and learning, as GenAI simultaneously disrupts traditional pedagogical and assessment practices and affords new pathways for educational innovation.

Alongside these debates, the general attitudes towards GenAI have evolved significantly. Countries and regions worldwide have moved from initial outright bans toward more structured, cautious approaches to embrace such technologies in schools, with policy frameworks being developed to guide implementation. The release of *Australia's Framework for Generative AI in Schools* (Department of Education, 2023) exemplifies this shifting position, as it seeks to provide guidance for the responsible and ethical use of GenAI tools to support positive outcomes for students, educators, and society at large.

Despite the transformative potential of GenAI and the emergence of supportive policy guidance, its integration into K–12 classrooms remains limited, with efforts largely confined to isolated, grassroots initiatives (Wang & Cheng, 2021). The discrepancy between the technology's promise, policy intentions, and actual classroom practice exemplifies a persistent implementation gap in the integration of GenAI technologies. A key contributing factor is the lack of sustained attention to teachers' diverse concerns and their professional development needs. Research from multiple contexts highlights this ambivalence: a large-scale survey in the United States found that one in four public K–12 teachers worried that using AI tools in education could do more harm than good, while only 6% expressed predominantly positive views (Pew Research Center, 2024). This reflects a broader pattern in educational technology adoption, where enthusiasm at the policy level often contrasts with hesitation among those expected to implement the tools. As the primary actors of implementation, teachers ultimately determine the success of educational innovation, yet they are frequently caught between top-down mandates to adopt emerging technologies and their own uncertainties about how to use them effectively in practice (Nixon et al., 2024).

A recent inquiry by the Parliament of Australia (2024) revealed that, despite growing access to AI tools, most Australian teachers felt unprepared to integrate them into their teaching. Their uncertainties range from academic integrity and equity of access to pedagogical alignment and the evolving nature of their professional roles in AI-enhanced classrooms. Within K–12 settings, these uncertainties carry additional weight; teachers working with younger learners must consider developmental appropriateness, maintain visibility over students' thinking, and safeguard children's emerging cognitive and social capacities. These contexts often require more cautious and context-sensitive approaches to technological adoption, with teachers needing clarity about how GenAI fits within existing learning processes and expectations. Recognising these developmental and pedagogical realities is crucial for understanding how GenAI might be introduced responsibly across different stages of schooling.

Meanwhile, research on educational change consistently highlights that successful implementation depends on meaningfully engaging with teachers' concerns about proposed innovations (Fuller, 1969; Hall & Hord, 2015). These concerns naturally evolve as teachers gain experience with new technologies, necessitating differentiated support at various stages of adoption. However, few studies have specifically and systematically examined K–12 teachers' concerns on GenAI integration at the moment.

This gap is particularly pressing given the developmental diversity within the K–12 sector, which requires tailored approaches to technology integration. Early childhood and primary teachers often need to prioritise age-appropriate GenAI introduction, while secondary teachers may face distinct challenges around academic integrity and digital citizenship development. This complexity makes it essential to understand how K–12 teachers perceive and respond to GenAI integration, as their concerns are likely shaped by the specific developmental needs.

The absence of such understanding also hampers the development of responsive teachers professional learning initiatives. Without insight into what teachers are actually concerned about, professional development risks being misaligned—based on assumptions rather than grounded realities. Gaining this understanding is a critical starting point for the meaningful integration of GenAI, as it enables the design of capacity-building approaches that are grounded in teacher perspectives and needs rather than imposed through top-down mandates.

This study, therefore, addresses this critical gap by investigating the following research question: *What are the predominant concerns of K–12 teachers regarding GenAI integration in their teaching practices?*

By systematically examining the nature and intensity of teachers' concerns about GenAI, this research aims to provide an empirical foundation for developing targeted support strategies that acknowledge teachers' perspectives and professional expertise. The findings will contribute to both scholarly understanding of GenAI adoption and the development of practical strategies for supporting teachers during this significant technological transition, ultimately enhancing K–12 education through the meaningful and pedagogically sound integration of GenAI.

Literature Review

Generative AI in Education

GenAI, particularly LLMs, has catalysed a paradigm shift in education worldwide. GenAI broadly refers to machine learning models capable of producing novel content—text, code, images, audio, video, and even multimodal artefacts—based on learned patterns from large datasets. Characterised by its multi-modality, interaction, flexibility, and productivity, GenAI introduces possibilities for dynamic, dialogic interactions, including personalised feedback, content creation, and collaborative problem-solving in real-time (Ronge et al., 2025). This technological leap has significant implications for pedagogy, curriculum design, assessment, and teacher roles, thus warranting an in-depth enquiry into how teachers perceive and adapt to its integration.

As reported in the literature, the potential of GenAI to enhance teaching and learning has been met with cautious optimism (Bower et al., 2025). On the one hand, studies have shown that GenAI can support differentiated instruction by tailoring explanations to individual learner profiles (Kohnke et al., 2025), assisting with scaffolding (Chien et al., 2024), generating formative assessments (Huang et al., 2024), and fostering more inclusive learning environments (Huang et al., 2024). On the other hand, substantial concerns persist around pedagogical integrity, student agency, academic honesty, and equity in access (Samala et al., 2025; Wang, 2023).

Central to this discourse is the evolving role of teachers, who are no longer solely knowledge transmitters but also take on the role of learning designers and facilitators (Laurillard, 2013), while increasingly working alongside AI as *Observers*, *Adopters*, *Collaborators*, or *Innovators*, depending on their level of engagement with the technology (Zhai, 2024). However, the extent to which teachers assume these roles varies considerably across contexts and individuals. Research indicates that teachers' beliefs, technological self-efficacy, and prior exposure to digital innovations shape their readiness to engage with GenAI tools (Cheah et al., 2025; Collie & Martin, 2024; Wang & Cheng, 2021).

The ethical dimensions of GenAI adoption present particularly complex challenges for K–12 education (Holmes et al., 2022). Teachers are likely to encounter a range of critical ethical tensions, including the balance between transparency and opacity, conflicts between attribution and originality, considerations of autonomy verses dependency, and the paradoxes of equity and accessibility, among others (Fu & Weng, 2024). These tensions manifest in classroom practice as teachers attempt to establish ethical boundaries while leveraging AI affordances (Norman, 1988).

Stage of Concerns

The Stages of Concern (SoC) is a theoretical construct that identifies and measures the feelings, perceptions, and attitudes individuals experience when faced with implementing change (Hall & Hord, 2015). SoC has its conceptual origins in the work of Frances Fuller (1969), who identified developmental patterns in the concerns expressed by teachers at different career stages. Fuller observed that beginning teachers primarily focused on self-concerns related to their adequacy and classroom control, while experienced teachers expressed greater concern about student learning and impact. Building on Fuller's research, Hall et al. (1973) developed the Concerns-Based Adoption Model (CBAM) that helps leaders and researchers understand, lead, and monitor the complex process of change in education, with SoC as a central dimension that includes distinct concern stages that individuals experience when implementing innovations. Specifically, SoC organises concerns into three broad categories encompassing seven developmental stages, as shown in Table 6.1:

SoC outlines a developmental progression through which individuals typically advance as they engage with an innovation. While concerns often follow a predictable pattern, they may also coexist at different stages and vary in intensity (Hall & Hord, 2015). The framework is underpinned by several key assumptions: that change is a process rather than a single event; individuals are central to the implementation process; concerns evolve in identifiable ways; and addressing these concerns is crucial for successful adoption (George et al., 2006). These assumptions collectively highlight the importance of attending to the human dimensions of change by implementing targeted strategies that respond to individuals' evolving concerns.

To assess individuals' progression through the SoC, researchers and practitioners employ a combination of quantitative and qualitative methodologies. The most

Table 6.1 Stage of Concerns

Categories	Stages		Descriptions
Impact concerns	6	Refocusing	Exploration of wider benefits and potential modifications
	5	Collaboration	Interest in coordinating with others regarding implementation
Task concerns	4	Consequence	Attention to innovation impact
	3	Management	Focus on processes, tasks, and resource requirements
Self concerns	2	Personal	Concerns about personal ability to implement the innovation
	1	Informational	Interest in learning the general characteristics of the innovation
	0	Awareness	Little concern about or involvement with the innovation

widely used quantitative tool is the Stages of Concern Questionnaire (SoCQ), originally developed by Hall et al. (1979) and later revised by George et al. (2006). This instrument measures the relative intensity of concerns across seven defined stages. In addition to the SoCQ, the SoC framework incorporates qualitative methods such as open-ended written responses and structured interviews. These qualitative approaches enrich the data by offering contextual insights that help interpret the numerical patterns identified by the SoCQ. By integrating both quantitative and qualitative methods, researchers are better equipped to triangulate findings and gain a more comprehensive understanding of how individuals experience and respond to innovation implementation.

Methodology

Research Design and Research Instrument

This study employed a mixed-methods approach (Creswell & Plano Clark, 2018) to investigate K–12 teachers' concerns over GenAI integration in their teaching practices.

The primary research instrument used was the SoCQ, adapted from George et al. (2006) to focus specifically on GenAI integration. The adapted questionnaire consisted of 49 items across seven stages of concern (five items per stage), measured on a 5-point Likert scale ranging from 1 (Strongly Disagree) to 5 (Strongly Agree). To supplement the quantitative data, three open-ended questions were asked at the end of the SoCQ.

The adapted SoCQ was pilot-tested with a small group of teachers (n = 10) not included in the main study to ensure clarity, relevance, and reliability of the items in the context of GenAI. These participants represented diverse teaching backgrounds, experience levels, and subject areas similar to the target population. Following completion of the questionnaire, participants provided written feedback on item wording, comprehensibility, and relevance. Minor revisions were made based on this feedback to enhance item clarity while maintaining the conceptual integrity of the original instrument.

Content validity was established through expert review and quantitative assessment using the Content Validity Index (CVI). A panel of four experts in educational technology integration, teacher professional development, and GenAI applications in education independently evaluated each item's relevance using a dichotomous scale (0 = not relevant, 1 = relevant). The Item-Content Validity Index (I-CVI) was calculated as the proportion of experts rating each item as relevant. Items with I-CVI values below 0.75 (representing agreement among at least three of the four experts) were either revised or eliminated, following recommendations for small expert panels (Lynn, 1986). The Scale-Content Validity Index (S-CVI/Ave), calculated by averaging all I-CVI values, was 0.88, indicating good content validity across the instrument.

Internal consistency reliability was assessed using Cronbach's alpha coefficients (Cronbach, 1951) for each of the seven stages of concern. The pilot data yielded satisfactory reliability coefficients ranging from 0.76 to 0.89 across the subscales, comparable to those reported in previous adaptations of the SoCQ for technological innovations (George et al., 2006).

This validation process ensured that the adapted SoCQ was psychometrically sound and contextually appropriate for measuring teachers' concerns regarding GenAI implementation, establishing a solid foundation for the main study's data collection and subsequent analyses.

Participants and Data Collection Process

The study consisted of 58 K–12 teachers ($n = 58$) from an independent school in South Australia, recruiting teachers who were readily available and willing to participate in the study through a convenience sampling strategy. While this approach facilitated efficient data collection within the school setting, we still monitored demographic representation. Demographic information collected included gender, age group, teaching experience, subject specialisation, teaching levels (primary and secondary), subject areas, and prior exposure to AI technologies.

Data collection occurred during the Term 1 of the 2025 school year. The SoCQ was administered online using Google Forms, with an average completion time of 20 minutes. Participants were informed about the study's purpose and assured of confidentiality and anonymity.

Data Analysis

The SoCQ data were analysed using descriptive statistical methods to identify patterns and trends across the seven stages of concern. For each stage (Awareness, Informational, Personal, Management, Consequence, Collaboration, and Refocusing), mean scores and standard deviations were calculated to establish the relative intensity of concerns among participants. This analytical approach provided a structured examination of how concerns were distributed across the different stages of the adoption process, revealing areas requiring targeted intervention.

Responses to open-ended questions were analysed using thematic analysis (Braun & Clarke, 2006). The analysis process involved six steps: familiarisation with the data, generating initial codes, searching for themes, reviewing themes, defining and naming themes, and producing the report. To ensure the reliability of the coding process, two researchers from our team independently coded the qualitative data.

Following independent coding, the researchers compared their analyses, discussed discrepancies, and reached consensus through collaborative dialogue. This investigator triangulation approach enhanced the credibility and trustworthiness of our findings by minimising individual researcher bias and ensuring analytical rigour (Lincoln & Guba, 1985). The high level of agreement between the independent coding processes indicated strong intercoder reliability.

Findings

The 58 teachers who responded to the survey ranged from one to 37 years in service ($M = 17.2$, $SD = 9.7$). Gender representation was generally even (30 Female, 27 Male, one unreported), giving a balanced view of teachers confronting GenAI adoption in education. Participants' self-reported familiarity with GenAI spanned from no prior exposure to regular use, meaning that both novices and early adopters of GenAI were captured.

Across the 49 scored Likert items, the full scale showed good internal consistency (Cronbach's $\alpha = .81$), so stage-level means can be interpreted with confidence Table 6.2.

The mean value for each SoC construct was calculated, as shown in Table 2. The mean scores provide insight into the overall intensity of concern for each stage across all participants; the 'percentage with stage highest' indicates the proportion of teachers for whom a particular stage represented their primary concern. Together, these metrics offer complementary perspectives: mean scores reflect general concern patterns, while the percentage highlights where individuals are developmentally situated in the adoption process.

The means ranged across all seven categories, indicating that teachers experienced a broad spectrum of concerns related to integrating GenAI into their teaching practice.

Stage 1 (Informational) emerged as the most salient concern. Teachers recorded an average rating of M = 3.65, SD = 0.77 — clearly above the neutral midpoint — indicating an active search for authoritative knowledge about how GenAI works and

Table 6.2 Univariate descriptive statistics of the SoC constructs

Stage		Mean	Standard Deviation	% with Stage Highest
6	Refocusing	3.21	0.79	6.9%
5	Collaboration	3.50	0.75	6.9%
4	Consequence	3.50	0.77	27.6%
3	Management	3.12	0.72	6.9%
2	Personal	3.22	0.55	3.4%
1	Informational	3.65	0.77	46.6%
0	Awareness	2.58	0.60	1.7%

how it might be introduced into practice. Stage 4 (Consequence) followed closely at M = 3.50, SD = 0.77, reflecting widespread concern about GenAI's potential impact on student learning, equity, and assessment integrity. A comparable mean (M = 3.50, SD = 0.75) for Stage 5 (Collaboration) suggests moderate, though not dominant, interest in collegial experimentation. The remaining stages clustered closer to the scale midpoint: Stage 2 (Personal) averaged 3.22 (SD = 0.55), Stage 3 (Management) averaged 3.12 (SD = 0.72), and Stage 6 (Refocusing) averaged 3.21 (SD = 0.79)—scores that point to emerging, but still secondary, concerns about individual capability, day-to-day logistics and transformational redesign. Stage 0 (Awareness) registered the lowest endorsement at M = 2.58 (SD = 0.60), suggesting that while a small number of teachers may still be relatively unfamiliar with GenAI, the majority have at least some degree of exposure or awareness.

Classifying each respondent by the single stage on which they scored highest showed the same hierarchy. Nearly half of the sample (27 of 58; 46.6%) peaked in Stage 1 (Informational), and another 16 teachers (27.6%) peaked in Stage 4 (Consequence), together accounting for almost three-quarters of the cohort. Much smaller groups identified Stage 3 (Management), Stage 5 (Collaboration) or Stage 6 (Refocusing) as their chief concern (four teachers, 6.9%, in each case), while only two teachers (3.4%) were dominated by Stage 2 (Personal) concerns and a single teacher (1.7%) remained anchored in Stage 0 (Awareness).

In summary, the quantitative findings suggest that while teachers are acutely aware of GenAI and express a strong understanding both in its technical functions and educational implications, the majority have not yet progressed to the stages characterised by collaborative implementation or curriculum refocusing.

Complementing the quantitative findings, the qualitative data reinforce this pattern of concern. Open-ended responses frequently include requests for "plain-language explanations of how large language models actually generate content", calls for "discipline-specific exemplars showing genuine learning gains", and questions regarding "hidden bias or plagiarism". These comments align with the quantitative finding that teachers' primary concerns centre on Stage 1 (Informational) and Stage 4 (Consequence) - seeking concrete understanding of how GenAI functions alongside apprehension about its educational benefits and associated risks.

The qualitative analysis also revealed the following themes:

GenAI as a tool for efficiency and workload relief—Teachers repeatedly framed GenAI as a timesaving assistant that could "*streamline assessment, planning and reporting*" or "*take the admin load off so I can spend more time with students.*" Approximately one in four respondents mentioned faster feedback cycles or automated preparation of lesson materials.

Academic integrity issues—A comparable proportion voiced apprehension about plagiarism and the erosion of authentic work: "*The challenge will be knowing what the student's own thinking is and what is AI-generated.*" Concerns about diminished critical thinking and over-reliance on automated answers were coupled with worries that GenAI might "*discourage independent and creative thought.*"

Potential loss of the human touch—Several teachers feared that personalised relationships could be diluted. One respondent cautioned that GenAI might "*take* *over the personal touch between students and teachers,*" while another expressed concern that it could "*reduce real conversation and nuanced feedback.*"

Variable relevance across subjects—Some teachers doubted the applicability of GenAI in certain disciplines, especially hands-on or performance-based subjects: "*It is used only for writing text and will not advantage practical subjects such as drama or physical education.*"

Professional learning needs—The most frequently cited support request was hands-on, technically focused training. Twenty-one respondents asked for workshops that walk-through prompt design, ethical safeguards and troubleshooting. Fourteen highlighted the need for time and mentoring to experiment safely, often phrased as "*faculty-based sessions that tackle subject-specific use-cases.*" Others called for showcases of successful classroom practice: "*I want to see concrete examples of how colleagues have used it without encouraging plagiarism.*"

Taken together, the findings reveal a clear pattern in teachers' engagement with GenAI: while awareness of the technology is high, deep pedagogical understanding and confidence in its classroom application remain limited. Qualitative responses highlight this knowledge gap through explicit requests for clear explanations and concrete, discipline-specific examples. The prominence of Stage 4 (Consequence) in the quantitative data is mirrored in the narrative concerns, which frequently centre on issues such as plagiarism, bias, and educational equity. Lower scores for Stage 3 (Management), Stage 5 (Collaboration) and Stage 6 (Refocusing) align with qualitative evidence that while the technology feels accessible, teachers lack sufficient understanding to confidently engage in collaborative curriculum redesign or transformative pedagogical practices.

Discussion

The simultaneous presence of concerns across all developmental stages suggests that the adoption of GenAI in education may follow a more complex and non-linear trajectory than that observed with previous technological innovations. Unlike previous education technologies that primarily require technical and pedagogical knowledge, GenAI immediately raises profound questions about the nature of teaching and learning, pedagogy, assessment, and professional identity that teachers must consider even before full implementation. From the theoretical perspective, this finding supports an interpretation of SoC as a dynamic, non-linear framework where concerns across different stages may intensify simultaneously or cyclically rather than sequentially.

The notably low average score for Stage 0 (Awareness) concerns at $M = 2.58$—the lowest among all stages—with only one teacher (1.7%) identifying it as their dominant concern, suggests that, despite being a relatively recent innovation, GenAI has achieved widespread recognition among K–12 teachers. This rapid awareness likely stems from extensive media coverage, policy discussions, and the consumer-oriented release of tools like ChatGPT. The low prevalence of Stage 0 concerns indicates that the initial hurdle of awareness has largely been overcome, distinguishing GenAI from earlier technologies where many practitioners remained unaware of what they were or if they could be used in education (Hall & Hord, 2015).

The prevalence of Stage 1 (Informational) concerns among nearly half of the participants suggests that, despite the widespread awareness of GenAI, many teachers still lack a fundamental understanding of how these tools function and their potential educational applications. This finding echoes broader research indicating that while teachers are aware of GenAI, many feel ill-prepared to integrate it effectively (Parliament of Australia, 2024). The strong interest in "plain-language explanations" and "discipline-specific exemplars" that emerged from our qualitative data indicates that teachers desire both technical knowledge and contextually relevant pedagogical examples.

The relatively lower intensity of Stage 2 (Personal) concerns in the sample ($M = 3.22$), with only 3.4% of teachers identifying it as their primary concern, contrasts with traditional technology adoption patterns where self-efficacy concerns often dominate early implementation phases (Hall & Hord, 2015). This deviation may reflect the unique nature of GenAI tools, which feature increasingly user-friendly interfaces but raise complex ethical and pedagogical questions that transcend technical proficiency. As one participant noted, the challenge is not using the tools themselves but "knowing what the student's own thinking is and what is AI-generated," highlighting how GenAI shifts concerns from technical competence to maintaining meaningful assessment, student voice, and learning visibility in a context where GenAI can easily obscure a student's own thinking.

Stage 3 (Management) concerns, clustering near the scale midpoint ($M = 3.12$), indicate that practical implementation challenges represent emerging but not yet dominant concerns for most teachers. This pattern suggests that most participants have not yet reached the implementation phase, where logistical issues become paramount. However, the qualitative theme of "efficiency and workload relief" indicates an anticipation of management benefits, with teachers envisioning GenAI as a tool that could "streamline assessment, planning and reporting" or "take the admin load off so I can spend more time with students." This perspective aligns with Kohnke et al.'s (2025) finding that teachers often conceptualise GenAI as an administrative assistant before experiencing its actual classroom implementation.

The prominence of Stage 4 (Consequence) as the second most dominant concern indicates that many teachers are already moving beyond basic awareness to critically consider the implications of GenAI for student learning outcomes, assessment integrity and education equity. These consequence concerns could also extend to cognitive and social-emotional developmental considerations during formative years, including how GenAI might impact children's development of independent problem-solving skills, and their ability to distinguish between human creativity and artificial content generation. This finding reflects a nuanced and forward-looking engagement with the technology, challenging prevailing narratives that position teachers as resistant to innovation. The substantial proportion of teachers expressing concerns about academic integrity aligns with previous research highlighting ethical tensions teachers need to navigate, including "attribution-originality conflicts" and "autonomy-dependency considerations", as identified by Fu and Weng (2024).

The comparable rating of Stage 5 (Collaboration) concerns alongside Stage 4 (Consequence) concerns (M = 3.50), despite only 6.9% of respondents identifying it as their peak concern, suggests an emerging recognition among teachers that effective GenAI integration necessitates collective professional dialogue rather than isolated experimentation. This finding aligns with Zhai's (2024) conceptualisation of evolving teacher roles in the GenAI era, particularly the transition from *Observer* and *Adopter* to *Collaborator* and *Innovator*. However, the qualitative data indicate that although teachers recognise the value of collaboration, many feel they a lack of structured opportunities for collective experimentation and professional dialogue about the integration of GenAI.

Stage 6 (Refocusing) concerns averaged 3.21, with only 6.9% of teachers identifying it as their primary concern, indicating that most participants have not yet reached the stage of reimagining their pedagogical approaches to fully leverage GenAI's affordances. This finding suggests that the transformative potential of GenAI remains largely theoretical rather than operationalised in current teaching practices. The limited manifestation of Refocusing concerns aligns with Chien et al.'s (2024) observation that teachers typically progress through extended periods of experimentation before achieving transformative implementation of new technologies.

Implications for Empowering K–12 Teachers' GenAI Integration

Given the prominence of Stage 1 (Informational) concerns among 46.6% of participants and coupled with strong Stage 4 (Consequence) concerns among 27.6% of teachers, teacher capacity-building initiatives should prioritise foundational knowledge-building and impact analysis. This targeted approach addresses teachers' most immediate concerns and enhances the efficiency of professional development by aligning support with demonstrated need. Focusing first on the concerns shared by nearly three-quarters of teachers can accelerate implementation readiness more effectively than generic, one-size-fits-all strategies. This staged approach acknowledges that effective GenAI integration requires addressing teachers' most pressing concerns sequentially, creating a strong foundation before advancing to more sophisticated implementation considerations.

Specifically, the primary focus of initial TPD efforts should be addressing the widespread Stage 1 (Informational) concerns through comprehensive GenAI literacy development. This should include conceptual understanding workshops that demystify GenAI through accessible explanations of how LLMs work, their capabilities, and limitations, avoiding technical jargon while providing sufficient depth to enable informed decision-making for GenAI adoptions. These workshops should be complemented by discipline-specific demonstrations showing concrete applications across different curriculum areas, directly addressing the perception of "uneven relevance across subjects" that emerged in our qualitative data. Critical analysis sessions enabling teachers to evaluate GenAI outputs and identify potential biases or inaccuracies would further strengthen this foundational understanding, helping teachers move beyond basic awareness to more nuanced comprehension of GenAI affordances and limitations.

Once foundational understanding is established, TPD should progress to addressing the significant Stage 4 (Consequence) concerns by exploring pedagogical implications through assessment redesign workshops, equity-focused discussions, and impact analysis frameworks. These components directly respond to teachers' anxieties about academic integrity, student autonomy, and potential inequality of access identified in our qualitative findings. For early childhood and primary teachers, this stage requires additional focus on evaluating GenAI tools for developmental appropriateness, maintaining authentic play-based assessment practices, and establishing transparent communication protocols with families about GenAI use in educational settings. Crucially, this phase should also include explicit attention to data privacy—particularly when using GenAI tools with younger learners—by guiding teachers on safeguarding student information, evaluating platform policies, and complying with privacy regulations. By providing structured approaches to evaluating GenAI's effects on student learning and designing sound integration strategies, these TPD elements would help teachers navigate the ethical complexities of GenAI implementation while maintaining a focus on educational quality, equity, and developmental appropriateness across the K-12 spectrum.

Although Stage 3 (Management) concerns were less prominent in the findings, practical implementation support remains essential as teachers transition from conceptual understanding to classroom application. This should focus on providing easily accessible resources such as curated collections of effective prompts, sample lesson plans that integrate GenAI meaningfully, and straightforward implementation guides tailored to different subject areas. By offering these ready-to-use materials alongside basic technical support, schools can significantly lower the barrier to initial implementation, helping teachers apply their conceptual understanding in practical classroom contexts without being deterred by logistical challenges.

As teachers progress from foundational understanding to practical implementation, collaborative learning structures become increasingly critical to support sustained integration of GenAI. Although only 6.9% of teachers identified Stage 5 (Collaboration) concerns as their primary focus, qualitative findings reveal an emerging interest in sharing experiences and co-developing strategies, underscoring the importance of collaborative learning structures in supporting GenAI integration. Communities of Practice (Wenger, 2011) centred around subject disciplines or grade levels provide ideal environments for collective experimentation and knowledge-building, allowing teachers to leverage diverse perspectives when navigating implementation challenges. The Lesson Study approach, with its emphasis on collaborative planning, observation, and reflective analysis, offers a particularly effective framework for developing shared expertise with GenAI tools (Wang, 2024). Rather than being positioned as separate from following foundational knowledge-building, such collaborative structures should be viewed as integrated contexts in which that knowledge can be applied, tested, and refined through collective practice.

Finally, although Stage 6 (Refocusing) concerns were relatively low among participants, longer-term TPD planning should include pathways for transformative practice with GenAI. Fostering environments in which teachers can reimagine how GenAI might fundamentally reshape educational experiences may enable meaningful innovation through action research targeting persistent challenges, curriculum redesign that leverages AI's unique affordances and teacher-led initiatives. These advanced components would serve two purposes: supporting the small cohort of early adopters already at the Refocusing stage while simultaneously establishing clear developmental pathways for other teachers as their concerns evolve. This approach recognises that while most teachers are currently focused on understanding and evaluating GenAI, professional development frameworks should anticipate and prepare for their eventual progression toward more transformative implementation, creating a continuous innovation pipeline that respects varied readiness levels and adoption timelines.

Conclusions and Limitations

This study investigated K–12 teachers' concerns regarding GenAI integration, with results showing a concentration around Stage 1 (Informational) and Stage 4 (Consequence) considerations. Although GenAI has become highly visible in public and professional discourse, awareness alone did not translate into pedagogical understanding or practical readiness. Teachers therefore remained in the early stages of adoption, seeking foundational knowledge about how GenAI functions and how it may influence teaching, learning, and assessment. The simultaneous presence of both basic and outcome-oriented concerns challenges linear models of technology adoption and highlights the need for differentiated, stage-sensitive support. Our recommendations towards school TPD respond directly to this concern hierarchy by prioritising foundational GenAI literacy and impact analysis before progressing to practical implementation support, collaborative experimentation, and transformative practice. This targeted approach enhances the effectiveness of TPD by addressing the most prevalent concerns first, creating a solid foundation for teachers' deeper GenAI integration.

Building on this, the findings also highlight the importance of creating conditions that allow teachers to explore GenAI safely and in ways that are directly relevant to their contexts. Opportunities to trial the technology, examine its pedagogical value, and work through concerns such as academic integrity, subject relevance, and the preservation of meaningful teacher–student interaction can support teachers' movement from awareness toward informed readiness. When schools make space for this kind of guided exploration, teachers are better positioned to integrate GenAI in ways that complement their professional judgement and enhance everyday teaching and learning.

This study has several limitations. Participants were drawn from a single independent school in South Australia, which may differ from public schools or other regions in terms of resources, professional culture and technological infrastructure. Additionally, the research captures teachers' concerns at a specific moment, meaning these perceptions could evolve rapidly as GenAI technology and its educational applications continue to develop.

Despite these contextual constraints, this research contributes valuable insights into the human dimensions of GenAI adoption in education. By systematically identifying teachers' concerns through the SoC framework, we establish an empirical foundation for designing targeted TPD that respects teacher perspectives and builds on their existing knowledge and concerns. Future research should extend this work through longitudinal studies tracking how teachers' concerns evolve over time, comparative analyses across diverse educational settings, and intervention studies examining the effectiveness of differentiated TPD approaches in enhancing GenAI integration and, ultimately, student learning experiences and outcomes.

Acknowledgments The authors extend their heartfelt gratitude to Paul Weinart, Mathew Disher, Jack Egan, and colleagues at Concordia College for their kind support in facilitating this research.

Ethics and Permissions This study received ethics approval from the Flinders University Human Research Ethics Committee. All participating teachers were informed about the purpose of the research, assured of confidentiality and anonymity, and provided informed consent before completing the questionnaire. No copyrighted third-party figures, tables, or datasets are reproduced in this chapter. All materials presented are original to the authors.

Appendix 1

GenAI in Education Stages of Concern Questionnaire

Introduction

This Questionnaire is designed to identify and explore any concerns you may have about integrating Generative AI (GenAI) technologies into your teaching practices. GenAI refers to computer programs that can produce text, images, or other content by learning from large datasets. For example, ChatGPT is a well-known GenAI tool that helps users with tasks, such as answering questions, generating creative content and providing insights.

There are a total of 49 items in this questionnaire. Please read each statement carefully and indicate your level of agreement using the following five-point Likert scale: **1 = Strongly Disagree (SD)**; **2 = Disagree (D)**; **3 = Neither agree nor disagree (N)**; **4 = Agree (A)**; **5 = Strongly Agree (SA)**. There are no "right" or "wrong" answers; your honest responses will help identify your primary concerns regarding GenAI adoption in teaching.

Demographic Information

Before completing the questionnaire, please provide some information about yourself. This data will be kept **anonymous** and **confidential** and will be used **solely for the research purposes of this study**.

Years of Teaching Experience: ______________.
Gender: ______________.
Highest Educational Qualification and Studying Area: ______________.
Familiarity with GenAI technologies: ______________.
Teaching Grade/Education Stage: ______________.
Subject Area(s): ______________.
The Questionnaire.

Statement	**1 SD**	**2 D**	**3 N**	**4 A**	**5 SA**
1. I worry that reliance on GenAI might diminish the essential human element in education.					
2. I am curious about the potential benefits of using GenAI in my classroom.					
3. I would like to modify my current teaching methods to incorporate advancements in GenAI					
4. I am not concerned about the use of GenAI in my classroom practice					
5. I actively seek information about how GenAI technologies can work in teaching and learning					
6. I sometimes question whether I have the necessary technical skills to use GenAI tools effectively in my teaching.					
7. I feel uncertain about my ability to effectively use GenAI tools in my classroom.					
8. I look forward to collaborative efforts to develop innovative, GenAI-based teaching strategies.					
9. I have concerns about the availability of adequate resources and support for using GenAI in education.					
10. I am interested in learning more knowledge about the capabilities and issues of GenAI technologies relevant to my teaching.					
11. I wonder if integrating GenAI could compromise the effectiveness of my teaching methods.					
12. I am concerned about the possible additional workload of incorporating GenAI into my teaching while managing my regular teaching responsibilities.					
13. I frequently reflect on ways to optimize the integration of GenAI to better align with my teaching objectives.					

(continued)

(continued)

Statement	1 SD	2 D	3 N	4 A	5 SA
14. I would like to have more information on the time and energy commitments required by this innovation.					
15. I believe that collective problem-solving can help overcome challenges in GenAI adoption.					
16. I sometimes question whether I have the necessary pedagogical skills to implement GenAI in ways that enhance student learning.					
17. I am anxious about unforeseen consequences that might arise from using GenAI in the classroom.					
18. I am concerned about the practical aspects of implementing GenAI in my teaching.					
19. I actively seek new ideas to maximize the benefits of GenAI in my teaching.					
20. I am concerned about how GenAI might challenge my role as a teacher.					
21. I seek opportunities to work together with other teachers to effectively integrate GenAI into teaching.					
22. I am concerned about the organizational changes required for effective GenAI integration					
23. I question whether GenAI will enhance or detract from the quality of education my students receive.					
24. I have not given much thought to integrating GenAI tools into my teaching practice.					
25. I am exploring ways to repurpose GenAI to further enhance teaching and learning in my classroom.					
26. I would like to know how GenAI might change my daily teaching practices.					
27. I am anxious about the time and effort required to learn and integrate GenAI into my teaching routine.					
28. I would welcome training or workshops that explain how GenAI can support my teaching.					
29. I worry that the use of GenAI in teaching could lead to negative effects on student engagement.					
30. I am not aware of any potential issues related to using GenAI in teaching and learning.					
31. I appreciate the potential for shared learning experiences when adopting GenAI tools.					
32. I am open to experimenting with innovative GenAI strategies to improve educational outcomes.					
33. I am worried about potential disruptions to my classroom management when using GenAI tools.					
34. I feel personally threatened by the rapid development of GenAI in the educational field.					
35. I want to know more about the different GenAI tools available for educators.					

(continued)

(continued)

Statement	1 SD	2 D	3 N	4 A	5 SA
36. I seldom reflect on the possible implications of GenAI in educational settings.					
37. I value discussions with colleagues about the successes and setbacks of GenAI in the classroom.					
38. I am concerned that GenAI might inadvertently disadvantage certain groups of students.					
39. I am interested in understanding the personal implications of integrating GenAI into my teaching practices.					
40. I am concerned about managing the technical challenges associated with GenAI tools.					
41. I would like to learn about the resources available to deepen my understanding of GenAI applications in education.					
42. I am considering alternative approaches to using GenAI beyond its current applications.					
43. I am concerned about how GenAI might impact my students' learning outcomes.					
44. I am interested in collaborating with colleagues to share best practices on using GenAI in education.					
45. I am eager to participate in professional learning communities focused on GenAI in education.					
46. I would like to understand what the immediate future requirements for using GenAI will be.					
47. I am curious about future possibilities of GenAI that could transform education in innovative ways.					
48. I have limited interest in exploring how GenAI can be applied in my teaching					
49. I rarely consider how GenAI might change the educational landscape.					

Open-Ended Questions.

In this section, you are invited to provide open-ended responses to several questions regarding your perceptions on GenAI. Please answer each question in your own words, offering as much detail as you feel comfortable sharing. Your thoughtful responses will help us gain a deeper understanding of the context behind your concerns and support needs.

1. What does GenAI mean to you, and in what ways do you believe its widespread adoption will impact both teachers and students?
2. What potential benefits or challenges do you foresee as GenAI becomes integrated in teaching and learning?
3. What types of training, resources, or support would help you feel more confident and prepared to use GenAI in your teaching? Why?

Thank you for your participation and for sharing your insights!

References

Bower, M., Henderson, M., Slade, C., Southgate, E., Gulson, K., & Lodge, J. (2025). What generative Artificial Intelligence priorities and challenges do senior Australian educational policymakers identify (and why)?. *The Australian Educational Researcher*, 1–26. doi:https://doi.org/10.1007/s13384-025-00801-z.

Cheah, Y. H., Lu, J., & Kim, J. (2025). Integrating generative artificial intelligence in K–12 education: Examining teachers' preparedness, practices, and barriers. *Computers and Education: Artificial Intelligence, 8*, 100363. https://doi.org/10.1016/j.caeai.2025.100363

Chien, C. C., Chan, H. Y., & Hou, H. T. (2024). Learning by playing with generative AI: design and evaluation of a role-playing educational game with generative AI as scaffolding for instant feedback interaction. *Journal of Research on Technology in Education*, 1–20. doi:https://doi.org/10.1080/15391523.2024.2338085.

Collie, R. J., & Martin, A. J. (2024). Teachers' motivation and engagement to harness generative AI for teaching and learning: The role of contextual, occupational, and background factors. *Computers and Education: Artificial Intelligence, 6*, 100224. https://doi.org/10.1016/j.caeai.2024.100224

Creswell, J. W., & Plano Clark, V. L. (2018). *Designing and conducting mixed methods research* (3rd ed.). SAGE.

Cronbach, L. J. (1951). Coefficient alpha and the internal structure of tests. *Psychometrika, 16*, 297–334. https://doi.org/10.1007/BF02310555

Department of Education. (2023). *Australian Framework for Generative Artificial Intelligence (AI) in Schools*. Commonwealth of Australia: Department of Education. https://www.education.gov.au/schooling/resources/australian-framework-generative-artificial-intelligence-ai-schools

Fu, Y., & Weng, Z. (2024). Navigating the ethical terrain of AI in education: A systematic review on framing responsible human-centered AI practices. *Computers and Education: Artificial Intelligence*, 100306. doi:https://doi.org/10.1016/j.caeai.2024.100306.

Fuller, F. F. (1969). Concerns of teachers: A developmental conceptualization. *American Educational Research Journal, 6*(2), 207–226. https://doi.org/10.3102/00028312006002207

George, A. A., Hall, G. E., & Stiegelbauer, S. M. (2006). *Measuring implementation in schools: The Stages of Concern Questionnaire*. SEDL.

Hall, G. E. (2010). Technology's Achilles heel: Achieving high-quality implementation. *Journal of Research on Technology in Education, 42*(3), 231–253. https://doi.org/10.1080/15391523.2010.10782550

Hall, G. E., George, A. A., & Rutherford, W. L. (1979). *Measuring stages of concern about the innovation: A manual for use of the SoC questionnaire*. The University of Texas at Austin, Research and Development Center for Teacher Education.

Hall, G. E., & Hord, S. M. (2015). *Implementing change: Patterns, principles, and potholes* (4th ed.). Pearson.

Hall, G. E., Wallace, R. C., & Dossett, W. A. (1973). *A developmental conceptualization of the adoption process within educational institutions*. Research and Development Center for Teacher Education, The University of Texas.

Holmes, W., Porayska-Pomsta, K., Holstein, K., Sutherland, E., Baker, T., Shum, S. B., et al. (2022). Ethics of AI in education: Towards a community-wide framework. *International Journal of Artificial Intelligence in Education, 32*, 504–526. https://doi.org/10.1007/s40593-021-00239-1

Huang, D., Huang, Y., & Cummings, J. J. (2024). Exploring the integration and utilisation of generative AI in formative e-assessments: A case study in higher education. *Australasian Journal of Educational Technology, 40*(4), 1–19. https://doi.org/10.14742/ajet.9467

Kohnke, L., Zou, D., & Su, F. (2025). Exploring the potential of gen AI for personalised English teaching: Learners' experiences and perceptions. *Computers and Education: Artificial Intelligence, 100371*. https://doi.org/10.1016/j.caeai.2025.100371

Laurillard, D. (2013). *Teaching as a design science: Building pedagogical patterns for learning and technology*. Routledge.

Lincoln, Y. S., & Guba, E. G. (1985). *Naturalistic inquiry*. Sage.
Lynn, M. R. (1986). Determination and quantification of content validity. *Nursing Research, 35*(6), 382–385. https://doi.org/10.1097/00006199-198611000-00017
Nixon, N., Lin, Y., & Snow, L. (2024). Catalysing equity in STEM teams: Harnessing generative AI for inclusion and diversity. *Policy Insights From the Behavioral and Brain Sciences, 11*(1), 85–92. https://doi.org/10.1177/23727322231220356
Norman, D. A. (1988). *The design of everyday things*. Doubleday.
Parliament of Australia. (2024). *Study buddy or influencer: Inquiry into the use of generative AI in the Australian education system*. Retrieved April 1st, 2025, from https://www.aph.gov.au/Parliamentary_Business/Committees/House/Employment_Education_and_Training/AIineducation/Report
Pew Research Center. (2024). *A quarter of U.S. teachers say AI tools do more harm than good in K-12 education*. Retrieved April 1st, 2025, from https://www.pewresearch.org/short-reads/2024/05/15/a-quarter-of-u-s-teachers-say-ai-tools-do-more-harm-than-good-in-k-12-education/
Ronge, R., Maier, M., & Rathgeber, B. (2025). Towards a definition of generative artificial intelligence. *Philosophy & Technology, 38*(1), 31. https://doi.org/10.1007/s13347-025-00863-y
Samala, A. D., Rawas, S., Wang, T., Reed, J. M., Kim, J., Howard, N. J., & Ertz, M. (2025). Unveiling the landscape of generative artificial intelligence in education: A comprehensive taxonomy of applications, challenges, and future prospects. *Education and Information Technologies, 30*(3), 3239–3278. https://doi.org/10.1007/s10639-024-12936-0
Wang, T. (2023). Navigating generative AI (ChatGPT) in higher education: Opportunities and challenges. In C. Anutariya, D. Liu, A. Kinshuk, J. Y. Tlili, & M. Chang (Eds.), *Smart learning for a sustainable society: Proceedings of the 7th international conference on smart learning environments* (pp. 215–225). SpringerNature.
Wang, T. (2024). Using lesson study as a strategy to build in-service teacher's capacity of K-12 AI education in Hong Kong. In E. C. K. Cheng & B. Lander (Eds.), *Implementing a 21st century competency-based curriculum through lesson study* (pp. 202–219). Routledge.
Wang, T., & Cheng, E. C. K. (2021). An investigation of barriers to Hong Kong K-12 schools incorporating artificial intelligence in education. *Computers and Education: Artificial Intelligence, 2*, 100031. https://doi.org/10.1016/j.caeai.2021.100031
Wenger, E. (2011). *Communities of practice: A brief introduction*. National Science Foundation.
Zhai, X. (2024). Transforming teachers' roles and agencies in the era of generative AI: Perceptions, acceptance, knowledge, and practices. *Journal of Science Education and Technology, 1-11*. https://doi.org/10.1007/s10956-024-10174-0

Dr Tianchong Wang is a Senior Lecturer in STEM in Innovative Education Futures at Flinders University's College of Education, Psychology and Social Work. He holds an EdD from the Chinese University of Hong Kong, an MSc from the University of Hong Kong, and a BA from Hong Kong Baptist University, along with various ICT qualifications. His work centres on technology-enhanced learning and teaching, with a particular focus on Artificial Intelligence (AI) in Education. Tianchong is an Associate Editor for *Education and Information Technologies*, a Q1 SSCI journal. He developed and taught Hong Kong's first master-level course on AI in Education at the University of Hong Kong in 2020. An advocate for the UN's SDG4, Tianchong's research aims to enhance education equity, quality, and inclusiveness, foster positive change in learning environments, and empower educators and learners in underprivileged communities. He actively engages with international and regional stakeholders such as UNESCO, The World Bank Group, and The Commonwealth of Learning in various capacities. In 2016, Tianchong co-developed UNESCO's framework for quality blended learning adoption and contributed to large-scale development projects addressing urban—rural disparities in STEM education quality in developing Asia. He also authored UNESCO's reports on transforming teaching and learning with new digital technologies in 2022, and served as Consultant and Chief Rapporteur for UNESCO's roundtable on generative AI and education in Asia—Pacific in 2023, and recently worked as an international expert for UNESCO's Fostering STEM Education in Africa and Small Island Developing States (SIDS) initiative. Tianchong is committed to empowering girls in STEM and is co-CI of the 2023 Google Award for Inclusion Research, promoting female inclusion in generative AI in K–12 schools in Australia. Besides research, he conducts teacher capacity-building activities in the Global South. His media commentaries on AI in education have been featured in international higher education platforms and national media outlets, contributing to public understanding of this fascinating field.

Chapter 7
Using ChatGPT to Differentiate Tasks: What Works and What Doesn't? A Guide for Early Educators

Tobias Bahr

Abstract Teachers are increasingly using generative AI tools like ChatGPT-4 in K-12 classrooms worldwide. However, teacher education often lacks foundational knowledge in computer science (CS), particularly in AI, especially in the context of early education (K-4). To harness the potential of generative AI like ChatGPT-4 effectively, educators must be equipped with the necessary knowledge and strategies to integrate these tools into their teaching practice. This chapter presents an approach to differentiating tasks using ChatGPT-4. Building on prior research, several pedagogical criteria were selected to adapt existing tasks in order to address the diverse levels of students' prior knowledge. This approach was piloted in two workshops with teachers and researchers from various backgrounds, including early education. Following a revision of the prompts, the method was tested again with pre-service teachers from a range of disciplines. Based on the insights gained from these trials, this chapter serves as a guide for early educators, offering a pedagogically grounded method to differentiate tasks for homework, classroom activities, and exams. By increasing the adaptability of their lessons, educators can better address students with varying levels of prior knowledge. The limitations of this approach are discussed at the conclusion of the chapter.

Keywords K-4 education · Task differentiation · AI

Introduction

The Heterogeneity regarding student's language skills and prior knowledge in early education (from kindergarten to grade 4, K-4) is high especially after the COVID-19 pandemic, according to the recent IQB results (Stanat et al., 2022). In Germany, the number of students with special pedagogical needs and different native language

T. Bahr (✉)
Didactics of Computer Science, Institute of Computer Science, University of Potsdam, Potsdam, Germany
e-mail: tobias.bahr@uni-potsdam.de

S. Papadakis (ed.), *AI Applications in Preschool and Primary Education*, Advances in Artificial Intelligence in Education 5, https://doi.org/10.1007/978-3-032-17190-0_7

(e. g. students from the Ukraine) in K-4 is rising as well (Sauerborn, 2022; SWK, 2022). Those factors are leading to a callout for a bigger focus on the basic competences supported by assessment of students in K-4 (SWK, 2022). A constructive approach to heterogeneity that can be implemented by *every* K-4 teacher is therefore more important than ever. Artificial Intelligence (AI), that has increasingly been integrated into early education as shown by the literature review of Aravantinos et al. (2024), could be a beneficial tool for early educators. Generative AI, especially AI-chatbots, such as ChatGPT-4, have the potential to support teachers in task generation (Manzocco et al., 2025; Trautmann, 2024). Finding good examples on a topic, restructuring texts, providing definitions at various levels of difficulty and more (Miller, 2023) have been identified as good use cases of AI-chatbots. Thus, the generation, differentiation and translation of tasks seem to be beneficial use cases for teachers (Wacker et al., 2025). However, AI-chatbots have challenges such as providing false or misleading responses (Sarsa et al., 2022). As AI-chatbots such as ChatGPT-4 generates not deterministic answers based on patterns from its training data and not factually true knowledge, it can generate inaccurate information (called hallucinations) that sound plausible but are incorrect (e. g. inventing poems by authors that exist). Based on the training data, misinformation or even misconceptions could be reinforced. Bahr et al. (2024) and Lohr et al. (2024) concluded that it still requires significant human intervention to generate sensible tasks that can be used by teachers. Uğraş et al. (2024) showed that primary school teachers might benefit from using AI tools such as ChatGPT by meeting specific curricula needs. Hence, analyzing and differentiating tasks might be a beneficial use case for early educators as well. This article tries to address these aforementioned challenges by introducing a guide for early educators, how to differentiate tasks using ChatGPT-4 as a working example. Grounded in theory about the differentiation of tasks (Sect. 7.2) and two working examples (Sect. 7.3), as well as findings in from the workshops and literature (Sect. 7.4), ending with a discussion highlighting limitations and future work (Sect. 7.5).

Task Differentiation

Several general didactical criteria of tasks have been identified that can be used to generate, differentiate or analyze them.

Matching the Tasks to the Curriculum

The main criteria, or the common criteria, that all teachers agreed on both workshops, was the alignment with the curricula of the specific subject (Bahr et al., 2024). The accuracy of the analysis by ChatGPT-4 was tested with the Computer science (CS) curriculum of Baden-Württemberg, Germany from grade 7 to 12 as a use case. The tasks from the CS curriculum commission that were specifically designed for the curriculum served as the ground truth (accurate, real-world data used as a benchmark for validating the accuracy). The prompt was to match the task to a learning outcome from the CS curriculum. In 97.5% of the cases the correct learning outcome was matched. Therefore, we have some evidence that shows that ChatGPT-4 can accurately match a task to a learning outcome.

Cognitive Process Dimension and Types of Knowledge

Cognitive processes can be seen as the primary characteristic of a task. According to Bloom et al. (1956) and later revised by Anderson and Krathwohl (2001) tasks can be differentiated into six different levels that are characterized by operators: (1) *remember*, (2) *understand*, (3) *apply*, (4) *analyze*, (5) *evaluate*, and (6) *create.*

Furthermore, there exist different types of knowledge: *factual knowledge* (knowledge that is domain specific and can be verbalized), *procedural knowledge* (implicit knowledge ranging from behaviors and domain specific procedures), *conceptual knowledge* (interconnected knowledge of different concepts that can be verbalized and implicit), and lastly *metacognitive knowledge* (knowledge about cognition and learning strategies).

The following example from CS in primary education shows the application of the taxonomy with the cognitive process and type of knowledge (Anderson & Krathwohl, 2001):

1. When you have 6 grapes and eat 2 how many grapes do you have left? (Remember, Factual knowledge)
2. Describe where you can find subtraction in your daily life based on one example. (Understand, Factual knowledge)
3. What pattern do you notice with does numbers 0, 5, 10, 15, 20? (Understand, Conceptual knowledge)
4. Explain to Alex how you solve this problem: Ben has three boxes with 8 apples inside each box. How many apples does Ben have? (Understand, Procedural knowledge)
5. Analyze the following calculation by Sven: $4 + 3 = 10$. Is it correct? If not help him. (Analyzing, Procedural knowledge)
6. Complete the house with numbers. (Applying, Procedural knowledge)
7. Read this story and solve it. (Evaluating, Procedural knowledge)

   a. Anna has 17 stickers. She gives 3 to her friend. How many does she have now?

8. Create your own story with addition or subtraction and ask a classmate to solve it. (Create, Procedural Knowledge)

This example shows that various levels of cognitive processes and different types of knowledge can be identified. When generating tasks these different levels should be considered. While there exists a discussion around the hierarchy of this taxonomy (Fuller et al., 2007) the taxonomy can serve as a criterion for differentiation for AI-chatbots and was used in the evaluation of tasks before (Bahr et al., 2024). There could be more elaborate analysis on taxonomy. That given this article has the main focus it the usage for task differentiation with AI-chatbots. However, learning outcomes stated in curricula in Germany, and other countries as well, build on the taxonomy (Fraefel, 2023). Therefore, connecting the curriculum-based approach (in Sect. 7.2.1) with this taxonomy.

Other Didactical Criteria

Several didactical criteria are mentioned in this section. Not all of them turned out to provide sensible tasks after the pilot phase.

Language Complexity

When creating a task for students, tasks in various language complexities can be developed (Jordan et al., 2006; Maier et al., 2010). From a very simple language complexity by using only short sentences, simple vocabulary and no technical term to a very advanced language complexity including complex sentence structures, distractors, many technical terms and possibly abstract concepts. Thus, the language complexity was included into the task differentiation using a five-point Likert scale from 1 = "very simple language complexity" to 5 = "very advanced language complexity" (Bahr et al., 2024). While the level of language complexity in primary education could in most cases be not very high, the analysis of the task at hand might be helpful to differentiate too complex tasks from a language level perspective to lower levels. According to Van Grop and Bogaert (2006) tasks should contain a gap between "the zone of next potential" and the current language proficiency. Too difficult tasks, from a language complexity level perspective, could decrease students' motivation. Tasks that were perceived as difficult and challenging but are still within the reach of students' competencies led to higher performance than goals that were perceived easy according to the meta-analysis from Locke and Kristof (1996). Hence, a step-by-step increase in language complexity could be achieved by the differentiation of tasks with AI-chatbots.

Convergent or Divergent Solutions

Tasks can be defined regarding their possible solutions (Maier et al., 2010). If a task has a fixed answer that can clearly be categorized in right or false it can be described as a task with a *convergent solution*, e. g. "find the mistake in the sequence of commands so that the Bee-Bot moves to the intended goal". To stimulate students' creativity

(Romeike, 2006), it can be beneficial to use tasks with a *divergent solution.* That means tasks with multiple solutions, for example writing a letter about how much they use digital devices such as the mobile phone in their free time and reflecting on that. Specifically, as the use of mobile phones is very prominent in Germany primary schools tasks like that address the relevance of everyday life.

Relevance to Everyday Life

For the relevance to everyday life in tasks Maier et al. (2010) defined four categories: tasks *without a connection to everyday life*, task with a *constructed connection to everyday life* (e. g., tasks with examples that are hardly recognizable by the students such as "a pricey orange thrown into the air by a market vendor, only to be skewered by a bird. Calculate the acting forces"), tasks with a *constructed but seemingly authentic connection to everyday life* (e. g., "you want to buy three oranges one costs 2 euros. How much do you have to pay? "), and lastly tasks with *a real-life connection* (e. g., "you want to buy five flowers for your mother on Mother's Day, one flower costs 2 euros. How much do you have to pay?).

Conclusion

There might be other didactical criteria that could be integrated to differentiate tasks such as the *tasks complexity* (including facts, procedures, concepts or even metacognition, Maier et al., 2010), the *openness of the formulated tasks* (analogues to the solution described in Sect. 7.2.3.2), or different forms of representation (Maier et al., 2010). However, the more complex parameters are used in prompts the more time the AI-chatbot needs to generate a response and the more time the user needs to think about the task at hand. The approach for this article is the differentiation and translation of tasks to support teachers by addressing the heterogeneity in students' prior knowledge and language skills and not the comprehensive development of an assessment instrument using AI-tools. Therefore, only the parameters mentioned in the sections above: (1) *learning outcome from the curriculum*, (2) *Bloom's revised taxonomy*, (3) *type of knowledge*, (4) *language complexity*, (5) *convergent or divergent solution* and (6) *real-life connection* are used in the working example below.

The Working Example

At the start, the first prompt introduces the AI-chatbot, in these working examples ChatGPT-4, with the scenario and the definitions from the previous section. Two tasks for primary students grade 4 are used as working examples.

The prompts are shown in the following structured by the subsections: initialization, response from ChatGPT-4, prompt to differentiate the task, and result.

Initialization

You are an experienced educator and an expert in task differentiation in primary education. Your task is to create an adapted assignment based on a detailed task analysis. The original task and the analyses provide insights into the existing structure and learning objectives.

Your goal is to develop a new assignment tailored to the updated values and learning profile of the students, ensuring that the same content competencies are conveyed at a modified level.

Definitions for the Metrics:

Bloom's Taxonomy:

1. Remembering (Recollection of facts, basic terms, and simple concepts without understanding)
2. Understanding (Explaining ideas or concepts, interpreting material)
3. Applying (Using information in new situations, applying concepts and theories)
4. Analyzing (Distinguishing between different components, recognizing patterns)
5. Evaluating (Justifying decisions, choosing between different alternatives)
6. Creating (Producing new material or ideas, combining concepts)

Linguistic Complexity:

1. Very simple language level (Short sentences, simple vocabulary, no technical terms)
2. Simple language level (Basic sentence structures, occasional use of technical terms with explanations)
3. Medium language level (More complex sentence structures, frequent use of technical terms but still understandable)
4. Advanced language level (Long sentences, advanced vocabulary, technical terms without explanations)
5. Very advanced language level (Complex sentence structures, rich vocabulary, many technical terms, and possibly abstract concepts)

Divergent solution:

If a task has a fixed answer that can clearly be categorized in right or false it can be described as a task with a convergent solution. Divergent solutions mean tasks with multiple solutions.

Relevance to Everyday Life:

A key component in designing teaching materials is the connection of the learning content to real-life, everyday situations.

Next Steps:

Ask sequentially for the following details:

- Task
- Learning Objective

- Bloom's Taxonomy Level
- Linguistic Complexity
- Divergent solution
- Relevance to Everyday Life
- Desired Differentiation:

BLOOM =
Linguistic Complexity =
Divergent solution =
Relevance to Everyday Life =

Based on the original task, the detailed analysis results, and the desired values for differentiation, create a concept for how the given task can be adapted so that the new values align. Ensure that the adapted task still covers all learning objectives.

Response from ChatGPT-4

Great, let's go step by step! To ensure a precise and effective adaptation of the task, I will need the following details from you to proceed:

- Task: Can you provide me with the original task or assignment you'd like to adapt?
- Learning Objective: What are the key learning objectives for the task?
- Bloom's Taxonomy Level: What cognitive level does this task currently aim to address (e.g., Remembering, Understanding, Applying, Analyzing, Evaluating, Creating)?
- Linguistic Complexity: What level of linguistic complexity should the task reflect (e.g., Very simple, Simple, Medium, Advanced, Very advanced)?
- Divergent Solution: Should the task have a fixed answer (convergent) or allow for multiple possible answers (divergent)?
- Relevance to Everyday Life: How is the task connected to real-life situations? Should the task be adapted to make it more relevant to students' everyday experiences?

Once I have these details, I'll be able to create an adapted version of the task that aligns with the desired differentiation values while ensuring all learning objectives are still met.

Prompt to Differentiate the Task

See Table 7.1.

Table 7.1 Prompts used to differentiate two tasks one for mathematics (left) and one for English as a second language (right)

Mathematics example	Language example
Original Task: There are 4 dogs running in the yard. How many legs are there in total? Write down how you solved the problem!	**Original Task:** Change this sentence into a question: 'German is fun.'
Learning Objective: Understanding multiplication as repeated addition Applying knowledge of real-world contexts to math Problems	**Learning Objective:** To understand how to change a statement into a question
Original Metrics: BLOOM = 3 (Applying) Linguistic Complexity = 1 Divergent solution = No Relevance to Everyday Life = yes	**Original Metrics:** BLOOM = 1 Linguistic Complexity = 1 Divergent solution = No Relevance to Everyday Life = No
Desired Differentiation: BLOOM = 4 Analyzing Linguistic Complexity = 1 Divergent solution = Yes Relevance to Everyday Life = yes	**Desired Differentiation:** BLOOM = 6 Linguistic Complexity = 1 Divergent solution = Yes Relevance to Everyday Life = yes

Result: The Differentiated Task

Adapted Task: Mathematics Example

You are helping at an animal shelter. In the yard, there are dogs, birds, and one cat playing. Some animals have more or fewer legs than others. You count 2 dogs, 3 birds, and 1 cat.

How many legs might there be in total? Can there be more than one correct answer? Explain how you found your total and if there could be other totals.

This adaptation maintains the essence of the original task but challenges students to engage in reflection and analysis. Besides the less realistic scenario of a cat playing with birds, the tasks engage students to think about different outcomes.

Adapted Task: English as a Foreign Language

You're planning a fun project about German for your class and want to ask people if they agree with you. Create a few different questions to ask others about German.

While the number of words is increasing, the task now provides a relevance to students everyday life and can be used to engage students into creating multiple questions about that topic, here German as a subject.

Discussion

The tasks from the working examples have room for improvement as they contain a lot of words that might be overwhelming for primary school students. However, from the analysis of the taxonomy level the differentiation seemed plausible. The task at hand was translated from German into English and back translated to check for the accuracy. No differences were found.

As reasoning models become more popular, it can be beneficial to ask the AI-chatbot for advice on how to generate a more effective prompt. Lastly, to add to the discussion the possibilities and challenges using AI-chatbots for task differentiation and translation findings from the teacher workshops are reported in the following subsections.

Findings from the Teacher Workshops

Researchers in the field of didactics of mathematics identified revising prompts with a step-by-step approach (chain of thought, only good for non-reasoning models) and letting ChatGPT ask questions regarding needed information (query loop) to solve a task can yield better outcomes (Schorcht et al., 2023). We found the same result in a workshop with K-12 teachers from various fields (Manzocco et al., 2025). Another result was that it might be beneficial to receive directly three tasks (based on the original one) for a basic, intermediate and advanced level. Regarding the task's complexity, one finding was that ChatGPT was better in generating more complex tasks than making tasks easier. A positive remark was that the tool directly mapped the tasks to the curricula or learning outcome confirming our analysis from the beginning. Furthermore, benefits of the task differentiation were seen in the generation of tasks for tests or homework were its clear or intended that the students must work alone at the task (Manzocco et al., 2025). Task differentiation in mathematics revealed the most heterogeneous results in conformance with the finding from Schorcht et al. (2023). Some teachers stated that with changing curricula and sometimes now ideas were to start with tasks for a new (interdisciplinary) subject, AI-chatbots can provide first suggestions. Another useful addition is the translation of a task after the differentiation (Wacker et al., 2025). However, there is still a need for user intervention and critical thinking as the qualitative analysis pointed out that "despite restrictions and preset settings,' to correctly adjust the level for students and produced overly abstract content and questions. These tasks, therefore, still present a significant challenge for some students, which in turn highlights the current limitations of the tool's capabilities." (Manzocco et al., 2025, p. 16).

Implications for Practice and Ethics

Reflecting the tasks is a must, as discussed above. Some examples from Stern (2003, p. 120) stated that tasks such as "Maria had 6 marbles. Then she gave Hans 4 marbles. How many marbles does Maria have now?" are easy (high solution rates) for preschool students whereas tasks such as "Maria has 9 marbles. She has 4 more marbles than Hans. How many marbles does Hans have?" are difficult (low solution rates). Therefore, cognitive process and implication of tasks for the students should be considered when applying AI-tools for task differentiation. Lastly, ethical considerations should be made when presenting students with these tasks. Private data from students should not be used in prompts. Translation of tasks should be at least back translated to ensure that they do not change the original task. Tasks could include gender stereotypes and should be reflected. When using the differentiated tasks educators should ensure that they remain in the pedagogical boundaries provided by the criteria presented in the theoretical framework in this chapter and enhance learning rather than provide unnecessary challenges for the students. With these limitations the aim of this chapter was to provide educators with a tool, with its benefits and challenges, which could support students.

References

Anderson, L. W., & Krathwohl, D. R. (2001). *A taxonomy for learning, teaching and assessing: A revision of bloom's taxonomy of educational objectives.*

Aravantinos, S., Lavidas, K., Voulgari, I., Papadakis, S., Karalis, T., & Komis, V. (2024). Educational approaches with AI in primary school settings: A systematic review of the literature available in scopus. *Education Sciences, 14*(7), 744. https://doi.org/10.3390/educsci14070744

Bahr, T., Manzocco, M., & Schuster, D. (2024). Differentiated tasks by ChatGPT for secondary computer science education: Useful or not? In *Proceedings of the 19th WiPSCE Conference on Primary and Secondary Computing Education Research (WiPSCE '24)*, Article 34, 1–2. Association for Computing Machinery. https://doi.org/10.1145/3677619.3678092

Bloom, B. S., Engelhart, M. D., Furst, E. J., Hill, W. H., & Krathwohl, D. R. (1956). *Taxonomy of educational objectives: The classification of educational goals. Handbook I: Cognitive domain.* David McKay Company.

Fraefel, U. (2023). *Erfolgreichen Unterricht planen: Pragmatisch, praktisch, professionell.* UTB.

Fuller, U., Johnson, C. G., Ahoniemi, T., Cukierman, D., Hernán-Losada, I., Jackova, J., Lahtinen, E., Lewis, T. L., McGee Thompson, D., Riedesel, C., & Thompson, E. (2007). Developing a computer science-specific learning taxonomy. In *Working group reports on ITiCSE on Innovation and technology in computer science education (ITiCSE-WGR '07)* (pp. 152–170). Association for Computing Machinery. https://doi.org/10.1145/1345443.1345438

Jordan, A., Ross, N., Krauss, S., Baumert, J., Blum, W., Neubrand, M., Löwen, K., Brunner, M., & Kunter, M. (2006). *Klassifikationsschema für Mathematikaufgaben: Dokumentation der Aufgabenkategorisierung im COACTIV-Projekt.* MPI.

Locke, E., & Kristof, A. (1996). Volitional choices in the goal achievement process. In P. Gollwitzer & J. Bargh (Eds.), *The psychology of action: Linking cognition to motivation and behaviour* (pp. 363–384). Guilfod Press.

Lohr, D., Berges, M., Chugh, A., Kohlhase, M., & Müller, D. (2024). Leveraging large language models to generate course-specific semantically annotated learning objects. *Journal of Computer Assisted Learning.* https://doi.org/10.48550/arXiv.2412.04185

Maier, U., Kleinknecht, M., Metz, K., & Bohl, T. (2010). Ein allgemeindidaktisches Kategoriensystem zur Analyse des kognitiven Potenzials von Aufgaben. *Beiträge zur Lehrerbildung, 28*, 84–96. https://doi.org/10.25656/01:13734

Manzocco, M., Schuster, D., Weisse, T., & Wacker, A. (2025). Ein digitales Tool zur Unterrichtsplanung. *Pädagogik*, 2, 14–18. https://doi.org/10.3262/PAED2502014

Miller, M. (2023). *AI for educators: Learning strategies, teacher efficiencies, and a vision for an artificial intelligence future*. Dave Burgess Consulting, Inc.. ISBN: 9781956306484.

Romeike, R. (2006). Creative students: What can we learn from them for teaching computer science? In *Proceedings of the 6th Baltic Sea conference on computing education research: Koli Calling 2006* (Baltic Sea '06) (pp. 149–150). Association for Computing Machinery. https://doi.org/10.1145/1315803.1315835

Sarsa, S., Denny, P., Hellas, A., & Leinonen, J. (2022). Automatic generation of programming exercises and code explanations using large language models. In *Proceedings of the 2022 ACM conference on international computing education research—volume 1 (ICER '22), 1* (pp. 27–43). Association for Computing Machinery. https://doi.org/10.1145/3501385.3543957

Sauerborn, H. (2022). Sprachlicher Heterogenität begegnen: Ein Fallbeispiel. *Leseräume: Deutschunterricht in der Postmigrationsgesellschaft*, *9*(8), 1–26. Retrieved March 8, 2025, from https://leseraume.de/wp-content/uploads/2022/12/lr-2022-1-Sauerborn.pdf

Schorcht, S., Baumanns, L., Buchholtz, N., Huget, J., Peters, F., & Pohl, M. (2023). Ask smart to get smart: Mathematische Ausgaben generativer KI-Sprachmodelle verbessern durch gezieltes Prompt Engineering. *Mitteilungen der Gesellschaft für Didaktik der Mathematik*, (115).

Stanat, P., Schipolowski, S., Schneider, R., Sachse, K. A., Weirich, S. & Henschel, S. (2022). *IQB Bildungstrend 2021. Kompetenzen in den Fächern Deutsch und Mathematik am Ende der 4.* Jahrgangsstufe im dritten Ländervergleich. Waxmann. Retrieved November 2, 2022, from https://www.iqb.hu-berlin.de/bt/BT2021/Bericht/

Ständige Wissenschaftliche Kommission der Kultusministerkonferenz (SWK) [Hrsg.]: *Basale Kompetenzen vermitteln—Bildungschancen sichern. Perspektiven für die Grundschule.* Gutachten der Ständigen Wissenschaftlichen Kommission der Kultusministerkonferenz (SWK). Bonn: SWK 2022, 190 S. - URN: urn:nbn:de:0111-pedocs-255420 - https://doi.org/10.25656/01:25542

Stern, E. (2003). Früh übt sich: Neuere Ergebnisse aus der LOGIK-Studie zum Lösen mathematischer Textaufgaben. In A. Fritz-Stratmann, G. Ricken, & S. Schmidt (Eds.), *Rechenschwäche: Lernwege, Schwierigkeiten und Hilfen bei Dyskalkulie: Ein Handbuch* (pp. 116–130). Beltz. https://hdl.handle.net/11858/00-001M-0000-0025-8E9D-D

Trautmann, M. (2024). Thema: KI in der Schule. *Pädagogik, 76*, H. 3, 7–10. ISBN: 9783407472939.

Uğraş, H., Uğraş, M., Papadakis, S., & Kalogiannakis, M. (2024). ChatGPT-supported education in primary schools: The potential of ChatGPT for sustainable practices. *Sustainability, 16*(22), 9855. https://doi.org/10.3390/su16229855

Van Gorp, K., & Bogaert, N. (2006). *Developing language tasks for primary and secondary education. Task-based language education: From theory to practice* (pp. 76–105). Retrieved March 9, 2025, from https://www.academia.edu/download/94019926/Task_Based_Language_Education_From_Theory_to_Practice_Cambridge_Applied_Linguistics_PDFDrive_.pdf#page=87

Wacker, A., Manzocco, M., & Bahr, T. (2025). Arbeitserleichterung mit KI? Ein Tool zur Differenzierung und Übersetzung von Aufgaben. *Lehren & Lernen. Die unabhängige Zeitschrift für Schule und Innovation aus Baden-Württemberg*. KI—Intelligenz aus der Steckdose. 1/2025.

Chapter 8
Play to Pedagogies: Building AI Literacy and Teacher Competencies in Early Years Education

Karen Murcia, Sarsha Mennell, Kimberly Maslin, and Emma Cross

Abstract This chapter explores learning design and teacher competencies for the effective integration of artificial intelligence (AI) tools and devices in early childhood education (ECE) by drawing on insights from digital learning experiences conducted with children aged 4 and 5 years. We begin by examining the potential of AI in early childhood education, outlining curriculum aligned with competency frameworks and reviewing existing research on how AI-driven educational tools potentially shapes young children's emerging digital literacy. A synthesis of current AI literacy frameworks informs the development of a play-based inquiry learning program grounded in the *Five Big Ideas of AI*: Perception, Representation & Reasoning, Learning, Natural Interaction, and Societal Impact. Example learning experiences are provided to illustrate how children actively explore AI concepts through hands-on activities, such as storytelling with AI, interacting with voice assistants, and role-playing AI-driven problem-solving scenarios. These experiences highlight how AI systems process information, learn patterns, and interact with users, fostering both computational thinking and ethical awareness in young children. Using this foundation, we then identify the specific competencies early childhood educators require to critically engage with AI-powered devices, platforms, and interactive experiences designed for young learners. The chapter further articulates pedagogical principles for integrating AI into early years education, emphasizing a child-centered inquiry approach, balancing digital and non-digital interactions, and ethical considerations in AI use. The recommended AI-specific digital competencies, aligned with quality

K. Murcia (✉) · S. Mennell · K. Maslin · E. Cross
Australian Research Council Centre of Excellence for the Digital Child, Curtin University, Perth, WA, Australia
e-mail: Karen.murcia@curtin.edu.au

S. Mennell
e-mail: s.mennell@curtin.edu.au

K. Maslin
e-mail: kimberly.maslin@curtin.edu.au

E. Cross
e-mail: emma.cross1@curtin.edu.au

S. Papadakis (ed.), *AI Applications in Preschool and Primary Education*, Advances in Artificial Intelligence in Education 5, https://doi.org/10.1007/978-3-032-17190-0_8

pedagogical practices aim to strengthening early childhood educators' capacity to navigate AI's role in early learning. This chapter contributes to building a future-ready framework for AI literacy in early years education.

Keywords AI literacy · Early childhood education · Digital pedagogy · Teacher AI competencies

Introduction

As artificial intelligence (AI) increasingly shapes daily lives, there is a growing awareness of the need to equip young learners with foundational AI literacy. Early childhood education provides a crucial opportunity to introduce foundation AI concepts in developmentally appropriate ways. However, effective AI integration in early years education hinges on educators' ability to guide and scaffold children's learning experiences. This chapter explores the essential teacher competencies required to introduce AI and smart coding devices in early childhood programs, fostering critical computational thinking through inquiry-based learning. Despite the increasing emphasis on AI education, there is currently no dedicated competency framework for early childhood teachers. Existing AI competency models primarily focus on K-12 educators, with limited attention given to early years pedagogical strategies or the unique developmental needs of young learners. Given that AI literacy is not merely about technical proficiency but also involves ethical reasoning, critical thinking, and problem-solving, it is essential that early childhood educators receive targeted guidance. To bridge the gap, this chapter examines the core skills, knowledge, and attitudes teachers need to effectively integrate AI into early learning environments. This chapter argues that an AI competency framework for early childhood educators is critical, not only to enhance teacher confidence but also to ensure that young learners develop the foundational skills necessary to navigate an AI-driven world.

AI Literacy in Early Childhood Education

The growing integration of AI into education has led to increasing calls for AI literacy to be recognized as a fundamental competency for all learners (Ng et al., 2021), including young children (Su & Yang, 2024a; Su et al., 2023). AI literacy encompasses a set of knowledge, skills, values, and attitudes that enable individuals to critically evaluate AI technologies, engage effectively with AI systems, and understand their limitations and ethical implications (Long & Magerko, 2020). It is often positioned as an extension of data literacy or digital literacy (Sperling et al., 2024; Yang, 2022). In early childhood settings, AI education is reported to primarily occur through interactive digital tools and games, smart devices and toys including codable robots which introduce young learners to foundation AI concepts.

Recent studies highlight a range of effective strategies for teaching AI in ECE, including embodied instruction (Yang, 2022), hands-on activities (Druga et al., 2019; Williams, 2018; Williams et al., 2019), project-based learning (Yang et al., 2024), and also with a view to include culturally responsive approaches (Eguchi et al., 2021). These reported strategies already being used align with established early childhood pedagogies that emphasize inquiry, computational thinking, and collaborative exploration. AI education has been shown to foster computational thinking, and emotional inquiry in young learners (Kewalramani et al., 2021a, 2021b; Vartiainen et al., 2020) when experiences are intentionally designed. While research suggests that early exposure to AI can enhance children's understanding of knowledge-based systems, generative AI, and machine learning (Lin et al., 2020; Su & Yang, 2024a; Williams, 2018; Williams et al., 2019), it is insufficient for children to develop AI literacy through unstructured interaction alone. Instead, a structured, scaffolded approach, aligned with play-based and inquiry-driven pedagogies, is necessary for meaningful learning (Druga et al., 2019; Williams et al., 2019; Yang, 2022).

Curriculum and Pedagogical Considerations for AI in Early Childhood Education

As AI technologies become more prevalent in everyday life, children are increasingly incorporating digital tools into their play (Berson et al., 2023). Guided, interactive learning experiences, such as cooperative play and hands-on exploration, support children in developing foundational AI literacy (Su & Yang, 2024a). Educators play a crucial role in facilitating these experiences, ensuring that digital interactions are balanced with human engagement (Berson et al., 2023). To effectively integrate AI into early childhood education, teachers require a combination of technical, pedagogical, and critical thinking competencies. A foundational understanding of AI tools and platforms is essential for making informed decisions about how these technologies should be introduced in play-based inquiry learning environments.

A review of key curriculum documents governing the Australian early childhood sector underscores the importance of AI-related competencies for educators. The Australian Curriculum: Technologies embeds digital literacy as a general capability across learning areas, emphasizing the need for ethical and informed technology use, including privacy, security, and intellectual property (Australian Curriculum, Assessment & Reporting Authority (ACARA), 2024). It also highlights computational thinking and problem-solving as foundational skills. Additionally, the Early Years Learning Framework (EYLF) Outcome 5.5 explicitly acknowledges the role of digital technologies in young children's learning (Australian Government Department of Education (AGDE), 2022). The National Quality Framework (NQF) Quality Area 1 further reinforces the need for early childhood services to incorporate digital technologies in meaningful and developmentally appropriate ways (Australian Children's Education & Care Quality Authority (ACECQA), 2023).

AI education in early childhood should extend beyond technical skills to encompass broader cognitive and creative competencies. Studies have shown that integrating AI concepts and robotic toys into children's play nurtures creativity, emotional inquiry, and collaborative problem-solving skills (Kewalramani et al., 2021a). Building on Papert's and Harel (1991) theory of constructionism, children learn most effectively when they actively create tangible objects, whether physical or digital. By engaging in coding, robotics, and interactive AI experiences, young learners could develop critical communication, problem-solving, and collaboration skills. Introducing AI technologies through open-ended, play-based experiences could make abstract AI concepts more tangible, supporting young children's development of digital literacy.

The success of AI education experiences in early childhood depends on teachers' ability to design and facilitate developmentally appropriate learning experiences. Many early childhood educators report a lack confidence in teaching AI due to limited professional development opportunities and unclear guidelines on how to introduce AI concepts meaningfully (Eguchi et al., 2021; Su, 2024; Su et al., 2023). Addressing this challenge requires not only defining key AI-related competencies for teachers but also identifying strategies for building their AI literacy. They not only require technical knowledge of AI but also pedagogical strategies to integrate AI meaningfully into young children's learning experiences.

A Gap in Existing Teacher AI Competency Frameworks

Despite the increasing push for AI education in K-12 settings, research on AI-specific teacher competencies remains limited (Kim et al., 2021; Mikeladze et al., 2024; Ng et al., 2023; Sperling et al., 2024). Existing AI competency frameworks predominantly address elementary (Kim & Kwon, 2023) or secondary school teachers (Filo et al., 2024; Younis, 2025), or take a broad, K-12 perspective (Kim et al., 2021; Long & Magerko, 2020; Lorenz & Romeike, 2023; Ng et al., 2023; Olari & Romeike, 2021; Sattelmaier & Pawlowski, 2023; Schüller, 2022). These models pay little attention to early childhood educators, their specific pedagogical approaches, or the distinct skills required to introduce AI concepts to young learners.

In Australia, the Australian Framework for Generative AI in Schools (2023) provides broad guidance on the ethical and responsible use of AI in education. It is structured around six guiding principles—teaching and learning, human and social well-being, transparency, fairness, accountability, and privacy. While comprehensive, this framework does not directly address the professional learning needs of early childhood educators. Similarly, state-based AI guidelines for schools primarily focus on integrity and ethical concerns rather than specifying teacher competencies (BSSS, 2023; Queensland Curriculum & Assessment Authority, 2024). Institutions such as the Australian Institute for Teaching & School Leadership (AITSL) and the International Society for Technology in Education (ISTE) have yet to explicitly update their standards to incorporate AI-related teaching competencies, though aspects of AI education could be implicitly aligned with existing digital literacy frameworks. The DigCompEdu framework (European Commission, 2022) is one of the few international standards that has explicitly updated its competencies to include AI considerations.

Other AI competency models, such as the TPACK for K-12 AI Education framework (Kim et al., 2021) and the Teachers' AI Digital Competencies and 21st Century Skills framework (Ng et al., 2023), attempt to extend existing teacher competency guides to specify AI-related skills. However, these frameworks again remain general, lacking a focus on early childhood pedagogy. One exception is the AI Competencies for Elementary School Teachers (Kim & Kwon, 2023), which developed an AI competency framework prototype informed by teacher experiences. Of the 67 teachers involved, only seven taught early years (Grades 1 and 2), highlighting some consideration of early childhood perspectives but falling short of a dedicated focus on early childhood education.

The UNESCO AI Competency Framework for Teachers (2024) provides a structured approach to equipping educators with AI-related skills (see Introduction). It takes a holistic perspective, viewing AI as a tool that supports, rather than replaces, human decision-making. It focuses on building knowledge, skills, and values across several domains to ensure effective and ethical AI use in education. The framework outlines five key competency areas:

1. A Human-Centered Mindset: Reinforcing human agency, accountability, and social responsibility in AI use.
2. Ethics of AI: Promoting responsible AI engagement aligned with ethical principles.
3. AI Foundations and Applications: Developing knowledge and skills to use and create AI technologies.
4. AI Pedagogy: Integrating AI into teaching and learning.
5. AI for Professional Development: Leveraging AI for lifelong learning.

These competencies are further categorized into three progression levels: Acquire, Deepen, and Create, allowing teachers to advance their AI understanding over time. This structure acknowledges the complexity of AI literacy and accommodates teachers at different levels of familiarity with AI. However, while comprehensive, this framework is also not tailored to early childhood educators and does not address the unique pedagogical strategies required for teaching AI to young children.

In response to this identified gap, we explored the competencies that educators need to integrate artificial intelligence (AI) and smart coding devices in early childhood educational programs that support children aged 4 and 5 years in fostering critical and computational thinking in child-centered inquiry learning experiences.

The Children's Technology Cove

As part of a wider research program which explores early childhood educators' pedagogical practices with digital technologies, an innovative AI education program for young children was designed and trialed within a Western Australian University's living laboratory, the *Children's Technology Cove* (CTC). Importantly, operations of the CTC are funded by the Australian Research Council (ARC) Centre of Excellence for the Digital Child.

The CTC offers an innovative learning environment for educators and families aiming to foster young children's creativity and connectedness with digital technologies. The CTC allows for real-time, semi-naturalistic observation of early childhood specialist teachers guiding and supporting children's engagement with digital technologies. For research and teaching purposes, with university ethics approval and consent from participating children and their parents-caregivers, digital play experiences run in the CTC are captured with photographs, video, and audio recordings using camera infrastructure built into the CTC.

The design and infrastructure of the CTC enables researchers and early years education specialists to test digital devices and products for their age appropriateness and safety considerations for the participating children. Once identified, devices are embedded into intentionally designed play and learning experiences that are based on social constructivist learning theory. Through repeat trials and cycles of critical reflection by educators and researchers, pedagogical principles are identified for engaging young children with computational thinking and the foundational, big ideas in AI.

Designing AI Experiences for Young Children

The "5 Big Ideas of AI", as outlined by Su and Yang (2024b), aim to make AI concepts accessible and engaging for young children. These ideas include *Perception*, where AI systems use sensors to see, hear, or feel the world; *Representation & Reasoning*, explaining how AI understands information and makes decisions; *Learning*, where AI improves over time by recognizing patterns; *Natural Interaction*, focusing on how AI can communicate with humans using language or gestures; and *Societal Impact*, encouraging children to think about the positive and negative effects of AI on people and society. Together, these big ideas when curated into meaningful play and learning experiences, can foster young children's development of foundation understandings of AI in relatable ways.

Additionally, by aligning children's early AI experiences with early years education curriculum frameworks, educators can design developmentally appropriate learning experiences that support both digital literacy and foundational STEM competencies. For example, activities that explore AI's ability to sense the environment (Perception) can be linked to science and technology outcomes related to sensory awareness and data. Engaging children in conversations about how AI systems learn from data can also support early mathematical and critical thinking outcomes, while talking with children about fairness and responsibility in AI (Societal Impact) promote ethical reasoning and align with personal and social capability learning areas in early years curricula.

Hence, based on these big ideas in AI, curriculum aligned learning experiences with selected digital devices were designed within the CTC to engage young children in active learning that connected AI used to the world around them. For example, using robotic toys, voice assistants and AI story telling toys, children investigate how robots perceive the world through sensors, interact with humans using voice commands and solve problems through collaborative tasks. These experiences start with everyday tasks that children are confident in doing and discuss their reasoning, such as sorting objects, storytelling and asking questions. They then can extend their knowledge with a connection to basic AI concepts. Whether role playing with a robot to assist in daily tasks or using an AI application to create stories, children explore AI concepts in an open-ended way that encourages exploration and deepens their understanding of digital technologies and AI in their world.

The design of the experiences was based on the assumptions that children learn effectively when actively creating tangible objects, which can be physical or digital (Papert & Harel, 1991). Therefore, when children are engaging with each other, interacting, coding and using digital technologies and robot toys, they are developing important skills such as communication, critical thinking, collaboration and creativity (Murcia et al., 2024). Interactive experiences that are hands-on, create opportunities for children to experiment, reflect and learn from trial and error, which are fundamental aspects of problem solving and the creative process (Murcia et al., 2022). Introducing basic AI technologies in these open-ended experiences can assist in making abstract concepts more tangible, teaching children about digital technology and AI concepts in an engaging and developmentally appropriate way. The educator's involvement in facilitating the learning experiences is recognized as critical to ensuring the balance of human interaction with digital technology (Berson et al., 2023).

The following are examples of the AI experiences designed by the research team and then trialed within the CTC with participating children aged 4 and 5 years, who were accompanied either by their educators from an early learning center or parents.

Big Idea One: Perception

AI systems use sensors to receive and respond to the world around them.

Inquiry Focus:

How do AI systems use sensors to interact with their surroundings? How do they respond to different types of input?

Playful Investigation:

1. Discovering AI in Action

    - Children will experiment with Bluebot, observing how it reacts to touch, sound, and proximity.

- They will explore how different inputs trigger responses, such as flashing lights when it detects an obstacle or movement when a button is pressed.

2. Designing & Experimenting

- Children are encouraged to collaborate and navigate their Bluebots towards one another, noticing how the robots detect each other and respond.
- They will build a bridge from blocks and use coding commands to program the robots to move underneath, experiencing how sensors can influence movement.

3. Connecting to Everyday AI

- Children can explore familiar AI technologies that use sensors, such as voice assistants responding to spoken commands and face recognition on mobile devices.

Big Idea Two: Representation & Reasoning

AI systems process, analyse, and interpret data to recognize patterns and generate meaningful responses.

Inquiry Focus:

How do AI systems process information to recognize and recreate visual representations? How do algorithms help AI classify objects and identify patterns?

Playful Investigation:

1. Discovering AI in Action

- Children will engage in a role-play activity where one child acts as a 'robot' while their partner provides step-by-step instructions to guide them in drawing a simple image (e.g., a rocket).
- The instructor holds an undisclosed picture card and provides structured commands related to shape, color, size, and position.
- The "robot" follows the given instructions to replicate the drawing, helping children explore how AI processes data through algorithms.

2. Designing & Experimenting

- Children are encouraged to reflect on how the "robot" interpreted and executed the drawing task based on the given instructions.
- They will discuss how AI systems follow step-by-step processes to analyse and classify patterns in images.
- To extend their understanding, children will experiment with Google Quick Draw, observing how AI identifies patterns and categorizes their sketches using machine learning algorithms.

3. Connecting to Everyday AI

- Children will explore familiar AI technologies that process and classify visual data, such as AI-powered drawing and image recognition apps and smart assistants that recognize objects through a camera.
- Through guided discussions, they will consider how AI algorithms help systems "see" and interpret the world by recognizing patterns in shapes, lines, and spatial elements.

Big Idea Three: Learning

AI systems learn by recognizing patterns, processing large amounts of data, and adapting based on user interactions.

Inquiry Focus:

How does AI learn from patterns in stories? How do AI systems adapt their responses based on user interactions?

Playful Investigation:

1. Discovering AI in Action
    - Children will listen to a well-known story, identifying patterns in language, sequencing, and expression.
    - They will imitate the story by collaboratively creating movements and sounds to retell it together, reinforcing their understanding of structure and storytelling elements.
2. Designing & Experimenting
    - Children will innovate a new version of the story, changing characters, settings, or events while maintaining the structure.
    - Children will then engage with an AI storytelling toy, contributing ideas about characters, settings, and problems.
    - They will observe how the AI generates a new narrative, demonstrating how AI learns and adapts by recognizing patterns in language and sequencing.
3. Connecting to Everyday AI
    - Children will discuss real-world AI applications that generate and adapt stories, such as AI-powered chatbots and virtual assistants that respond to conversations and language-based AI tools that generate stories, poems, or songs.
    - They will explore how AI systems analyse large amounts of data, learn from interactions, and generate creative content in ways that mirror human creativity.

Big Idea Four: Natural Interaction

AI systems interact with humans in ways that seem natural, responding to voice, text, and other inputs while simulating conversation and communication.

Inquiry Focus:

How do AI systems communicate with humans? What are the limitations of AI interactions?

Playful Investigation:

1. Discovering AI in Action

    - Children will be introduced to a voice assistant smart speaker and observe how it responds to spoken commands and questions.
    - They will explore how AI simulates human communication by recognizing speech and providing responses.
    - Through guided interactions, children will ask the voice assistant questions such as, *"What is the weather today?" "Can you tell me a joke?"*
    - They will discuss and reflect on the AI's responses, recognizing how it follows programmed rules rather than understanding meaning.

2. Designing & Experimenting

    - Children will draw a picture in response to the question: *"What does Siri look like?"*
    - Through this activity, they will realize that Siri is not a physical entity, reinforcing the idea that AI can simulate interaction without having a body or emotions.
    - They will test different commands and questions to observe when the AI provides appropriate responses and when it does not.
    - Educators will guide discussions about AI's limitations, such as it can respond but does not actually understand and it lacks emotions.

3. Connecting to Everyday AI

    - Children will explore real-world AI interactions beyond voice assistants, such as AI-powered language translation tools and automated responses in smart devices (e.g., touch screen assistants).
    - They will discuss how AI mimics conversation and why it might feel like talking to a friend, even though it does not experience emotions or personal relationships.

Big Idea Five: Societal Impact

AI systems influence and shape the way we live, work, and interact with the world, assisting humans in problem-solving, decision-making, and daily tasks.

Inquiry Focus:

How do AI systems assist humans in everyday life? How do humans and AI collaborate to solve problems?

Playful Investigation:

1. Discovering AI in Action

- Children will explore real-world AI systems that assist humans, such as navigation apps (e.g., Google Maps giving step-by-step directions) and robot vacuum cleaners (e.g., sensing and moving around obstacles).
- They are encouraged to share ideas about how AI could be designed to assist humans with instructions and solving problems.

2. Designing & Experimenting

    - Children will engage in a role-playing activity where one child acts as the AI robot helper, providing step-by-step instructions to their partner to complete a task such as building a block tower using precise instructions (e.g., "Pick a red square block, place it on top of the yellow triangle block").
    - Children will collaborate, taking turns playing the role of the AI, experiencing how clear communication and structured instructions help complete tasks efficiently.

3. Connecting to Everyday AI

    - Children will reflect on their experiences and discuss how AI could help people complete tasks in daily life.
    - Educators will introduce real-world AI applications, such as self-driving cars, robotic assistants in hospitals, and AI-powered smart homes, highlighting AI's growing role in society.

Taking a similar play-based inquiry approach, early childhood teachers could tailor experiences to the interests of the children in their classroom and the learning context. It is recommended that teachers use the following 5 steps in designing AI experiences for young children:

1. *Choose a big idea* to focus on and review the concept in child-friendly terms.
2. *Identify curriculum links*, looking for cross curricula learning opportunities such as exploring technology, problem solving and algorithmic thinking.
3. *Design the activity*, deciding on an inquiry focus which can be explored by children through play and uses developmentally appropriate pedagogies such as storytelling, imaginative play and open questioning.
4. *Facilitate and observe* the experience with a focus on encouraging children's curiosity, questioning, and sharing of thinking.
5. *Reflect and extend* by capturing children's exploration, ideas and questions to inform follow-up activities based on their interests. Extend the experience to a child-centered learning journey.

AI Competency Framework for Early Childhood Specialist Teachers

The Five Big Ideas in AI (Su & Yang, 2024b) provided a strong foundation for the early childhood education program, as each concept was introduced through play-based, exploratory learning. The experiences outlined in this chapter are developmentally appropriate, fostering curiosity and foundational computational thinking skills. However, the successful implementation of these experiences requires specific competencies from early childhood educators to ensure ethical, meaningful, and responsible AI engagement.

When examined through the UNESCO AI Teacher Competency Framework, it becomes clear that a Human-Centered Mindset is essential for these learning experiences. The activities encourage children to interact with AI systems critically, such as understanding Siri's limitations in Natural Interaction and recognizing AI's role in society in Societal Impact. However, teachers must reinforce the understanding that AI is a tool rather than a replacement for human relationships. Guiding children to distinguish between real friendships and AI-driven interactions is crucial in fostering healthy perspectives on technology use. Ethical concerns may also arise in the use of AI storytelling apps and voice assistants, as young children may unconsciously trust AI-generated responses without questioning their accuracy or bias. Teachers can navigate these discussions, ensuring that children engage with AI in a way that promotes critical thinking and digital literacy.

To guide young children's engagement with big AI ideas, educators require a strong foundation in AI concepts and applications themselves. They require an understanding of AI concepts such as sensors, algorithms, and pattern recognition. Without this knowledge, educators may struggle to scaffold discussions beyond surface-level engagement, limiting children's ability to grasp AI's deeper functionalities. Effective AI Pedagogy is an essential consideration, as integrating AI into teaching and learning requires thoughtful and developmentally appropriate strategies. The experiences outlined adopted child-led, play-based, and inquiry-driven learning approaches, aligning with best practices in early childhood education. However, educators must also be prepared to differentiate AI learning for children with diverse needs.

Importantly, for ethical and responsible use of AI in early childhood education contexts, educators require clear and practical guidelines on the responsible use of AI technologies with and by young children. This includes understanding how to protect children's personal information, ensuring they provide informed consent and tools are avoided that collect unnecessary or intrusive information. By including discussions of digital ethics and child safety into professional learning, educators should be supported to critically assess AI tools before integrating them into their practice. Prioritizing a culture of transparency and accountability would help ensure AI is used in ways that fosters learning without compromising the human nature of learning relationships and children's rights and data privacy.

An AI competency framework for early childhood specialist teachers should address the unique developmental needs of young learners while ensuring that educators are equipped to facilitate meaningful, ethical, and inquiry-based AI learning experiences. Based on a review of the literature, existing competency frameworks and the AI learning experiences trialed in the CTC, the following elaborated key competencies are recommended for early childhood specialist educators (Table 8.1).

While the Five Big Ideas in AI provide an excellent framework for introducing AI concepts in early childhood education, their success depends on the competencies of teachers. Educators must possess a human-centered mindset, ethical awareness, foundational AI knowledge, effective pedagogical strategies, and access to professional development to facilitate meaningful AI learning experiences. Strengthening these competencies will ensure young children engage with AI in ways that are ethical, critical, and developmentally appropriate. By embedding AI competencies into early childhood teacher training, educators will be empowered to shape AI-literate, ethically aware, and critically engaged learners from an early age. As AI becomes increasingly embedded in everyday life, ensuring that early childhood educators are prepared to teach AI literacy is essential. Future research should focus on developing and testing AI competency frameworks, as well as identifying effective strategies for teacher training.

Implications for Practice and Ethics

In an increasingly AI shaped world, there are implications for early childhood educators' practice as education plays a critical role in building the foundations of essential digital literacy. The 5 Big Ideas in AI, Perception, Representation & Reasoning, Learning, Natural Interaction, and Societal Impact, offer a powerful framework for educators helping young children explore how intelligent technologies work, how they learn and how they influence our lives. Embedding these ideas into playful, inquiry-driven activities not only fosters critical thinking and creativity but also aligns with early learning outcomes across STEM. To achieve quality learning with and about AI, educators require support to develop the competencies needed to select, use and critically evaluate AI tools. Ethical and responsible use of AI tools would ensure they are used in ways that respect the developmental needs of young children and maintain safe and inclusive learning environments. This involves building ethical awareness understanding data privacy, and designing experiences where children are not passive users but active creators in a digital world. By embracing AI literacy as an essential aspect of early education, we empower children to navigate their futures with curiosity, critical thinking and digital confidence. As this chapter has shown, early childhood settings are not too early, but rather the important beginning to vital professional dialogue and quality pedagogical practices.

Table 8.1 AI competencies for early childhood educators

Domain	Key competencies
1. Human Centered AI Awareness	(a) Ability to discuss AI's presence in children's daily life in a developmentally appropriate way (b) Capacity to facilitate discussions on AI's limitations, such as voice assistants lack of emotions or self-awareness (c) Skills to support children in distinguishing between real and AI-generated interactions, fostering digital literacy
2. Ethical and Responsible AI Engagement	(a) Understanding ethical concerns in AI, including bias, privacy, and misinformation (b) Ability to guide children in questioning AI-generated responses rather than accepting them uncritically (c) Skills to create e-safe AI learning environments, ensuring AI tools are used responsibly with and by children
3. AI Literacy and Applications	(a) Understanding basic AI concepts such as pattern recognition, sequencing, and machine learning in ways that can be made accessible to young children (b) Ability to use AI-powered educational tools effectively and explain their functioning in simple terms (c) Knowledge of AI's applications in daily life, such as voice assistants and recommendation systems, to facilitate relevant discussions with children
4. AI Pedagogy and Play-Based Learning Integration	(a) Ability to design and implement AI learning experiences that align with play-based inquiry pedagogy (b) Capacity to differentiate AI instruction for diverse learners and critically assess AI for cultural appropriateness (c) Skills to foster curiosity, problem-solving, and computational thinking through AI-related activities
5. AI Professional Growth and Life-long Learning	(a) Commitment to continuous learning and adaptation of AI knowledge (b) Ability to engage with AI-specific professional development opportunities (c) Capacity to collaborate with peers, researchers, and AI experts to enhance AI teaching strategies

References

Australian Children's Education & Care Quality Authority. (2023). *Quality Area 1—Educational program and practice*. https://www.acecqa.gov.au/nqf/national-quality-standard/quality-area-1-educational-program-and-practice

Australian Curriculum, Assessment & Reporting Authority. (2024). *Digital literacy*. https://v9.australiancurriculum.edu.au/f-10-curriculum/general-capabilities/digital-literacy?element=0&sub-element=DLDSWA

Australian Government Department of Education. (2022). *Early years learning framework*. https://www.education.gov.au/early-childhood/about/national-quality-framework/approved-learning-frameworks

Berson, I. R., Berson, M. J., Luo, W., & He, h. (2023). Intelligence augmentation in early childhood education: A multimodal creative inquiry approach. International Conference on Artificial Intelligence in Education. In *International conference on artificial intelligence in education* (pp. 756–763). Springer. https://link.springer.com/chapter/ https://doi.org/10.1007/978-3-031-36336-8_116

BSSS. (2023). *Teacher guide: AI and academic integrity*. https://www.bsss.act.edu.au/__data/assets/pdf_file/0006/571722/BSSS_Teacher_Guide_AI_and_Academic_Integrity.pdf

Druga, S., Vu, S. T., Likhith, E., & Qiu, T. (2019). Inclusive AI literacy for kids around the world. In *Proceedings of FabLearn 2019* (pp. 104–111). https://dl.acm.org/ https://doi.org/10.1145/3311890.3311904

Eguchi, A., Okada, H., & Muto, Y. (2021). Contextualizing AI education for K-12 students to enhance their learning of AI literacy through culturally responsive approaches. *KI-Künstliche Intelligenz, 35*(2), (pp. 153–161). https://link.springer.com/content/pdf/ https://doi.org/10.1007/s13218-021-00737-3.pdf

European Commission. (2022). *Digital competence framework for educators (DigCompEdu)*. https://joint-research-centre.ec.europa.eu/digcompedu_en

Filo, Y., Rabin, E., & Mor, Y. (2024). An artificial intelligence competency framework for teachers and students: Co-created with teachers. *European Journal of Open, Distance & E-Learning, 26*(1). https://doi.org/10.2478/eurodl-2024-0012

Kewalramani, S., Palaiologou, I., Dardanou, M., Allen, K. A., & Phillipson, S. (2021a). Using robotic toys in early childhood education to support children's social and emotional competencies. *Australasian Journal of Early Childhood, 46*(4), 355–369. https://search.informit.org/doi/10.3316%2Finformit.186678071472224

Kewalramani, S., Kidman, G., & Palaiologou, I. (2021b). Using artificial intelligence (AI)-interfaced robotic toys in early childhood settings: A case for children's inquiry literacy. *European Early Childhood Education Research Journal, 29*(5), (pp. 652–668). https://www.tandfonline.com/ https://doi.org/10.1080/1350293X.2021.1968458

Kim, S., Jang, Y., Choi, S., Kim, W., Jung, H., Kim, S., & Kim, H. (2021). Analyzing teacher competency with TPACK for K-12 AI education. *KI-Kunstliche Intelligenz, 35*(2), 139–151. https://doi.org/10.1007/s13218-021-00731-9

Kim, K., & Kwon, K. (2023). Exploring the AI competencies of elementary school teachers in South Korea. *Computers and Education: Artificial Intelligence*, (v.4). https://www.sciencedirect.com/science/article/pii/S2666920X23000164

Lin, P., Van Brummelen, J., Lukin, G., Williams, R., & Breazeal, C. (2020). Zhorai: Designing a conversational agent for children to explore machine learning concepts. In *Proceedings of the AAAI Conference on Artificial Intelligence, 34*(9), (pp. 13381–13388). https://ojs.aaai.org/index.php/AAAI/article/view/7061

Long, D., & Magerko, B. (2020). What is AI literacy? Competencies and design considerations. *Proceedings of the 2020 CHI conference on human factors in computer systems*. Article 3376727 (pp. 1–16). https://dl.acm.org/ https://doi.org/10.1145/3313831.3376727

Lorenz, U., & Romeike, R. (2023). What is AI-PACK? Outline of AI competencies for teaching with DPACK. *International Conference on Informatics in Schools: Situation, Evolution, and Perspectives*. https://ebookcentral.proquest.com/lib/curtin/reader.action?pq-origsite=primo&c=UERG&ppg=29&docID=30882881

Mikeladze, T., Meijer, P. C., & Verhoeff, R. P. (2024). A comprehensive exploration of artificial intelligence competence frameworks for educators: a critical review. *European Journal of Education, 59*(3). https://doi.org/10.1111/ejed.12663

Murcia, K., Campbell, C., Joubert, M. M., & Wilson, S. (2022). *Children's creative inquiry in STEM*. Springer. https://doi.org/10.1080/03004279.2023.2287532

Murcia, K., Cross, E., & Lowe, G. (2024). Young children's computational thinking: Educator pedagogy fostering children's play and learning with a tangible coding device. *The Australian Educational Researcher, 52*(2), 1261–1279. https://doi.org/10.1007/s13384-024-00762-9

Ng, D. T. K., Leung, J. K. L., Chu, K. W. S., & Qiao, M. S. (2021). AI literacy: Definition, teaching, evaluation and ethical issues. *Proceedings of the Association for Information Science and Technology, 58*(1), 504–509. https://doi.org/10.1002/pra2.487

Ng, D. T. K., Leung, J. K. L., Su, J., Ng, R. C. W., & Chu, S. K. W. (2023). Teachers' AI digital competencies and twenty-first century skills in the post-pandemic world. *Educational Technology Research and Development, 71*(1), 137–161. https://doi.org/10.1007/s11423-023-10203-6

Olari, V., & Romeike, R. (2021). Addressing AI and data literacy in teacher education: A review of existing educational frameworks. In *Proceedings of the 16th workshop in primary and secondary computing education* (pp. 1–2). https://doi.org/10.1145/3481312.3481351

Papert, S., & Harel, I. (1991). Situating constructionism. *Constructionism, 36*(2), 1–11. http://www.papert.org/articles/SituatingConstructionism.html

Queensland Curriculum & Assessment Authority. (2024). *Developing artificial intelligence capabilities: Guidance for schools*. https://www.qcaa.qld.edu.au/downloads/p_10/factsheet_ai_guidance_schools.pdf

Sattelmaier, L., & Pawlowski, J. M. (2023). Towards a generative artificial intelligence competence framework for schools. In *Proceedings of the International Conference on Enterprise and Industrial Systems*. https://doi.org/10.2991/978-94-6463-340-5_26

Schüller, K. (2022). Data and AI literacy for everyone. *Statistical Journal of the IAOS, 38*(2), 477–490. https://doi.org/10.1016/j.caeo.2024.100169

Sperling, K., Stenberg, C.-J., McGrath, C., Åkerfeldt, A., Heintz, F., & Stenliden, L. (2024). In search of artificial intelligence (AI) literacy in teacher education: A scoping review, 6. *Computers and Education*. https://doi.org/10.1016/j.caeo.2024.100169

Su, J. (2024). Kindergarten teachers' perceptions of AI literacy education for young children. *International Journal of Technology and Design, 34*, 1–21. https://doi.org/10.1007/s10798-024-09876-8

Su, J., Ng, D. T. K., & Chu, S. K. W. (2023). Artificial Intelligence (AI) literacy in early childhood education: The challenges and opportunities. *Computers and Education: Artificial Intelligence*. https://doi.org/10.1016/j.caeai.2023.100124

Su, J., & Yang, W. (2024a). Artificial Intelligence (AI) literacy in early childhood education: An intervention study in Hong Kong. *Interactive Learning Environments, 32*(9), 5494–5508. https://doi.org/10.1080/10494820.2023.2217864

Su, J., & Yang, W. (2024b). Artificial Intelligence and robotics for young children: Redeveloping the five big ideas framework. *ECNU Review of Education, 7*(3), 685–698. https://doi.org/10.1177/20965311231218013

UNESCO. (2024). *AI competency framework for teachers*. https://www.unesco.org/en/articles/ai-competency-framework-teachers

Vartiainen, H., Tedre, M., & Valtonen, T. (2020). Learning machine learning with very young children: Who is teaching whom?. *International Journal of Child-Computer Interaction*. https://doi.org/10.1016/j.ijcci.2020.100182

Williams, R. (2018). *PopBots: Leveraging social robots to aid preschool children's artificial intelligence education*. Doctoral dissertation, Massachusetts Institute of Technology. https://dspace.mit.edu/handle/1721.1/122894

Williams, R., Park, H. W., & Breazeal, C. (2019). A is for artificial intelligence: The impact of artificial intelligence activities on young children's perceptions of robots. In*Proceedings of the 2019 CHI conference on human factors in computing systems*. https://doi.org/10.1145/3290605.3300677

Yang, W. (2022). Artificial Intelligence education for young children: Why, what, and how in curriculum design and implementation. *Computers and Education: Artificial Intelligence*. https://doi.org/10.1016/j.caeai.2022.100061

Yang, W., Hu, X., Yeter, I. H., Su, J., Yang, Y., & Lee, J. C. K. (2024). Artificial Intelligence education for young children: A case study of technology-enhanced embodied learning. *Journal of Computer Assisted Learning, 40*(2), 465–477. https://doi.org/10.1111/jcal.12892

Younis, B. (2025). The artificial intelligence literacy (AIL) scale for teachers: A tool for enhancing AI education. *Journal of Digital Learning in Teacher Education, 41*(1), 37–56. https://doi.org/10.1080/21532974.2024.2441682

Part III
Pedagogical Resources, Tools and Prompting

Chapter 9
AI-Integrated Platforms for Generating Educational Digital Narratives

Nerea López-Bouzas, M. Esther del-Moral-Pérez, and Jonathan Castañeda-Fernández

Abstract Immersive digital narratives represent a valuable resource in the educational field. Therefore, teachers require guidelines for their creation, supported by emerging technologies such as Artificial Intelligence (AI). This chapter presents various AI-integrated platforms (free, accessible online, and compatible with various operating systems) that can contribute to the design of digital narratives for educational purposes. Specifically, they are grouped into five categories based on their purpose: (1) Character creation: images, portraits, and visual art; 3D animation; conversational characters and simulations; (2) Creation of settings and fictional elements: images and environments based on digital art; 3D environment simulation; and landscapes; (3) Incorporation and modification of voices: text-to-speech conversion, voice generation and customisation; and voice modification and transformation; (4) Video production: creation of videos and animated presentations; video editing; and text-to-video generation; and (5) Creation of interactive stories: visual and multimedia content; choice-based simulations; and tools for planning, writing, and developing narratives. Additionally, various didactic applications of the products created with these platforms are described, highlighting the opportunities they offer teachers to integrate them into the school context by designing playful environments that foster student engagement. Furthermore, the ethical responsibilities and appropriate use of these tools are underscored, ensuring privacy protection, preventing identity fraud, respecting copyright, and properly acknowledging the tools used to avoid improper appropriation.

Keywords Artificial Intelligence · Digital storytelling · Digital platforms · Educational context

N. López-Bouzas (✉) · M. E. del-Moral-Pérez · J. Castañeda-Fernández
Department of Educational Sciences, University of Oviedo, Oviedo, Spain
e-mail: lopeznerea@uniovi.es

M. E. del-Moral-Pérez
e-mail: emoral@uniovi.es

J. Castañeda-Fernández
e-mail: castanedajonathan@uniovi.es

S. Papadakis (ed.), *AI Applications in Preschool and Primary Education*, Advances in Artificial Intelligence in Education 5, https://doi.org/10.1007/978-3-032-17190-0_9

Introduction

This chapter provides teachers with Artificial Intelligence (AI) tools for designing digital narratives with an educational purpose. The creation of content aimed at fostering students' reflection and the development of critical thinking can begin by following both technical and ethical guidelines that respect the rights of others, acknowledge original authorship and sources, comply with copyright regulations, and cite the applications used, among other considerations.

Undoubtedly, immersive digital narratives hold great educational potential by transforming teaching–learning processes into playful and engaging scenarios. Therefore, teachers should receive training on how to design them, taking advantage of AI's potential. These resources enhance student engagement with learning tasks by immersing them in settings where they interact directly with content while becoming protagonists of these stories (Mariani & Ciancia, 2023). The integration of AI in the design of such narratives further amplifies their educational impact by enabling the personalisation of learning experiences (Fan et al., 2024).

Specifically, the personalisation of interactive narratives plays a crucial role in adapting content to the specific educational context, students' interests, the classroom topics, and the learners' age group. This alignment with users' interests fosters a deeper connection with the content (Papadimitriou & Virvou, 2025). Furthermore, the design of AI-enhanced immersive digital narratives facilitates the creation of more inclusive, flexible, and motivating learning environments. For this reason, it is essential to establish clear design guidelines and compile a selection of platforms that support teachers and educators in the development of such narratives (Fig. 9.1).

In this regard, Antony and Huang (2024) highlight the importance of selecting appropriate digital resources to ensure effective and inclusive learning experiences. As noted by Madaan et al. (2024), numerous platforms are currently available for storytelling design, integrating AI tools to create interactive experiences without requiring expertise in programming or digital design. These platforms typically offer user-friendly interfaces, pre-designed templates, and customisation options, enabling teachers to tailor their narratives to the specific needs of their students.

According to Liang et al. (2024), it is crucial to align the design of characters, settings, voices, and other elements within these stories with the intended educational objectives. To ensure narrative effectiveness, each element must support the user's emotional and cognitive connection. For instance, characters should be designed with distinct visual, psychological, and emotional traits that allow students to identify with and empathise with the protagonists, thereby fostering a deeper and more meaningful experience (Tang & Chen, 2024). Likewise, voices should be carefully selected to convey authentic emotions, bringing the stories to life and providing a fully multisensory experience (Dai et al., 2024).

Furthermore, as noted by Fan et al. (2024), the development of immersive settings is essential for enhancing narrative engagement. This requires a deliberate selection of visual and auditory elements that situate users in specific contexts, whether realistic or fantastical, creating an atmosphere that promotes emotional involvement. Given

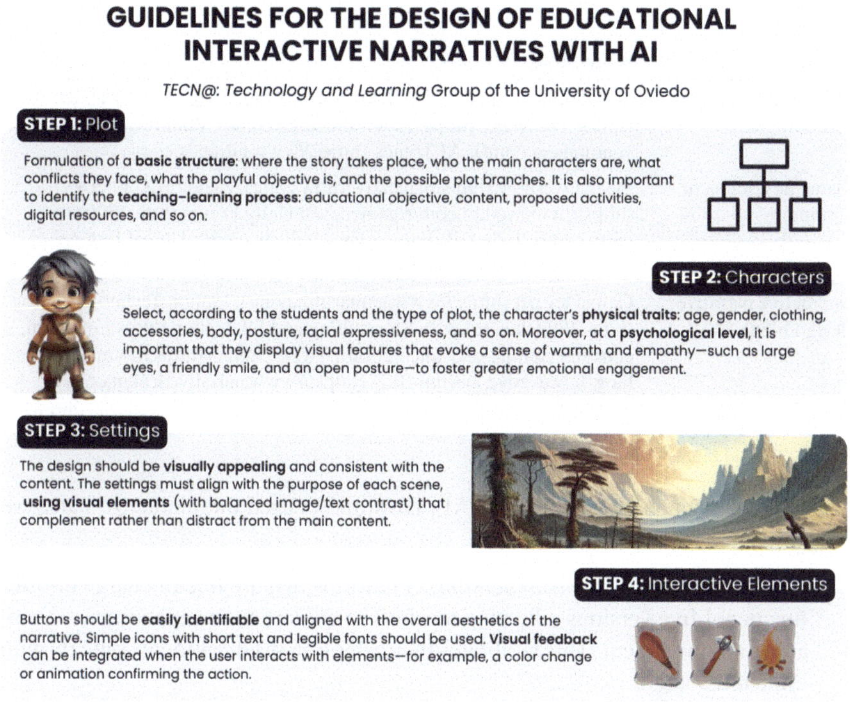

Fig. 9.1 Guidelines for designing educational interactive narratives using AI tools. *Source* Created by the authors

these considerations, the present study provides an in-depth analysis of various AI platforms for designing immersive digital narratives, focusing on their application within the educational context.

Methodology

While AI-integrated platforms have proliferated in recent years, this qualitative study is based on content analysis (Shava et al., 2021) of 100 AI-driven platforms focused on the design of interactive digital narratives to identify their intended purpose.

Procedure

AI platforms were identified through various specialised search engines (Table 9.1).

Table 9.1 Search sources

Source	Search Engine (Link)
Websites on emerging technologies	TechCrunch (https://techcrunch.com/); Wired (https://www.wired.com/); The Verge (https://www.theverge.com/); VentureBeat (https://venturebeat.com/); AI Trends (https://www.aitrends.com/)
Game development forums	Stack Overflow (https://stackoverflow.com/); Reddit (r/GameDev) (https://www.reddit.com/r/gamedev/); Unity Forum (https://forum.unity.com/); IndieDB (https://www.indiedb.com/); Unreal Engine Forum (https://forums.unrealengine.com/)
Interactive narrative design blogs	GameDev.net (https://www.gamasutra.com/); Fiction Technology Blog (https://iftech.carrd.co/); Storytelling and Interaction (https://medium.com/storytelling-and-interaction); Twine Stories (https://twinery.org/blog/); Narrative Design Blog (https://www.narrativedesign.com/)
Academic platforms	Google Scholar; ResearchGate; Academia.edu; IEEE Xplore; JSTOR

The criteria adopted for selecting AI platforms focused on interactive narrative design were as follows:

(1) *Free or with accessible trial versions:* Platforms that are free of charge or offer functional free versions, allowing teachers to explore their capabilities without an initial investment. This facilitates their adoption in educational contexts with limited resources.
(2) *Ease of use and intuitive interface*: The tools needed to offer simple interfaces, with templates and drag-and-drop features, enabling teachers to use them without advanced technical knowledge.
(3) *Compatibility and flexibility*: The platforms needed to be accessible via web browsers or apps on iOS/Android, allowing their use across different devices and operating systems. This supports implementation in diverse educational environments.

Five categories were established to classify the platforms based on their purpose: character creation, fictional settings and elements, video production, voice incorporation and modification, and interactive storytelling. Ultimately, the sample was composed of 100 platforms, with 20 assigned to each category (see "Appendix"). After reviewing the selected platforms, they were analysed to determine their primary functionality and subsequently regrouped into various subcategories (Fig. 9.2).

Sample

Table 9.2 identifies the platforms that integrate AI for narrative design, grouped based on categories and subcategories.

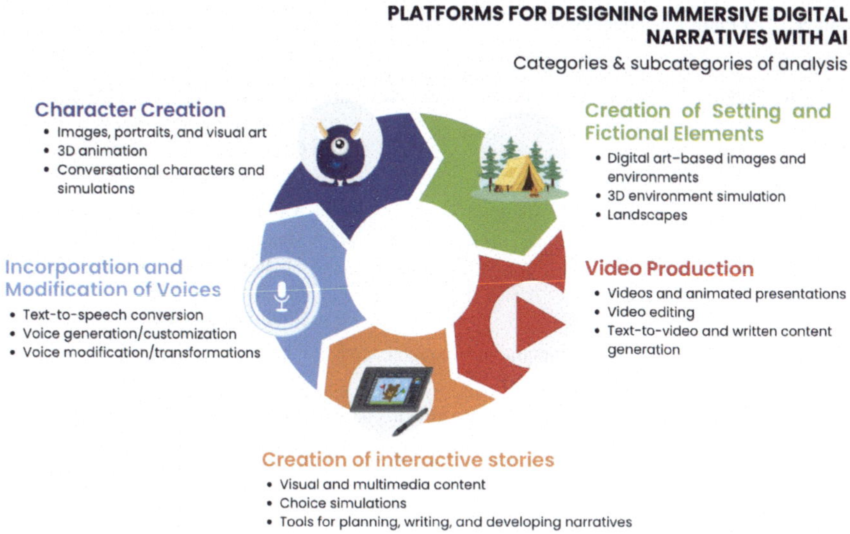

Fig. 9.2 Pre-established analysis categories. *Source* Created by the authors

Results

Platforms Integrating AI for Character Creation

Generation of Images, Portraits, and Visual Art

These platforms are designed for the creation of 2D images, whether of characters or visual art. They utilise AI to generate portraits, human faces, or stylised art from textual inputs or pre-existing images. Specifically, *Artbreeder, DALL·E* (Fig. 9.3), and *Deep Dream Generator* allow users to create new images by combining existing ones or using textual descriptions. Artbreeder primarily focuses on the fusion and modification of existing images, allowing users to blend features from different portraits to generate unique characters. It offers a collaborative approach where users can reuse and modify creations made by others. *Deep Dream Generator* specialises in creating psychedelic or abstract visual art, transforming images to produce unique works of art with an idyllic aesthetic. Meanwhile, *Generated Photos* and *This Person Does Not Exist* enable the creation of realistic human faces, which is useful for projects requiring realistic photos without image rights. Generated Photos provides greater control to users over the characteristics of the faces, such as age, gender, and expression, while *This Person Does Not Exist generates* portraits randomly. Additionally, *Toonify* transforms human faces into stylised versions resembling cartoons.

Table 9.2 AI Platforms under study

Category	Subcategory	Platforms
Character Creation	Images, portraits, and visual art	Artbreeder, DALL·E, Deep Dream Generator, Fotor, Generated Photos, This Person Does Not Exist, and Toonify
	3D Animation	Anima, Headshot (Reallusion), MakeHuman, MetaHuman Creator, Mixamo, Ready Player Me, Sims 4 Create-a-Sim, Vroid Studio, and ZEPETO
	Conversational characters and simulations	Character.ai, Replika, Promethean AI, and Runway ML
Creation of scenes and fictional elements	Images and environments based on digital art	Artbreeder, DALL·E, Deep Dream Generator, Fotor, MidJourney, and Runway ML
	3D environment simulation	Blender, CityEngine, Google Earth Studio, Houdini, Terragen, Unreal Engine, Vue, and Terrain.party
	Landscapes	FlowScape, Gaea, Lumion, Promethean AI, and World Creator
Incorporation and modification of voices	Text-to-speech conversion	Amazon Polly, Balabolka, Google Text-to-Speech, iSpeech, Microsoft Azure Speech, Murf AI, NaturalReader, Play.ht, SpeechGen.io, and Speechify
	Voice generation and customization	CereVoice, Descript, Lyrebird AI, Replica Studios, Synthesia, and Voicogen
	Voice modification and transformation	Altered Studio, Voice Changer, Voicemod, and Vocaloid
Video production	Animated videos and presentations creation	Animaker, Biteable, Doodly, Powtoon, Renderforest, Vyond, and Wideo
	Video editing	Descript, Filmora, Kapwing, Magisto, Runway ML, Veed.io, and Wave.video
	Video generation from text and written content	DeepBrain, FlexClip, InVideo, Lumen5, Pictory, and Synthesia
Creation of interactive stories	Visual and multimedia content	Agartha, Fungus, Genially, Ren'py, Visual Novel Maker, and StorymapJS

(continued)

Table 9.2 (continued)

Category	Subcategory	Platforms
	Choice simulations	Alter Ego, ChoiceScript, Talespire, Zombies, Run!, and Hypertextopia
	Planning, writing, and narrative development tools	Campfire, ChatMapper, Inklewriter, Narrative Designer, Twine, Write and Transformer, TiddlyWiki, Choose Your Own Adventure, and Ink

Fig. 9.3 Examples of AI-generated characters. *Source* Created with DALL·E. *Source* Created by the authors

Generation and Animation of 3D Characters

These platforms focus on the creation and manipulation of 3D characters, allowing users to adjust physical features, postures, and, in some cases, create animations. *Anima, Mixamo*, and *Vroid Studio* offer automatic animation options, making the process easier for users without experience in manual animation. They also allow users to export characters for integration into digital environments such as video games, simulations, or virtual worlds, in various 3D formats (obj., stl., gltf., etc.). *Anima* and *Mixamo* specialise in character animation. *Anima* creates characters for architectural environments or large scenes, while *Mixamo* animates pre-created characters and includes a library of pre-set movements and animations. *MetaHuman Creator* and *MakeHuman* design hyper-realistic characters, focusing on details such as skin textures, hair, facial expressions, and gestures. *Ready Player Me* and *ZEPETO* allow users to create more cartoonish, stylised, and customisable 3D avatars. On the other hand, *Vroid Studio* focuses on the creation of anime-style characters, distinguishing it from other applications that aim for more realism.

Creation of Conversational Characters and Simulations

Platforms in this category focus on the creation of interactive characters that can simulate conversations or respond to user interactions. They utilise conversational AI to generate coherent responses and simulate dialogues in real-time. *Character.ai* and *Replika* simulate human interactions using natural language, whether for entertainment, education, or emotional support. *Character.ai* is more flexible, allowing the creation of characters with diverse personalities, while *Replika* is more focused on relationships and deeper, emotional dialogues, simulating a "virtual friend". *Promethean AI* and *Runway ML* allow the creation of characters within interactive environments. *Promethean AI* generates autonomous characters within 3D environments, while *Runway ML* generates images and edits videos.

Platforms Integrating AI for Creating Environments and Fictional Elements

Generation of Images and Environments Based on Digital Art

These platforms utilise AI to generate images and environments, typically from textual descriptions or pre-existing images. *DALL·E, MidJourney, Artbreeder,* and *Deep Dream Generator* create surreal, fantastical, or abstract environments. These tools do not require advanced design skills. *Artbreeder* blends pre-existing images, allowing users to combine landscapes, portraits, and objects to create new environments or characters. *DALL·E* and *MidJourney* (Fig. 9.4) stand out for their detail and complexity. While *DALL·E* is more flexible and realistic, *MidJourney* tends to generate images with a more artistic and surreal style. *Deep Dream Generator* specialises in abstract visual art, with a more psychedelic approach, using neural networks to modify existing images. On the other hand, *Fotor* and *Runway ML* are oriented towards image editing, with the option to generate backgrounds or environments, but with additional tools for retouching or modifying the generated images.

Creation and Simulation of Realistic 3D Environments

These applications allow the creation of 3D environments with a high level of detail and precision. *Blender, Unreal Engine, Houdini, Terragen,* and *Vue* offer the ability to model, texture, and animate 3D terrains and environments. Specifically, *Houdini* specialises in complex simulations, such as particle effects, liquids, etc. *Terragen* and *Vue* focus on the creation of natural landscapes. *CityEngine, Google Earth Studio,* and *Terrain.party* enable the design of environments based on real data, such as

Fig. 9.4 Examples of AI-generated characters. *Source* Created with MidJourney. *Source* Created by the authors

topographic maps or satellite images, for projects related to urban visualization or simulations in geographical settings. *Unreal Engine* is one of the most advanced graphic engines for the creation of open worlds and hyper-realistic environments, though it requires specialised training in 3D modelling and animation.

Specialized Landscape and Terrain Generators

These platforms are designed for the creation of detailed landscapes, offering complete control over geography and terrain, allowing users to generate natural environments such as mountains, rivers, forests, etc. All platforms have customisation options for flora, fauna, and geographical elements. *FlowScape* and *Lumion* are the easiest to use, with intuitive interfaces that allow for the quick creation of detailed natural landscapes. *FlowScape* is particularly suitable for creating scenes with flora and fauna, while *Lumion* focuses on architectural visualisation, allowing for real-time rendering of architectural structures. *Gaea* and *World Creator* design hyper-realistic environments, adjusting erosion, geological formations, and other natural elements. *World Creator* specialises in custom terrains, while *Terragen* adopts a more cinematic aesthetic, enabling the creation of either fantastic or realistic landscapes with dynamic skies. *Promethean AI* differentiates itself with its focus on creating complete environments for video games or visual narratives, inserting objects and elements within the environment to facilitate interaction.

Platforms Integrating AI for Incorporating and Modifying Voices

Text-to-Speech Conversion

These platforms are designed to transcribe written text into speech in a fluid and natural manner, mimicking human speech. *Balabolka* and *iSpeech* allow text-to-speech conversion using voices already installed on the system. *Amazon Polly, Google Text-to-Speech,* and *NaturalReader* utilise cloud storage to generate natural and realistic voices, supporting multiple languages and accents, making them optimal tools for voicing characters in different languages or narrating stories in specific contexts. They also offer customisation options for adjusting the tone and speed of the generated voices. *Meanwhile, Microsoft Azure Speech, Murf AI,* and *Play.ht* facilitate text-to-speech conversion with advanced personalisation. They provide synthetic voices with adjustable tone, speed, and emphasis, allowing their use in chatbots, virtual assistants, and digital content. Additionally, platforms such as *SpeechGen.io* are designed specifically for the educational context, converting voices for videos, presentations, and other multimedia content, while *Speechify* is tailored to assist individuals with dyslexia or reading difficulties by enabling better text comprehension through natural and customisable voices.

Generation and Personalisation of Voices Through AI

These platforms specialise in the creation of synthetic voices that can be personalised for various applications, such as video games, animated characters, and multimedia content. Some of these platforms allow voice cloning and advanced speech synthesis. *Synthesia* and *Voxygen* offer a wide range of voices with different styles and intonations, adapting to the needs of each user. On the other hand, *Descript* and *Lyrebird AI* modify and enhance audio quality, including features such as automatic transcription and text-based editing. They can be used for creating podcasts, narrations, and other multimedia content. Likewise, *Replica Studios* generates expressive and natural voices for video games and animation.

Modification and Transformation of Voices

These tools enable real-time voice alteration or the application of modification effects. *Altered Studio* and *Voicemod* create virtual character voices with varying vocal characteristics, making them useful for audiovisual production, gaming, and dubbing. *Voice Changer* offers a simpler interface and provides a broad range of voice modification effects, including distortions and changes in tone and speed. Additionally, *Vocaloid* is a voice synthesis software designed to create songs performed by virtual voices.

Platforms Integrating AI for Video Creation

Creation of Animated Videos and Presentations

Animaker, Biteable, Powtoon, Renderforest, and *Wideo* are animated video creation tools designed for users without experience in video editing. These platforms generate animated content in various styles, including explainer videos, presentations, and advertisements. They feature a "drag-and-drop" interface, an extensive library of customisable characters, animation effects, and multiple pre-designed templates. *Doodly,* on the other hand, is specialised in the creation of animated videos in the style of whiteboard animation. It draws characters, graphics, and text on different background styles, such as whiteboards, blackboards, glassboards, and coloured backgrounds. It can be used to design explainer videos and educational presentations, offering a broad library of images, the ability to import custom graphics, and an option to add voiceovers. *Vyond* also facilitates character animation by synchronising lip movement with facial expressions.

Video Editing

Descript is a comprehensive audio and video editing platform that enables users to modify multimedia content through text transcription, editing videos as if they were text documents, removing words, pauses, and errors by simply editing the transcription. It also offers advanced features such as voice cloning, automatic dubbing, and real-time subtitle generation. *Filmora, Magisto*, and *Runway ML* provide intuitive interfaces for applying visual effects, transitions, animated titles, and filters without requiring technical knowledge. They also offer features such as split-screen, colour correction, audio editing, and compatibility with multiple video formats. *Kapwing* and *Veed.io* make video editing easier by offering tools for trimming, adding text, generating automatic subtitles, transcribing audio, applying filters, inserting animated text, and adjusting video speed. Their interfaces also facilitate real-time team collaboration in the cloud, allowing editing without the need for downloads. Finally, *Wave.video* also offers live streaming and hosts videos on its own server.

Video Generation from Text and Written Content

DeepBrain and *Synthesia* specialise in converting text into video using realistic avatars, with the script being interpreted and narrated by avatars with lip-syncing. These platforms also support multiple languages and avatar personalisation. *FlexClip, InVideo*, and P*ictory* facilitate video creation from customisable templates and written content. Their cloud-based system offers an intuitive interface with drag-and-drop functions, making it easy to convert scripts into dynamic videos with images, transitions, and animated effects. They include advanced tools such as automatic subtitle generation and video clip editing. Additionally, they offer personalisation tools, including colour adjustments, fonts, and background music, to tailor content to various needs. Lumen5 is a platform specialised in transforming articles, blog posts, and other written content into visually engaging videos. Its natural language processing system identifies the most relevant parts of the text and converts them into slides with automatically suggested images and animations.

Platforms Integrating AI to Generate Interactive Stories

Visual and Multimedia Content

Genially employs AI to assist in the creation of interactive presentations and multimedia narratives, making it easy for users to develop interactive stories intuitively. It recommends templates and visual resources that align with the themes selected by the user. *Agartha, Ren'Py*, and *Visual Novel Maker* utilise AI to enhance the creation of dynamic interactive stories, enabling the automatic generation of plots and branching dialogues that adapt based on user choices. Furthermore, the AI optimises multimedia integration by suggesting images and sounds that match the tone and direction of the story, making it easier to create more immersive narrative experiences without the need for advanced programming skills. Fungus operates similarly, helping manage in-game interactions, and requires no technical expertise for the creation of visual and narrative content. *StoryMapJS*, on the other hand, focuses on storytelling based on interactive geographical locations, integrating algorithms to generate interactive maps with text and other multimedia elements.

Decision Simulations

Alter Ego, ChoiceScript, and *Hypertextopia* employ AI to create life-like decision simulations, allowing users to make choices that affect the development of a branching narrative. While AI does not autonomously generate content, it optimises decision paths and creates an adaptive system where the user's choices dynamically alter the events of the story, providing a unique and personalised experience in each session. *Talespire* is a platform for creating and playing interactive narratives in a 3D digital environment, where AI facilitates the creation of dynamic maps and scenarios, adjusting visual elements and interactions to align with player decisions. *Zombies, Run!* generates an immersive experience that combines interactive storytelling with physical exercise. The AI personalises missions according to the player's progress and choices, creating a unique story each time the user participates in an exercise session. Additionally, the AI adjusts the pace and difficulty of the missions based on data collected, such as the player's speed and decisions made during running or walking, enhancing the personalisation of the experience.

Tools for Planning, Writing, and Developing Narratives

Campfire, Ink, Inklewriter, Narrative Designer, and *Twine* focus on the planning and organisation of complex stories, using algorithms to efficiently manage plots, characters, and relationships. AI allows for dynamic suggestions and adjustments of connections between characters, events, and timelines, helping maintain narrative coherence and facilitating the creation of more complex and branching plots. These platforms also enable the generation of alternative paths by adapting the narrative according to the player's previous choices. Similarly, *ChatMapper* is centred on the design of interactive dialogues and branching narratives, utilising AI to optimise the creation of non-linear dialogues, allowing interactions between characters to evolve smoothly according to the user's decisions. *Choose Your Own Adventure* allows users to create and read interactive stories following the classic "Choose Your Own Adventure" style.

Specifically, it uses AI to suggest new routes or endings based on the player's choices, enhancing the interactive experience and replayability of the stories. Write with *Transformer* is a tool that uses AI to generate text, facilitating the creation of interactive narratives. It is based on advanced language models like GPT-3, where AI helps generate narrative content, adapting and extending stories based on the user's instructions. AI allows the narrative to evolve dynamically, providing continuation suggestions, creating dialogues, or even completing scenes according to the creator's inputs. A similar function is offered *by TiddlyWiki*, which allows for collaborative design.

Discussion and Conclusions

In light of the numerous AI platforms created for the design of digital narratives, specific training is required to assist teachers, in general, and future educators in particular, in selecting the most appropriate tools to apply in the classroom, thus contributing to the optimisation of the teaching–learning process. Undoubtedly, the selection of AI-integrated platforms presented here offers a wide range of opportunities for their didactic implementation.

Specifically, the platform *Genially* is a versatile tool that uses AI to create visual environments from interactive scenarios and stories, enabling the design of tales, mini-games, and other educational activities. Its intuitive interface allows for the incorporation of images, videos, links, sounds, and animations, enriching the immersive experience (Del Moral et al., 2024). Furthermore, it allows interactive buttons to be added, which students can click to progress through the story, promoting autonomy and decision-making within the narrative. On the other hand, Vyond helps create videos intuitively by combining images, characters, audio, etc. It also offers a library of backgrounds, objects, and animated gifs, which enhance the narrative and allow for thematic adaptation in educational stories.

Regarding the personalised design of characters, *Ready Player Me* is an ideal platform as it does not require advanced modelling skills. It also provides options to modify facial features, clothing, and expressions, enabling students to create their own characters. In terms of assigning voices to different characters, *Google Text-to-Speech* offers an accessible and effective solution to enrich interactive stories with voices, as it allows the conversion of text to audio and includes natural, expressive voices in multiple languages and accents, which can facilitate storytelling in different contexts.

After selecting the most intuitive, visual, and accessible platforms for designing interactive narratives with AI in the school context, it is necessary to analyse how to integrate them for didactic purposes. For example, they could assist in designing learning situations (supported by a digital narrative) where characters, acting as a thread throughout the story, guide students through various activities.

As can be seen, there are numerous tools that can facilitate language learning through the presentation of dialogues in other languages, helping to learn pronunciation, syntax, semantic fields, idiomatic expressions, metaphors, etc., elements inherent in different languages. They can also be used to bring characters to life, develop scripts for animation, and create videos based on narratives that consider the various plots defined by Tobías (2012). Additionally, creating advertising campaigns could be particularly useful as it allows the incorporation of transversal areas of the curriculum, such as environmental respect, peace education, visual education, interculturality, etc.

Moreover, audio conversion platforms can be used in literary activities, reading animation, or to foster oral comprehension, stimulate narrative skills and/or creativity, such as identifying alternative endings in the same story. These tools also serve as ideal resources for students with Special Educational Needs (ACNEAE), both for communication tasks and for establishing specific dialogues between characters in concrete contexts, stimulating the learning of appropriate responses to various everyday situations, as suggested by Hesami et al. (2025). For educators with more advanced design skills, there could be a focus on creating educational video games, incorporating specific mechanics, dynamics, and aesthetics, similar to the research by Del Moral et al. (2023). Activities aimed at the creation of transmedia products could also be promoted, such as turning stories and/or films into Serious Games, transforming a comic into a video where characters come to life, etc.

Ultimately, the suitability of platforms varies depending on the educational level and the degree of student autonomy. It is advisable to select tools that consider accessibility, the level of customization, and the developmental needs of each stage. Therefore, for younger learners, tools that allow for the creation of visually engaging environments and easily customizable characters, without requiring advanced technical skills, are particularly useful. For example, *Genially* enables the development of multimedia stories and interactive narratives with clickable buttons that students can activate themselves, promoting autonomy and decision-making.

Doodly, by using whiteboard-style animations, helps capture the attention of Early Childhood Education students and can be used to reinforce routines, rules, or simple narrative sequences. *Ready Player Me* and *Toonify* allow students to create their own avatars or see themselves reflected in playfully styled characters, enhancing emotional identification. Additionally, *Speechify*, a text-to-speech tool, is designed for students with reading difficulties and could be especially helpful in Early Childhood settings, particularly in inclusive proposals or reading motivation activities.

On the other hand, in Primary Education, platforms that support greater narrative customization, decision-making, and transmedia content development become more relevant. *Twine* and *Inklewriter* allow students to interact with non-linear stories, choose different paths, and explore new narrative structures, encouraging critical thinking. *Campfire* is suitable for planning complex plots and maintaining textual coherence, skills typically developed in the upper grades of Primary Education. *Vyond* and *Powtoon* animate characters, backgrounds, and sound effects, allowing students to create audiovisual products that can be integrated into interdisciplinary projects, emphasizing both written and oral expression. Finally, *Google Text-to-Speech* stands out for its usefulness in narrating stories in different languages.

The activities that can be carried out in the classroom using these platforms should be tailored to the educational stage. For instance, in Early Childhood Education, photographs of the students could be transformed into animated characters who become the protagonists of personalized stories, supporting identity building and the recognition of oneself and others. Fantastic landscapes (such as a farm, a city, or the ocean floor) could also be created using visual tools that allow for the depiction of spaces where different stories unfold, fostering environmental exploration and imagination development. In addition, voiceovers could be added based on the students' own oral creations, reinforcing linguistic communication skills by enhancing verbal expression, active listening, and the temporal sequencing of their own narratives.

In Primary Education, students can create avatars that participate in stories set within specific subject contexts, for example, an adventure through the solar system in Science, or a historical journey in Social Studies. They can plan each scene, write the dialogues, and incorporate synthesized voices, thereby developing both language and digital skills. Students can also produce videos to bring their stories or school reports to life, integrating images, music, and voiceovers. As a final activity, they could design interactive stories in which each reader's decision, such as whether to save a character or choose one path over another, alters the course of the narrative. This promotes logical thinking, creative writing, and decision-making. These types of activities enable the integration of curricular content in a cross-disciplinary way, enhancing students' digital competence, oral and written expression, and creativity.

Undoubtedly, there are many possible applications of these AI-integrated platforms in the school environment, which is why future teachers should use these emerging tools as allies, responding to the needs of their students and the curricular area in which they teach. However, it is essential that these educators are fully aware of the ethical responsibilities that come with their use. First and foremost, they must take great care to avoid the unnecessary exposure of personal data, both their own and that of their students, ensuring the privacy and protection of sensitive information. This involves not only complying with current data protection legislation (such as the GDPR in Europe) but also adopting best practices to prevent any leaks or misuse of data that could compromise the safety of minors.

Implications for Practice and Ethics

It is essential to emphasize that teachers must avoid disclosing their own personal data or that of their students in order to protect privacy. Likewise, educational policy makers should establish a clear set of guidelines for the responsible use of these tools, ensuring compliance with ethical standards. Such guidelines should explicitly prohibit the impersonation of others through the use of their image and/or voice, as well as the recreation of degrading situations that may promote hate speech. They should also include the recognition of copyright and authorship rights of existing artistic works and the proper referencing of such materials. Furthermore, it is necessary to list the tools employed in the design of the produced materials, thereby preventing the misappropriation of works, images, videos, or audio content. Ultimately, a clear and rigorous commitment to digital ethics and educational responsibility is required to harness the advantages of Artificial Intelligence while safeguarding the security, respect, and well-being of the educational community.

Appendix

See Tables 9.3, 9.4, 9.5, 9.6, and 9.7.

Table 9.3 AI platforms for generating characters

Platform (link)	Utility	Features
Anima (https://animaapp.com/)	Generation of 3D human characters and animations for architecture and video games	Facial animation, advanced customisation, integration with design tools
Artbreeder (https://www.artbreeder.com/)	Generation of characters and portraits by blending images	Image blending, feature customisation, access to an artist community
Character.ai (https://beta.character.ai/)	Creation of conversational characters simulating interactions	Real-time responses, character customisation
DALL·E (https://openai.com/dall-e)	Generation of images from textual descriptions	Creation of visual art, unique interpretations, ability to combine concepts
Deep Dream Generator (https://deepdreamgenerator.com/)	Generation of art and visual characters based on neural networks	Surreal art style, customisable filters, community for sharing creations
Fotor (https://www.fotor.com/)	Platform that includes avatar and portrait generation with AI	Photo editor, portrait creation, graphic design templates
Generated Photos (https://generated.photos/)	Generates realistic human faces with AI for various uses	Library of faces, image customisation, commercial use
Headshot (Reallusion) (https://cutt.ly/Ie5t07B2)	Generates 3D characters from a photo	Image-to-3D transformation, customisation tools, game use
MakeHuman (http://www.makehumancommunity.org/)	Software to create 3D human characters with advanced customisation	Detailed 3D modelling, texturing options, support for rigging and animation
MetaHuman Creator (https://www.unrealengine.com/en-US/metahuman)	Create hyper-realistic human characters for video games and productions	High visual fidelity, integration with Unreal Engine, detailed customisation
Mixamo (https://www.mixamo.com/)	3D animation platform that generates characters and animates them automatically	Character library, automatic animations, integration with design software
Promethean AI (http://www.prometheanai.com/)	Generation of 3D environments and characters for video games or visual narratives	Creation of interactive environments, character customisation, easy integration
Ready Player Me (https://readyplayer.me/)	Create customisable 3D avatars for virtual worlds and video games	Integration across various virtual reality platforms
Replika (https://replika.com/)	Creation of AI avatars that simulate human conversations	Conversational interaction, focus on emotional well-being
Runway ML (https://runwayml.com/)	AI tool for generating and editing character images and videos	Real-time editing, advanced visual effects
Sims 4 Create-a-Sim (https://www.ea.com/games/the-sims/the-sims-4)	Tool for creating detailed characters within the Sims 4 game	Customisation of physical traits, clothing, and personality, game integration

(continued)

Table 9.3 (continued)

Platform (link)	Utility	Features
This Person Does Not Exist (https://thispersondoesnotexist.com/)	Automatic generation of realistic human faces with AI	Infinite AI-generated faces, commercial use allowed
Toonify (https://toonify.justinpinkney.com/)	Converts human portraits into cartoon-style characters	Cartoon effect, instant transformation, easy to use
Vroid Studio (https://vroid.com/en/studio)	Creation of 3D anime characters, primarily for video games and animations	Anime character modelling, customisations and clothing, various export formats
ZEPETO (https://zepeto.me/)	Creation of customisable 3D avatars and characters	Online social interaction, avatar customisation, social media compatibility

Source Created by the authors

References

Antony, V. N., & Huang, C. M. (2024). Co-creating visual stories with generative AI. *ACM Transactions on Interactive Intelligent Systems, 14*(3), 1–29. https://doi.org/10.1145/3672277

Dai, Y., Lee, J., & Kim, J. W. (2024). AI vs. human voices: How delivery source and narrative format influence the effectiveness of persuasion messages. *International Journal of Human-Computer Interaction, 40*(24), 8735–8749. https://doi.org/10.1080/10447318.2023.2288734

Del Moral, M. E., López-Bouzas, N., & Castañeda, J. (2023). Activating teacher competencies through designing gamified stories with augmentative reality. In E. Podovšovnik, T. De Giuseppe, & F. Corona (Eds.), *Handbook of research on establishing digital competencies in the pursuit of online learning* (pp. 230–252). IGI Global. https://doi.org/10.4018/978-1-6684-7010-7.ch012

Del Moral, M.E., López Bouzas, N. & Castañeda, J. (2024). Transmedia skill derived from the process of converting films into educational games with augmented reality and artificial intelligence. *Journal of New Approaches in Educational Research, 13*(15). https://doi.org/10.1007/s44322-024-00015-8

Fan, M., Cui, X., Hao, J., Ye, R., Ma, W., Tong, X., & Li, M. (2024). StoryPrompt: Exploring the design space of an AI-empowered creative storytelling system for elementary children. In *Extended abstracts of the CHI conference on human factors in computing systems* (pp. 1–8). https://doi.org/10.1145/3613905.3651118

Hesami, E., Bakhshani, N. M., Dahouie, M. A., & Zaheri, Y. (2025). Evaluation of the effectiveness of a serious game titled "Kookism" on the receptive lexicon in 4–9-year-old autistic children. *Heliyon, 11*(1). https://doi.org/10.1016/j.heliyon.2024.e41036

Liang, Z., Zhang, X., Ma, K., Liu, Z., Ren, X., Goucher-Lambert, K., & Liu, C. (2024). StoryDiffusion: How to support UX storyboarding with generative-AI. *arXiv preprint* arXiv:2407.07672. https://doi.org/10.48550/arXiv.2407.07672

Madaan, G., Asthana, S. K., & Kaur, J. (2024). Generative AI: Applications, models, challenges, opportunities, and future directions. *Generative AI and Implications for Ethics, Security, and Data Management*. https://doi.org/10.4018/979-8-3693-8557-9.ch004

Mariani, I., & Ciancia, M. (2023). Design for narrative change. A pedagogical model for interactive digital narratives. *International Journal of Art & Design Education, 42*(3), 384–401. https://doi.org/10.1111/jade.12468

Table 9.4 AI platforms for generating environments

Platform (link)	Utility	Features
Artbreeder (https://www.artbreeder.com/)	Mixes images to create surreal landscapes and environments	Collaborative image generation through visual element blending
Blender (https://www.blender.org/)	Creation and design of realistic or fantastic 3D environments	3D modelling software with sculpting, texturing, and animation tools
CityEngine (https://www.esri.com/en-us/arcgis/products/arcgis-cityengine/overview)	Generation of 3D cities for simulations, video games, and urban visualisation	City creation with parametric modelling and geospatial data
DALL·E (https://openai.com/dall-e)	Generation of scenario images from textual descriptions	Creation of original images from text with customisable visual styles
Deep Dream Generator (https://deepdreamgenerator.com/)	Generation of abstract and surreal environments based on AI	Transformation of images into creations with dream-like and psychedelic styles
FlowScape (https://pixelforest.itch.io/flowscape)	Creation of detailed natural 3D landscapes with flora, fauna, and terrain	Interactive simulation with brush tools for modelling terrain and vegetation
Fotor (https://www.fotor.com/)	Generation of backgrounds and landscapes using AI and image editing	Image editing platform with filters and composition tools
Gaea (https://quadspinner.com/gaea)	3D terrain and landscape generator for video games and movies	Terrain creation with erosion tools and advanced texturing
Google Earth Studio (https://www.google.com/earth/studio/)	Generation of 3D tours based on satellite images	3D map animation using satellite imagery and geospatial data from Google Earth
Houdini (https://www.sidefx.com/products/houdini/)	3D animation and simulation software used for generating complex environments in films and games	Modelling, advanced simulations, and customisable filters for environment generation
Krita (https://krita.org/en/)	Digital art tool for creating detailed illustrated environments	Digital painting software with advanced brushes and composition tools
Lumion (https://lumion.com/)	Tool for rendering 3D architectural environments in real-time	Real-time rendering with material libraries and environmental effects
MidJourney (https://www.midjourney.com/)	Generation of images and landscapes from textual descriptions in a unique artistic style	Creation of images with varied artistic styles from textual prompts

(continued)

Table 9.4 (continued)

Platform (link)	Utility	Features
Promethean AI (http://www.prometheanai.com/)	Generation of detailed 3D environments for video games and visual narratives	AI assistant that suggests and organises design elements in 3D environments
Runway ML (https://runwayml.com/)	Tool for generating and modifying scenario images and videos	Image and video editing with AI, background generation, and overlay tools
Terragen (https://planetside.co.uk/)	Creation of realistic or fantastic landscapes and environments in 3D	Atmospheric simulation software and terrain generation
Terrain.party (http://terrain.party/)	Platform for generating topographic maps from real data	Download topographic maps based on real geospatial data for 3D modelling
Unreal Engine (https://www.unrealengine.com/)	Graphics engine for designing hyper-realistic 3D scenarios and open-world environments	Real-time rendering with advanced lighting and physics tools
Vue (https://info.e-onsoftware.com/vue)	Tool for creating 3D natural and architectural environments	Ecosystem simulation with advanced control over atmosphere, water, and vegetation
World Creator (https://www.world-creator.com/)	Generation and customisation of 3D terrain and environments	Procedural terrain modelling with texturing and weather simulation tools

Source Created by the authors

Papadimitriou, S., & Virvou, M. (2025). User-player and student modeling in personalized educational games: A literature review. *Artificial intelligence—based games as novel holistic educational environments to teach 21st century skills*, 63–94. https://doi.org/10.1007/978-3-031-77464-5_3

Shava, G. N., Hleza, S., Tlou, F., Shonhiwa, S., & Mathonsi, E. (2021). Qualitative content analysis, utility, usability and processes in educational research. *International Journal of Research and Innovation in Social Science, 5*(7), 553–558.

Tang, M., & Chen, Y. (2024). AI and animated character design: Efficiency, creativity, interactivity. *The Frontiers of Society, Science and Technology, 6*(1), 117–123. https://doi.org/10.25236/FSST.2024.060120

Tobías, R. B. (2012). *20 Master plots: And how to build them.* Writer's Digest Books.

Table 9.5 AI platforms for generating and modifying voices

Platform (link)	Utility	Features
Altered Studio (https://altered.studio/)	Voice modification and creation of virtual characters for multimedia content	Real-time voice transformation with multiple effects and customizable adjustments
Amazon Polly (https://aws.amazon.com/polly/)	Text-to-speech service that converts text into realistic audio	Generation of natural voices in multiple languages
Balabolka (http://www.cross-plus-a.com/balabolka.htm)	Free software to convert text to speech in various formats	Compatible with multiple file formats and allows customization of voice speed and pitch
CereVoice (https://www.cereproc.com/)	Generation of customized, high-quality voices for various applications	Creation of synthetic voices with emotional intonations and personalized accents
Descript (https://www.descript.com/)	Voice generation and modification using AI, with audio editing features	Allows text-based audio editing, voice cloning, and noise removal
Google Text-to-Speech (https://cloud.google.com/text-to-speech)	AI-based voice generation in multiple languages, ideal for applications	Uses Google AI to offer realistic voices with speed and pitch control
iSpeech (https://www.ispeech.org/)	Platform to convert text to speech and modify voices	Supports multiple platforms, including web, mobile, and enterprise applications
Lyrebird AI (https://www.descript.com/lyrebird)	Generation of personalized voices using AI, voice cloning	Advanced AI to replicate voices with high precision and generate custom dialogues
Microsoft Azure Speech (https://azure.microsoft.com/en-us/services/cognitive-services/speech/)	Platform to convert text to speech and customize voices	Includes neural voice generation with intonation and speed adjustments
Murf AI (https://murf.ai/)	Generation of natural voices for presentations and narrations	Voice library in multiple languages with customization and tone options
NaturalReader (https://www.naturalreaders.com/)	Text-to-speech conversion with multiple voice and accent options	Compatible with documents, PDFs, and web pages for smooth read-aloud functionality
Play.ht (https://play.ht/)	Text-to-speech conversion with realistic voices for podcasts and audiobooks	Allows exporting audio files in MP3 and WAV with high-quality synthetic voices
Replica Studios (https://replicastudios.com/)	Generation of realistic voices for video game characters and animation	Specializes in voices for characters with emotions and realistic modulation
SpeechGen.io (https://speechgen.io/)	Text-to-speech generator, useful for videos and presentations	Online platform with multiple languages and adjustable voice effects

(continued)

Table 9.5 (continued)

Platform (link)	Utility	Features
Speechify (https://speechify.com/)	Tool to convert text to speech and enhance content accessibility	Compatible with mobile devices and browsers, with variable speed functions
Synthesia (https://www.synthesia.io/)	Video platform that allows creating videos with AI-generated voices	Generation of virtual avatars with precise lip-syncing
Vocaloid (https://www.vocaloid.com/en/)	Voice synthesis for singing and creation of voices for virtual characters	Voice synthesis engine capable of creating songs with digital voices
Voice Changer (https://voicechanger.io/)	Online voice modifier with multiple effects and options	Free tool with customization options for pitch and tone
Voicemod (https://www.voicemod.net/)	Real-time voice modifier with effects for games and content creation	Compatible with Discord, Twitch, and video games, with live dynamic effects
Voxygen (https://www.voxygen.fr/)	Generation of customized voices for different applications	Specializes in voices with expressive intonations and advanced customization

Source Created by the authors

Table 9.6 AI platforms for generating videos

Platform (link)	Utility	Features
Animaker (https://www.animaker.com/)	Tool for creating animated videos with multiple customization options	Animated templates, customizable characters, drag-and-drop tools
Biteable (https://biteable.com/)	Animated and marketing video creator with customizable templates	Video templates, social media integration, easy-to-use editor
DeepBrain (https://www.deepbrain.io/)	Video generation with AI avatars that can speak entered text	Text-to-video conversion, AI-generated avatars, customization
Descript (https://www.descript.com/)	Video and audio editing platform for creating multimedia content from text	Text-based editing, dubbing functions, collaborative tools
Doodly (https://www.doodly.com/)	Creation of whiteboard-style animated videos	Drawing styles, animated characters and objects, voice-over option
Filmora (https://filmora.wondershare.com/)	Easy-to-use video editing software with options to create engaging videos	Special effects, animated titles, support for multiple video formats
FlexClip (https://www.flexclip.com/)	Online video creator for marketing and personal projects	Customizable templates, editing tools, media library
InVideo (https://invideo.io/)	Platform for creating promotional videos, presentations, and more using templates	Advanced editing tools, access to video and music libraries
Kapwing (https://www.kapwing.com/)	Video editing platform and multimedia content generation	Video editing, subtitle generation, meme tools
Lumen5 (https://www.lumen5.com/)	Video creation from articles or written content using AI	AI for content creation, image and video libraries, easy to use
Magisto (https://www.magisto.com/)	Automated video generator that uses AI to edit multimedia content	Smart templates, automatic editing, music options
Pictory (https://pictory.ai/)	Generation of short videos from scripts or text	Automatic generation, simple editing features, royalty-free images
Powtoon (https://www.powtoon.com/)	Tool for creating animated videos and visual presentations	Animated templates, export options, online collaboration
Renderforest (https://www.renderforest.com/)	Generation of animated videos, presentations, and logos online	Video templates, branding, marketing tools
Runway ML (https://runwayml.com/)	Tool for creating and editing videos with AI capabilities	Real-time editing, collaboration tools, AI-generated effects

(continued)

Table 9.6 (continued)

Platform (link)	Utility	Features
Synthesia (https://www.synthesia.io/)	Video generation from text with virtual avatars	Avatar customization, multiple languages, rapid video creation
Veed.io (https://www.veed.io/)	Online video editor that allows easy generation and customization of videos	Simple editing, subtitle generation, graphic design tools
Vyond (https://www.vyond.com/)	Platform for creating animated videos for businesses and presentations	Character animation, story templates, content library
Wave.video (https://wave.video/)	Video editing tool and content creation for social media	Editing tools, media library, social media integration
Wideo (https://wideo.co/)	Creation of animated and promotional videos through an easy-to-use interface	Animation templates, online collaboration, easy export

Source Created by the authors

Table 9.7 AI platforms for generating interactive stories

Platform (link)	Utility	Features
Agartha (https://agartha.io/)	Tool for creating interactive and dynamic stories using templates and custom options	Allows the creation of visual and dynamic interactive stories with options to integrate multimedia
Alter Ego (http://www.mindgames.com/alterego)	Interactive narrative game exploring life decisions, with options to create stories from scratch	Focused on designing real-life simulations and exploring personal decisions through branching choices
Campfire (https://www.campfiretechnology.com/)	Tool for planning and organizing stories, characters, and plots from scratch	Structuring complex plots, creating detailed characters, and managing multiple timelines and relationships
ChatMapper (https://chatmapper.com/)	Software for creating interactive dialogues and branching narratives using templates	Designing nonlinear dialogues for video games and interactive narratives with a focus on branching
ChoiceScript (https://www.choiceofgames.com/make-your-own-games/choicescript-intro/)	Programming language for creating text-based games and interactive narratives from scratch	Creating stories from text with deep choices and complex mechanics
Choose Your Own Adventure (https://www.cyoa.com/)	Platform for creating and reading interactive stories using templates	Creation of simple narratives in the style of classic "Choose Your Own Adventure" books with direct branching choices
Fungus (http://fungusdocs.itch.io/fungus)	Tool for creating interactive story games in Unity with available templates	Creating visual interactive stories without programming experience
Genially (https://www.genially.com/)	Tool for creating interactive presentations and multimedia narratives using templates	Creation of interactive presentations, infographics, and multimedia narratives with innovative visual elements
Hypertextopia (http://hypertextopia.com/)	Platform for creating interactive and nonlinear narratives from scratch	Allows the development of nonlinear stories with options for unstructured and branching navigation
Ink (https://www.inklestudios.com/ink/)	Scripting language for creating interactive narratives and text games from scratch	Offers a flexible programming language for interactive stories that mix narrative and decisions
Inklewriter (https://www.inklestudios.com/inklewriter/)	Platform for writing and publishing interactive stories easily using templates	Intuitive and accessible, allows easy creation of branching stories without advanced programming

(continued)

Table 9.7 (continued)

Platform (link)	Utility	Features
Narrative Designer (https://narrativedesigner.com/)	Tool for designing interactive narratives and choice systems from scratch	Focused on creating and managing complex choice systems with clear and detailed story branches
Ren'Py (https://www.renpy.org/)	Visual novel engine for creating interactive stories from scratch or with templates	Creation of visual novels with an intuitive interface, ideal for developing graphic adventure games
StoryMapJS (https://storymap.knightlab.com/)	Creates interactive narratives combining maps and text, with available templates	Integration of interactive geographical maps into stories, ideal for telling location-based and travel narratives
Talespire (https://talespire.com/)	Platform for creating and playing interactive narratives in a digital environment using templates	Creation of stories with 3D visualization, suitable for role-playing games and interactive narratives with settings
TiddlyWiki (https://tiddlywiki.com/)	Personal wiki that allows creating and organizing interactive narratives from scratch	Offers a nonlinear organization system ideal for developing collaborative or open-structured stories
Twine (https://twinery.org/)	Tool for creating interactive and nonlinear stories from scratch	Creation of nonlinear stories with easy customization options and an intuitive visual system
Visual Novel Maker (https://visualnovelmaker.com/)	Software for creating interactive visual novels from scratch or using templates	Creation of visual novels with graphic tools and templates to integrate stories and visual art
Write with Transformer (https://transformer.huggingface.co/)	Text generator using AI to help write interactive narratives from scratch	Generates interactive narrative content, allowing stories to evolve dynamically
Zombies, Run! (https://zombiesrungame.com/)	Interactive storytelling game that allows creating custom stories from scratch	Combines interactive storytelling with physical exercise, creating an immersive experience while running or walking

Source Created by the authors

Chapter 10
Guide to Generate AI Educational Resources for Primary Mathematics Education

Jin Su Jeong, Ana Isabel Montero-Izquierdo, and David González-Gómez

Abstract The increasing number of Artificial Intelligence (AI) applications has sparked interest in the potential pedagogical uses of Generative AI (GenAI) technologies and Large Linguistic Models (LLM) based chatbots. The use of AI tools in education offers promising opportunities to enhance teaching–learning strategies and can support personalized learning by adapting to students' needs, offering tailored explanations, and providing immediate feedback. However, many teachers are inexperienced with AI and face significant obstacles to integrating into their educational practice. This chapter provides detailed guidance for educators, facilitating the use of GenAI for the creation of lesson plans and evaluation tools. Furthermore, it explains how LLM based chatbots can be used by students to personalize their learning process for the mathematics subject in primary education, ensuring ethical use and privacy of children's data.

Keywords Generative Artificial Intelligence (GenAI) · Large Linguistic Models (LLM) · Chatbot · Mathematics education · Primary education

J. S. Jeong (✉) · A. I. Montero-Izquierdo · D. González-Gómez
Departamento de Didáctica de las Ciencias Experimentales y Matemáticas, Facultad de Formación del Profesorado, Universidad de Extremadura, Cáceres, Spain
e-mail: jin@unex.es

A. I. Montero-Izquierdo
e-mail: ana_montero@unex.es

D. González-Gómez
e-mail: dggomez@unex.es

S. Papadakis (ed.), *AI Applications in Preschool and Primary Education*, Advances in Artificial Intelligence in Education 5, https://doi.org/10.1007/978-3-032-17190-0_10

Introduction

As Artificial Intelligence (AI) continues to transform the educational landscape, its integration into early and primary education presents both exciting opportunities and ethical challenges. The book *AI Applications in Preschool and Primary Education* explores this transformative shift and offers insights into how AI can enhance pedagogical practices, personalize learning experiences, and assist educators. In this context, this chapter *Guide to Generate AI Educational Resources for Primary Mathematics Educatio*n provides educators and learners with a structured approach to create AI-enhanced resources tailored according to the cognitive and developmental needs of young learners and considering ethical issues.

The term AI can be defined as computer systems capable of performing activities that typically require human intellect, such as reasoning, decision-making, problem-solving, situational adaptation, and experience-based improvement (Fügener et al., 2022; Yang et al., 2018). In the education field, AI is being introduced with the aim to improve teaching–learning strategies. Specifically, AI has the capacity to generate personalized educational resources in real-time (Bernacki et al., 2020; Macfadyen & Dawson, 2010), and, thereby, enabling educators to customize teaching methods with greater efficacy (Hasibuan & Azizah, 2023; Jeong & González-Gómez, 2025a; Pesovski et al., 2024). While the integration of AI holds great potential to transform the educational scenery, it is important to acknowledge the challenges posing to educational institutions (Coccoli et al., 2016; Zawacki-Richter et al., 2019). Nonetheless, it has become evident that there has been a proliferation of AI platforms and tools for education in recent years. As a result, research studies are being conducted into the potential use of AI in education (Holmes & Miao, 2024), with a particular focus on the implications of Generative Artificial Intelligence (GenAI) for teaching–learning strategies in mathematics education at primary education.

In the field of AI, GenAI has had a significant impact on a wide range of research and application areas in recent years. It is a type of AI technology that enables the generation of synthetic content and data by learning from existing human-created samples (Abukmeil et al., 2021; Gui et al., 2021; Pérez et al., 2020). GenAI responds to textual instructions in natural language conversational interfaces (prompts) by automatically producing new material. In addition, GenAI may assist educators in creating instructional materials immediately and provide guidance to tailor a lesson plan according to the learning objectives and educational content (Holmes & Miao, 2024; Pesovski et al., 2024; Sabzalieva & Valentini, 2023). Currently, GenAI correctness is unreliable despite its fluidity and remarkable production capacity (Stefanova & Georgiev, 2024; Tlili et al., 2023). This requires learning to create effective prompts for various tasks and developing critical skills for analyzing and improving AI output, and it is recommended to utilize concise and simple terminology, provide context, refine and iterate, and provide examples that demonstrate the desired response (Jeong & González-Gómez, 2025b; Stefanova & Georgiev, 2024). Therefore, there is a growing demand to learn how to use GenAI correctly.

There is limited research on GenAI in the field of mathematics education. However, some studies have been found that address this field of research. For instance, Canonigo (2024) examined how AI technologies can influence students' perceptions of the mathematics learning process and explores students' level of engagement with the subject matter as well as their conceptual knowledge of mathematics. Other studies have reported positive results, such as an increase of teaching effectiveness, students' engagement level, and understanding of intricate concepts (Egara & Mosimege, 2024). Hwang (2022) and Usluoğlu and Toptaş (2025) revealed that the application of AI had a significant and positive impact on the performance of primary school mathematics students. Regarding the creation of lesson plans with AI, Karaman (2024) has indicated substantial improvement in academic performance using lesson plans that have been developed with the support of AI. Moreover, as demonstrated by several studies, AI has also the capacity to facilitate the creation of evaluation instruments congruent with didactic and curricular objectives (Al Braiki et al., 2020; Fernández-Sánchez et al., 2025). Nonetheless, the teachers' supervision is essential to assess the data generated by GenAI and to make decisions that are in line with the educational needs (Fernández-Sánchez et al., 2025).

The potential applications of GenAI are manifold. Another such notable application is that of real-time information provision, thereby aiding students in comprehending fundamental mathematical concepts (Stefanova & Georgiev, 2024). Specifically, AI chatbots are a subcategory of GenAI, distinguished by their interaction with Large Language Models (LLMs) in a complex process that results in the generation of text responses to queries and prompts. These responses are crafted to closely resemble those of a human being, what is achieved using deep learning techniques (Tili et al., 2023). LLMs are AI models that have been trained with large volumes of data to analyze language and produce natural language text responses (Yigci et al., 2024). Significant data growth and advances in computational insights have improved the utility of LLM-based chatbots (Alazzam et al., 2023; Khosravi et al., 2024; Lin et al., 2023), leading to their increasing popularity and widespread adoption in fields such as education. The AI LLM-based chatbots provide immediate answers to academic questions and act as personal virtual tutors, facilitating personalized learning support (Schei et al., 2024). The extant literature indicates that chatbots have been employed in the domain of mathematics education (Nguyen et al., 2019).

In recent years, research has been conducted into the potential benefits of using AI in early childhood and primary education settings. Language processing and machine learning are some components of AI, which can be leveraged to develop engaging, customized learning opportunities for young children (Jin, 2019). For instance, AI-powered virtual assistants can converse naturally with children and offer them tailored help and feedback by using natural language processing and machine learning algorithms that can analyze students' learning habits, modify the content, and instructional techniques accordingly to ensure that each student receives the support required to progress (Mohamed et al., 2020). However, there exists a scarcity on literature about how teachers can properly use GenAI. Thus, several recommendations that educators should consider in the implementation of GenAI in education are that teachers must be trained to use AI-based technologies to proper tailor lesson plans to age-content of students, implement data security measures together with parents to safeguard pupils' privacy, ensure that there is a balance between AI and teacher-student interaction during the lessons and use AI applications in the classroom maintaining students' engagement while fostering student' creativity, problem-solving, and curiosity (Avan & Aydinli, 2024).

In early childhood education settings, data privacy is a particular concern due to their limited capacity to comprehend the possible consequences of sharing data (Yilmaz et al., 2024). In education, AI systems frequently depend on data collection and its evaluation to customize learning experiences (Ayyıldız & Yılmaz, 2021; Holmes et al., 2019). The use of AI applications can collect children's information, which encompasses personal identifiers, learning styles, and emotions. Therefore, various strategies can be adopted to use AI and effectively protect children's privacy. These include data minimization, anonymization, pseudonymization, and local processing, which are effective ways of protecting privacy (El Emam & Arbuckle, 2013). Thus, ensuring the protection of children's data is a responsibility shared by parents and educators (Powers & Green, 2018; Yılmaz, 2021; Zilka, 2017). Moreover, a further measure that should be taken into consideration to cultivate safety-conscious environment is the training of educators in ethical use of AI (Alshammari & Singh, 2018; Johnson, 2012).

Notwithstanding the commencement of research endeavors to explore the potential of AI to enhance teaching and learning practices (George, 2023; Srinivasa et al., 2022), there exists a scarcity on literature about how teachers can adopt GenAI in primary and early childhood education settings. Therefore, there is a need for research and proposing best practices for teachers and young learners to use GenAI to support the educational process. The present chapter has therefore reviewed the use of GenAI strategies in education providing practical guidance for primary education teachers in the use of GenAI applications for mathematics education: (1) creating a lesson plan using GenAI and a mathematical problem story, (2) building assessment tools such as a rubric and content quiz, and for students (3): using an LLM-based chatbot as a personalized learning tutor for primary school students in mathematics education. Finally, some recommendations for ensuring the privacy of young children's data and recommendations for educators to use GenAI in mathematics education are provided. However, the guidance provided in this chapter can be used to customize any other subject.

Creation of a Lesson Plan with GenAI for Mathematics in Primary School

This section explores the potential of GenAI for primary school teachers to design lesson plans and personalize them according to the learners' grade and content. In addition, a comprehensive guide is provided to facilitate teachers' use of this GenAI tool in their teaching practice. In particular, the examples are proposed for the subject of mathematics but can be used to customize any subject. Many AI platforms have now been developed to facilitate the process of creating lesson plans. In this guide, the Magic School AI website has been selected to generate an AI lesson plan since it is free, open access, and offers a wide range of educational tools. To start the lesson plan creation process, it is necessary to register on the Magic School website. Thereafter, the lesson plan generator tool must be selected from the control panel, which gives access to the platform for the creation of the corresponding lesson plan, as depicted in Fig. 10.1.

To generate a lesson plan, there are several items that need to be completed within the platform. First, the grade must be indicated. Second, the objective, standard or topic must be specified. Third, additional information must be outlined. Finally, any information aligned with the previously selected standard should be provided. As demonstrated in the current example, sixth grade has been introduced in the

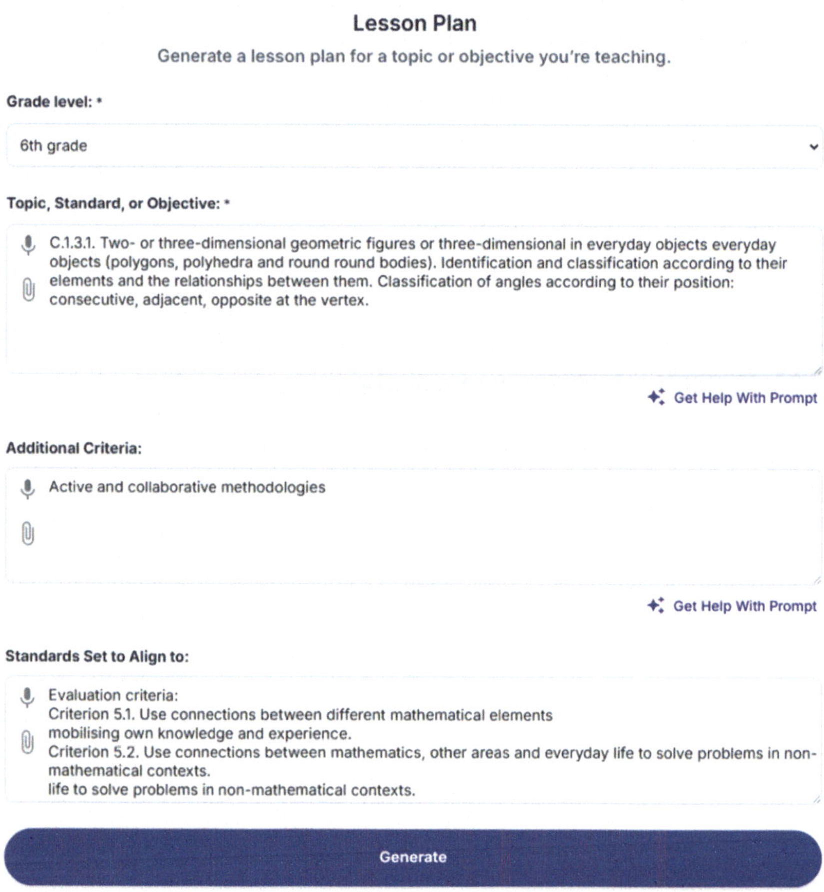

Fig. 10.1 AI-generated mathematics lesson plan

initial box. The curriculum topic was placed in the subsequent box and described as follows: 'Two- or three-dimensional geometric figures or three-dimensional in everyday objects (polygons, polyhedral, and round bodies). Identification and classification according to their elements and the relationships between them. Classification of angles according to their position: consecutive, adjacent, and opposite at the vertex. In the following section, within the 'additional criteria' section, the description of the type of methodology to be used in the lesson plan was added: 'active and collaborative methodologies'. Finally, two assessment criteria from the curriculum were selected for consideration in the assessment of the lesson. These criteria are included in the box entitled 'Set of standards to align with': 'Use connections between different mathematical elements by mobilizing their own knowledge and experiences' and, 'use the connections between mathematics, other areas, and everyday life to solve problems in non-mathematical contexts'. Incorporating the data, the GenAI platform produced the following mathematics lesson plan (see Table 10.1).

There is also another very useful GenAI feature for mathematics within Magic School, the 'Math Story Word Problems', which can be very interesting to motivate students and involve them in the proposed lesson plan with thematic mathematical problems. This tool generates a narrative that suggests problems related to the content to be covered. In this instance, the grade level and topic are identical to those in the previous example. Finally, the topic introduced as the story topic for primary school students was 'Aliens' (see Fig. 10.2). The 'Math story word problems' generated with Magic School is shown in Table 10.2.

Creation of Evaluation Instruments with GenAI for Mathematics in Primary Education

The application of AI in the creation of assessment tools for mathematics education holds considerable potential. It is imperative to ascertain the methods by which educators can personalize and adapt these assessment tools to align with learners' pedagogical requirements. This section elucidates the methodology for the construction of evaluation instruments with GenAI for mathematics in primary education, encompassing the development of assessment rubric and a content questionnaire. These instruments were designed considering the curricular content and the evaluation criteria that were previously selected in the examples presented in the first section. For the initial case study, the creation of an evaluation rubric utilizing a GenAI tool, the website Canva has been selected, given its status as a free tool. Initially, it is necessary to register and select the 'Doc' option to create a new document, and then to select the 'Magic Write' option. The following prompt was introduced to create the rubric tool: 'Create an evaluation rubric in table format (list of criteria in column and the levels in row) for the following evaluation criteria': (1) Use connections between different mathematical elements by mobilizing their own knowledge and experiences and (2) Use the connections between mathematics, other areas, and

Table 10.1 Lesson plan generated by Magic School GenAI platform

Geometric Figures in Everyday Objects
Learning objectives:
Students will be able to identify and classify two-dimensional and three-dimensional shapes, including polygons, polyhedral, and spherical bodies. Students will also be able to classify angles based on their positions: consecutive, adjacent, and opposite at the vertex
Assessments:
Students will complete a classification activity where they will identify and categorize various geometric figures using real-life objects. Additionally, a quiz assessing their understanding of angle classifications will be administered at the end of the lesson
Key points:
•Two-Dimensional Shapes: Definition and examples of polygons (triangles, quadrilaterals, among others) •Three-Dimensional Shapes: Understanding polyhedral (cubes, pyramids) and spherical bodies (spheres) •Angle Classification: Definitions and examples of consecutive, adjacent, and opposite angles •Real-Life Connections: How geometric figures are found in everyday objects (e.g. buildings, furniture, nature)
Opening:
•Begin with a short video showcasing various geometric shapes found in everyday life (e.g. buildings, furniture) •Ask students to think of an object they see every day and identify its geometric shapes •Pose the question: "What shapes do you notice around you, and how can we classify them?"
Introduction to new material:
•Discuss the definitions of two-dimensional and three-dimensional shapes, providing visual aids and physical examples •Introduce angle classifications, using diagrams on the board to illustrate each type •Anticipate the misconception that all angles in a polygon are the same; clarify that angles can vary based on the shape
Guided practice:
•Divide students into small groups and provide a mix of objects (both pictures and real items) to classify shapes •Scaffold questioning: Start with simple identification (e.g., "What shape is this?") and progress to classification (e.g. "How many vertices does this shape have?") •Monitor student performance by walking around and observing group discussions, providing feedback as necessary Independent practice: •Assign students a worksheet where they must identify and classify shapes from a series of images of everyday objects •Include a section where they must classify different types of angles from given diagrams •Set clear expectations for quiet, focused work and encourage them to use their previous group discussions to assist in their classifications
Closing:
•Hold a quick discussion where students share one new shape or angle, they learned about and where they might see it in their daily lives •Ask students to reflect on the importance of understanding shapes and angles in real-world applications

(continued)

Table 10.1 (continued)

Extension activity:
•For students who finish early, provide them with a challenge to create a poster that showcases geometric figures they find in their homes or neighborhoods, including labels and classifications for each shape
Homework:
•Assign students to take pictures of three different geometric shapes they find in their environment and write a short description of each, including its classification (2D or 3D) and any angles they can identify
Standards aligned:
Evaluation criteria: •Criterion 5.1: Use connections between different mathematical elements mobilizing own knowledge and experience •Criterion 5.2: Use connections between mathematics, other areas, and everyday life to solve problems in non-mathematical contexts

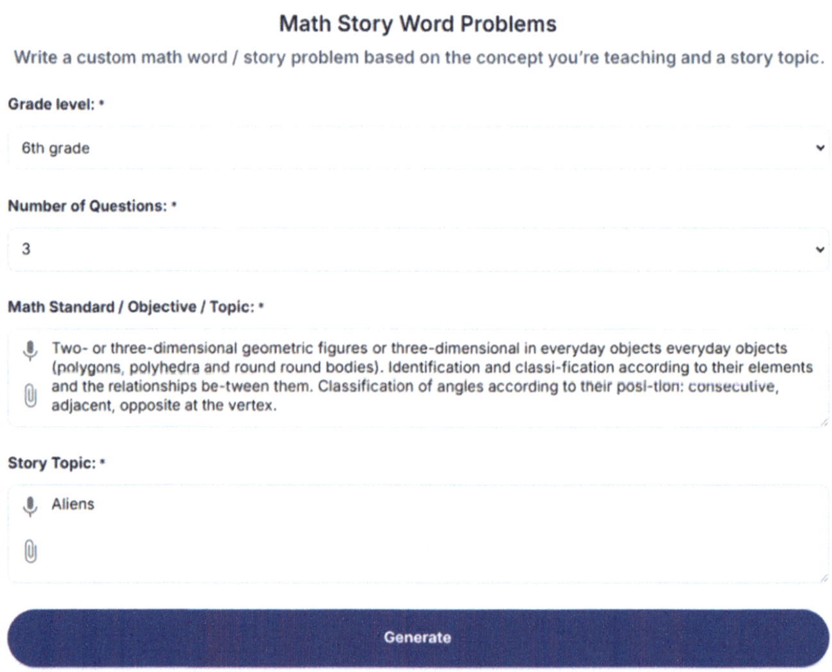

Fig. 10.2 AI-Generated mathematical Story Word Problems

Table 10.2 'Math story word problems' generated with Magic School

Alien Geometry Adventures
The alien spaceship Zeta-X has landed on Earth! Scientists notice it has a unique hexagonal base with all sides measuring 12 m each. The ship's walls rise straight up 15 m and meet at a point at the top, forming triangular faces. How many edges does this entire alien spacecraft have? Can you also identify what type of three-dimensional shape this spacecraft represents?
On Planet Geometra, alien buildings are constructed only using regular polygons. An alien architect is designing a new community center with a room that has 8 equal sides and 8 equal angles. Two adjacent walls meet at an angle, and the architect needs to know this angle measurement to ensure proper construction. What is the measure of the angle where any two adjacent walls meet in this octagonal room?
The alien species Mathematicus has discovered a mysterious crystal on their home planet. The crystal is a perfect polyhedron with 6 square faces of equal size, where three faces meet at each vertex. The length of each edge is 4 cm. If you were a scientist studying this crystal, what three-dimensional shape would you classify it as? How many vertices does this crystal have?

everyday life to solve problems in non-mathematical contexts. I need the rubric to assess at the following levels: inadequate (1 to 4 out of 10), sufficient (5 to 6 out of 10), good (6 to 7 out of 10, very good (7 to 8 out of 10), and outstanding (9 to 10 out of 10)'. Therefore, the generated rubric was designed to evaluate five levels of performance: inadequate, sufficient, good, very good, and outstanding. After entering the prompt, this GenAI tool automatically generates the rubric table to evaluate the activity (see Table 10.3). It is recommended that teachers determine the consistency of the elements involved and adapt the rubric once generated accordingly to their needs.

Lastly, for the creation of a content questionnaire with a GenAI tool, it was used as a tool within the Magic School platform, known as 'Math Spiral Review'. This feature allows teachers to generate different types of review questions tailored to each group of students by entering the grade level, the mathematical content and the number of questions required. In this example the grade level and the selected content were the same as in the previous example. Finally, it was defined to generate a total of 5 questions to create the example for the review questionnaire (see Table 10.4).

Use of LLM-Based Chatbot as a Virtual Assistant for Primary School Mathematics Students

There are promising applications in the use of LLM-based chatbots as virtual assistants for primary school mathematics students, and it would be useful to know how students can use them correctly to learn autonomously and in accordance with their pedagogical needs. As an example, the CK-12 platform was selected as an AI tool to illustrate how an LLM-based chatbot can be used as a personalized learning tutor for students in primary mathematics education. This platform is an open educational resource, free and easily accessible to teachers and students. Regardless of

Table 10.3 Rubric of evaluation generated with Canva GenAI

Performance level	Criterion 5.1	Criterion 5.2
Inadequate (1–4)	Struggles to identify connections between mathematical elements and rarely apply personal knowledge or experiences effectively	Rarely identifies or uses connections between mathematics and other areas; struggles to apply mathematical concepts to everyday problems
Sufficient (5–6)	Occasionally identifies connections with limited application of personal knowledge and experiences	Sometimes identifies connections between mathematics and other areas; demonstrates limited ability to apply concepts to everyday problems
Good (6–7)	Identifies connections between elements and sometimes uses personal knowledge and experiences to enhance understanding	Often identifies relevant connections and apply mathematical concepts to solve problems in non-mathematical contexts with some effectiveness
Very good (7–8)	Frequently identifies and utilizes connections between elements, effectively integrating personal knowledge and experiences	Frequently identifies and effectively uses connections to solve non-mathematical problems, demonstrating a strong understanding of interdisciplinary applications
Outstanding (9–10)	Consistently excels in identifying and utilizing complex connections, seamlessly integrating extensive personal knowledge and experiences for profound understanding	Consistently excels in identifying and leveraging connections across disciplines, demonstrating outstanding ability to solve complex, non-mathematical problems

the educational resources available to a student or location, the CK-12 Foundation aims to provide free access to content through digital platforms to support students' learning (CK-12, 2012). In addition, it is a user-friendly website that provides information for mathematics and science at all levels (Owens, 2016; Pradhan et al., 2023) and offers a personalized learning system that assists with user-generated materials and up-to-date resources. Additionally, a virtual chatbot assistant has been integrated, which provides detailed explanations of mathematics and science concepts, acting as a free AI tutor (helping students with homework, teaching concepts and providing step-by-step solutions to a problem). As an example of use, the web address must be first accessed. Next, the CK-12 Flexi chatbot must be selected to use the chatbot where the learner can request the detailed steps needed to get a solution to understand the concept in depth. In this example, the virtual assistant chatbot was asked to solve a step-by-step problem from the previously chosen content, and the prompt entered was as follows: I need a step-by-step solution of how to solve the degrees of the triangle that has two angles of 21 degrees and another of 121 degrees' (see Fig. 10.3). The chatbot can not only generate the result with detailed explanation, but it can also generate images providing visual support for students, which may be a valuable tool for facilitating the comprehension of mathematical concepts.

Table 10.4 Review questions generated with Magic School 'Math spiral review'

Geometric Figures and Angles Review
1. Look around your classroom and identify three different three-dimensional shapes. For each shape: • Write its name • Count the number of faces • Count the number of edges • Count the number of vertices
2. In the figure below, angles A and B share a common vertex. If angle A measures 45° and angle B measures 45°, are these angles: • Adjacent angles • Consecutive angles • Opposite angles at the vertex • Explain your reasoning
3. Draw a regular hexagon and identify: • The number of sides • Three pairs of parallel sides • Two pairs of consecutive angles • Label all the angles using capital letters
4. A cereal box represents a rectangular prism. List: • The number of faces that are rectangles • The number of faces that are squares (if any) • The total number of edges • Whether any faces are adjacent to each other
5. Look at the corners of your desk or table. The three edges that meet at each corner form three angles. Are these angles: • Adjacent • Consecutive • Perpendicular • Explain how you know and measure one of these angles with a protractor

Discussion

Diverse studies revealed that GenAI may have great potential in educational field. Thus, several GenAI tools have been proposed along with this chapter to support teachers and students. In particular, the examples are proposed for the subject of mathematics education but can be customized to apply for any subject. The use of AI in primary education has been the subject of research (Hwang, 2022), concluding that the use of AI has a positive effect on the performance of primary school students in mathematics. Also, AI technologies have been shown to have a favorable impact on students' perspectives of the mathematics learning process (Canonigo, 2024), revealing positive outcomes, including increased teaching effectiveness, student engagement, and comprehension of complex ideas (Egara & Mosimege, 2024). In this chapter, the process of creating a lesson plan using GenAI tools for primary mathematics education was introduced, which can serve as a practical guide for teachers in early education settings. As previously mentioned, AI is capable to instantly creating

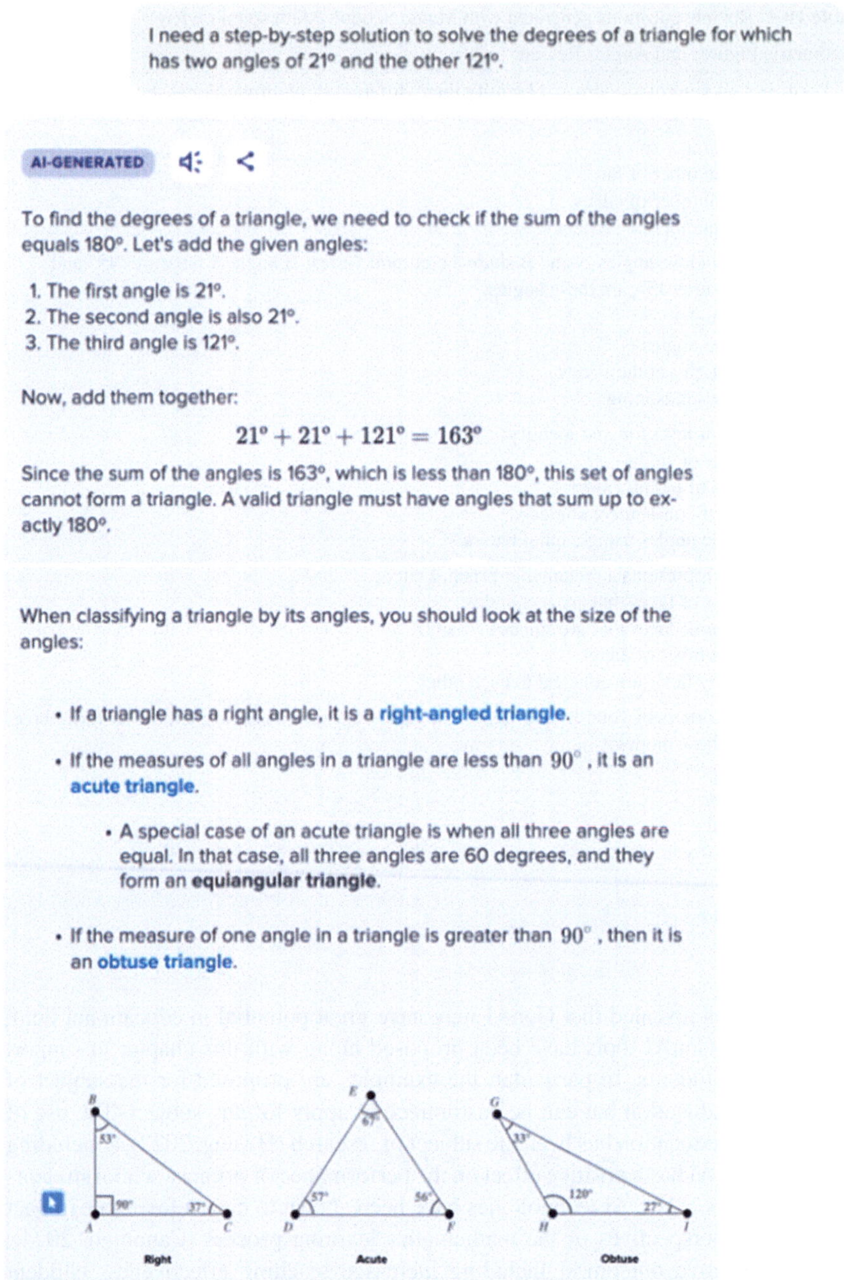

Fig. 10.3 CK-12 Flexi chatbot assistant

customized learning materials (Bernacki et al., 2020; Macfadyen & Dawson, 2010) with increased teachers' effectiveness (Hasibuan & Azizah, 2023; Pesovski et al., 2024). These is consistent with previous studies how GenAI can be used to create a lesson plan based on the learning objectives and educational content with the assistance of GenAI, which could help teachers create instructional materials instantly (Holmes & Miao, 2024; Pesovski et al., 2024). Moreover, utilizing lesson plans created with AI has demonstrated notable enhancement in academic achievement (Karaman, 2024). Here, it was proposed that GenAI can be utilized in the creation of evaluation instruments, as evidenced by extant literature which demonstrates the capacity of AI to facilitate the generation of assessment instruments (Al Braiki et al., 2020; Fernández-Sánchez et al., 2025). However, a paucity of specific studies on the creation of mathematics rubrics in primary education has been found. In addition, the use of LLM-based chatbot has been proposed, as according to the body of existing research, chatbots have been used in the field of mathematics education (Nguyen et al., 2019). Nevertheless, only a limited number of studies have addressed how chatbots can be used in primary mathematics education. The present work offers concrete guidance, as well as a detailed explanation of how students could benefit from it. Moreover, there is a scarcity literature on how GenAI can be properly used in education. Thus, this chapter provides educators with recommendations on how to implement AI in education and use GenAI effectively while maintaining student engagement and balancing AI and human interaction. Finally, the privacy of children's data is a particular concern when using AI. Various methods have been proposed to protect their privacy, such as local processing, anonymization, pseudonymization, and data reduction (El Emam & Arbuckle, 2013). Furthermore, both educators and parents are responsible for ensuring the protection of children's data (Powers & Green, 2018; Yılmaz, 2021; Zilka, 2017). In conclusion, despite the growing focus on AI in recent years, research into its application and on best practices for mathematics teachers and students in primary education remains limited. The present chapter thus seeks to address this research gap by offering teachers and students a practical guide to generating GenAI educational resources, while ensuring the ethical use of AI and the protection of children's data.

Conclusions

The integration of GenAI into the field of mathematics education in primary education presents potential benefits for teachers and students that need to be further investigated. In this chapter, diverse possibilities of using GenAI for creating lesson plans and evaluation instruments were examined. It also provides a detailed guide for students on the use of a chatbot teaching assistant for learning mathematics in primary education. Moreover, it aims to facilitate educational agents, teachers, and students, with a practical guide to use GenAI educational resources. In addition, this chapter includes recommendations to ethically use GenAI and to guarantee children data privacy in educational settings. As demonstrated in this chapter, GenAI models have the capacity to assist teachers in the creation of lesson plans and didactic resources customized according to the objectives, contents, and methodologies to be applied. In addition, the GenAI tools allow teachers to create instruments to assess students' performance. Finally, the use of chatbots allows students to learn autonomously, providing explanations and offering visual support for difficulties students may encounter during learning. This chapter has several implications; it provides a solid foundation on which future research in this area can be built, thus paving the way for exploring new possibilities and improving education. However, the successful application of GenAI in education requires adequate training for teachers and learners. The inherent limitations of the chapter are clearly delineated by its narrow focus on specific practices, as the conclusions and practices proposed in this chapter are based on the use of a restricted selection of only three GenAI tools. In future research, it would be advisable to compare a larger number of GenAI tools to be applied to mathematics education. In addition, it would be of interest to conduct research to find out the perceptions of students and teachers on the use of AI to create lesson plans, assessment instruments, and the use of virtual chatbot assistants as tools to support educational agents in teaching–learning practices. Ultimately, the application of GenAI for mathematics in primary education and the continuous adoption of AI-based educational solutions promise to transform the future of learning and teaching in the digital age that needs to be addressed. Finally, it is imperative that educators develop a comprehensive understanding of the potential and limitations of AI before integrating it into the educational context (Su & Yang, 2023).

Implications for Practice and Ethics:

Educators who wish to use GenAI in their teaching should consider the following recommendations for proper use:

(1) Train teachers in the use of AI: educators must learn how to use AI-based tools effectively to generate specific and age-appropriate content for students.
(2) Establish children's data security measures: teachers and parents must be aware of the ethical use of AI and have a shared responsibility to protect students' personal information.
(3) Balance the use of AI with human interaction: teachers should supervise the use of AI and ensure a balance between teacher-student interaction during lessons.
(4) Engage students with GenAI applications: the AI use in education should encourage students' participation, curiosity, and problem-solving thinking skills.

Ethics Statements

This chapter was conceived and written entirely by the authors without the assistance of artificial intelligence tools or generative technologies.

Acknowledgements This work has been 85% co-financed by the European Union, the European Regional Development Fund and the Regional Government of Extremadura, the Managing Authority and the Ministry of Finance, through project IB24004. A.I.M.I. thanks the Ministry of

Universities of the Government of Spain for the scholarship of her FPU predoctoral contract (FPU22/04217).

References

Abukmeil, M., Ferrari, S., Genovese, A., Piuri, V., & Scotti, F. (2021). A survey of unsupervised generative models for exploratory data analysis and representation learning. *ACM Computing Surveys, 54*(5), 1–40.

Al Braiki, B., Harous, S., Zaki, N., & Alnajjar, F. (2020). Artificial intelligence in education and assessment methods. *Bulletin of Electrical Engineering and Informatics, 9*(5), 1998–2007.

Alazzam, B. A., Alkhatib, M., & Shaalan, K. (2023). Artificial intelligence chatbots: A survey of classical versus deep machine learning techniques. *Information Sciences Letters, 12*(4), 1217–1233.

Alshammari, R., & Singh, D. (2018). A framework to integrate cybersecurity into education. *Journal of Theoretical and Applied Information Technology, 96*(15), 4910–4922.

Avan, Ç., & Aydinli, B. (2024). STEM and AI integration in early childhood: First steps for future scientists. In B. Aydınlı, B. D. Altunoğlu (Eds.), *Transforming early childhood education: Technology, sustainability, and foundational skills for the 21st century* (pp. 159–173). Özgür Publications.

Ayyıldız, P., & Yılmaz, A. (2021). Putting things in perspective: The COVID-19 pandemic period, distance education and beyond. *Anemon Muşalparslan Üniversitesi Sosyal Bilimler Dergisi, 9*(6), 1631–1650.

Bernacki, M. L., Chavez, M. M., & Uesbeck, P. M. (2020). Predicting achievement and providing support before STEM majors begin to fail. *Computers & Education, 158*, Article 103999.

Canonigo, A. M. (2024). Levering AI to enhance students' conceptual understanding and confidence in mathematics. *Journal of Computer Assisted Learning, 40*(6), 3215–3229.

CK-12. (2012). CK-12. https://www.ck12info.org/wp-content/uploads/2012/10/ck12-vision-document.pdf

Coccoli, M., Maresca, P., & Stanganelli, L. (2016). Cognitive computing in education. *Journal of E-learning and Knowledge Society, 12*(2).

Egara, F. O., & Mosimege, M. (2024). Exploring the integration of artificial intelligence-based ChatGPT into mathematics instruction: Perceptions, challenges, and implications for educators. *Education Sciences, 14*(7), 742.

El-Emam, K., & Arbuckle, L. (2013). *Anonymizing health data: Case studies and methods to get you started*. O'Reilly Media, Inc.

Fernández-Sánchez, A., Lorenzo-Castiñeiras, J. J., & Sánchez-Bello, A. (2025). Navigating the future of pedagogy: The integration of AI tools in developing educational assessment rubrics. *European Journal of Education, 60*(1), Article e12826.

Fügener, A., Grahl, J., Gupta, A., & Ketter, W. (2022). Cognitive challenges in human–artificial intelligence collaboration: Investigating the path toward productive delegation. *Information Systems Research, 33*(2), 678–696.

George, A. S. (2023). Preparing students for an AI-driven world: Rethinking curriculum and pedagogy in the age of artificial intelligence. *Partners Universal Innovative Research Publication, 1*(2), 112–136.

Gui, J., Sun, Z., Wen, Y., Tao, D., & Ye, J. (2021). A review on generative adversarial networks: Algorithms, theory, and applications. *IEEE Transactions on Knowledge and Data Engineering, 35*(4), 3313–3332.

Hasibuan, R., & Azizah, A. (2023). Analyzing the potential of artificial intelligence (AI) in personalizing learning to foster creativity in students. *Enigma in Education, 1*(1), 6–10.

Holmes, W., Bialik, M., & Fadel, C. (2019). *Artificial Intelligence in Education: Promises and implications for teaching and learning*. Center for Curriculum Redesign.
Holmes, W., & Miao, F. (2024). *Guidance for generative AI in education and research*. UNESCO.
Hwang, S. (2022). Examining the effects of artificial intelligence on elementary students' mathematics achievement: A meta-analysis. *Sustainability, 14*(20), 13185.
Jeong, J. S., & González-Gómez, D. (2025a). AI-driven chatbots in flipped-classroom mathematics education: Enhancing learning achievement and self-efficacy in pre-service primary teachers. In S. Papadakis (Ed.), *Teaching with Artificial Intelligence. A guide for primary and elementary educators*. Routledge.
Jeong, J. S., & González-Gómez, D. (2025b). Examining the impact of flipped classroom learning (FCL) and gamified-flipped classroom learning (G-FCL) on students' attitudes and emotions toward learning in a university course. *Active Learning in Higher Education*, 14697874251347184.
Jin, Y. (2019). Artificial intelligence in education: A review. *International Journal of Artificial Intelligence in Education, 29*(1), 1–31.
Johnson, D. G. (2012). *Computer ethics*. Prentice Hall.
Karaman, M. R. (2024). Are lesson plans created by ChatGPT more effective? An experimental study. *International Journal of Technology in Education, 7*(1), 107–127.
Khosravi, H., Shafie, M. R., Hajiabadi, M., Raihan, A. S., & Ahmed, I. (2024). Chatbots and ChatGPT: A bibliometric analysis and systematic review of publications in Web of Science and Scopus databases. *International Journal of Data Mining, Modelling and Management, 16*(2), 113–147.
Lin, C. C., Huang, A. Y., & Yang, S. J. (2023). A review of ai-driven conversational chatbots implementation methodologies and challenges (1999–2022). *Sustainability, 15*(5), 4012.
Macfadyen, L. P., & Dawson, S. (2010). Mining LMS data to develop an "early warning system" for educators: A proof of concept. *Computers & Education, 54*(2), 588–599.
Mohamed, A. M., Ibrahim, A. H., & El-Metwally, E. M. (2020). AI-based personalized learning systems for children: A review. *International Journal of Intelligent Engineering and Systems, 13*(2), 102–114.
Nguyen, H. D., Pham, V. T., Tran, D. A., & Le, T. T. (2019). Intelligent tutoring chatbot for solving mathematical problems in High-school. In *Proceedings of the 11th international conference on knowledge and systems engineering (KSE)* (pp. 1–6).
Owens, A. D. (2016). Review: The CK-12 foundation. *The American Biology Teacher, 78*(1), 83–83.
Pérez, J. Q., Daradoumis, T., & Puig, J. M. M. (2020). Rediscovering the use of chatbots in education: A systematic literature review. *Computer Applications in Engineering Education, 28*(6), 1549–1565.
Pesovski, I., Santos, R., Henriques, R., & Trajkovik, V. (2024). Generative AI for customizable learning experiences. *Sustainability, 16*(7), 3034.
Powers, J., & Green, M. F. (2018). Principals' perspectives on social media in schools. *NASSP Bulletin, 102*(4), 279–292.
Pradhan, S., Zam, S., & Zangmo, Y. (2023). How can ck-12 (an open educational resource, oer) enhance the attitude and academic performance of class vii students in science? *Journal of Educational Action Research, 1*(7), 1–16.
Sabzalieva, E., & Valentini, A. (2023). *ChatGPT and artificial intelligence in higher education: Quick start guide*. UNESCO. https://unesdoc.unesco.org/ark:/48223/pf0000385146
Schei, O. M., Møgelvang, A., & Ludvigsen, K. (2024). Perceptions and use of AI chatbots among students in higher education: A scoping review of empirical studies. *Education Sciences, 14*(8), 922.
Srinivasa, K. G., Kurni, M., & Saritha, K. (2022). Harnessing the power of AI to education. In K. G. Srinivasa, M. Kurni, & K. Saritha (Eds.), *Learning, teaching, and assessment methods for contemporary learners: Pedagogy for the digital generation* (pp. 311–342). Springer.
Stefanova, T., & Georgiev, S. (2024). Possibilities for using AI in mathematics education. *Mathematics and Education in Mathematics, 53*, 117–125.

Su, J., & Yang, W. (2023). Unlocking the power of ChatGPT: A framework for applying generative AI in education. *ECNU Review of Education, 6*(3), 355–366.

Tlili, A., Shehata, B., Adarkwah, M. A., Bozkurt, A., Hickey, D. T., Huang, R., & Agyemang, B. (2023). What if the devil is my guardian angel: ChatGPT as a case study of using chatbots in education. *Smart Learning Environments, 10*(1), 15.

Usluoğlu, B., & Toptaş, V. (2025). Increasing mathematical curiosity using simple AI instruction in primary school. *Journal of Innovation and Research in Primary Education, 4*(1), 42–50.

Yang, G. -Z., Bellingham, J., Dupont, P. E., Fischer, P., Floridi, L., Full, R., Jacobstein, N., Kumar, V., McNutt, M., Merrifield, R., Nelson, B. J., Scassellati, B., Taddeo, M., Taylor, R., Veloso, M., Wang, Z. L., & Wood, R. (2018). The grand challenges of Science Robotics. *Science Robotics, 3*(14), eaar7650.

Yigci, D., Eryilmaz, M., Yetisen, A. K., Tasoglu, S., & Ozcan, A. (2024). Large language model-based chatbots in higher education. *Advanced Intelligent System, 7*(3), 2400429.

Yılmaz, A. (2021). Fen bilimleri eğitimi kapsamında uzaktan eğitimde kalite standartları ve paydaş görüşleri (Quality standards and stakeholder opinions in distance learning within the scope of science education). *Atatürk Üniversitesi Kazım Karabekir Eğitim Fakültesi Dergisi, 42*, 26–50.

Yilmaz, A., Nacar, M., & Uysal, G. (2024). Ethical use of Artificial Intelligence applications in early childhood education. In B. Aydınlı, B. D. Altunoğlu (Eds.), *Transforming early childhood education: Technology, sustainability, and foundational skills for the 21st century* (pp. 159–173). Özgür Publications.

Zawacki-Richter, O., Marín, V. I., Bond, M., & Gouverneur, F. (2019). Systematic review of research on artificial intelligence applications in higher education—where are the educators? *International Journal of Educational Technology in Higher Education, 16*(1), 1–27.

Zilka, G. C. (2017). Awareness of eSafety and potential online dangers among children and teenagers. *Journal of Information Technology Education: Research, 16*, 319–338.

Chapter 11
Empowering Early Educators and Learners: Integrating AI in Mathematics Education

Xinyue Li and Rachad Zaki

Abstract Artificial Intelligence (AI) has evolved from a novel idea in education to a powerful element in teaching and learning. However, effectively integrating AI tools into school contexts remains challenging for many educators, especially in early years education. This chapter addresses these challenges by providing ethical, responsible, and practical strategies to help early years educators navigate obstacles and seize opportunities presented by such new technologies. We focus particularly on mathematics education, which poses unique challenges for adopting large language models (LLMs) due to various technical and pedagogical factors. We present a series of high-level summaries outlining innovative AI applications that could facilitate teaching in early childhood education, such as adaptive learning and personalised education. To help educators understand real-world applications of responsible AI use, we present a list of use cases and classroom activity examples that focus on practical strategies for integrating AI into early childhood mathematics education. We conclude by discussing several ethical considerations for young children, including screen time, age-appropriate content, and critical media literacy.

Keywords Artificial intelligence in education (AIED) · Digital technology · Personalisation · Scaffolding · Technology uses in mathematics education

Introduction

The origin of artificial intelligence (AI) can be traced back to the mid-twentieth century when pioneers such as Alan Turing and Marvin Minsky laid the groundwork for the discipline. AI in education (AIED) is not that recent either; it is not something that emerged only after the public release of ChatGPT. For instance, the International

X. Li (✉) · R. Zaki
Cambridge University Press & Assessment, University of Cambridge, Cambridge, UK
e-mail: xinyue.li@cambridge.org

R. Zaki
e-mail: rachad.zaki@cambridge.org

S. Papadakis (ed.), *AI Applications in Preschool and Primary Education*, Advances in Artificial Intelligence in Education 5, https://doi.org/10.1007/978-3-032-17190-0_11

Journal of Artificial Intelligence in Education (IJAIED) has, to April 2025, already published 35 volumes, with the earliest issue dating back to 1989. In fact, generative pre-trained transformer (GPT) models have existed for a few years, with GPT-1 being introduced in 2018, but it was the introduction of ChatGPT in 2022 that provided users with the opportunity to interact directly with a GPT (e.g., by asking questions and requesting specific tasks), thus sparking heated discussions about its use in many aspects of our daily lives (Li et al., 2024).

The debates surrounding ChatGPT have sparked significant discussions on the ethical and responsible use of generative AI (GenAI). In response, several institutions have developed guidance and policies and are continuing to refine and update them. In the UK, for example, University College London (UCL) published in February 2023 the first of a series of student briefings, "Engaging with AI in your education and assessment", aimed at helping students understand the effective and ethical use of AI tools. Cambridge University Press launched the first AI research ethics policy in 2023, applicable to research papers, books, and other scholarly works. Additionally, the Russell Group (an association of 24 leading research-intensive universities including the University of Cambridge, the University of Oxford, and UCL) released its principles on the use of GenAI tools in education on 4th July 2023.

Higher education institutions and publishers are leading the way potentially because they are under time pressure to address academic integrity, particularly in relation to AI-generated assignments, essays and research. While the use of GenAI is increasingly regulated in higher education, and although certain entities are attempting to also include K-12 teachers and students (e.g., UNESCO, 2024a, 2024b), there is a scarcity in universally applicable frameworks and guidelines for use in early years education. This chapter aims to help address this gap. Focusing specifically on mathematics education, we explore innovative applications of AI to enhance early childhood education, along with use cases that demonstrate the ethical and responsible use of AI in this context. We conclude by highlighting key concerns and challenges in the field.

The Potential of AI in Mathematics Education

One of the key strengths of AI lies in its adaptability to diverse audiences, both within and beyond educational contexts. In educational settings specifically, AI tools can be designed or trained to accommodate a range of factors, including students' age, educational level, language of instruction, cultural background and social environment. For young learners, for instance, gamification has proven to be a particularly effective strategy for enhancing engagement and supporting learning outcomes. This includes the use of AI-integrated toys and robotic kits (Kewalramani et al., 2021), which can provide interactive, age-appropriate learning experiences tailored to early developmental needs. Moreover, AI can enhance the learning of languages; promote curiosity through experimentation; and also facilitate self-expression, leading to the discovery of learners' creativity (Berson & Berson, 2024). In the context of mathematics, there has been considerable speculation about AI models' ability to successfully solve mathematical problems (Garisto, 2022). While strong mathematical capabilities and reasoning skills are prerequisites for AI tools to effectively support mathematics teaching and learning, they do not necessarily guarantee a meaningful or effective educational experience.

In this section, we present findings from a systematic literature review that provides insights into the current landscape of AI-assisted mathematics education. These findings inform the discussions that follow on conversational AI and chatbots, AI-powered adaptive learning platforms, the integration of AI with Augmented Reality (AR) and Virtual Reality (VR), and the use of AI for early diagnostics.

A Systematic Literature Review

Mixed results are beginning to emerge regarding the effectiveness of GenAI tutoring in mathematics. Some researchers have found that while both safeguarded (with knowledge of correct solutions, student mistakes, and instructions to not give students direct answers) and unsafeguarded versions of GPT-4 improved students' immediate performance in mathematics, the version without safeguards negatively impacted later exam performance by 17%; in addition, further analysis suggested that students were using GPT-4 as a shortcut, frequently requesting answers without engaging in meaningful constructive dialogue (Bastani et al., 2024).

AI tools could help teachers with the design of lessons, ensuring that content is suitable for the students and that the material is engaging. However, research comparing pre-service teachers' responses to hints generated by educators versus those generated by GPT-4 revealed mixed preferences: educator-generated hints were preferred for their use of visuals, while GPT-4's hints were preferred for being more detailed and comprehensive (Gattupalli et al., 2023).

To establish an understanding of the landscape of AI-assisted early childhood mathematics education, we conducted a systematic literature review using the Web of Science database. The search was performed using the following query: TS = ("artificial intelligence" OR AI) AND TS = ("early childhood" OR "primary school" OR "elementary education") AND TS = ("mathematics education" OR "maths education"). This returned seven results. Only one of these research studies, which presented findings from an empirical study involving Year 1 students from a primary school in England (Rumbelow & Coles, 2024), is directly relevant to the focus of the present chapter. In their study, the researchers challenged primary school students with a prototype AI-based object-recognition app to identify Cuisenaire rods placed on a tabletop. However, their study mainly focused on the technical design of the child–rods–app–task system, rather than on the mathematical learning outcomes.

We then used the following query to explore the topic in a broader context: TS = ("artificial intelligence" OR AI) AND TS = ("mathematics education" OR "math education" OR "maths education" OR "mathematics teaching and learning" OR "maths teaching and learning"). This returned 122 results. Given the fast-paced evolution of AI technologies, we believe that focusing on recent literature would allow us to reflect the tools, practices, and applications most relevant to today's educators. Therefore, we limited the publications to those published between 2FF022 (when ChatGPT was introduced) and 2025 to highlight the emerging trends in AI-assisted mathematics education. This level of refinement returned 93 results. As we scanned the abstracts of these studies, we noticed that not all of them were focused on educational contexts. Therefore, we further refined the results by "Research Areas" to include only "Education Educational Research", which returned 65 results, and we reviewed all of these (N = 65). Out of the 65 publications, one article appeared twice in the search results, and six articles were not relevant to the focus of the present chapter, so 58 publications were reviewed in depth (N = 58).

As shown in Table 11.1, the majority of the studies are empirical (65.5%, N = 38), followed by literature reviews (29.3%, N = 17) (e.g., Awang et al., 2025; bin Mohamed et al., 2022). Although not all research studies have focused on specific educational levels, it seems that higher education (N = 10) (e.g., Nikolova, 2024) and secondary/high/middle school education (N = 9) (e.g., Egara & Mosimege, 2024) are the most frequently studied educational levels. One study, which focused on the context of the Philippines, used the term "Basic Education" (Magat & Sangalang, 2024), and we have retained this original description. Additionally, three articles used the more general term "K-12", which we have also adopted as is. It is important to clarify that only two empirical studies focused on preservice level, and both of them focused on teachers' perspectives. Only a limited number of studies focused on one or several specific AI tools, with ChatGPT being the most frequently studied (N = 14) (e.g., Egara & Mosimege, 2024). It is important to note that some researchers examined multiple tools within a single study (e.g., Canonigo, 2024; Torres-Peña et al., 2024); therefore, the numbers in the AI Tools section of Table 11.1 reflect the number of times these tools were studied, not the number of publications.

It is clear that the use of AI in early childhood mathematics education remains an under-researched field based on our systematic literature review. We believe that one of the key reasons for this might be early childhood educators' limited AI literacy, lack of confidence in their competencies, and concerns about infrastructure and privacy, as well as uncertainty around pedagogically sound applications for young learners, as demonstrated by other researchers (Kölemen & Yıldırım, 2025).

Our review found that conversational AI and chatbots are the most commonly studied applications of AI tools in the existing literature. In addition, AI-powered adaptive learning platforms, the integration of AI with Augmented Reality (AR) and Virtual Reality (VR), and the use of AI for diagnostic purposes also show significant potential to enhance the educational landscape. Each of these areas is briefly discussed in the following subsections.

It is important to note that, due to time constraints, we had to prioritise the systematic literature review to using one specific database as well as a limited number of grey literature resources. While this approach allowed for a more focused and manageable review process, future research could benefit from a broader database search and the

Table 11.1 Literature Review—summary

Theme	Amount
Type of Publication	
Literature Review	17
Empirical Research	38
Workshop Report	1
Technical Solutions (e.g., platforms, tools)	2
Educational Level	
Preservice (e.g., PSTs)	2
Primary/Elementary School	5
Secondary/High/Middle School	9
Higher Education	10
Basic Education (in Philippines)	1
K-12	3
AI Tools	
Intelligent Tutoring System (ITS)	3
ChatGPT	14
Photomath	2
Snatchbot	1
MathGPT, Gemini & Wolfram Alpha	1
GeoGebra	1
Blockplay.ai	1
AIEDN AI Assistant	1
Chatbot (name not specified)	2

inclusion of a diverse range of grey literature to ensure an even more comprehensive understanding of the topic.

Conversational AI and Chatbots

An AI chatbot's ability to provide personalised and differentiated responses enables teachers to support the individualised needs of each student; its interactive and conversational design also encourages the development of inquiry and critical questioning skills (Bettayeb et al., 2024; Labadze et al., 2023). Moreover, chatbots can continuously reinforce important concepts through reminding leaners of key information. They also provide a more relaxed environment, hence encouraging shy students in the learning process and assisting in building their confidence, which is also emphasised through immediate feedback. Furthermore, chatbots are easily accessible to students, including at a young age, which removes the pressure of the need to study at a specific time and location.

Several online learning platforms have introduced GenAI chatbots that could serve as mathematics tutors (e.g., Khanmigo). Some of these chatbots are student-facing and are usually operated without a professional teacher (i.e., a school teacher) directly involved in the student-AI interaction (although some teachers may be involved in the design and development of the AI chatbot), which means that students often interact directly with the GenAI conversational agent; as a result, these tools rely on the safeguards that technology developers put in place to prevent inappropriate or harmful interactions.

When it comes to mathematics, which can induce anxiety for learners from an early age (Carey et al., 2019), the interaction with a chatbot can help reduce stress to a certain extent, as it removes the fear of asking questions in a classroom setting and the potential anxiety about peer reactions. AI chatbots can support learners in various ways (Li et al., 2025), including serving as digitised tutoring companions that are always accessible and ready to interact with learners across different contexts. This support can help avoid potentially distressing experiences, such as the fear of being judged or criticised for asking a "basic" question, that some learners may associate with traditional classroom environments. Ultimately, this can contribute to the improvement of numeracy skills as an initial step, with potential benefits extending further. It is important to emphasise that the role of the teacher should never be eclipsed; ongoing monitoring of the interactions between students and chatbots, as well as the outcomes of those interactions, remains essential.

AI-Powered Adaptive Learning Platforms

In 1956, Gordon Pask designed the first Self Adaptive Keyboard Instructor (SAKI) for trainee keyboard operators (Pask, 1982). What set SAKI apart from other earlier teaching machines was its ability to adjust learning tasks based on each user's individual performance, using a dynamic probabilistic model that continuously updated to reflect the user's progress (Holmes et al., 2019). During the 1960s and 1970s, many Computer-Assisted Instruction (CAI) systems were developed, with an early influential example being PLATO (Programmed Logic for Automatic Teaching Operations) (Holt, 1983), in which students accessed materials via remote terminals, allowing a thousand students working at the same time.

Jaime Carbonell is often recognised for the first implementation of AI techniques in CAI, introducing a system called SCHOLAR, which was designed to allow a student to review their knowledge of the geography of South America (Carbonell, 1970). SCHOLAR is often considered the first example of Intelligent Tutoring Systems (ITS). ITSs provide step-by-step instructions personalised for each student (Alkhatlan & Kalita, 2019) and are considered one of the most common applications of AI in education (Holmes et al., 2019).

One of the most impactful applications of ITS lies in AI-powered adaptive learning platforms, such as Khan Academy Kids. These systems adjust instructional content and difficulty in real time based on a child's performance, creating individualised learning trajectories that support all learners, from those who are struggling through to those who are advanced. The adoption of adaptive learning technologies is reshaping the traditional role of teachers; rather than serving solely as the main providers of knowledge and information, teachers are increasingly taking on the roles of facilitators and guides, supporting students as they navigate personalised learning pathways (Abrasid, 2024).

In mathematics education, many platforms with AI-powered features are available to support both students and teachers. These include ALEKS, Desmos, Duolingo, GeoGebra, Khan Academy, Maple Calculator, Mathway, Microsoft Math Solver, Photomath, Socratic (its functionality was merged into Google Lens in 2025), Symbolab, Wolfram Alpha, etc. Many of these platforms offer content specifically designed for early learners. Several are inherently adaptive in design, enabling personalised learning experiences and more targeted instructional approaches, while also offering versatility and flexibility. Interactivity is a key feature of these platforms, helping to sustain student engagement and motivation. By encouraging learners to persist in problem-solving, these tools can foster perseverance and a genuine enjoyment of learning.

If a student is asked to identify a shape on a screen, for example, they can click on it, rotate it, and ask questions about it which the system will answer immediately, activating another key feature which is direct feedback. If a student fails to provide the correct answer, the system can suggest a question at a lower level of difficulty before prompting them to try again. The use of virtual manipulatives has been proven to be widely effective for early learners, even more than concrete ones in certain cases (Shurr et al., 2021). When it comes to number sense—for example, if a student is asked to count to 10 or 100—the system can assist them through real-time support such as number recognition, identification of errors, and adaptation to the student's individual learning pace and needs. In addition, gamification and a well-designed reward system can serve as features that engage students and motivate them to persist with challenging questions, thereby boosting their self-confidence. These benefits are often delivered through realistic simulations and virtual experiments adapted to each student's profile.

AI with Augmented Reality, Virtual Reality

Many research studies have demonstrated that AR and VR tools can effectively improve learning motivation and engagement, enhance spatial reasoning and visualisation skills, and have a positive impact on long-term memory retention (e.g., Bertrand et al., 2024; Li & Zaki, 2024). For instance, AR-powered mathematics apps allow children to interact with two-dimensional (2D) and three-dimensional (3D) digital content, offering benefits in understanding spatial data; therefore, they can be effectively used as a supplement to traditional curriculum materials (Billinghurst & Duenser, 2012). It is believed that the integration of AR and VR in adaptive learning could make seemly abstract ideas more concrete and understandable for early years learners (Abrasid, 2024). Because of AI's potential to offer real-time diagnostics and support personalised learning pathways, students' diverse and individual needs could be catered to. When thoughtfully combined with the immersive capabilities of AR and VR, these technologies present a powerful opportunity to create more engaging, adaptive, and immersive mathematics learning experiences for young learners. However, the integration of AI with AR and VR in early childhood mathematics education remains underdeveloped and under-researched at the time of writing this chapter; more research studies and collaboration between educators, developers, and researchers will be essential in shaping tools that not only enhance students' mathematical understanding but also support meaningful, student-centred teaching practices.

AI for Early Diagnostics

AI can support early years teachers by streamlining assessment and progress monitoring. AI-powered platforms that offer real-time analytics can provide valuable insights into student performance, helping teachers identify learning trends, tailor instruction, and offer timely support from early on. Moreover, AI can assist in the early identification of potential learning challenges, allowing for prompt interventions tailored to individual student needs which can also be detected through AI-driven analysis (Strielkowski et al., 2024; Walter, 2024).

Moreover, certain tools can assist in screening and addressing specific learning disorders, such as dyslexia (Derbyshire, 2023) and dyscalculia (Bhushan et al., 2024), thereby helping students manage and overcome these challenges. The data-driven approach underpinning AI enables the identification of patterns that may be easily overlooked by humans, thereby leveraging teachers' ability to make informed decisions based on students' individual learning needs.

Ethical and Responsible Use of AI in Mathematics Education

In mathematics education, AI tools offer powerful opportunities to support teaching and learning, but they must be used in ways that are transparent, inclusive, and pedagogically sound. In this section, we begin with strategies for creating effective prompts for teachers, followed by approaches to assessment and progress monitoring. We then look at how to build AI literacy in simple terms and highlight the importance of professional development, empowering both students and educators to understand and critically engage with these tools with confidence and ethical awareness.

Creating Effective Prompts

In the field of AIED, one critical skill teachers and students need to develop is the ability to create effective instructions for the AI model to generate content; a practice known as prompt engineering. The OpenAI Platform (n.d.) provides six strategies for getting better results: "Write clear instructions", "Provide reference text", "Split complex tasks into simpler subtasks", "Give the model time to 'think'", "Use external tools", and "Test changes systematically". In addition, there are four main areas to consider when constructing an effective prompt (Google, 2024, p. 2):

Persona; *Task*; ***Context***; <u>Format</u>.

Here is an example:

You are an enthusiastic early childhood teacher who is passionate about making mathematics fun and interactive for young children. You believe in hands-on activities that help children grasp fundamental mathematics concepts through play. *Your task is to design a mathematics activity for a group of 4-year-old children that introduces them to the concept of shapes: specifically circles, squares, and triangles.* ***The children in your group are just beginning to recognise and identify shapes. They enjoy using manipulatives like blocks, clay, and drawing tools. The classroom is set up with plenty of space for movement and exploration, and you have access to large paper and markers***. <u>Create a detailed activity plan that includes an introduction to shapes, hands-on activities for exploring these shapes, and a closing activity to reinforce learning</u>.

It is important to note that while the four suggested areas should be covered to create effective prompts, they do not need to be addressed in four separate sentences or sections, nor is there a requirement to follow a specific order (see Sect. 11.4 for classroom examples).

Assessment and Progress Monitoring

AI can be leveraged in various aspects of assessment, from the design of test items to automated marking and feedback provision, and this has proven to be a positive experience for educators (Ciampa et al., 2025). With emerging technologies, assessment is evolving not only in terms of content but also in the way it is administered. Features such as speech recognition, touch screen capabilities, and adaptive testing modes are now being integrated to move beyond the traditional static model, particularly in formative and continuous assessment contexts. For instance, if a student advans with an addition or multiplication question, the system can present alternative examples, helping to uncover the main areas of concern. These features are especially valuable in early years assessments, alongside the gamification of tests, which can help reduce fear and stress associated with traditional evaluations.

That being said, various elements are important to consider while embedding AI in any type of assessment, such as transparency, privacy of data, potential bias, over-reliance on the automated outputs, and lack of accountability. Indeed, AI-powered platforms have access to personal and sensitive data, and such data should be safely guarded and used in an ethical manner, without any biases or disadvantaging of certain student populations. Fairness, inclusivity, and diversity should be carefully prioritised in the design and implementation of AI-driven assessments.

Furthermore, teachers should remain in the driving seat and should not fully rely on these tools (Cambridge University Press & Assessment, 2023). They must remain the ones making the final call, at least at this early stage of using AI; their judgment and feedback should ensure fairness and protect academic integrity.

Build AI Literacy in Simple Terms

AI is now part of our daily lives, and everyone is exposed to it in various forms; from chatbots, to social media content, to educational platforms and much more. In order to ensure that educators and students are using it well, it is important to consider various factors like AI literacy (TeachAI, 2025). One approach is to devise new curricula specifically developed for AI or to integrate AI-related elements across the existing system, through, for example, a project-based approach that creates interdisciplinary connections between subjects. This growing emphasis on AI literacy is increasingly evident in several education systems around the world, including those in China, Finland, South Korea, Singapore, the UAE, the UK, the USA, and others.

It is important to talk to children about AI literacy in simpler language to foster an early understanding of AI. It has been recommended to introduce content that focuses on a playful approach tailored to young learners (Gennari et al., 2023), and some researchers suggest approaching it from different angles such as technological, cognitive, cultural, and even philosophical (Trifonova et al., 2024). The key is to make sure it is introduced at an early age, in a way that captures students' attention and makes it relatable to their daily lives and experiences. But it is not just about students being exposed to AI: teachers also need support to manage classrooms and monitor student work.

While numeracy, or mathematical literacy, and literacy have been the focus over the past decades, there should be a more systematic focus on digital literacy and AI literacy, including prompt literacy, as they are all now an integral part of educational models.

Professional Development

AI literacy is not restricted to learners, it should also include educators who should be encouraged to pursue professional development opportunities focused on AI.

This can be done through online courses (e.g., Coursera, EdX), webinars, and workshops. Alternatively, existing educator networks could provide powerful platforms to develop further understanding of AI, share best practices, and reflect critically on the pedagogical implications of AI use.

It is the responsibility of policymakers to ensure that such training is encouraged, accessible, and adapted to teachers' needs. While a general theoretical knowledge of AI is needed, suitable infrastructure and resources are required to ensure proper practical support for teachers, and also for their students. Moreover, there are specificities to certain subjects that should be considered; for example, in mathematics, this ranges from how to include and use data, how to manipulate graphs and charts, how to build digitised assessments, etc. Such training should be ongoing to keep pace with technological advances, especially in AI. Teachers should be encouraged to experiment, while being aware of the ethical considerations and pitfalls to avoid.

Despite the need for such training and the importance of having well-researched approaches to support teachers and students in early years education, there is not enough research on the matter, which should be quickly addressed to avoid a large-scale adoption without proper foundations (Mustafa et al., 2024).

Practical Classroom Activities

AI tools can support learners and teachers alike through practical classroom activities that can be directly used to address certain topics. For instance, large language models (LLMs), such as ChatGPT, Gemini, etc., could integrate step-by-step guidance into exercises related to counting, basic arithmetic, or shape recognition. One approach to achieve that would be using interactive storytelling, with the help of an LLM which can create a fictitious engaging story that is mathematics focused. Such an approach is proven to support young students' learning, through a conversational model adapted to the needs and level of each student (Ruan et al., 2020; Zhang et al., 2024).

For instance, the teacher could use the following prompt to create an activity which focuses on the topic of counting:

You are an enthusiastic early childhood teacher who is passionate about making mathematics fun and interactive for young children. You believe in hands-on activities that help children grasp fundamental mathematics concepts through play and storytelling. Your task is to create a mathematics-related activity involving "Rob the Rabbit" who needs to collect 10 carrots for a party with his friends. The activity should target children aged 4–5 and should focus on counting, addition and subtraction. The classroom is set up with plenty of space for movement and exploration, and you have access to paper and markers.

Another example is the following prompt that could be used by a teacher who wants to design a classroom activity which focuses on the topic of shapes:

You are an enthusiastic early childhood teacher who is passionate about making mathematics fun and interactive for young children. You believe in hands-on activities that help children grasp fundamental mathematics concepts through play and storytelling. Your task is to create a mathematics-related activity involving drawing a castle for King Geo using the following shapes: square, rectangle, triangle, and circle. The activity should target children aged 4–5 and should focus on shape recognition, properties and relationships. The classroom is set up with limited space for movement and exploration, and you have access to paper and markers.

Challenges and Considerations

While acknowledging the potential added value of AI tools, it is important to remain aware of the challenges that the use of such resources pose, and we discuss some of these challenges in this section.

Screen Time and Exposure to AI-Powered Content

Sanders et al. (2024) conducted a comprehensive umbrella review synthesising data from 102 meta-analyses, encompassing 2,451 primary studies and 1,937,501 participants, examining the effects of screen-based technology on children and adolescents. Their findings revealed a mix of outcomes. For example, they found that screen use was associated with lower literacy, but had positive effects when parents watched with their children. As AI is increasingly integrated into devices and online platforms, longer screen time could be associated with increased exposure to AI-powered content and experiences. Therefore, it is essential for educators and parents to monitor young people's screen time and ensure that they are developing the critical thinking skills necessary to understand the sources and intentions behind the information they consume.

Critical Media Literacy

AI is primarily trained on data generated by humans, much of which is sourced from publicly available content on the internet. This raises important concerns, especially considering how easily young people can be exposed to unfiltered harmful information and ideologies online. The recently-released Netflix TV show *Adolescence*, created by Jack Thorne and Stephen Graham (Herbert et al., 2025), has sparked national and global debates about online safety and the role parents and teachers should play in educating young people, highlighting concerns shared not only within the education section but across society as a whole. With "Hallucinate" named the Word of the Year by the Cambridge Dictionary in 2023 (Cambridge University Press & Assessment, n.d.), the discussion should not centre on whether young children should be allowed to use social media, because in reality, they are highly likely to find ways to access it, even if it is banned at school or at home; instead, it is crucial to equip young people with critical media literacy, empowering them from an early age with the critical thinking skills needed to discern credible information from misinformation.

We believe that educators in early childhood education must be aware of the potential harms young children may face in today's digital society and must actively engage with them on these issues. Both educators and parents should be aware of the online environments young people are exposed to. As AI tools continue to evolve based on this vast pool of online content, it becomes increasingly important to consider the ethical implications, particularly for vulnerable users like children. However, this issue cannot be addressed by the education sector alone; it requires a multi-stakeholder collaborative effort involving educators, tech developers, policymakers, parents, and communities (UNESCO, 2022).

Ethical and Responsible Use of AI—a Collaborative Effort

The ethical and responsible use of AI requires a collaborative effort from both the field of education and the technology industry. As AI continues to impact everyday life, ensuring its alignment with human values and transparency becomes a shared responsibility. While it is important for educators to equip students with the necessary AI literacy and critical thinking skills to navigate and engage with AI tools thoughtfully, it is equally essential for AI developers to embed ethical considerations and safeguards into the design and deployment of these technologies. This means going beyond technical efficiency and novelty to consider the broader societal impacts of AI, such as bias, misinformation, data privacy, and accessibility.

It is promising to see major tech firms like Google making efforts from this perspective. In March 2025, Google introduced Gemma 3, a suite of lightweight, open models optimised to run on a single GPU or TPU (Farabet & Warkentin, 2025). Notably, the fully on-device Gemma 3 1B model enables users to process data that is unable to leave the device or is end-to-end encrypted, ensuring enhanced privacy and security (Ikonomidis et al., 2025). This move reflects a growing shift toward AI systems that prioritise user control and data protection, which are critical pillars of ethical AI use.

Conclusion

What makes humans unique on this planet is our ability to create and utilise tools. Throughout history, from the invention of the hammer, paper, and printing techniques to the development of trains, airplanes, computers, smartphones, and AR and VR, we have continually advanced both the technology behind our tools and the techniques used to develop them. While some jobs and skills have become unnecessary as a result, these innovations have also served as catalysts for new kinds of jobs and different skill sets; it is through this ongoing process that civilisation has progressed.

One of the primary goals of education is to prepare young people for a future with jobs that do not yet exist, tools that have yet to be developed, and a world where many essential skills are not yet part of today's curriculum. AI has the potential to support and inspire the next generation of learners, preparing them for a future that our generation once only saw in fictional films. Integrating AI into early childhood mathematics education presents both opportunities and challenges; as educators and parents navigate the integration of AI in early learning environments, it is essential to balance the opportunities these tools offer with a critical awareness of their limitations and potential risks.

Implications for Practice and Ethics

AI tools have the potential to support early mathematics education by scaffolding personalised teaching and learning. However, several ethical and well-being considerations should be taken into account, such as safeguarding data privacy, ensuring age-appropriate use, and preventing excessive screen time. Addressing these issues could help ensure that AI tools enhance young children's learning experiences without compromising their safety or overall development.

Acknowledgements **Disclaimer** The tools and platforms referenced in this chapter are presented solely for demonstration and research-related purposes. Their inclusion does not imply promotion or criticism by the authors. Readers are encouraged to critically assess the suitability and implications of any tool within their own educational and institutional contexts.

References

Abrasid, A. (2024). Personalizing education for young minds through adaptive learning. In: Vidyapati & J. P. Sahae (Eds.), *Teaching and learning of values: Necessity of humankind* (pp. 151–164). Manglam Publications.

Alkhatlan, A., & Kalita, J. (2019). Intelligent tutoring systems: A comprehensive historical survey with recent developments. *International Journal of Computer Applications, 181*(43), 1–20. https://www.ijcaonline.org/archives/volume181/number43/30402-2019918451/

Awang, L. A., Yusop, F. D., & Danaee, M. (2025). Current practices and future direction of artificial intelligence in mathematics education: A systematic review. *International Electronic Journal of Mathematics Education, 20*(2), em0823. https://doi.org/10.29333/iejme/16006

Bastani, H., Bastani, O., Sungu, A., Ge, H., Kabakcı, O., & Mariman, R. (2024). Generative AI can harm learning. *Social Science Research Network*. https://doi.org/10.2139/ssrn.4895486

Berson, I. R., & Berson, M. J. (2024). Fragments of the past: The intersection of AI, historical imagery, and early childhood creativity. *Future in Educational Research, 2*(4), 403–421. https://doi.org/10.1002/fer3.46

Bertrand, M. G., Sezer, H. B., & Namukasa, I. K. (2024). Exploring AR and VR tools in mathematics education through culturally responsive pedagogies. *Digital Experiences in Mathematics Education, 10*, 462–486. https://doi.org/10.1007/s40751-024-00152-x

Bettayeb, A. M., Abu Talib, M., Sobhe Altayasinah, A. Z., & Dakalbab, F. (2024). Exploring the impact of ChatGPT: Conversational AI in education. *Frontiers in Education, 9*, 1379796. https://doi.org/10.3389/feduc.2024.1379796

Billinghurst, M., & Duenser, A. (2012). Augmented reality in the classroom. *Computer, 45*(7), 56–63. https://doi.org/10.1109/MC.2012.111

bin Mohamed, M. Z., Hidayat, R., binti Suhaizi, N. N., binti Mat Sabri, N., bin Mahmud, M. K. H., & binti Baharuddin, S. N. (2022). Artificial intelligence in mathematics education: A systematic literature review. *International Electronic Journal of Mathematics Education, 17*(3), em0694. https://doi.org/10.29333/iejme/12132

Bhushan, S., Arunkumar, S., Eisa, T. A. E., Nasser, M., Singh, A. K., & Kumar, P. (2024). AI-enhanced dyscalculia screening: A survey of methods and applications for children. *Diagnostics, 14*(13), 1441. https://doi.org/10.3390/diagnostics14131441

Cambridge University Press. (n.d.). AI contributions to research content. In Publishing ethics: *Authorship and contributorship for journals*. https://www.cambridge.org/core/services/publishing-ethics/authorship-and-contributorship-journals

Cambridge University Press & Assessment. (n.d.). Hallucinate. In *Cambridge Dictionary*. https://dictionary.cambridge.org/dictionary/english/hallucinate?q=Hallucinate

Cambridge University Press & Assessment. (2023, March 27). *The Cambridge approach to generative AI and assessment*. https://www.cambridge.org/news-and-insights/The-Cambridge-approach-to-generative-AI-and-assessment

Canonigo, A. M. (2024). Levering AI to enhance students' conceptual understanding and confidence in mathematics. *Journal of Computer Assisted Learning, 40*(6), 3215–3229. https://doi.org/10.1111/jcal.13065

Carbonell, J. R. (1970). AI in CAI: An artificial-intelligence approach to computer-assisted instruction. *IEEE Transactions on Man-Machine Systems, 11*(4), 190–202. https://doi.org/10.1109/TMMS.1970.299942

Carey, E., Devine, A., Hill, F., Dowker, A., McLellan, R., & Szucs, D. (2019). *Understanding mathematics anxiety: Investigating the experiences of UK primary and secondary school students*. Centre for Neuroscience in Education. https://doi.org/10.17863/cam.37744

Ciampa, K., Wolfe, Z., & Hensley, M. (2025). From entry to transformation: Exploring AI integration in teachers' K–12 assessment practices. *Technology Pedagogy and Education, 34*(2), 141–160. https://doi.org/10.1080/1475939x.2024.2413378

Derbyshire, E. (2023, September 29). *Dyslexia and artificial intelligence*. BERA Blog series: Artificial Intelligence in educational research and practice. https://www.bera.ac.uk/blog/dyslexia-and-artificial-intelligence

Egara, F. O., & Mosimege, M. (2024). Exploring the integration of artificial intelligence-based ChatGPT into mathematics instruction: Perceptions, challenges, and implications for educators. *Education Sciences, 14*(7), 742. https://doi.org/10.3390/educsci14070742

Farabet, C., & Warkentin, T. (2025, March 12). *Introducing Gemma 3: The most capable model you can run on a single GPU or TPU*. Google The Keyword. https://blog.google/technology/developers/gemma-3/

Garisto, D. (2022, October 12). *AI language models are struggling to "get" math: Should this be telling us something?* IEEE Spectrum. https://spectrum.ieee.org/large-language-models-math

Gattupalli, S., Lee, W., Allessio, D., Crabtree, D., Arroyo, I., & Woolf, B. (2023, July 7). *Exploring pre-service teachers' perceptions of large language models-generated hints in online mathematics learning* [Paper presentation]. AIED2023 Empowering Education with LLMs—the Next-Gen Interface and Content Generation. https://ceur-ws.org/Vol-3487/paper10.pdf

Gennari, R., Melonio, A., Pellegrino, M. A., & D'Angelo, M. (2023). How to playfully teach AI to young learners: A systematic literature review. In C. Gena (Ed.), *CHItaly '23: Proceedings of the 15th biannual conference of the Italian SIGCHI chapter* (pp. 1–9). Association for Computing Machinery. https://doi.org/10.1145/3605390.3605393

Google. (2024, October). *Gemini for Google Workspace. Prompting guide 101. A quick-start handbook for effective prompts.* https://services.google.com/fh/files/misc/gemini-for-google-workspace-prompting-guide-101.pdf

Herbert, M., Feller, E., Graham, S., Walters, H., Thorne, J., Barantini, P., Pitt, B., Gardner, D., Kleiner, J., & Wolarsky, N. (Executive Producers). (2025–2025). *Adolescence* [TV series]. Warp Films; It's All Made Up Productions; Matriarch Productions; Plan B Entertainment; One Shoe Films.

Holmes, W., Bialik, M., & Fadel, C. (2019). *Artificial intelligence in education: Promises and implications for teaching and learning.* Center for Curriculum Redesign. http://bit.ly/AIED-BOOK

Holt, R. W. (1983). An introduction to the PLATO CAI system. *Behavior Research Methods & Instrumentation, 15*, 142–144. https://doi.org/10.3758/BF03203536

Ikonomidis, M., Alumbaugh, T. J., Sherwood, M., & Brick, C. (2025, March 12). *Gemma 3 on mobile and web with Google AI Edge.* Google for Developers. https://developers.googleblog.com/en/gemma-3-on-mobile-and-web-with-google-ai-edge/

Kewalramani, S., Kidman, G., & Palaiologou, I. (2021). Using artificial intelligence (AI)-interfaced robotic toys in early childhood settings: A case for children's inquiry literacy. *European Early Childhood Education Research Journal, 29*(5), 652–668. https://doi.org/10.1080/1350293X.2021.1968458

Kölemen, E. B., & Yıldırım, B. (2025). A new era in early childhood education (ECE): Teachers' opinions on the application of artificial intelligence. *Education and Information Technologies.* https://doi.org/10.1007/s10639-025-13478-9

Labadze, L., Grigolia, M., & Machaidze, L. (2023). Role of AI chatbots in education: Systematic literature review. *International Journal of Educational Technology in Higher Education, 20*, 56. https://educationaltechnologyjournal.springeropen.com/articles/ https://doi.org/10.1186/s41239-023-00426-1

Li, X., Gould, T., & Zaki, R. (2024). The impact of artificial intelligence on learners and teachers: A mathematics education perspective. In S. Papadakis & M. Kalogiannakis (Eds.), *Education, development and intervention: Toward participatory and integrated solutions* (pp. 133–148). Springer. https://doi.org/10.1007/978-3-031-60713-4_9

Li, X., Morley, F., & Zaki, R. (2025). *Mind the knowledge gap: Evaluating AI tutors' ability to detect mathematical prior knowledge and misconceptions.* EasyChair Preprint 15939. https://easychair.org/publications/preprint/4C1J

Li, X., & Zaki, R. (2024). Harnessing the power of digital resources in mathematics education: The potential of augmented reality and artificial intelligence. In S. Papadakis (Ed.), *IoT, AI and ICT for educational applications: Technologies to enable education for all* (pp. 191–223). Springer. https://doi.org/10.1007/978-3-031-50139-5_10

Magat, R. J. B., & Sangalang, E. M. (2024). Teachers' familiarity, perceptions, and training needs on the use of ChatGPT in mathematics instruction. *International Journal of Education in Mathematics, Science and Technology, 12*(4), 1471–1487. http://files.eric.ed.gov/fulltext/EJ1465795.pdf

Mustafa, M. Y., Tlili, A., Lampropoulos, G., Huang, R., Jandrić, P., Zhao, J., Salha, S., Xu, L., Panda, S., Kinshuk, López-Pernas, S., & Saqr, M. (2024). A systematic review of literature reviews on artificial intelligence in education (AIED): A roadmap to a future research agenda. *Smart Learning Environments, 11*, 59. https://doi.org/10.1186/s40561-024-00350-5

Nikolova, E. (2024). Artificial intelligence tools into higher mathematics education: Opportunities, challenges and student perceptions. *Mathematics & Informatics, 67*(4). https://philosophy.azbuki.bg/en/uncategorized/artifical-intelligence-tools-into-higher-mathematics-education-opportunities-challenges-and-student-perceptions/

OpenAI Platform. (n.d.). *Prompt engineering.* Retrieved May 30, 2025, from https://platform.openai.com/docs/guides/prompt-engineering/six-strategies-for-getting-better-results

Pask, G. (1982). SAKI: Twenty-five years of adaptive training into the microprocessor era. *International Journal of Man-Machine Studies, 17*(1), 69–74. https://doi.org/10.1016/S0020-7373(82)80009-6

Ruan, S., He, J., Ying, R., Burkle, J., Hakim, D., Wang, A., Yin, Y., Zhou, L., Xu, Q., AbuHashem, A., Dietz, G., Murnane, E. L., Brunskill, E., & Landay, J. A. (2020). Supporting children's math learning with feedback-augmented narrative technology. In *IDC '20: Proceedings of the interaction design and children conference* (pp. 567–580). https://doi.org/10.1145/3392063.3394400

Rumbelow, M., & Coles, A. (2024). The promise of AI object-recognition in learning mathematics: An explorative study of 6-year-old children's interactions with Cuisenaire rods and the Blockplay.ai app. *Education Sciences, 14*(6), 591. https://doi.org/10.3390/educsci14060591

Russell Group. (n.d.). *Russell Group principles on the use of generative AI tools in education.* https://russellgroup.ac.uk/media/6137/rg_ai_principles-final.pdf

Sanders, T., Noetel, M., Parker, P., Del Pozo Cruz, B., Biddle, S., Ronto, R., Hulteen, R., Parker, R., Thomas, G., De Cocker, K., Salmon, J., Hesketh, K., Weeks, N., Arnott, H., Devine, E., Vasconcellos, R., Pagano, R., Sherson, J., Conigrave, J., & Lonsdale, C. (2024). An umbrella review of the benefits and risks associated with youths' interactions with electronic screens. *Nature Human Behaviour, 8*, 82–99. https://doi.org/10.1038/s41562-023-01712-8

Shurr, J., Bouck, E. C., Bassette, L., & Park, J. (2021). Virtual versus concrete: A comparison of mathematics manipulatives for three elementary students with autism. *Focus on Autism and Other Developmental Disabilities, 36*(2), 71–82. https://doi.org/10.1177/1088357620986944

Strielkowski, W., Grebennikova, V., Lisovskiy, A., Rakhimova, G., & Vasileva, T. (2024). AI-driven adaptive learning for sustainable educational transformation. *Sustainable Development, 33*(2), 1921–1947. https://doi.org/10.1002/sd.3221

TeachAI. (2025). *Foundational policy ideas for AI in education.* World Economic Forum. https://www.teachai.org/media/foundational-policy-ideas-for-ai-in-education-6yie2o

Torres-Peña, R. C., Peña-González, D., Chacuto-López, E., Ariza, E. A., & Vergara, D. (2024). Updating calculus teaching with AI: A classroom experience. *Education Sciences, 14*(9), 1019. https://doi.org/10.3390/educsci14091019

Trifonova, A., Destéfano, M., & Barajas, M. (2024). Teaching AI to the next generation: A humanistic approach. *Digital Education Review, 45*, 115–123. https://doi.org/10.1344/der.2024.45.115-123

UCL. (n.d.). *Engaging with AI in your education and assessment.* https://www.ucl.ac.uk/students/exams-and-assessments/assessment-success-guide/engaging-ai-your-education-and-assessment

UNESCO. (2022). *Recommendation on the ethics of Artificial Intelligence.* https://unesdoc.unesco.org/ark:/48223/pf0000381137

UNESCO. (2024a). *AI competency framework for teachers.* https://doi.org/10.54675/ZJTE2084

UNESCO. (2024b). *AI competency framework for students.* https://doi.org/10.54675/JKJB9835

Walter, Y. (2024). Embracing the future of Artificial Intelligence in the classroom: The relevance of AI literacy, prompt engineering, and critical thinking in modern education. *International Journal of Educational Technology in Higher Education, 21*, 15. https://educationaltechnologyjournal.springeropen.com/articles/ https://doi.org/10.1186/s41239-024-00448-3

Zhang, C., Liu, X., Ziska, K., Jeon, S., Yu, C.-L., & Xu, Y. (2024). Mathemyths: Leveraging large language models to teach mathematical language through child-AI co-creative storytelling. In

F. F. Mueller (Ed.), *CHI '24: Proceedings of the 2024 CHI conference on human factors in computing systems* (No. 274, pp. 1–23). https://doi.org/10.1145/3613904.3642647

Chapter 12
Applications of Large Language Models in Automatic Item and Feedback Generation for Early Elementary Education

Okan Bulut, Bin Tan, and Elisabetta Mazzullo

Introduction

Recent discussions around artificial intelligence (AI) in education have shifted from "if" to "how" these tools can meaningfully support learning. In early elementary classrooms, where teachers must balance instruction, assessment, and individualized support, time and resources are often limited. AI-powered tools, particularly large language models (LLMs), offer a new way to streamline high-effort tasks by handling routine generative tasks, allowing teachers to focus on observation, relationship-building, and responsive teaching. Within this broader landscape of AI integration in education, assessment is a particularly promising area where LLMs can create value.

Generative AI, particularly LLMs, has demonstrated impressive capabilities in content generation. In education, these capabilities unlock new possibilities for supporting teachers in creating effective assessments and enhancing student learning in classroom settings. This chapter examines two promising applications of LLMs in early elementary education (typically, from kindergarten to Grade 3; Ma et al., 2016): automatic item generation and automatic feedback generation (AFG). Our goal is to equip teachers with knowledge, useful strategies, and tools needed to thoughtfully

O. Bulut (✉)
Centre for Research in Applied Measurement and Evaluation, Faculty of Education, University of Alberta, Edmonton, AB, Canada
e-mail: bulut@ualberta.ca

B. Tan · E. Mazzullo
Measurement, Evaluation, and Data Science, Faculty of Education, University of Alberta, Edmonton, AB, Canada
e-mail: btan4@ualberta.ca

E. Mazzullo
e-mail: mazzullo@ualberta.ca

S. Papadakis (ed.), *AI Applications in Preschool and Primary Education*, Advances in Artificial Intelligence in Education 5, https://doi.org/10.1007/978-3-032-17190-0_12

apply LLMs to support high-quality assessment and feedback practices tailored to early learning contexts.

In the first part of this chapter, we begin by exploring how LLMs can be used to generate standardized tests, which are especially amenable to automation due to their structured format and scalability. Although early childhood assessments often include observational tools, checklists, and informal assessments, standardized tests remain a common format of literacy and numeracy screening. This section reviews the goals and approaches of automatic item generation and identifies considerations specific to early learners. We also provide practical strategies for teachers to use LLMs to create assessment items suitable for early elementary education contexts.

In the second part of the chapter, we shift our focus to AFG. We begin by discussing the critical role of feedback in early elementary education. Next, we trace the evolution of AFG, from the early rule-based feedback generation systems to the LLM-enhanced systems. Additionally, we present recent research demonstrating how effective practices can improve the quality of LLM-generated feedback in early elementary contexts. Lastly, we showcase promising practices for AFG, discuss common challenges and explore ethical considerations in implementing AFG.

Automatic Item Generation

A Primer on LLMs for Automatic Item Generation

The goal of automatic item generation is to generate a large number of high-quality items while reducing overall costs (Gierl & Lai, 2012). This approach aims to satisfy the growing demand for high-quality items in the development of many modern educational assessment theories and technologies, such as formative assessment (Beerepoot, 2023) and personalized learning and assessment (Bulut, 2024). Traditional approaches to automatic item generation often require custom-built software and close collaboration between subject matter experts and assessment specialists (Gierl & Lai, 2012). However, the recent emergence of publicly accessible LLMs, such as ChatGPT, has broadened access to automatic item generation, allowing teachers to create a large number of assessment items with far less technical support.

LLMs have demonstrated their effectiveness for automatic item generation across a variety of educational contexts (e.g., Nguyen et al., 2022; Wang et al., 2022). A recent scoping review showed that the use of LLMs in item generation is not limited by subject domain, language, or item types, offering remarkable flexibility (Tan et al., 2024). For instance, Wang et al. (2022) systematically tested different prompts (i.e., the instruction given to an LLM to elicit responses) using OpenAI's GPT-3 to generate practice questions for biology and identified an approach that produced items comparable in quality to those created by human experts. In another study, Kıyak and Kononowicz (2024) developed a GPT-based tool for medical education. This tool allows teachers to generate Multiple-Choice Questions (MCQs) by selecting from built-in prompt templates and entering a learning objective. By minimizing the need for technical expertise, these types of AI tools lower the barrier to entry for teachers and streamline the item generation process.

While LLMs have made it significantly easier to generate a large number of assessment items, quantity alone is not sufficient. High-quality items are essential for both instructional and assessment purposes, whether in summative or formative contexts (Tan et al., 2024). Formative assessments, often used in classroom settings, require items that are educationally sound, aligned with learning goals, and able to identify student misconceptions (Gierl et al., 2021). To ensure quality in automatic item generation, practitioners should begin by clearly defining the assessment context and measurement goals. It is also important to evaluate the generated items for both their measurement properties and their educational value as a key part of the generation process.

Automatic Item Generation in Early Elementary Education

The context of early elementary education presents unique challenges for automatic item generation, distinct from those associated with older learners. At this age, children are still developing foundational cognitive, linguistic, and motor skills (Piaget, 1962; Tieman et al., 2005). Therefore, selecting developmentally appropriate item types and formats is critical for effective automatic item generation in early elementary education. Many formats commonly used with older students, such as lengthy open-ended questions or tasks requiring abstract reasoning, often exceed the abilities of younger children (Snow & Hemel, 2008). In contrast, more suitable formats for this age group include picture-based MCQs, matching tasks that pair images with corresponding words or sounds, and short reading passages followed by simple comprehension questions. In digital environments, interactive formats such as touchscreen responses or drag-and-drop activities can further enhance accessibility and engagement.

Attention span is also a critical consideration in assessments for early elementary education. Young learners have limited attention spans and are likely to disengage from tasks that are repetitive, overly complex, or lack personal relevance (Gregory & Kaufeldt, 2015). To maintain engagement during assessments, items should be concise, visually stimulating, and rooted in familiar, concrete themes such as daily routines or animals. Traditional item development for early literacy has long prioritized developmental appropriateness, relevance to children's interests, and alignment with key learning domains (Iyer et al., 2019). Automated item generation systems should adhere to these same principles to ensure that the items they produce are not only developmentally accessible but also engaging and effective for young learners.

Cultural relevance is another essential consideration in automatic item generation for early elementary education. Children's language acquisition and conceptual development are profoundly influenced by their cultural and linguistic environments (Schieffelin & Ochs, 2013). Therefore, assessment items must be culturally appropriate and based on concepts that are familiar to the children being assessed (Shepard, 1994). For instance, references to snowball fights or subway rides may confuse children who have never encountered such experiences. To prevent unintended barriers to understanding, item content should reflect children's everyday lives and avoid region-specific references or unfamiliar idioms (Darling-Hammond et al., 2013). Furthermore, developmental trajectories in early childhood vary considerably based on factors such as age, socio-cultural background, and the presence of special educational needs. To ensure the appropriateness and relevance of generated content, teachers may need to provide contextual information, such as the child's first language, learning interests, or instructional goals, to help LLMs tailor items effectively.

Lastly, automatic item generation practices should align with the pedagogical values of early elementary education. Unlike high-stakes assessments common in later grades, assessments for early elementary education are often low-pressure and formative. Their primary purposes are to inform instruction, identify special educational needs, facilitate communication with families, and support program evaluation and policy development (Shepard, 1994; Snow & Hemel, 2008). The focus is on promoting each child's growth and fostering learning rather than ranking, sorting, or excluding them. Shepard (1994) cautions against assessment practices that lead to retention or stigmatization, emphasizing their role in guiding support instead. Similarly, Meisels and Atkins-Burnett (2000) argue that assessment should be the starting point for potential intervention rather than a final judgment. Therefore, automatically generated items should embody these values by producing information that supports assessment purposes.

A Three-Stage Framework for High-Quality Item Generation

The effectiveness of LLMs in generating assessment items relies not only on their underlying capabilities but also on how strategically they are utilized. Recent research and practical experimentation have led to a set of emerging practices that improve the quality and pedagogical relevance of generated assessment items. According to a scoping review by Tan et al. (2024), the use of LLMs in item generation can be divided into three key stages: pre-generation, generation, and post-generation, each playing a crucial role in producing high-quality assessment items. In this study, we adapted this three-stage framework to explain how teachers can effectively engage in automatic item generation.

In the **pre-generation** stage, teachers focus on thinking and preparing suitable materials for the subsequent item generation. This involves identifying the assessment goal (e.g., diagnostic, formative, or summative use), selecting the item type, identifying the construct to be measured by considering the expected learner outcomes and instructional objectives, defining content coverage, planning the cognitive complexity, and specifying the weight or emphasis of various item types.

During the **item generation** stage, teachers begin by selecting a suitable LLM. Most LLMs are trained on general language corpora and are not optimized for educational content, especially for early elementary education. Nevertheless, providing high-quality prompts can guide LLMs to produce more desirable and relevant outputs and improve accuracy (Brown et al., 2020). In general, high-quality prompts are often characterized by four attributes (White et al., 2023): clarity (avoiding ambiguity), context (providing background), precision (clearly stating the task and expected output), and role-play (assigning the model to a specific persona, such as a Grade 3 teacher or subject expert). Moreover, breaking the task into multiple steps (e.g., asking the model to first generate a reading passage and then create questions based on it) helps improve the overall coherence and alignment of generated content (Cheng et al., 2024). Another useful practice is prompt iteration, in which teachers can assess the quality of initial outputs and revise prompts to refine the results. For instance, an initial prompt may yield overly complex items; revising the prompt to simplify language or restructure examples can yield more appropriate content. This reflective process allows teachers to fine-tune prompts based on trial and error, ultimately improving item quality over iterations.

In addition to general prompt quality, teachers can also adopt specific prompt patterns—structured strategies that guide how prompts are formulated and delivered to LLMs. These prompt patterns are not rigid rules but flexible strategies that teachers can adopt, adapt, and combine to fit their assessment needs. Used thoughtfully, they enable more desired, pedagogically useful, and developmentally appropriate item generation. In the next section, we will showcase four prompt patterns that can be useful for automatic item generation.

As the final step in the automatic item generation framework, the **post-generation** stage involves evaluating and selecting the automatically generated items. High-quality output cannot be assumed after one generation cycle. As such, a growing body of research has focused on identifying quality criteria and developing robust methods for evaluating automatically generated items (Bulut et al., 2025; Falcão et al., 2023). Gorgun and Bulut (2024) classified item evaluation methods into two broad categories: judgment-based and statistical evaluation. Between the two, judgment-based evaluation involves stakeholders such as subject-matter experts, researchers, and teachers reviewing the generated items for linguistic clarity, content alignment, fairness, and cognitive appropriateness. Statistical evaluation, by contrast, is further divided into metric-based and post-hoc methods. Metric-based evaluations use standardized, automated metrics—often embedded within item-generation systems—to assess aspects such as similarity between generated and reference items. Post-hoc evaluations rely on psychometric analyses, including the analysis of item difficulty and discrimination parameters, distractor performance, and experimental validation studies to determine how well the items function in practice. In classroom settings, it may be challenging for teachers to conduct either metric-based or post-hoc evaluations due to time and resource constraints. However, teachers are uniquely positioned to assess the contextual relevance, content validity, and pedagogical value of test items. As such, judgment-based evaluation is often more accessible, meaningful, and considered more appropriate and cost-effective for classroom use.

Effective Prompt Patterns for Automatic Item Generation

Designing high-quality prompts is arguably one of the most important steps in automatic item generation using LLMs. To support this process, we introduce four effective prompt patterns that have been shown to help generate high-quality assessment items. For each pattern, we provide an example using ChatGPT, a widely used platform for interacting with OpenAI's GPT models, to create items specifically designed for early elementary education. These examples include simple counting questions, number operation questions, phonics-based exercises, and basic reading comprehension tasks.

One-Shot or Few-Shot Pattern

These prompt patterns involve presenting the model with one (one-shot) or a small set (few-shot) of example items before asking it to generate new content (Radford et al., 2019). These examples serve as templates or demonstrations, helping the model infer the desired characteristics of the output. This is particularly useful when generating a series of similar assessment items. Below is an example of generating a number operation question using the one-shot pattern.

Example.

User prompt:

Here is a number operation (subtraction) question for Grade 2 students:

Emma has 15 apples. She gave 7 to her friend and then ate 2 herself. How many apples does she have now?

Now, please generate another addition question of similar difficulty.

Response (GPT-4o):

Liam has 8 toy cars. His mom bought him 5 more, and then his dad gave him 3 more. How many toy cars does Liam have now?

Role-Play/persona Pattern

In this pattern, the LLM is instructed to take on the persona of a specific type of educator, such as a Grade 1 teacher or an early childhood literacy specialist. In doing so, the LLM understands the context of the assigned role, such as an early classroom setting, and mimics the language and priorities associated with that role. This enhances the relevance and usability of the generated content in the classroom while saving time by reducing the need to provide additional contextual information. Below is an example of generating a phonics-based exercise using this pattern.

Example.

User prompt:

You are a Grade 1 teacher with a warm and encouraging tone. You are helping your students practice their phonics skills. Please create a short fictional story (60–80 words) that includes simple phonics patterns (e.g., CVC words and blends such as "sh," "ch," or "st"). Then, ask two questions that focus on phonics awareness. Keep the language child-friendly and developmentally appropriate.

Response (GPT-4o):

Story: Sam and his dog, Ben, went to the park. They sat on the soft grass and played with a red ball. Sam said, "Catch, Ben!" Ben ran fast and caught the ball with a whoosh! They laughed and had fun all day.

Questions:

1. What sound does the "sh" in "s-h" make in the word "sat"?
2. Can you find a word in the story that has the "st" sound, like in "st-ick"? What is it?

Flipped-Interaction Pattern

This pattern reverses the typical direction of prompting by having the LLM ask the user clarifying questions before completing the task (White et al., 2023). Instead of the user figuring out all the details upfront, the LLM asks clarifying questions (e.g., about students' level, learning goals, or desired item type and format) before generating content. Therefore, this approach becomes more suitable when teachers are still refining the lesson plan or need help aligning questions with content or curriculum standards. Below is an example of using this pattern to generate a reading passage along with two comprehension questions.

Example.

User prompt (1st turn):

Ask me questions about my assessment needs and other relevant details until you are ready to generate a short reading passage along with two comprehension questions suitable for Grade 3 students. Ask one question at a time and wait for my response before proceeding.

Response (GPT-4o; 1st turn):

Great! To start, what is the main topic or theme you want the reading passage to focus on?

User prompt (2nd turn):

Let's go with a theme that's both age-appropriate and engaging for Grade 3 students: "Helping Others".

Response (GPT-4o; 2nd turn):

Awesome choice! Helping others is a wonderful theme. Next question: Do you want the passage to be fiction (a story) or nonfiction (informative)? Or maybe a mix of both?

User prompt (3rd turn):

I suggest we go with fiction—a short story.

Response (GPT-4o; 3rd turn):

Perfect! A short fictional story it is. Now, what kind of setting do you prefer for the story? For example, should it take place at school, at home, in a park, or somewhere else?

User prompt (4th turn):

For this story about helping others, a school setting would work really well. It's a familiar environment for Grade 3 students.

Response (GPT-4o; 4th turn):

Great! A school setting will be easy for the kids to relate to. Next, how long do you want the passage to be? Something like 100–150 words, or shorter, or maybe a bit longer?

User prompt (5th turn):

A passage of around 150–180 words.

Response (GPT-4o; 5th turn):

Got it—around 150 to 180 words. Now, for the two comprehension questions: Would you prefer questions that focus more on recalling facts from the story, or questions that encourage students to think about the message and meaning (like the lesson about helping others)? Or maybe one of each?

User prompt (6th turn):

I Recommend Doing One of Each.

Response (GPT-4o; 6th turn):

Perfect. Last quick question before I draft: Should the language be fairly simple and straightforward, or would you like to include a few new vocabulary words with context clues to help students learn?

User prompt (7th turn):

Let's go with simple and clear language overall, but include these two new vocabulary words for the students: "Frustrated" and "Encouraged".

Response (GPT-4o; 7th turn):

Excellent! Here's a short fictional reading passage about helping others, with the two target vocabulary words included, followed by two comprehension questions—one fact-based and one that encourages reflection:

Reading Passage: One sunny morning, Mia was feeling frustrated. She had a big art project to finish, but her paintbrush broke just as she started. She didn't know what to do.

Her friend Liam saw Mia's problem and walked over. "Don't worry," he said, "I have extra paintbrushes you can use." Mia smiled and felt encouraged. With Liam's help, she finished her painting on time.

Later that day, Mia saw another classmate struggling to carry a heavy box of books. Mia remembered how Liam helped her, so she ran over and offered to help. The classmate smiled and said, "Thank you!"

Mia learned that helping others not only makes them feel better, but it also makes you feel good too.

Comprehension Questions:

1. What did Liam do to help Mia with her art project?
2. Why do you think Mia felt encouraged when Liam helped her?

Template Pattern

This pattern involves instructing the model to follow a fixed structure or format when generating new items. Teachers can provide one or two example templates, and the LLM can generate multiple variations that adhere to the same structure. This approach is particularly effective for creating uniform practice sheets, flashcards, or skill-based assessments in areas such as phonemic awareness and basic arithmetic. Below is an example of using this pattern to generate addition-focused word problems for Grade 1 students.

Example.

User prompt:

You are a Grade 1 math teacher creating addition-focused word problems. Generate 5 unique questions following this exact template:

"[NAME] has [NUMBER 1] [OBJECTS]. [They/He/She] gets [NUMBER 2] more. How many now?"

Rule:

Names: Use kid-friendly names (e.g., Sam, Maya, Leo, Zoe).

Objects: Choose from toys (e.g., cars, dolls), animals (e.g., dogs, frogs), or snacks (e.g., apples, cookies).

Numbers: Sums must be $\leq$ 10.

Diversity: Vary names, objects, and numbers across questions.

Response (GPT-4o):

Sure! Here are 5 addition-focused word problems following your template:

1. Sam has 3 cars. He gets 4 more. How many now?
2. Maya has 5 apples. She gets 2 more. How many now?
3. Leo has 2 dogs. He gets 3 more. How many now?
4. Zoe has 1 doll. She gets 6 more. How many now?
5. Amir has 4 cookies. He gets 5 more. How many now?

Automatic Feedback Generation

Advancing Feedback Practices: The Role of LLMs in Automatic Feedback Generation

Feedback plays a vital role in supporting student learning by enhancing performance, motivation, and the development of effective learning strategies (Hattie & Timperley, 2007). To be effective, feedback should be timely, actionable, and personalized. When delivered during or soon after a task, feedback is more likely to sustain students' engagement and help them stay focused on their goals (Jia et al., 2022). Actionable feedback enables students to identify their strengths and areas for improvement, while also guiding their next steps (D'Antoni et al., 2015). Personalized feedback further supports conceptual understanding by helping learners bridge the gap between their current performance and desired outcomes (Hattie & Timperley, 2007).

However, providing timely, personalized, and actionable feedback remains a significant challenge for teachers, who often manage heavy workloads and operate with limited resources (Jomuad et al., 2021). To address this issue, researchers have developed AFG systems to support students during and after task completion. Prior to the emergence of LLMs, AFG systems typically relied on either expert-driven or data-driven approaches. Expert-driven methods used predefined libraries of correct answers, common errors, or rule-based templates. While these approaches offered teachers a degree of control, they often lacked the flexibility needed for personalized feedback. In contrast, data-driven systems provided more adaptability but frequently struggled to align feedback with task content and individual learner needs (Deeva et al., 2021). This limitation is particularly evident in early elementary education, where feedback must be highly personalized and developmentally appropriate. For instance, Wilson et al. (2021) reported that although teachers found an automated writing evaluation tool helpful, they were critical of its rigid rubric and inability to adjust to students' needs or instructional goals.

LLMs provide a promising foundation for the next-generation AFG because of their ability to understand context, follow instructions, and generate human-like text. Recent studies exploring this potential have primarily focused on state-of-the-art ChatGPT models and various prompting strategies. The findings are encouraging: LLMs have been shown to generate feedback that closely resembles that of expert teachers (Fokides & Peristeraki, 2025; Jacobsen & Weber, 2023; Steiss et al., 2024) and outperforms feedback provided by novice teachers (Jacobsen & Weber, 2023). Moreover, LLM-generated feedback has been linked to improved revision performance, increased task motivation, and more positive emotional responses (Meyer et al., 2024).

Despite these promising outcomes, notable limitations remain. For instance, Meyer et al. (2024) reported only modest gains in student performance. Jacobsen and Weber (2023) found that one of the 20 feedback outputs evaluated was of poor quality. Similarly, Azaiz et al. (2024) noted that the latest version of ChatGPT produced correct and complete feedback in just 52% of cases, with the remainder exhibiting issues such as misclassifications, redundancy, inconsistency, or inaccurate explanations. Furthermore, most existing research on AFG systems has focused on postsecondary contexts. Only a limited number of studies have examined the use of LLMs for AFG in early elementary education. For instance, in a systematic review by Deeva et al. (2021), just 4.6% of the 109 analyzed articles addressed automatic feedback for elementary school students.

Effective Prompting Practices for AFG: Lessons Learned so Far

An essential element for the success of AFG is the quality of the instructions (or prompts) provided to the model. Prompting offers a low-cost and accessible method to generate high-quality feedback, but identifying effective prompts requires careful design, domain knowledge, and iterative refinement. A highly effective prompt is often the result of multiple trials and revisions. Generally, prompts are most successful when they are clear, focused yet sufficiently detailed, descriptive, directive, and explicit (Lo, 2023). In the context of AFG research, Jacobsen and Weber (2023) identify four core elements that contribute to high-quality prompts: context, question, format, and example. Building on this, Jacobsen et al. (2025) developed a coding manual to support teachers in designing effective prompts. This resource helps users construct prompts that: (1) specify the role the AI should assume, the target audience of the response, and the channel (i.e., context); (2) define a mission for the model to solve (i.e., question); and (3) do so with clarity and specificity, for instance, specifying the desired format and including clear emotional components. The correct use of domain-specific terminology is also emphasized, as it helps the model incorporate accurate and relevant content in its responses.

Emerging studies further support the value of crafting effective prompts. For instance, Steiss et al. (2024) found that prompting the model to adopt the persona of a secondary school teacher and to provide 2–3 pieces of actionable feedback resulted in outputs that more closely aligned with the authors' expectations. The prompt included details about the educational context (persona and grade level), the task (feedback based on evaluation criteria), and the tone (positive and supportive), illustrating the importance of clarity and specificity in prompt design. Similarly, Meyer et al. (2024) used a structured prompt to generate feedback for Grade 10 s-language learners' essays. The prompt specified the students' grade level and learner status (context), asked the model to evaluate three aspects of writing (question), and requested three hints and three examples for each aspect (format). These were presented in a table, and the prompt also included a sample feedback entry (example), demonstrating an effective case of one-shot prompting.

In addition to these structural elements, certain prompting strategies can further enhance output quality. One such approach is Chain-of-Thought (CoT) prompting, which encourages the model to articulate its reasoning process. As noted by Jacobsen and Weber (2023), CoT prompting can be implemented either by including sample responses that show the reasoning or by simply appending the phrase "let's think step by step" to the prompt (Kojima et al., 2022). This strategy has been found to improve the coherence and transparency of generated feedback.

Because generating high-quality feedback with LLMs requires detailed and context-specific instructions, effective prompts are often lengthy and tailored to specific classroom needs. While many successful prompts share common principles, there is no one-size-fits-all template that guarantees high-quality results. Thus, teachers are encouraged to consult examples from the literature, adapt them to their own instructional contexts, and iteratively refine their prompts based on the model's performance. With thoughtful design and ongoing testing, prompting can serve as a powerful tool for AFG systems to deliver timely, actionable, and personalized feedback.

Considerations for AFG in Early Elementary Education

As with automatic item generation, designing AFG systems for young learners requires thoughtful consideration. To align with their developmental needs, feedback should be delivered in formats and language that are appropriate for early elementary students. Formats commonly used with older learners—such as dashboards or detailed performance reports—may be too complex for younger students, who often face challenges with reading fluency, interpreting visual data (Peterman et al., 2015), sustaining attention (Asprilia et al., 2020), and understanding complex text (Amendum et al., 2018). For this age group, effective feedback should prioritize simplicity, clarity, and relevance. The language should be age-appropriate and the content should focus on key aspects of performance tied directly to learning goals. When using LLMs to generate feedback, it is essential to provide contextual details such as the learner's age, learning environment, instructional objectives, and evaluation criteria, to help the model produce developmentally appropriate responses.

In addition to design considerations, the ethical use of AI in education must address three key areas: data privacy, the balance of benefits and potential harms (beneficence), and fairness or equity (Ferguson et al., 2016). These considerations are especially important when applying AFG practices in early elementary contexts, where students may be particularly vulnerable. The following section briefly explores how each of these ethical issues applies to AFG in practice and offers potential solutions to address them.

Benefits and Potential Harms

The literature shows that feedback generated by LLMs can enhance student performance and motivation (Meyer et al., 2024). However, it can also be of poor quality, at times containing incorrect, incomplete, or misleading information (Jacobsen & Weber, 2023; Azaiz et al., 2024). This risk is especially concerning when feedback is delivered directly to elementary students, who may not yet have the critical thinking skills needed to evaluate or question such information. To address this issue, prompting strategies that encourage the model to explain its reasoning, such as CoT prompting, may help reduce factual errors in generated outputs (Kojima et al., 2022). Even so, technical solutions alone are not sufficient. Teachers play a crucial role in helping students make sense of feedback, identify what is useful, and critically engage with the content. As AI tools become more integrated into educational practice, it is important to guide students in how to interact with AI-generated knowledge. Rather than treating feedback as infallible, students should be encouraged to reflect on it, discuss it with their teachers, and use it as a starting point for learning. This approach not only helps mitigate harm but also supports the development of digital literacy and responsible use of AI in the classroom.

Equality

Most current applications of AFG with LLMs rely on well-crafted prompts to harness their generative capabilities. Although prompting is a low-cost and scalable solution, some researchers caution that it may present a barrier for teachers who lack familiarity with effective prompting strategies (Jacobsen & Weber, 2023). As an alternative, researchers and developers have explored fine-tuning pre-trained models on task-specific data. This approach can reduce reliance on prompt quality by enabling models to generate high-quality feedback more consistently (Bergmann, 2024). However, fine-tuning comes with substantial costs, including the need for human-annotated datasets and greater computational resources. To date, few studies have examined this method, and findings remain mixed. While fine-tuned models can closely replicate training examples, they still produce occasional inaccuracies, raising concerns about whether the benefits justify the costs, particularly in data-scarce educational contexts (Mazzullo et al., 2025a, 2025b, under review).

Another equity concern relates to the performance of LLMs in underrepresented languages, which often suffer from limited representation in training data. Fokides and Peristeraki (2025) explored this issue by prompting ChatGPT to generate feedback on short essays written by primary students in two linguistic contexts: English and Greek. Their results showed that the model's feedback was superior in both quality and quantity compared to instructor-generated feedback, but only for the English-language essays. The model's weaker performance in Greek highlights the unequal distribution of LLM capabilities across languages and underscores the need for greater linguistic inclusivity in model development and deployment.

Data Privacy

In the current research landscape, where most studies use proprietary GPT models for AFG, data privacy concerns remain prominent. These models typically operate through external servers, meaning that any data input (e.g., student responses or assessment materials) is transmitted beyond the control of teachers. This raises important questions about how such data may be stored, accessed, or used for future model training, potentially exposing sensitive information related to students, assessments, or educational practices. To address these risks, teachers and researchers can consider using open-source alternatives to proprietary LLMs, such as Meta's Llama (Touvron et al., 2023) or Mistral (Jiang et al., 2023). These models allow for local deployment, which keeps data processing within institutional boundaries and offers greater control over how educational data is handled, thereby protecting student privacy.

Conclusion

LLMs present valuable opportunities to enhance early elementary education through the automatic generation of assessment items and feedback. As demonstrated throughout this chapter, when used thoughtfully, LLMs can enable teachers to quickly and flexibly create high-quality items that span a wide range of subjects, languages, and formats. In addition, LLMs can support learning by delivering timely, actionable, and personalized feedback during or after task completion. However, to fully realize this potential, it is essential to go beyond technical strategies and consider both the developmental needs of young learners and the pedagogical goals of early childhood education. Ethical considerations must also guide the adoption of LLMs in these sensitive educational contexts.

For automatic item generation, the process should begin with clearly defined instructional goals and the selection of developmentally appropriate item types. The quality of the generated content can be significantly improved through effective prompt design. Teachers can use a variety of prompt patterns to guide the model's output and should iteratively evaluate the quality and pedagogical relevance of the generated items. Similarly, effective feedback generation depends on providing sufficient context. Prompts should specify not only the type of feedback desired but also details about the learner's age, skill level, and classroom environment. The resulting feedback should be framed in simple, supportive language that promotes student reflection and growth.

In both item and feedback generation, educator involvement is indispensable. LLMs can serve as helpful tools, but they cannot replace the teacher's role in ensuring developmental appropriateness, instructional alignment, and emotional sensitivity. Teachers must actively review, adapt, and interpret the model's outputs to ensure they are pedagogically meaningful and supportive of each child's learning journey. This also includes helping students understand that AI-generated feedback is a starting point for reflection and dialogue. Ultimately, with thoughtful design, ethical implementation, and educator involvement, LLMs can meaningfully enhance assessment and feedback practices supporting children's learning experiences and outcomes.

Implications for Practice and Ethics

LLMs can reduce teachers' workload by quickly generating developmentally appropriate assessment items and personalized feedback, allowing teachers more time for observation and instructional decisions. Yet, there are important implications for both practice and ethics. First, teachers should carefully review AI-generated outputs because even state-of-the-art AI models can produce inaccurate, biased, or inappropriate content. Second, teachers should focus on data privacy and fair access, especially when student work or personal data are involved. Lastly, we recommend that schools establish clear protocols for teacher oversight, language inclusivity, and local data management to ensure AI supports, rather than replaces, teachers' professional judgment.

References

Amendum, S. J., Conradi, K., & Hiebert, E. (2018). Does text complexity matter in the elementary grades? A research synthesis of text difficulty and elementary students' reading fluency and comprehension. *Educational Psychology Review, 30*, 121–151. https://doi.org/10.1007/s10648-017-9398-2

Asprilia, M. T., Qodariah, L., & Purba, F. D. (2020). First grader's attention span during in-class activity. *GUIDENA: Jurnal Ilmu Pendidikan, Psikologi, Bimbingan dan Konseling, 10*(2), 144–150. https://doi.org/10.24127/gdn.v10i2.3151

Azaiz, I., Kiesler, N., & Strickroth, S. (2024). Feedback-generation for programming exercises with GPT-4. *arXiv*. https://doi.org/10.48550/arXiv.2403.04449

Beerepoot, M. T. (2023). Formative and summative automated assessment with multiple-choice question banks. *Journal of Chemical Education, 100*(8), 2947–2955. https://doi.org/10.1021/acs.jchemed.3c00120

Bergmann, D. (2024, April 5). What is instruction tuning? *IBM Think*. https://www.ibm.com/think/topics/instructiontuning

Brown, T., Mann, B., Ryder, N., Subbiah, M., Kaplan, J. D., Dhariwal, P., & Amodei, D. (2020). Language models are few-shot learners. *arXiv*. https://doi.org/10.48550/arXiv.2005.14165

Bulut, O. (2024). From adaptive testing to personalized adaptive testing: Applications of recommender systems. In H. Jiao & R. W. Lissitz (Eds.), *Machine learning, natural language processing, and psychometrics* (pp. 177–199). Information Age Publishing.

Bulut, O., Beiting-Parrish, M., Casabianca, J., Slater, S., Jiao, H., Song, D., & Morilova, P. (2025). Application of artificial intelligence in educational measurement: Opportunities and ethical challenges. *Chinese/English Journal of Educational Measurement and Evaluation, 5*(3). https://doi.org/10.59863/SFEB5996

Cheng, X., Li, J., Zhao, W. X., & Wen, J. R. (2024). ChainLM: Empowering large language models with improved chain-of-thought prompting. *arXiv*. https://doi.org/10.48550/arXiv.2403.14312

D'antoni, L., Kini, D., Alur, R., Gulwani, S., Viswanathan, M., & Hartmann, B. (2015). How can automatic feedback help students construct automata? *ACM Transactions on Computer-Human Interaction, 22*(2), 1–24. https://doi.org/10.1145/2723163

Darling-Hammond, L., Herman, J., Pellegrino, J., Abedi, J., Aber, J. L., Baker, E., & Steele, C. M. (2013). *Criteria for high-quality assessment*.

Deeva, G., Bogdanova, D., Serral, E., Snoeck, M., & De Weerdt, J. (2021). A review of automated feedback systems for learners: Classification framework, challenges and opportunities. *Computers & Education, 162*, Article 104094. https://doi.org/10.1016/j.compedu.2020.104094

Falcão, F., Pereira, D. M., Gonçalves, N., De Champlain, A., Costa, P., & Pêgo, J. M. (2023). A suggestive approach for assessing item quality, usability and validity of Automatic Item Generation. *Advances in Health Sciences Education, 28*(5), 1441–1465. https://doi.org/10.1007/s10459-023-10225-y

Ferguson, R., Hoel, T., Scheffel, M., & Drachsler, H. (2016). Guest editorial: Ethics and privacy in learning analytics. *Journal of Learning Analytics, 3*(1), 5–15. https://doi.org/10.18608/jla.2016.31.2

Fokides, E., & Peristeraki, E. (2025). Comparing ChatGPT's correction and feedback comments with that of educators in the context of primary students' short essays written in English and Greek. *Education and Information Technologies*. https://doi.org/10.1007/s10639-024-12912-8

Gierl, M. J., & Lai, H. (2012). The role of item models in automatic item generation. *International Journal of Testing, 12*(3), 273–298. https://doi.org/10.1080/15305058.2011.635830

Gierl, M. J., Lai, H., & Tanygin, V. (2021). *Advanced methods in automatic item generation*. Routledge.

Gregory, G., & Kaufeldt, M. (2015). *The motivated brain: Improving student attention, engagement, and perseverance*. ASCD.

Gorgun, G., & Bulut, O. (2024). Exploring quality criteria and evaluation methods in automated question generation: A comprehensive survey. *Education and Information Technologies*. https://doi.org/10.1007/s10639-024-12771-3

Hattie, J., & Timperley, H. (2007). The power of feedback. *Review of Educational Research, 77*(1), 81–112. https://doi.org/10.3102/003465430298487

Iyer, S., Do, D., Akshoomoff, N., Malcarne, V. L., Hattrup, K., Berger, S. P., & Needlman, R. (2019). Development of a brief screening tool for early literacy skills in preschool children. *Academic Pediatrics, 19*(4), 464–470. https://doi.org/10.1016/j.acap.2018.11.008

Jacobsen, L. J., & Weber, K. E. (2023). The promises and pitfalls of ChatGPT as a feedback provider in higher education: An exploratory study of prompt engineering and the quality of AI-driven feedback. Preprint. https://doi.org/10.31219/osf.io/cr257

Jacobsen, L. J., Rohlmann, J., & Weber, K. E. (2025). AI feedback in education: The impact of prompt design and human expertise on LLM performance. Preprint. https://doi.org/10.31219/osf.io/fx5qz

Jia, Q., Young, M., Xiao, Y., Cui, J., Liu, C., Rashid, P., & Gehringer, E. (2022). Insta-Reviewer: A data-driven approach for generating instant feedback on students' project reports. *Zenodo*. https://doi.org/10.5281/zenodo.6853099

Jiang, A. Q., Sablayrolles, A., Mensch, A., Bamford, C., Chaplot, D. S., De Las Casas, D., Bressand, F., Lengyel, G., Lample, G., Saulnier, L., Lavaud, L. R., Lachaux, M., Stock, P., Scao, T. L., Lavril, T., Wang, T., Lacroix, T., & Sayed, W. E. (2023). Mistral 7B. *arXiv*. https://doi.org/10.48550/arXiv.2310.06825

Jomuad, P., Leah, M., Cericos, E., Bacus, J., Vallejo, J., Dionio, B., Bazar, J., Cocolan, J., & Clarin, A. (2021). Teachers' workload in relation to burnout and work performance. *International Journal of Educational Policy Research and Review, 8*(2). https://doi.org/10.15739/ijeprr.21.007

Kıyak, Y. S., & Kononowicz, A. A. (2024). Case-based MCQ generator: A custom ChatGPT based on published prompts in the literature for automatic item generation. *Medical Teacher, 46*(8), 1018–1020. https://doi.org/10.1080/0142159X.2024.2314723

Kojima, T., Gu, S. S., Reid, M., Matsuo, Y., & Iwasawa, Y. (2022). Large language models are zero-shot reasoners. *arXiv*. https://doi.org/10.48550/arXiv.2205.11916

Lo, L. S. (2023). The CLEAR path: A framework for enhancing information literacy through prompt engineering. *Journal of Academic Librarianship, 49*(4), Article 102720. https://doi.org/10.1016/j.acalib.2023.102720

Ma, X., Shen, J., Krenn, H. Y., Hu, S., & Yuan, J. (2016). A meta-analysis of the relationship between learning outcomes and parental involvement during early childhood education and early elementary education. *Educational Psychology Review, 28*, 771–801. https://doi.org/10.1007/s10648-015-9351-1

Mazzullo, E., Bulut, O., Jerez Garcia, D., Vo, K., Walsh, C., Sitarenios, G., & MacIntosh, A. (2025a). *Is it worth the effort? A comparison of automatic feedback generated by base and fine-tuned LLMs. [Manuscript submitted for publication]*. Faculty of Education, University of Alberta.

Mazzullo, E., Bulut, O., Walsh, C., Sitarenios, G., & MacIntosh, A. (2025b). Fine-tuning GPT-3.5-Turbo for automatic feedback generation. In *Proceedings of the 40th ACM/SIGAPP Symposium on Applied Computing (SAC '25)*. https://doi.org/10.1145/3672608.3707735

Meisels, S. J., & Atkins-Burnett, S. (2000). The elements of early childhood assessment. In J. P. Shonkoff & S. J. Meisels (Eds.), *Handbook of early childhood intervention* (2nd ed., pp. 231–257). Cambridge University Press.

Meyer, J., Jansen, T., Schiller, R., Liebenow, L. W., Steinbach, M., Horbach, A., & Fleckenstein, J. (2024). Using LLMs to bring evidence-based feedback into the classroom: AI-generated feedback increases secondary students' text revision, motivation, and positive emotions. *Computers and Education: Artificial Intelligence, 6*, Article 100199. https://doi.org/10.1016/j.caeai.2023.100199

Nguyen, H. A., Bhat, S., Moore, S., Bier, N., & Stamper, J. (2022, September). Towards generalized methods for automatic question generation in educational domains. In *European Conference on Technology Enhanced Learning* (pp. 272–284). Springer International Publishing. https://doi.org/10.1007/978-3-031-16290-9_20

Peterman, K., Cranston, K. A., Pryor, M., & Kermish-Allen, R. (2015). Measuring primary students' graph interpretation skills via a performance assessment: A case study in instrument development. *International Journal of Science Education, 37*(17), 2787–2808. https://doi.org/10.1080/09500693.2015.1105399

Piaget, J. (1962). The stages of the intellectual development of the child. *Bulletin of the Menninger Clinic, 26*(3), 120.

Radford, A., Wu, J., Child, R., Luan, D., Amodei, D., & Sutskever, I. (2019). Language models are unsupervised multitask learners. *OpenAI Blog, 1*(8), 9.

Schieffelin, B. B., & Ochs, E. (2013). A cultural perspective on the transition from pre-linguistic to linguistic communication. In *Becoming a person* (pp. 211–229). Routledge.

Shepard, L. A. (1994). The challenges of assessing young children appropriately. *The Phi Delta Kappan, 76*(3), 206–212. https://www.jstor.org/stable/20405297

Snow, C. E., & Van Hemel, S. B. (2008). *Early childhood assessment: Why, what, and how*. The National Academies Press.

Steiss, J., Tate, T., Graham, S., Cruz, J., Hebert, M., Wang, J., Moon, Y., Tseng, W., Warschauer, M., & Olson, C. B. (2024). Comparing the quality of human and ChatGPT feedback of students' writing. *Learning and Instruction, 91*, Article 101894. https://doi.org/10.1016/j.learninstruc.2024.101894

Tan, B., Armoush, N., Mazzullo, E., Bulut, O., & Gierl, M. (2024). A review of automatic item generation techniques leveraging large language models. *International Journal of Assessment Tools in Education, 12*(2), 317–340. https://doi.org/10.21449/ijate.1602294

Tieman, B. L., Palisano, R. J., & Sutlive, A. C. (2005). Assessment of motor development and function in preschool children. *Mental Retardation and Developmental Disabilities Research Reviews, 11*(3), 189–196. https://doi.org/10.1002/mrdd.20074

Touvron, H., Martin, L., Stone, K., Albert, P., Almahairi, A., Babaei, Y., Scialom, T. (2023). LLaMA 2: Open foundation and fine-tuned chat models. *arXiv*. https://doi.org/10.48550/arXiv.2307.09288

Wang, Z., Valdez, J., Basu Mallick, D., & Baraniuk, R. G. (2022, July). Towards human-like educational question generation with large language models. In *International Conference on Artificial Intelligence in Education* (pp. 153–166). Springer International Publishing. https://doi.org/10.1007/978-3-031-11644-5_13

White, J., Fu, Q., Hays, S., Sandborn, M., Olea, C., Gilbert, H., & Schmidt, D. C. (2023). A prompt pattern catalog to enhance prompt engineering with ChatGPT. *arXiv*. https://doi.org/10.48550/arXiv.2302.11382

Wilson, J., Ahrendt, C., Fudge, E. A., Raiche, A., Beard, G., & MacArthur, C. (2021). Elementary teachers' perceptions of automated feedback and automated scoring: Transforming the teaching and learning of writing using automated writing evaluation. *Computers & Education, 168*, Article 104208. https://doi.org/10.1016/j.compedu.2021.104208

Part IV
Co-creative Approaches with Generative AI

Chapter 13
Generative AI in Early Childhood Education: Teachers' Perspectives on Possibilities and Challenges

Marianne Undheim, Maria Dardanou, and Torstein Unstad Heimdal

Abstract The integration of digital technology and artificial intelligence (AI) in education has had an impact on early childhood education and care (ECEC). Generative AI (GAI) offers both opportunities and challenges, emphasizing the need for digital resilience among children. Teachers must develop digital competence to guide children in using technology creatively and critically. In Norway, ECEC focuses on children's participation, promoting democracy and inclusivity. Ethical considerations, such as algorithmic bias and data privacy, are crucial when using AI in education. This qualitative study explores seven Norwegian pre-service and in-service teachers' perspectives on GAI in ECEC, aiming to understand the possibilities and challenges they face. The analysis shows that the participants have a positive, yet at the same time critical, perspective towards using GAI in ECEC, focusing both on possibilities and challenges. The study highlights the importance of practice theory in developing professional digital competence. Through theory-based and ethical justifications and reflections on their actions, teachers can develop a more informed, critical, and discerning understanding of how and why to use GAI in their interactions with young children. This will help them navigate the complexities of digital technology in ECEC and nurture digitally resilient children.

Keywords Digital judgement · Early childhood education and care (ECEC) · Generative artificial intelligence (GAI) · Practice theory · Possibilities and challenges

M. Undheim (✉)
Department of Early Childhood Education, University of Stavanger, Stavanger, Norway
e-mail: marianne.undheim@uis.no

M. Dardanou · T. U. Heimdal
Department of Teacher Education and Pedagogy, UiT - The Arctic University of Norway, Tromsø, Norway
e-mail: maria.dardanou@uit.no

T. U. Heimdal
e-mail: torstein.heimdal@uit.no

S. Papadakis (ed.), *AI Applications in Preschool and Primary Education*, Advances in Artificial Intelligence in Education 5, https://doi.org/10.1007/978-3-032-17190-0_13

Introduction

The increasing integration of digital technology and artificial intelligence (AI) into various aspects of society has prompted significant changes in the landscape of education (Selwyn, 2019), including early childhood education. This evolution, particularly through the advent of generative AI (GAI), presents both unprecedented opportunities and multifaceted challenges for teachers and learners alike (Su et al., 2024). The findings in this chapter show that GAI can enhance participation and engagement when used collaboratively with young children, allowing them to co-create and reflect critically around the use of this tool. However, teachers must balance their use with critical judgement, using GAI as a supplement to, not substitute for, human collaboration, communication and imagination. The growing prevalence of GAI technology has underscored the need for teachers to help children develop digital resilience, enabling them to navigate this dynamic environment effectively and responsibly (OECD, 2023).

As early childhood education and care (ECEC) increasingly incorporates digital technologies, it is crucial that pre-service and in-service teachers possess a strong foundation in digital competence. Research emphasizes the importance of developing professional digital competence throughout their academic training (Dardanou et al., 2023; Madsen et al., 2023; Undheim & Ploog, 2024). Teachers must engage with digital technology not only as instruments for instruction but also as platforms for critical reflection, exploration, and dialogue (Papavlasopoulou et al., 2024). This engagement fosters both theoretical understanding and practical expertise, equipping teachers with the ability to guide children in utilizing these creatively and critically. In this way, digital technology becomes a way of thinking, not just a tool. Godhe (2019) suggested that a distinctive feature of Nordic curricula, compared with those of other countries, is the emphasis on societal issues and a critical, ethical approach to understanding the application of digital competence for both pre-service and in-service teachers. This is particularly relevant for the ECEC workforce (Dardanou et al., 2023). Moreover, AI can be leveraged to cultivate a range of cognitive, social, and emotional skills through appropriate pedagogical frameworks and carefully designed pedagogical practices (Voulgari et al., 2024).

Using GAI in education presents many opportunities and important issues that teachers need to be made aware of and acknowledge, such as social harms, societal implications and possible ethical consequences, as well as the environmental and ecological costs (Selwyn, 2022). Ethical considerations related to AI in ECEC have been reported by various studies (Berson et al., 2025; Crescenzi-Lanna, 2022) and are associated with algorithmic bias (Wang et al., 2024; Yang, 2022), data privacy (Kewalramani et al., 2023) or ethical challenges regarding children's autonomy or vulnerabilities (Adams et al., 2023; Kurian, 2023). Finally, AI-driven optimisation in supply chains can lead to overproduction and overconsumption by reducing costs and increasing the availability of goods, placing additional strain on environmental resources (UNICEF, 2018). To address these issues, it is essential to carefully manage AI's role in economic and environmental contexts. This ensures that technological advancements contribute positively to sustainability rather than worsening existing crises (Gupta et al., 2021).

Research Questions

Considering these pressing imperatives, this study investigates pre-service and in-service teachers' perspectives on GAI in ECEC. By exploring their experiences, we seek to identify the possibilities and challenges they encounter when they use these technologies in their pedagogical practices. Furthermore, to meet the increasing use of GAI in society, it is important to know more about what is actually being used within specific contexts, such as ECEC, and develop context-rich analyses of the practice (Selwyn, 2010). The research questions are as follows:

1. What are early childhood pre-service and in-service teachers' perspectives of GAI in ECEC?
2. What are the possibilities and challenges with GAI in ECEC?

The Norwegian ECEC Context and Children's Participation

In Norway, ECEC serves children aged one to five years prior to their formal schooling at the age of six. While attendance is not mandatory, a notable 94.4% of children in this age group are enrolled in ECEC institutions (kindergartens) (Statistics Norway, 2025). In Norwegian ECEC, children's participation is a fundamental principle that reflects the values of democracy, inclusivity, and individual agency, as stated in the *Framework Plan for Kindergartens* (Directorate for Education and Training, 2017). The framework plan emphasizes the importance of children's voices in shaping their learning experiences, ensuring they are active contributors to their environments. Teachers encourage participation by fostering an open dialogue where children can express their thoughts, preferences, and ideas, thereby promoting their autonomy and self-confidence. More specifically, "everyone shall have the same opportunities to be seen, heard and encouraged to participate in all shared activities" (Directorate for Education and Training, 2017, p. 10). This approach not only enhances children's social and emotional development but also empowers them to take ownership of their learning, facilitating a sense of belonging and community within ECEC settings (Bae, 2021).

Additionally, the use of digital technology in ECEC is emphasized as a method for everyday activities and practices with children (Directorate for Education and Training, 2017). Digital judgement is explicitly mentioned, such as being conscious of copyright issues, critically analysing sources and safeguarding children's privacy (Directorate for Education and Training, 2017, p. 45). Thus, the focus on participation is closely linked to the opportunities of digital technology, which underscores the relevance of children's perspectives in creating meaningful and engaging play and learning experiences (Shengjergji, 2024).

Practice Theory

ECEC teachers' professional digital competence can be viewed from different perspectives. In this study, we draw on Handal and Lauvås' (1999) practice theory. They describe teachers' practice theory as a dynamic construction of three elements: personal experience, transmitted knowledge, and values. These elements are intimately intertwined, and it is impossible to identify them as isolated elements. Values can be of a general ethical or philosophical nature, political (e.g., democratic values or children's participation) or related to ECEC. To work as an ECEC teacher, "knowing how" is as important as "knowing that", as emphasized in the term "practice", in which both action and reflection-on-action are central (Handal & Lauvås, 1999, p. 21).

Handal and Lauvås (1999, pp. 40–41) divided the teachers' practice theory into three levels. P1, the first level, is the level of action. At this level, teachers draw on their personal experiences and provide practice-based arguments for their actions. The next level, P2, is the level of reflection and justification. At this level, teachers provide professional justifications for their actions by drawing on theory-based arguments. The last level, P3, is the level of values. At this level, teachers provide ethical justifications for and reflect on their actions, which are rooted in values. To summarize, Handal and Lauvås' (1999) practice theory includes practice-based and theory-based justifications as well as ethical justifications of actions.

In line with findings in Undheim and Ploog (2024), it is important to engage pre-service and in-service teachers in reflections and didactic judgements of how, why and when to use technology, for example by first exploring technology in groups and then sharing their experiences with each other. To develop relevant professional digital competence, it is important to include and draw on a combination of practice-based, theory-based and ethical justifications of actions when discussing the use of digital technology in ECEC. In the early childhood teacher education curriculum, both theoretical and practical aspects of digital competence need to be included (Undheim & Ploog, 2024). To develop a high-quality pedagogical use of digital technology, reflections and discussions of attitudes, usefulness and usage among the teachers and staff in ECEC is required (Dardanou et al., 2023).

Methods

Research Design

This study employs a qualitative research design to explore the reflections and opinions of ECEC pre-service and in-service teachers. We draw on an interpretive and constructivist paradigm (Creswell & Poth, 2018), understanding knowledge as co-constructed by the participants within the social, cultural and professional context. A qualitative approach is particularly well-suited for understanding the diverse views and professional practices of such a new and fast-developing field as GAI, as it allows participants to describe their thoughts and experiences in their own words (Creswell & Poth, 2018).

A total of seven participants, recruited through early childhood teacher education courses at UiT–The Arctic University of Norway and the University of Stavanger, participated in this study. Five of the participants were pre-service teachers in the final year of their bachelor's degree in ECEC. Two of the participants were in-service teachers in an extension course on digital technology. All participants had direct or recent practical experience working with children in ECEC settings. Three of the pre-service teachers had attended lectures on GAI prior to this study. Both sexes were included.

Data Construction

In this study, the participants' shared perspectives are explored in greater depth; therefore, group interviews with a semi–structured interview guide were chosen as the data collection method. Group interviews allow participants to build on each other's inputs and expand their collective reflections, often sparking deeper insights that might not surface in individual interviews (Brinkmann & Kvale, 2018). The method is particularly appropriate when collecting data with ECEC pre-service and in-service teachers since the participants are accustomed to working in a collaborative environment with collegial discussions and provide for practical insights and examples as well as enhanced comfort during discussions amongst peers (Brinkmann & Kvale, 2018).

An interview guide with a set of open-ended questions was used, allowing flexibility for follow-up questions and comments on the topic. The interview guide covered questions on knowledge of AI and GAI, the use of GAI in professional settings and attitudes towards GAI. This research design ensures that the voices of the participants are at the forefront of the discussion while also conducting in-depth explorations of some of their reflections.

Three digital group interviews were conducted, with two to three participants in each. The interviews were recorded in *Microsoft Teams* and lasted between 30 and

45 minutes each. *Autotekst*[1], a secure AI-driven transcription service, was used to transcribe the interviews, which were then manually reviewed by the first and third authors.

Analysis

Inspired by Braun and Clarke (2022), we conducted a thematic analysis of the transcribed interviews, guided by the research questions. The empirical knowledge constructed in this study is analysed and bound by the Norwegian ECEC context. The participants' perspectives of GAI can be categorised as: a focus on pedagogical, administrative, and critical and balanced use, digital judgement, and competence and experience.

We acknowledge that, as researchers, we play an active role in interpreting the data while striving not to let our expectations and assumptions colour the findings (Alvesson & Sköldberg, 2018).

Ethics

The study was approved by and conducted in line with the guidelines provided by Sikt[2] as well as the ethical commitments of the two universities. All participants were provided with detailed information regarding the purpose of the study as well as procedures and data handling before agreeing to participate, in line with the Norwegian National Research Ethics Committees (NESH, 2024). They were informed of their right to withdraw at any stage without explanation or consequence to themselves, per the principles of voluntary participation and respect for everyone's rights (NESH, 2024).

Given the relatively few participants, measures were taken to preserve confidentiality and anonymity. This was ensured through the pseudonymisation of each participant, avoiding limited demographic data, such as age, workplace and sex, in both transcripts and in this paper, and safe storage of all sensitive data. When presenting the results, we focus on what was said but not by whom.

[1] *Autotekst* by the University of Oslo, https://autotekst.uio.no.

[2] Norwegian Agency for Shared Services in Education and Research, https://sikt.no.

Results

Drawing on the analysis, we present the results according to five themes: (1) pedagogical use of GAI with children, (2) administrative use of GAI, (3) critical and balanced use of GAI, (4) digital judgement, and (5) competence and experience.

Pedagogical Use of GAI with Children

When we asked if and how the participants had used GAI in ECEC, they mostly spoke about how they had used it pedagogically with the children. Four of the participants had used GAI together with the children to generate pictures, colouring sheets, stories, songs and music.

> I have used it a lot in ECEC, to make some music, to make colouring sheets. It is a lot of fun to involve the children in making new motifs. But also texts, stories... stories where you give just a short... a few guidelines, and then the rest is made in its entirety by AI.

> I have used it for texts, such as fairy tales. (...) I have used AI to make a small fairy tale based on the children's input.

> I have made stories together with the children by using AI. First, we discussed what the story was going to be about. One of the children told me that it was me and him and her. I asked the children what they were going to do in the story. Then, we wrote, "Make a story of 500 words". We also wrote who the story was going to be about and what they were doing. Then, we added some more plot, and then we read it out loud. Very often, the children then said, "No, it was not like that, we want him to do...". It is fun to create a story based on the children's ideas.

One of the participants presented a new idea that he wanted to try with the children: "I am also thinking about using AI even more to generate maybe pictures, to make a picture book based on fairy tales that the children have made".

The participants who had tried GAI together with the children emphasized that GAI provided good opportunities to involve the children in the process. They underscored that children were given opportunities to participate in new ways, for example, by generating materials on the basis of their ideas. They all expressed that the children thought it was fun to do.

> In a way, it is easier to acknowledge the children's participation more when using AI. Because when you can generate pictures "here-and-now" of what the children are actually saying, you get a better picture of what it is they are really thinking of. (...) This makes it easier to get pictures directly focused on their actual ideas.

> I have experienced that there are many children who think it is a lot of fun when we are doing it. I have seen some children expressing both humour and sincere joy and emotions.

Three of the participants had not used GAI themselves with the children.

Administrative Use of GAI

Another aspect of using GAI in ECEC is in collaboration with parents. Three of the participants gave concrete examples of how they had used GAI to create information letters, to write monthly and daily reports and to translate text for parents.

> Just this last week, I sent out an information letter about vomiting disease, in which I had used AI to formulate the letter. AI came up with some very nice details that I, of course, reformulated and made my own before I sent out. But when writing an information letter, it is very good to get some guidance. It had even taken into account the Norwegian Institute of Public Health's recommendations in relation to infection control and measures and some information about what we do in ECEC to prevent the disease from spreading. This is not something I have included before when I have written similar letters to the parents, which I thought was a very good thing. It is important for the parents to know that we have sharpened our focus on hygiene on surfaces and things like that. Things that you say to them, but not always include in a written letter.

> It has helped me with the daily report. I added a few keywords on what had happened, and then AI generated some complementary sentences that I got some inspiration from.

Two participants had used GAI for inspiration when planning ECEC activities, while another participant had used it to make lists of responsibilities and everyday routines for the staff.

Critical and Balanced Use of GAI

All the participants emphasized that there are both possibilities and challenges in using GAI in ECEC. On the one hand, the participants expressed a positive attitude, but on the other hand, they also expressed that the most important thing is to use it critically and reflectively. Among the three groups that were interviewed, the two in-service teachers were the most specific when they talked about the opportunities to use GAI, whereas the five pre-service teachers expressed a greater degree of uncertainty, especially concerning using GAI with the children.

In addition to the practical possibilities that have already been presented, other possibilities highlighted by the participants were more general: "I see great possibilities in GAI. It is amazing… It feels so endless". Another participant described it as a way to provide "varied working methods to give the children different experiences", indicating that GAI may be one way to provide these experiences.

Many of the challenges the participants highlighted concerned the critical and balanced use of GAI in ECEC.

> I think that the challenge is to use GAI in a good way. To be familiar with it and understand some of the opportunities that lie in it.

> It is important not to become too dependent on GAI either, and let it take away all creativity. (…) It is easy to just ask GAI to generate a new song about something, instead of sitting together and thinking and pondering and making it with the children.

> I think that it is a bit similar to other digital tools, that you have to use it a little carefully. It should not be a dominant working method and only use that. Sometimes you use AI, sometimes you use your imagination. I think using different types of working methods is very important.
>
> It is about finding that balance, what is okay and what is not okay.

Digital Judgement

The participants also emphasized the importance of professional digital competence and digital judgement to be able to meet the challenges that might occur. One participant described a situation in which the children, on their own initiative, created three fictional characters that they constantly referred to during play. This participant became curious about these characters and what they looked like and talked with the children about them.

> When I talked to the children about these fictional characters, I actually got a really good description of them. So, then I thought I would use AI to generate some pictures of the characters. At first, I thought of doing it together with the children. But then I started thinking more about it. "No, ugh, the characters were witches and wolves and trolls". I was afraid of what AI would generate based on the descriptions, so I did not dare to do it directly with the children. I did not feel competent enough. I did not know what was coming. So, I ended up generating the pictures myself and then I presented them to the children. But I did not do it together with them, because I actually felt very insecure. The characters they had made were quite scary, with teeth and many scary details. I was a bit like... I could probably have added that the generated pictures should be as cartoonish as possible, for example, but at that time I had not tested it long enough for me to feel comfortable in doing it together with the children. However, this is one of those situations I think of as an example of a golden opportunity situation.

Another participant explained that he tested GAI at home with his own children first and then used these experiences when he involved the children in similar activities in ECEC.

> I found out that if I first added information that I was making pictures to be used together with children at the age of four or added several details in advance or during the activity, then I see that so far it has gone well when I have used it with the children. But you never know. There is always a chance, but that is a risk I am willing to take. It depends on what prompts you add, but personally I think it is great fun.

Several of the participants highlighted children's understanding of GAI. They expressed a concern that GAI can be challenging for adults to understand, and even more so for children. One participant presented one way to meet these challenges.

> From the children's perspectives, they probably get the most value from using GAI if they can relate it to themselves. And also, by being involved in the process itself, it will be easier for them to understand how it works, and not just make something and then say: "See what I have made for you!"

Another participant gave an example of a GAI activity making rhymes with 3–4-year-olds. This was a great way to show the children, through practical examples, that AI is making up words, among other things.

> I think that making rhymes with AI is a good way to use it together with the children. I think it is important, early on, to consciously show the children that AI makes mistakes. I have used it with the 3–4-year-olds in relation to language and rhyming. They learned that AI is wrong. "That is not a real word," the children said. Such small drops over a long period of time are important so that they see and experience that not all answers are real. It becomes… a tool.

The participants also highlighted various aspects regarding ethical issues and digital judgement as challenges, such as copyright, source criticism and privacy.

> Lately, I have heard a lot about copyright and such things regarding AI-generated pictures. This makes me a little sceptical about using GAI. I feel that I need to know a little more about it before I dare to use it.

> You have to think about the children's safety when using GAI. (…) You have to think before, during and after you use it.

To meet these challenges, one of the participants said that it is important to test the different programs before using them with the children and "check that they adhere to the guidelines you are giving".

Competence and Experience

The analysis shows that the participants' expertise and experience play a major role in how they view the use of GAI. The participants who had used GAI with the children and tried it out on their own were clearly enthusiastic about using it. The participants who had not yet tried it with children expressed that they wanted to try it, but that they felt insecure and wanted to learn more about it before involving the children.

> I am quite positive about it, but I also notice that I have to play a lot more with it before I start using it in ECEC.

> Copyright is one of the things that often stops me, because I do not have enough knowledge about copyright and such. (…) I think that I need to… I need to feel safer myself. Yes. I am very afraid of making a mistake.

One of the participants said, "If you just continue using it, and then it is not… then I do not teach the children to exercise digital judgement". The participant underscored the importance of knowledge to be a good role model for the children.

Several of the participants also emphasized the importance of informing both the parents and the rest of the staff of what they were doing and why.

> This is a bit like with other things; you might feel resistance from the parents, especially if they are not fully aware of what you are actually doing or are not fully informed of what you are using GAI for.

> I think it is very important to build a solid collaboration with the parents and explain what it is you actually use GAI for in ECEC. But also, to explain to the other staff, and challenge them. Maybe discuss GAI at a staff meeting and work in teams to experiment and check out how it can be used so that the staff together becomes a driving force.

The participants considered information as one way to overcome scepticism from parents and colleagues. However, providing comprehensive and knowledge-based information requires having the necessary knowledge and expertise, which several of the participants highlighted.

> I think it is important to exercise GAI with professional digital competence, to exercise it with judgement, among other things. And to remember that... it should be a supplement, not the standard in ECEC.

Discussion

Positive yet Critical

In answer to the first research question, the analysis shows that the participants have a positive, yet critical, perspective on GAI in ECEC. During their teacher education, they learned about using digital technology and expressed an interest in applying it to their practice. The participants presented several examples of how they had used GAI themselves, both pedagogically with the children and to perform administrative tasks. They focused on the importance of using GAI critically, with a balanced and reflective approach. However, in their examples, they focused mostly on what happened, the action, which we interpret as the first level of Handal and Lauvås' (1999) practice theory. The participants who had used GAI and tried it out themselves, were enthusiastic about using it. The participants who had not yet tried it with the children expressed that they wanted to try it but also felt insecure and wanted to learn more before using it with the children. The Norwegian framework plan focuses not only on using digital technology in creative and inventive ways together with children but also on using it with care and not allowing it to dominate as a practice (Directorate for Education and Training, 2017, pp. 44–45). The participants are clearly influenced by the framework plan.

Possibilities and Challenges

Possibilities

To answer the second research question, we first focus on the possibilities and then the challenges.

The participants presented several possibilities regarding the use of GAI in ECEC. These were mostly related to practical examples, such as generating new materials (e.g., pictures and texts) together with the children. Several of the participants spoke about the many opportunities for involving children in the process when generating materials with AI. Through the immediate response provided by AI, children are given new possibilities to participate and contribute "here-and-now", in line with the *Convention on the Rights of the Child* (United Nations, 1989). This is an innovative use of digital technology in which children are given various opportunities to participate in new ways, in line with the Norwegian framework plan (Directorate for Education and Training, 2017) and findings from other studies (e.g., Bae, 2021; Berson et al., 2025; Kurian, 2023; Su et al., 2024; Voulgari et al., 2024).

The participants also considered GAI to be helpful and inspiring in administrative tasks. They viewed the possibilities with GAI as endless, both pedagogically and administratively.

Challenges

In addition to these possibilities, several challenges with using GAI in ECEC were mentioned by the participants.

First, the participants found it challenging to use GAI in a good and balanced way. They highlighted the importance of using GAI when it adds value and not to become overly dependent on it. As noted by Berson et al. (2025, p. 8), there is a "potential for AI systems to limit children's autonomy and creativity". One way to meet this challenge is to use GAI in pedagogically appropriate ways (Adams et al., 2023), such as to collaborate and create together using their own and children's creativity.

Second, some participants raised concerns about children's understanding of GAI. It is difficult for adults to understand that something is generated by AI; thus, for children, it is even more challenging, which was also emphasized by other researchers (e.g., Adams et al., 2023; Berson et al., 2025; Kurian, 2023). AI can sometimes present incorrect information in a way that appears highly convincing. Awareness of this can be addressed by involving the children in the process and discussing what is happening, such as in the example where the children and teacher used GAI to make rhymes. Age-appropriate activities and learning experiences that scaffold children's understanding of AI constitute one way to meet this challenge (Yang, 2022). In this way, children can develop digital resilience, which is important in today's society (OECD, 2023).

Third, challenges related to ethical issues and digital judgement, such as copyright, source criticism, and privacy, were mentioned by all participants, in line with national and international policy documents (Directorate for Education and Training, 2017; OECD, 2023; UNICEF, 2018). These challenges are also emphasized by other studies (e.g., Adams et al., 2023; Berson et al., 2025; Crescenzi-Lanna, 2022). Additionally, the participants raised concerns regarding children's safety because it is difficult to know exactly what might be generated when using GAI. One way to address this challenge is to test relevant prompts prior to using them with the children and to inform GAI that anything created should be age-appropriate for children under the age of six. To use GAI safely with children, teachers require experience and knowledge (Yang, 2022). Children are vulnerable and have a right to protection; at the same time, they have a right to be heard (United Nations, 1989). It can be challenging to balance these contrasting dimensions (Adams et al., 2023; Kurian, 2023).

As discussed above, the participants mentioned several challenges, although none referred to social harms, algorithmic bias, sustainability or energy usage, which are urgent issues to be aware of (Adams et al., 2023; Kurian, 2023; Selwyn, 2022; Wang et al., 2024; Yang, 2022). For example, when AI is used to generate pictures, it is likely that certain groups of people will be empowered, while others may be disempowered, due to algorithmic bias. It is reasonable to assume that some of the participants were aware of these challenges, even if they did not reflect upon them during the interview. However, we did not ask explicitly about this, the questions were more general, such as "Which possibilities or challenges do you see when using GAI in ECEC?"

Conclusion

In this study, we explored pre-service and in-service teachers' perspectives on using GAI in ECEC to learn more about the "state-of-the-actual" within a specific context (Selwyn, 2010). This is a small-scale study with few participants. Nevertheless, the study contributes to this evolving field by providing rich descriptions of how and why participants use GAI in ECEC.

Drawing on Handal and Lauvås' (1999) practice theory, we consider that most participants' knowledge of GAI in ECEC is at the first level (P1). The participants focused mostly on what they had done and how they had done it. Some participants reflected on the why aspect by providing professional justifications for their actions, as described in the second level (P2). The only value-based reflections provided by the participants, which we interpret to be at the third level (P3), were about children's participation. No participants truly questioned if GAI should be used in ECEC.

The results of this study imply that ECEC teachers should explore, experience and reflect upon practices, if possible, together with colleagues, to become more confident users of GAI, as also emphasized by Yang (2022). Teachers need to develop professional digital competence to effectively guide children in using technology both creatively and critically (Dardanou et al., 2023), including GAI. Additionally, teachers must reflect on their practices by drawing on both theoretical and ethical foundations, as emphasized by Handal and Lauvås (1999). Through such reflections, teachers can build a more informed, critical, and discerning understanding of how and why to use GAI in their interactions with young children. This will help them navigate the complexities of digital technology in ECEC and nurture digitally resilient children.

Practical Guidelines for Teachers

Based on the participants' examples, we propose the following practical guidelines for teachers who want to use GAI in ECEC:

Familiarise yourself with GAI and the opportunities, for example, by generating pictures, colouring sheets, stories, songs or music.

Consider safety aspects, for example by testing the programs before including the children.

Use age-appropriate prompts, for example by including text such as, "a fairytale-inspired illustration of a troll to be used together with children at the age of four", when generating materials together with children.

Include the children in the process by generating materials based on their ideas.

Plan age-appropriate activities related to the children's experiences and interests, for example, asking GAI to make rhymes based on children's ideas, pictures based on the children's favourite book, or a story about the children going on a trip.

Talk about the generated materials with the children and discuss algorithmic bias, for example, by highlighting elements in an AI-generated picture: "Does the illustration of the troll look like a troll? Why/why not?", "What do the children think of the rhymes? Why did AI use those words?"

Implications for Practice and Ethics

Supporting teachers in their use of GAI as a creative and participatory tool could strengthen children's emerging digital competence and resilience. For teachers to become more confident users of GAI, it is important to practice hands-on exploration of GAI tools, but always with critical reflection and ethical awareness as a focus in their professional development. Ethically, attention must be on issues such as bias, data privacy and children's vulnerability as explorers of a powerful tool. Ensuring equitable access and safeguarding children's rights and well-being in all GAI-supported practices will be important in future practices everywhere.

Acknowledgments We thank the participants who so willingly shared their experiences with us.

Funding The research reported in this article was supported by the FILIORUM Centre for Research in Early Childhood Education and Care at University of Stavanger (https://www.uis.no/en/research/filiorum-centre-for-research-in-early-childhood-education-and-care), project grant no. 275576.

References

Adams, C., Pente, P., Lemermeyer, G., & Rockwell, G. (2023). Ethical principles for artifcial intelligence in K-12 education. *Computers and Education: Artificial Intelligence, 4*, 100131. https://doi.org/10.1016/j.caeai.2023.100131

Alvesson, M., & Sköldberg, K. (2018). *Reflexive methodology: New vistas for qualitative research* (3rd ed.). SAGE Publications Ltd.

Bae, B. (2021). Children's participatory rights at risk? Perspectives from Norway: Policy and practice in early childhood education and care. In A. Višnjić-Jevtić, A. R. Sadownik, & I. Engdahl (Eds.), *Young children in the world and their rights: International perspectives on early childhood education and development* (pp. 189–201). Springer. https://doi.org/10.1007/978-3-030-68241-5_14

Berson, I. R., Berson, M. J., & Luo, W. (2025). Innovating responsibly: Ethical considerations for AI in early childhood education. *AI, Brain & Child, 1*. https://doi.org/10.1007/s44436-025-00003-5

Braun, V., & Clarke, V. (2022). *Thematic analysis: A practical guide*. SAGE Publications Ltd.

Brinkmann, S., & Kvale, S. (2018). *Doing interviews* (2nd ed.). SAGE Publications Ltd.

Crescenzi-Lanna, L. (2022). Literature review of the reciprocal value of artificial and human intelligence in early childhood education. *Journal of Research on Technology in Education, 55*(1), 21–33. https://doi.org/10.1080/15391523.2022.2128480

Creswell, J. W., & Poth, C. N. (2018). *Qualitative inquiry and research design: Choosing among five approaches* (4th ed.). SAGE Publications Ltd.

Dardanou, M., Hatzigianni, M., Kewalramani, S., & Palaiologou, I. (2023). *Professional development for digital competencies in early childhood education and care: A systematic review*. OECD Education Working Papers, No. 295. https://doi.org/10.1787/a7c0a464-en

Directorate for Education and Training. (2017). *Framework plan for kindergartens: Regulations on the Framework plan for the content and tasks of kindergartens*. https://www.udir.no/laring-og-trivsel/rammeplan-for-barnehagen/

Godhe, A.-L. (2019). Digital literacies or digital competence: Conceptualizations in Nordic curricula. *Media and Communication, 7*(2), 25–35. https://doi.org/10.17645/MAC.V7I2.1888

Gupta, S., Langhans, S. D., Domisch, S., Fuso-Nerini, F., Felländer, A., Battaglini, M., Tegmark, M., & Vinuesa, R. (2021). Assessing whether artificial intelligence is an enabler or an inhibitor of sustainability at indicator level. *Transportation Engineering, 4*, 100064. https://doi.org/10.1016/j.treng.2021.100064

Handal, G., & Lauvås, P. (1999). *På egne vilkår—en strategi for veiledning med lærere* [On your own terms—a strategy for mentoring with teachers]. Cappelen Akademisk forlag.

Kewalramani, S., Palaiologou, I., & Dardanou, M. (2023). *The integration of Internet of Toys in early childhood education: Research from Australia, England and Norway*. Routledge.

Kurian, N. (2023). Toddlers and robots? The ethics of supporting young children with disabilities with AI companions and the implications for children's rights. *International Journal of Human Rights Education, 7*(1), 1–13. https://repository.usfca.edu/ijhre/vol7/iss1/9

Madsen, S. S., Unstad, T., Tveiterås, N. C., Dardanou, M., Habbestad, H., & Kosner, L. (2023). Planverkets blindsone? En analyse av profesjonsfaglig digital kompetanse i emneplanbeskrivelser for barnehagelærerutdanning [A blind spot in curricula? An analysis of professional digital competence in subject curricula for early childhood teacher education]. *Nordisk Barnehageforskning, 20*(4), 103–128. https://doi.org/10.23865/nbf.v20.531

NESH. (2024). *Guidelines for research ethics in the social sciences and the humanities* (5th ed.) The Norwegian National Research Ethics Committees. https://www.forskningsetikk.no/globalassets/dokumenter/4-publikasjoner-som-pdf/nesh-guidelines-en-2024/

OECD. (2023). *Starting Strong VII: Empowering young children in the digital age. OECD Publishing*. https://doi.org/10.1787/50967622-en

Papavlasopoulou, S., Undheim, M., Meaney, T., & Esmaeeli, S. (2024). Early childhood preservice teachers' preparation for using technology with children: A systematic literature review.

European Journal of Teacher Education, 1–18. https://doi.org/10.1080/02619768.2024.2341935

Selwyn, N. (2010). Looking beyond learning: Notes towards the critical study of educational technology. *Journal of Computer Assisted Learning, 26*(1), 65–73. https://doi.org/10.1111/j.1365-2729.2009.00338.x

Selwyn, N. (2019). *Should robots replace teachers?* Polity Press.

Selwyn, N. (2022). The future of AI and education: Some cautionary notes. *European Journal of Educational Research, 57*(4), 620–631. https://doi.org/10.1111/ejed.12532

Shengjergji, S. (2024). "Yeah, I am making new stuff!": Responsivity to and negotiations of agency during digital storytelling in preschool. *European Early Childhood Education Research Journal, 32*(5), 834–851. https://doi.org/10.1080/1350293X.2023.2301595

Statistics Norway. (2025). *Kindergartens.* Statistisk Sentralbyrå. Retrieved 15 March 2025 from https://www.ssb.no/en/utdanning/statistikker/barnehager

Su, J., Yang, W., Yim, I. H. Y., Li, H., & Hu, X. (2024). Early artificial intelligence education: Effects of cooperative play and direct instruction on kindergarteners' computational thinking, sequencing, self-regulation and theory of mind skills. *Journal of Computer Assisted Learning, 40*(6), 2917–2925. https://doi.org/10.1111/jcal.13040

Undheim, M., & Ploog, M. (2024). Digital competence and digital technology: A curriculum analysis of Norwegian early childhood teacher education. *Scandinavian Journal of Educational Research, 68*(6), 1105–1120. https://doi.org/10.1080/00313831.2023.2204109

UNICEF. (2018). *Children and AI: Where are the opportunities and risks?* UNICEF Innovation and World Economic Forum. https://www.unicef.org/innovation/sites/unicef.org.innovation/files/2018-11/Children%20and%20AI_Short%20Verson%20%283%29.pdf

United Nations. (1989). *Convention on the Rights of the Child.* https://www.ohchr.org/EN/ProfessionalInterest/Pages/CRC.aspx

Voulgari, I., Lavidas, K., Aravantinos, S., Sypsa, S., & Sfyroera, M. (2024). Exploring the role, implementation, and educational implications of AI in early childhood education. In A. M. Olney, I.-A. Chounta, Z. Liu, O. C. Santos, & I. I. Bittencourt (Eds.), *Artificial Intelligence in Education. AIED 2024* (Vol. 2151). Springer. https://doi.org/10.1007/978-3-031-64312-5_4

Wang, G., Zhao, J., Van Kleek, M., & Shadbolt, N. (2024). Challenges and opportunities in translating ethical AI principles into practice for children. *Nature Machine Intelligence, 6*(3), 265–270. https://doi.org/10.1038/s42256-024-00805-x

Yang, W. (2022). Artifcial intelligence education for young children: Why, what, and how in curriculum design and implementation. *Computers and Education: Artificial Intelligence, 3*, 100061. https://doi.org/10.1016/j.caeai.2022.100061

Chapter 14
Teaching with AI Personas: Designing for Co-CreAItivity in ECEC

Zacharias E. Andreadakis

Abstract This study explores the concept of *co-creAItivity*, i.e. the nexus of creativity and human-centered artificial intelligence for early childhood education and care. Drawing on recent developments in computational creativity and digital pedagogy, this chapter introduces four developmentally appropriate AI personas *Storyteller*, *Explorer*, *Playmate*, and *Mentor* designed to support creative engagement in early childhood settings. Each persona is analyzed through key interaction modalities *control*, *feedback*, *pace*, and *transparency* that structure meaningful human–AI collaboration and aligns with acceded and well-founded ECEC teaching and learning values. By situating these personas within established ECEC practices and theories, this study aims to offer a concrete, ethical framework for designing AI systems that amplify creativity in ECEC. The study concludes with a critical discussion of trade-offs, including risks of bias, over-personalization, and environmental costs, arguing for a co-creative, human-centered vision of AI that supports agency, equity, and exploration from the earliest years.

Keywords Artificial Intelligence · AI · Early Childhood Education · ECE · AI Personas · Co-Creation · Co-CreAItivity · computational creativity

Introduction

> Ἄνδρα μοι ἔννεπε, Μοῦσα, πολύτροπον
>
> Tell me, muse, of the man of many ways
>
> Odyssey, Book 1, verse 1.

Creativity, often regarded as a hallmark of human ingenuity our wiley, Odyssean self is typically defined as "the ability to generate novel and useful ideas" (Garcia, 2025; Rhodes, 1961). Its epistemic depth and conceptual range have long captivated

Z. E. Andreadakis (✉)
KINDknow Research Centre, Department of Pedagogy, Religion, and Social Studies, Western Norway University of Applied Sciences, Bergen, Norway
e-mail: zaan@hvl.no

S. Papadakis (ed.), *AI Applications in Preschool and Primary Education*, Advances in Artificial Intelligence in Education 5, https://doi.org/10.1007/978-3-032-17190-0_14

all aspects of scientific, technological and artistic reasoning—be that e.g. education, psychology, philosophy, mathematics- serving as a key driver of innovation, cultural development, and human problem-solving. Within education in particular, creativity has been celebrated not only as an individual trait but as a social and developmental imperative for all learners (Amabile, 2019; Sica et al., 2022). Creativity, as a sociocultural construct, is shaped by both individual and cultural factors, namely, cognitive flexibility, emotional insight, and sociocultural context, and in its essence is constituted of the core constructs of divergent and convergent thinking (Kumar et al., 2024; Garcia, 2025). Now, on the one hand, divergent thinking enables the generation of multiple, varied ideas by exploring different perspectives and possibilities. Conversely, convergent thinking involves synthesizing these ideas into coherent, valuable, and often tangible outcomes. Together, they represent the dynamic interplay between imagination and logic, spontaneity and structure in our creative thinking. As scholarship so far concedes (Garcia, 2025; Grilli and Pedota, 2024; Hubert et al., 2024), what ultimately characterizes creativity is not only the production of the new and the useful, but also the capacity to transcend conventional boundaries linking the abstract with the concrete, the personal with the collective. Traditionally, this synthesis of creativity has been seen as an exclusively human trait, rooted in our embodied consciousness and our sapiential capacity for meaning-making.

This anthropocentric view, however, has been challenged by the rapid ascent of *computational creativity*, which refers to the generation of novel and contextually meaningful outputs by machines (Grilli & Pedota, 2024; Colton & Wiggins, 2012). Recently, advanced AI systems such as ChatGPT-4, DALL-E, Gemini, and Stable Diffusion now routinely generate high-quality visual, linguistic, and conceptual artifacts which are almost inseparable from human-generated ones. Recently, in controlled tasks like the Alternative Uses Task and the Divergent Association Task, GPT-4 has been shown to outperform humans in originality and elaboration (Hubert et al., 2024), raising questions about what constitutes real creativity in the age of machine learning. AI's ability to sidestep human cognitive limitations such as fixation and explore expansive creative domains through probabilistic mechanisms has opened up new and highly unexplored possibilities for education (Liu et al., 2024).

In response to this shifting landscap of creativity, this chapter sets out to examine how AI might be meaningfully integrated into early childhood education and care (ECEC) through a pedagogically grounded framework of *co-creAItivity*. I begin by revisiting the historical discourse on creativity in education, providing conceptual context for the debate around AI's emerging creative roles. Then, I outline the core human-AI *interaction modalities* **control**, **feedback**, **pace**, and **transparency** that govern how AI systems engage with human users (Moruzzi & Margarido, 2024). These modalities are crucial for understanding the quality and developmental appropriateness of AI integration, as they define the rhythm, agency, and intelligibility of human-AI collaborations. To further elaborate on this co-creative potential, each modality is explored in relation to its pedagogical significance and potential for shaping future ECEC practices. In response to these modalities, the study then introduces a set of AI personas Storyteller, Explorer, Playmate, and Mentor each designed to support distinct domains of development and co-creative interaction between children, educators, and intelligent systems.

The chapter concludes with a critical discussion of the trade-offs involved in adopting co-creAItivity as a guiding framework for AI in education, on the narrower epiphemomena of AI personas, as well as on a broader picture. Ethical and sustainability concerns such as algorithmic bias (Bird et al., 2024), energy use (Bourzac, 2024), data privacy (Kumi-Yeboah et al., 2023), and the risk of over-personalization (Pariser, 2011; Brincker, 2021) are addressed alongside deeper philosophical tensions around human agency, mentorship, and creative autonomy (Vervaeke & Coyne, 2024; Lara & Muller, 2023).

Creativity in ECEC: From Pedagogy to Digital Innovation

Creativity has long been a foundational goal in early childhood education and care (Alves-Oliveira et al., 2022). Traditionally, one of the most influential frameworks in this context of fostering creativity has been **design thinking**. Design thinking has been construed as a set of pedagogical practices that incorporates learning stages such as empathizing, ideating, prototyping, and testing into playful learning environments, which supports children in exploring real or imagined problems, encouraging collaboration, iterative thinking, and creative expression (Chatzigeorgiadou et al., 2022; Grönman et al., 2024). Its human-centered approach blends multidisciplinary learning with empathy-driven inquiry, setting the stage for deeper cognitive and social engagement (Yalçin, 2022; Mize et al., 2022).

Building on this foundation of frameworks for fostering creativity, the next era of human-computer interaction for ECEC was **digital pedagogy,** a set of pedagogical practices which has extended these creativity principles by integrating technology into child-led exploration. Grounded in educational models like the SAMR framework (Substitution; Augmentation; Modification; Redefinition), educators have transformed traditional tasks into digital storytelling, animation, and early programming activities that enhance problem-solving and communication (Fleer, 2019; Fleer, 2020). This shift from a more passive consumption of digital or hybrid content to active creation allows children to co-construct content, expanding both digital fluency and their creative repertoire (Fleer, 2020; Undheim, 2022; Liu et al., 2024; OECD, 2023).

More recently, the next era of HCI for ECEC, namely, **technology-integrated pedagogy** has introduced tools such as AI, robotics, and augmented reality into everyday learning. These technologies are no longer simply add-ons but function as responsive, adaptive elements within play-based activities (Kewalramani et al., 2020). With real-time feedback and data-driven interaction, children's contributions are acknowledged and scaffolded not only actively, but in real time, enhancing their opportunities for creative experimentation and personalized exploration (Li et al., 2024).

To be sure, we must take a step back here and establish that these pedagogical and technological shifts are not merely atheoretical technical innovations. Rather, they are all theoretically grounded in a sociocultural perspective. From this theoretical point of view, creativity in early childhood education and care is understood as a mediated and collective process, inseparable from the cultural practices and relationships that sustain it (Vygotsky, 1978; Hopwood & Sannino, 2023). Children develop creative thought through participation in shared activities storytelling, exploration, and play that unfold within social contexts rich with cultural tools and symbols which transform and give a deep sense of agency. As Hedegaard and Ødegaard (2020), Fleer (2019) and Fleer and Hedegaard (2010) have repeatedly shown, meaning in education emerges not in isolation but through collaboration, dialogue, and the transformation of motives within these activity systems.

From that theoretical point of view, AI systems become part of the evolving ecology of mediation in early education. They are not autonomous agents but new **cultural artefacts** that extend how children and educators co-construct meaning. When used thoughtfully, AI personas can operate as mediational means within the **zone of proximal development**, supporting shared attention, language, inquiry and agency, rather than displacing them. The creative encounter between child, educator, and AI thus represents a continuation of the sociocultural tradition of guided participation and transformation through mediated action (Rogoff, 2003; Hopwood & Sannino, 2023). Situating AI personas in this framework ensures that co-creAItivity remains aligned with the pedagogical values that have long underpinned ECEC: purposeful play, collaboration, and the cultivation of agency through socially meaningful activity.

Lately, the latest and most transformative development in this continuum is **generative AI**, which combines digital pedagogy with computational creativity. For the first time, tools like GPT can operate as creative partners, generating prompts, feedback, and idea spaces that support real-time, collaborative engagement between children, educators, and machines (Kanders et al., 2024). This evolving synergy often described as "generative synesthesia" (Zhou & Lee, 2024) redefines creativity as a co-constructed process where AI acts not merely as a support, but as an active co-agent in children's imaginative learning and expressive development.

This evolving landscape of creativity in ECEC from design thinking to digital pedagogy and, most recently, to generative AI marks a shift not only in tools, but in the nature of pedagogical relationships themselves. As AI moves from the periphery of enhancement to the center of co-creative processes, educators are increasingly faced with the challenge of integrating these systems in ways that are both developmentally appropriate and pedagogically meaningful. This shift necessitates a more nuanced understanding of how AI can participate in learning not just as a tool, but as a responsive, interactive presence. To address this, researchers have begun to conceptualize **AI personas**: structured, role-based agents that embody specific functions within the learning environment (Moruzzi and Margarido, 2024). These personas offer a way to make AI's presence intelligible and relational for young learners, building on existing pedagogical foundations while opening new pathways for co-creAItivity.

Interaction Modalities: Structuring Human-AI Interaction

This chapter builds on the premise that the quality of AI's pedagogical contribution depends not solely on its functional role or narrative framing, but on the interactional structure that underpins it. That structure is defined by what are termed **interaction modalities** foundational dimensions that determine how agency, communication, responsiveness, and mutual intelligibility are distributed in the interaction between human and machine (Moruzzi & Margarido, 2024). These modalities are not merely technical parameters but constitute the very conditions under which co-creAItivity can occur. They define whether the AI guides or follows, whether it responds immediately or reflectively, and whether its operations are intelligible to users or remain opaque.

To understand how AI can meaningfully participate in co-creative educational processes, we must look beyond its surface functions and consider the underlying architecture of interaction. At the core of this architecture are four foundational **interaction modalities control**, **feedback**, **pace**, and **transparency** which together shape the rhythm, balance, and intelligibility of human–AI collaboration (Moruzzi & Margarido, 2024). These modalities are not mere technical parameters; they are the grammar through which co-creativity is negotiated. They determine when the AI speaks and when it listens, how it responds to the child's imagination, how quickly or slowly it moves through an activity, and whether its inner workings are revealed or concealed. Each modality, then, is a dimension of relational possibility a way in which agency, meaning, and pedagogy are distributed between human and machine. When orchestrated intentionally, these modalities give rise to AI personas: role-based configurations such as the **Storyteller**, **Explorer**, **Playmate**, and **Mentor**, each offering a distinctive way for AI to join the creative unfolding of thought and expression in early childhood settings. To think with a potentially elucidating metaphor here, one might think of these modalities as the strings of a marionette: not dictating a fixed performance, but allowing for nuanced, responsive movement sometimes led by the child, sometimes guided by the AI, always dependent on balance and timing. In what follows, we define each of these four modalities in turn, illustrating how they serve as the scaffolding through which AI personas participate in and shape co-creAItive learning.

Control refers to the degree of agency exercised by either the user or the AI in initiating, sustaining, and concluding an activity. In co-creative contexts, particularly with young children, shared control where the AI supports without dominating has been shown to foster autonomy and exploratory engagement (Haase and Hanel 2023; Haase & Pokutta, 2024). Conversely, feedback shapes the interactional quality of the system's responses how immediate, specific, or reflective they are in relation to the child's input. Tailored feedback has been linked to increased motivation and learning gains, especially when aligned with developmental needs (Liu et al., 2024). Next, pace refers to the rhythm and timing of exchanges, which can either enable deeper reflection or create friction in the flow of activity. In pedagogical settings, a well-calibrated pace supports both attentiveness and sustained engagement (Long et al.,

2019). Finally, transparency functions as a meta-modality, referring to how openly and intelligibly the AI system communicates the rationale behind its actions or decisions. This is particularly critical in educational environments where interpretability, trust, and accountability are foundational to effective learning relationships (Longo et al., 2024). As a case in point, the Storyteller persona may reduce user control while amplifying narrative feedback to spark imaginative engagement, whereas the Mentor persona increases educator control and system transparency to provide clear scaffolding and didactic support.

These four modalities, taken together, provide a theoretical and design-oriented scaffold for constructing AI systems that are not only technically capable but developmentally resonant and ethically sound. They bridge the gap between algorithmic capacity and pedagogical intention, ensuring that AI contributes to rather than undermines the social, imaginative, and relational foundations of early childhood education. With this conceptual foundation established, we now turn to the design of developmentally appropriate AI personas each embodying distinct interactional profiles and pedagogical affordances grounded in the modalities discussed above.

Framing AI Personas

While the concept of interaction modalities offers a robust analytical scaffold for structuring human–AI collaboration, it can often appear abstract or technically remote, particularly in the context of educational practices. To render these modalities more tangible and pedagogically interpretable, researchers have turned to the idea of **AI personas** role-based configurations that embody specific interactional dynamics within human–AI systems (Moruzzi & Margarido, 2024). These personas function as intuitive, developmentally grounded archetypes that translate the underlying modalities of control, feedback, pace, and transparency into distinct pedagogical roles.

The groundwork for such role-based thinking was laid by Lubart (2005), who proposed four foundational interactional roles **nanny, pen-pal, coach,** and **colleague** each reflecting a different balance of agency, responsiveness, and task orientation. Here is the breakdown of these roles in a nutsheel. First, the nanny emphasizes supervision and structure, aligning with high system control and low user autonomy. Then, the pen-pal privileges reflective dialogue, enabling the user to elaborate ideas in a more open-ended exchange. Alternatively, the coach offers formative feedback and motivational scaffolding, while the colleague engages as a near-equal in shared, co-creative processes. These roles helped to conceptualize the range of possible human–AI relationships, particularly in contexts requiring adaptive support. Think about it: this is a lot about how any kind of human interaction and relationship dynamics work.

So, expanding on this foundation from Lubart, Moruzzi and Margarido (2024) introduced a more differentiated taxonomy of AI personas **Assistant, Inspirational Source, Idea Challenger, Colleague, Quality Controller,** and **Director** tailored to adult creative workflows and nuancing the potential roles of these personas. In fact, these personas map the increasingly complex functions AI can fulfill in cognitive and design processes with humans for creativity. For instance, the Assistant streamlines repetitive tasks to enhance efficiency, while the Director takes a more assertive role in orchestrating creative directions. Intermediate roles, such as the Inspirational Source and Idea Challenger, are designed to provoke novel thinking and critical reflection, whereas the Colleague and Quality Controller facilitate co-production and iterative refinement.

Crucially, this expansion of AI personas is not arbitrary. Rather, it emerges from a deepening understanding over years of studying of how interaction modalities structure human–AI dynamics. These modalities control, feedback, pace, and transparency not only define how systems behave but also determine the kind of pedagogical relationships they afford. In adult learning contexts, they help us to mediate difficult trade-offs between autonomy and guidance, exploration and efficiency, or novelty and coherence each with implications for the nature and outcome of creative engagement. In other words, these AI personas can help us shape our very own creative fabric however we see fit. They can allow our supercharged creative selves to emerge.

Building on this lineage for adult human-computer interaction, and adapting it to the specific needs of early childhood education and care (ECEC), our current framework in turn proposes four **ECEC-aligned AI personas that can be used in ECEC classroom contexts**: **Storyteller, Explorer, Playmate,** and **Mentor**. Each persona is designed to reflect a distinct pedagogical role while operationalizing a unique configuration of interaction modalities. As I will showcase below, these AI personas can offer a developmentally appropriate and ethically grounded approach to integrating generative AI into early learning environments, not as a replacement for human creativity, but as a responsive and co-creative presence.

Four AI Personas for ECEC

Storyteller Persona: Fostering Language and Imagination

One of the pillars of ECEC interaction across all early childhood education and and care settings is storytelling and narrative skills, with long documented impacts on future school literacy, children´s inferential/representational skills, as well as their socio-cognitive and linguistic development (Shengjergji et al., 2024; Vretudaki, 2022). To further tap into the potential of honing narrative skills, the **Storyteller** persona is envisioned to co-create narratives with children, promoting language development, imaginative thinking, and comprehension. Its purpose is to engage children in storytelling activities where they contribute ideas, and the AI system integrates and expands these into cohesive narratives with them. In terms of **control**, the interaction is shared, with children suggesting story elements while the AI facilitates the narrative. Then, the **feedback** provided is immediate and positive, encouraging children to elaborate on their ideas and engage in dialogic exchanges. The **pace of interaction** is slow to moderate, allowing children time to reflect and verbalize their contributions effectively. And finally, transparency is **high**, with the AI explicitly explaining its actions, such as why a character was introduced or how the story's plot is progressing. This persona could mirror dialogic reading practices, which are proven to enhance language skills and imaginative capacities in young learner, as well as a holistic set of emergent skills and prosocial behavior.

Explorer Persona: Encouraging Inquiry and Discovery
Another foundational element of positive development in ECEC is the notion of exploration, a foundational learning and developmental mechanism in childhood, which allows for adaptive decision making and learning to infer probalistic associations between cues and outcomes (Xu et al., 2023), as well as infering the social world around them and acquiring cognitive flexibility (Blanco and Sloutsky, 2021; Meder et al., 2021; Hedegard and Ødegaard, 2020). In response to the well-documented benefits of explorative behavior in children, then, the envisioned **Explorer** persona is designed to stimulate curiosity and inquiry-based learning by guiding children through exploratory tasks (see Table 14.1). The explorer would be designed fosters critical thinking and creativity. The **control** dynamic is child-led, with the AI acting as a scaffold, providing subtle prompts and suggestions to guide exploration and hypothesis creation. Coversely, the **feedback** would indirect, reflective, and designed to encourage self-discovery rather than direct answers. The **pace of interaction** would be flexible, adapting to the child's engagement levels to ensure sustained interest without overwhelming them. Finally, transparency would be **moderate**, as the AI provides insights when needed, while keeping the focus on the child's exploration process. This aligns with Dewey's experiential learning theory, emphasizing the importance of discovery and hands-on learning (Na and Song, 2014), and testing further the well-documented benefits of exploration and explorative behavior in children.

Playmate Persona: Supporting Social and Emotional Development
Another foundational aspect of positive development in ECEC is play, which is well documented to foster emotional, physical, cognitive, and social development (Dankiw et al., 2023; Yogman et al., 2018), as well as autonomy and social interactions in say cases of risky play (Sando et al., 2021). In response to the well-documented benefits of encouraging play and playful behavior, the **Playmate** persona could be designed to engage in interactive play with children, supporting the development of social, emotional, and communication skills. This persona would foster collaborative play as a medium for fostering interpersonal interactions and problem-solving abilities, as well as social bonding. The **control** would be balanced, with both the child and the AI taking turns or collaborating equally in leading the play. **Feedback** may be immediate and multimodal, combining verbal encouragement with visual or auditory cues to maintain engagement and foster collaboration. The **pace of interaction** would be dynamic, adjusting to the rhythm of the child's play while maintaining a stimulating and responsive environment. Finally, transparency would be envisioned to be **low to moderate**, ensuring the child remains focused on the activity rather than the AI's underlying processes. This approach aligns with

Vygotsky's theories and a large host of recent data on play and collaborative learning, emphasizing the role of social interaction in cognitive and emotional development (Dankiw et al., 2023; Yogman et al., 2018).

Mentor Persona: Providing Scaffolding for Educators and Learners
Finally, older and newer scientific contributions have emphasized the importance of mentoring for young children, especially the ones at risk, for preventing trouble in educational facilities, and showcasing behavioral and emotional strenghts, as well as positive outcomes for children at risk for mental health, educational functioning and attainment, relationships amongst peers, placement outcomes, and life satisfaction (Tausig and Weiler, 2019). In response to the potential benefits of mentorship amongst yougn children, and particularly ones at risk, the **Mentor** persona may offer tailored scaffolding to both children and educators, enhancing learning experiences and classroom management. By providing structured guidance and activity suggestions, this personal could serve as an assistant in creating enriched educational environments which can help guide children through difficult. The **control** dynamic may vary, with the AI taking a more directive role when working with educators and adopting a shared-control model with children to provide adaptive scaffolding. **Feedback** is detailed and task-specific, offering clear explanations and contextual information to facilitate learning. The **pace of interaction** is moderate to fast, designed for efficiency in classroom settings while remaining adaptable to individual learning needs. Transparency can be **high**, ensuring educators understand the AI's decisions and processes, which helps integrate the AI seamlessly into teaching strategies. The Mentor persona reflects Vygotsky's zone of proximal development, providing the necessary support to help learners and educators achieve their goals. Here are two illustrative examples of AI personas in practice which can be useful for practitioners, as well as a summative overview table of the features of each AI persona.

It's mid-morning in a preschool classroom. Five children sit with their teacher in the reading corner, a tablet beside a picture book. The *Storyteller* persona begins: "Once there was a fox who found a shiny key."

"Maybe it opens a rocket!" says Theo.

The teacher smiles. "Let's ask our storyteller."

The AI system replies, "A rocket sounds exciting what should happen next?"

The teacher pauses the screen so children can build on one another's ideas, helping them use new words and connect sentences. When the story ends, they listen to the replay and retell it in their own words, proud of how their story grew together.

After a rainy morning, the class gathers near a puddle. "Why is it only here?" a child asks. The teacher kneels beside them, opening the *Explorer* persona on a tablet.

"Good observation," says the AI system. "What could you check to find out?"

Children dig a little soil while the teacher guides the tools and safety. They test two jars of dirt, noticing one stays wetter. The teacher prompts: "So what does that tell us?"

They shout, "The tree drinks the water!" The group races off to mark new spots to test next time it rains learning to look, wonder, and reason together (Table 14.1).

Table 14.1 AI personas and their respective modalities

AI Persona	Control	Feedback	Pace of interaction	Transparency
Storyteller	Low user control, AI takes initiative in co-creating narratives	Indirect feedback, AI adapts narrative style based on user engagement	Normal pace, AI adjusts speed of storytelling based on user engagement	Moderate transparency, AI explains narrative decisions when asked
Explorer	Shared control, AI provides prompts for exploration while user decides paths	Direct and indirect feedback, AI adjusts prompts based on user choices	Fast or normal, adaptable to user curiosity and task progress	High transparency, AI explains reasoning behind exploratory prompts
Playmate	Moderate control, turn-taking where AI responds dynamically to user actions	Direct feedback, AI responds to user actions with adaptive play responses	Normal to fast, encouraging dynamic and interactive play	Moderate transparency, AI shows reasoning behind actions in interactive play
Mentor	High user control, AI provides suggestions and scaffolding based on user input	Direct and detailed feedback, AI provides actionable suggestions tailored to educational needs	Slow to normal, allowing time for reflection and scaffolded learning	High transparency, AI offers detailed insights into pedagogical suggestions

Discussion and Conclusory Remarks: Trade-offs and Potential Limitations

To be sure, AI and co-creative AI processes are not a panacea. Rather, a growing body of research highlights significant limitations, discontents, and darker undercurrents that demand scrutiny both in specific educational practices, as well as on a broader scale with regards to AI (Crawford et al., 2024; Holmes & Porayska-Pomsta, 2023; Ivanov, 2023). Recently, scholars such as Holmes and Tuomi (2022) have underscored the risks of unchecked AI adoption, especially in pedagogical contexts aiming for co-creativity. To address these concerns, this section outlines the major trade-offs, beginning with the limitations of the AI personas themselves.

Let us start with AI Persona challenges. Despite the arguable pedagogical promise of the four AI personas Storyteller, Explorer, Playmate, and Mentor there are important caveats that must temper their implementation. First, one key challenge lies in developmental appropriateness and contextual sensitivity. To be sure, while personas may be carefully designed to scaffold specific learning processes, their efficacy depends heavily on how they are interpreted and operationalized in diverse educational settings and national frameworks of ECEC. For instance, the Storyteller persona, if left unchecked, may inadvertently constrain narrative openness by steering children's contributions toward algorithmically "coherent" paths, thereby reducing the spontaneity of emergent storytelling. Similarly, the Explorer persona, although designed to promote inquiry, risks unintentionally privileging certain cognitive styles of convergent thinking such as logical deduction or pattern recognition over others like aesthetic or kinesthetic learning or largely divergent thinking. These issues have not yet been empirically tested, and thusly call for nuanced implementation strategies that involve educators in co-designing persona behavior, ensuring alignment with pedagogical values, cultural norms, and learners' needs.

Moreover, a reliance on role-based personas may obscure the fluidity and unpredictability of real-life learning dynamics. While the personas offer structure and interpretability, their predefined modality configurations could limit the adaptability required for genuinely learner-centered experiences. For example, the Playmate persona may struggle to accommodate neurodiverse children who interpret social cues differently, or whose preferred modes of play are not easily modeled by current AI architectures. Likewise, the Mentor persona despite its benefits in structured guidance could unintentionally reinforce hierarchical classroom dynamics, diminishing opportunities for reciprocal learning between children and adults, or prioritizing the children´s voices. These potential blindspots suggest the need for flexible, context-aware systems of AI personas adoption that can transition fluidly between modalities or even co-evolve with the learners they support. Without such adaptability, AI personas risk becoming rigid templates that replicate, rather than enrich, the pedagogical status quo. Therefore, careful testing and proofs of concept of AI personas in ECEC are conditions sine qua non.

Then, let us examine some overarching, higher order trade-offs in using AI per se in education. First, the undeniable environmental toll of AI systems. The energy-intensive training and operation of large models have dramatically raised emissions Google's and Microsoft's environmental reports reveal increases of 48% and 30%, respectively over five years with a single model training run equating to the lifetime carbon output of five cars (Strubell et al., 2020). In education, where localization and frequent updates are often needed, the carbon footprint is only amplified. Recent efforts to prioritize efficiency such as low-latency models and carbon-neutral data centers are underway (Xie et al., 2024), but far from universal.

Equally troubling are the structural imbalances in AI development. Despite promises of democratization, the ecosystem remains dominated by a handful of profit-driven tech corporations, which are often monopolistic (Van der Vlist et al., 2024; Korinek & Vipra, 2024). These actors monopolize and feudalize tools, datasets, and infrastructures, creating dependencies that undermine institutional autonomy and equity. Proprietary algorithms may benefit well-resourced ECEC institutions while sidelining underfunded ones in lower-income regions. Therefore, even though open-source initiatives and public AI projects like Deep Seek offer new alternatives (Sicari et al., 2024; Ng et al., 2025), the extent to which they will disrupt this concentration remains uncertain. Big tech has yet to prove its not-for-profit motives.

Another risk concerns AI's potential to narrow rather than expand creativity. Algorithmic personalization can create filter bubbles or what Brincker (2021), drawing on Arendt, terms "epistemic bubbles," reinforcing existing preferences and undermining exposure to diverse perspectives (Pariser, 2011; Onitiu, 2022). This personalization trap risks reducing learners to passive recipients of tailored content, eroding critical thinking and agency offline. To avoid turning us into inane puppets ourselves, AI systems must be carefully designed to empower rather than automate. As argued by Muñoz et al. (2025), AI still lacks the essential ingredients of human intelligence generalization, world-modelling, and relevance realization while concerns like parasitic processing remain (Jaeger et al., 2024; Vervaeke & Coyne, 2024). Our role, then, is not to be mentored by machines, but to mentor them to ensure AI augments rather than diminishes human creativity. Children need systematic exploration and ways to tame uncertainty (Blanco and Sloutsky, 2021), and Co-creAItivity has to provide real answers to the choices of young children, and their adult menots.

These challenges also intersect with long-standing ethical concerns. Transparency remains elusive, as most systems function as opaque "black boxes," reducing trust and interpretability (Longo et al., 2024; Wang et al., 2024). Algorithmic bias inevitably inherited from training data has been well documented, especially in educational datasets that replicate structural inequalities (Adams-Prassl et al., 2023; Bird et al., 2024). If widely replicated, biased assessments can penalize underrepresented learners or exclude minority voices altogether. Moreover, the volume of personal data required to train and deploy educational AI raises acute privacy concerns (Kumi-Yeboah et al., 2023), especially for young children (Kanders et al., 2024). Unauthorized data access or misuse could have lasting consequences. In this context, explainable AI (XAI), along with technologies like federated learning, offers a path forward minimizing risk while preserving functionality (Loftus et al., 2022; Zhang et al., 2024), and require closer examination and scaling up.

Ultimately, the most profound risk may be the erosion of human agency itself a process Lara and Muller (2023) call the "zombie work force". If AI displaces decision-making and creative judgment, we risk fostering a generation of passive, consumerist, narcisistic ciphers rather than active, co-creative meaning-makers. To avoid this, regulatory and pedagogical safeguards are essential. As Vervaeke and Coyne (2024) have strongly argued, the future of co-creAItivity lies not in deferring to AI, but in guiding it ensuring that humans remain senior partners in shaping the creative and ethical contours of AI in education.

Like with all real innovations of knowledge, our AI path can be *per aspera ad astra*. Co-creAItivity marks a new horizon for education, offering profound potential while demanding careful navigation. Rather than automating creativity for efficiency, we must design AI in early childhood education to enhance children's imaginative, critical, and socio-emotional capacities. Developmentally grounded rAI personas Storyteller, Explorer, Playmate, and Mentor can, if implemented with care and ethical foresight, foster deeper engagement and agency for both learners and educators. Creativity, however, is a sharp double-edged sword: it can inspire and solve seemingly impossible problems, as AlphaGo and AlphaFold show, but if misdirected, it may deepen systemic biases and reinforce conformity, worsening our already fragile societal and planetary condition. Thus, integrating AI into early childhood education must prioritize diversity of thought, equitable access, and ethical co-creation, enabling higher levels of discourse and practice. Ultimately, the goal of such new plains of co-creAItivity is not to merely adapt to AI-driven change, but to thrive because of it and perhaps, just perhaps, cultivate a generation for whom creativity is not a tool for survival in a zombified "The Last of Us" dystopia, but a catalyst for flourishing and a Socratic gadfly against our creative myopia.

References

Adams-Prassl, J., Binns, R., & Kelly-Lyth, A. (2023). Directly discriminatory algorithms. *The Modern Law Review, 86*(1), 144–175. https://doi.org/10.1111/1468-2230.12759

Alves-Oliveira, P., Arriaga, P., Xavier, C., Hoffman, G., & Paiva, A. (2022). Creativity landscapes: Systematic review spanning 70 years of creativity interventions for children. *The Journal of Creative Behavior, 56*(1), 16–40. https://doi.org/10.1002/jocb.514

Amabile, T. M. (2019). *Creativity in context: Update to the social psychology of creativity* (1st ed.). Routledge. https://doi.org/10.4324/9780429501234

Bird, K. A., Castleman, B. L., & Song, Y. (2024). Are algorithms biased in education? Exploring racial bias in predicting community college student success. *Journal of Policy Analysis and Management.* https://doi.org/10.1002/pam.22569

Blanco, N. J., & Sloutsky, V. M. (2021). Systematic exploration and uncertainty dominate young children's choices. *Developmental Science, 24*(2), e13026. https://doi.org/10.1111/desc.13026

Bourzac, K. (2024). Fixing AI's energy crisis. *Nature.* https://doi.org/10.1038/d41586-024-03408-z

Brincker, M. (2021). Disoriented and alone in the "experience machine"—On Netflix, shared world deceptions and the consequences of deepening algorithmic personalization. *SATS, 22*(1), 75–96. https://doi.org/10.1515/sats-2021-0005

Chatzigeorgiadou, S., Hatzigianni, M., Ratkidou, F., & Toziou, S. (2022). Design thinking and digital technologies in the exploration of science in early childhood education. In *Lecture Notes in Educational Technology* (pp. 135–155). Springer Nature Singapore. https://doi.org/10.1007/978-981-19-0568-1_8

Colton, S., & Wiggins, G. A. (2012). Computational creativity: The final frontier? In L. De Raedt, C. Bessière, D. Dubois, P. Doherty, P. Frasconi, F. Heintz, & P. Lucas (Eds.), *ECAI 2012: Proceedings of the 20th European Conference on Artificial Intelligence* (pp. 21–26). IOS Press. https://doi.org/10.3233/978-1-61499-098-7-21

Crawford, J., Allen, K.-A., Pani, B., & Cowling, M. (2024). When artificial intelligence substitutes humans in higher education: the cost of loneliness, student success, and retention. *Studies in Higher Education, 49*(5), 883–897. https://doi.org/10.1080/03075079.2024.2326956

Dankiw, K. A., Kumar, S., Baldock, K. L., & Tsiros, M. D. (2023). Parent and early childhood educator perspectives of unstructured nature play for young children: A qualitative descriptive study. *PloS One, 18*(6), e0286468. https://doi.org/10.1371/journal.pone.0286468

Domain, P. (2025, April 3). *AI's $4.8 trillion future: UN warns of widening digital divide without urgent action.* UN News. https://news.un.org/en/story/2025/04/1161826

Fleer, M. (2019). Digitally amplified practices: Beyond binaries and towards a profile of multiple digital coadjuvants. *Mind Culture and Activity, 26*(3), 207–220. https://doi.org/10.1080/10749039.2019.1646289

Fleer, M. (2020). Digital pop-ups: Studying digital pop-ups and theorising digital pop-up pedagogies for preschools. *European Early Childhood Education Research Journal, 28*(2), 214–230. https://doi.org/10.1080/1350293x.2020.1735741

Fleer, M., & Hedegaard, M. (2010). *Early Learning and Development: Cultural-historical Concepts in Play.* Cambridge University Press. https://doi.org/10.1017/CBO9780511844836

Garcia, M. B. (2025). The paradox of artificial creativity: Challenges and opportunities of generative AI artistry. *Creativity Research Journal, 37*(4), 755–768. https://doi.org/10.1080/10400419.2024.2354622

Grilli, L., & Pedota, M. (2024). Creativity and artificial intelligence: A multilevel perspective. *Creativity and Innovation Management, 33*(2), 234–247. https://doi.org/10.1111/caim.12580

Grönman, S., Lindfors, E., & Rönkkö, M.-L. (2024). Design thinking in early childhood education and care. A literature review and consideration from the perspective of young learners' craft, design, and technology education. *International Journal of Technology and Design Education*, 1–21. https://doi.org/10.1007/s10798-024-09944-z

Haase, J., & Hanel, P. H. P. (2023). Artificial muses: Generative artificial intelligence chatbots have risen to human-level creativity. *Journal of Creativity, 33*(3), 100066. https://doi.org/10.1016/j.yjoc.2023.100066

Haase, J., & Pokutta, S. (2024). Human-AI co-creativity: Exploring synergies across levels of creative collaboration. In *arXiv [cs.HC].arXiv*. http://arxiv.org/abs/2411.12527

Hedegaard, M., & Ødegaard, E. E. (2020). *Children's exploration and cultural formation*. Springer Nature. https://doi.org/10.1007/978-3-030-36271-3

Holmes, W., & Tuomi, I. (2022). State of the art and practice in AI in education. *European Journal of Education, 57*(4), 542–570. https://doi.org/10.1111/ejed.12533

Hopwood, N., & Sannino, A. (Eds.). (2023). *Agency and transformation: Motives, mediation, and motion*. Cambridge University Press. https://doi.org/10.1017/9781009153799

Hubert, K. F., Awa, K. N., & Zabelina, D. L. (2024). The current state of artificial intelligence generative language models is more creative than humans on divergent thinking tasks. *Scientific Reports, 14*(1), 3440. https://doi.org/10.1038/s41598-024-53303-w

Ivanov, S. (2023). The dark side of artificial intelligence in higher education. *Service Industries Journal, 43*(15–16), 1055–1082. https://doi.org/10.1080/02642069.2023.2258799

Jaeger, J., Riedl, A., Djedovic, A., Vervaeke, J., & Walsh, D. (2024). Naturalizing relevance realization: Why agency and cognition are fundamentally not computational. *Frontiers in Psychology, 15*, 1362658. https://doi.org/10.3389/fpsyg.2024.1362658

Kanders, K., Stupple-Harris, L., Smith, L., & Gibson, J. L. (2024). Perspectives on the impact of generative AI on early-childhood development and education. *Infant and Child Development, e2514*. https://doi.org/10.1002/icd.2514

Kewalramani, S., Palaiologou, I., Arnott, L., & Dardanou, M. (2020). The integration of the internet of toys in early childhood education: A platform for multi-layered interactions. *European Early Childhood Education Research Journal, 28*(2), 197–213. https://doi.org/10.1080/1350293x.2020.1735738

Korinek, A., & Vipra, J. (2024). Concentrating intelligence: Scaling and market structure in artificial intelligence. *SSRN Electronic Journal.*. https://doi.org/10.36687/inetwp228

Kumar, H., Vincentius, J., Jordan, E., & Anderson, A. (2024). Human creativity in the age of LLMs: Randomized experiments on divergent and convergent thinking. In *arXiv [cs.HC].arXiv*. http://arxiv.org/abs/2410.03703

Kumi-Yeboah, A., Kim, Y., Yankson, B., Aikins, S., & Dadson, Y. A. (2023). Diverse students' perspectives on privacy and technology integration in higher education. *British Journal of Educational Technology: Journal of the Council for Educational Technology, 54*(6), 1671–1692. https://doi.org/10.1111/bjet.13386

Lara, J. A., & Muller, A. (2023). Zombie work force: Capitalism, sacrifice, and the virtual afterlife of labor. *Symplokē, 31*(1–2), 397–404. https://doi.org/10.1353/sym.2023.a914671

Li, H., He, H., Luo, W., & Li, H. (2024). Early childhood digital pedagogy: A scoping review of its practices, profiles, and predictors. *Early Childhood Education Journal*. https://doi.org/10.1007/s10643-024-01804-8

Liu, F., Lv, J., Cui, S., Luan, Z., Wu, K., & Zhou, T. (2024). Smart "error"! Exploring imperfect AI to support creative ideation. *Proceedings of the ACM on Human-Computer Interaction, 8*(CSCW1), 1–28. https://doi.org/10.1145/3637398

Loftus, T. J., Ruppert, M. M., Shickel, B., Ozrazgat-Baslanti, T., Balch, J. A., Efron, P. A., Upchurch, G. R., Jr., Rashidi, P., Tignanelli, C., Bian, J., & Bihorac, A. (2022). Federated learning for preserving data privacy in collaborative healthcare research. *Digital Health, 8*, 20552076221134455. https://doi.org/10.1177/20552076221134455

Long, D., Jacob, M., & Magerko, B. (2019, June 13). Designing co-creative AI for public spaces. *Proceedings of the 2019 on Creativity and Cognition.* C&C'19: Creativity and Cognition, San Diego CA USA. https://doi.org/10.1145/3325480.3325504

Longo, L., Brcic, M., Cabitza, F., Choi, J., Confalonieri, R., Ser, J. D., Guidotti, R., Hayashi, Y., Herrera, F., Holzinger, A., Jiang, R., Khosravi, H., Lecue, F., Malgieri, G., Páez, A., Samek, W., Schneider, J., Speith, T., & Stumpf, S. (2024). Explainable Artificial Intelligence (XAI) 2.0: A manifesto of open challenges and interdisciplinary research directions. *An International Journal on. Information Fusion, 106*(102301), 102301. https://doi.org/10.1016/j.inffus.2024.102301

Lubart, T. (2005). How can computers be partners in the creative process: Classification and commentary on the Special Issue. *International Journal of Human-Computer Studies, 63*(4–5), 365–369. https://doi.org/10.1016/j.ijhcs.2005.04.002

Meder, B., Wu, C. M., Schulz, E., & Ruggeri, A. (2021). Development of directed and random exploration in children. *Developmental Science, 24*(4), e13095. https://doi.org/10.1111/desc.13095

Mize, K., Arrington, L., & Willox, L. (2022). Design thinking: Blazing a trail for social and emotional learning in the early grades. *Kappa Delta Pi Record, 58*(4), 172–177. https://doi.org/10.1080/00228958.2022.2110820

Moruzzi, C., & Margarido, S. (2024, May 11). A user-centered framework for human-AI co-creativity. *Extended Abstracts of the CHI Conference on Human Factors in Computing Systems.* CHI '24: CHI Conference on Human Factors in Computing Systems, Honolulu HI USA. https://doi.org/10.1145/3613905.3650929

Muñoz, J. M., Bernacer, J., Noë, A., & Thompson, E. (2025). Why AI will never be able to acquire human-level intelligence. *Nature, 637*(8047), 794. https://doi.org/10.1038/d41586-025-00170-8

Na, J., & Song, J. (2014). Why everyday experience? Interpreting primary students' science discourse from the perspective of John Dewey. *Science & Education, 23*(5), 1031–1049. https://doi.org/10.1007/s11191-013-9637-y

Ng, K., Drenon, B., Gerken, T., & Cieslak, M. (2025). What is DeepSeek—and why is everyone talking about it? *BBC News.*. https://www.bbc.com/news/articles/c5yv5976z9po

OECD. (2023). *Empowering Young Children in the Digital Age.* (2023, April 17). OECD. https://www.oecd.org/en/publications/empowering-young-children-in-the-digital-age_50967622-en.html

Onitiu, D. (2022). Fashion, filter bubbles and echo chambers: Questions of privacy, identity, and governance. *Law, Innovation and Technology, 14*(2), 395–420. https://doi.org/10.1080/17579961.2022.2113672

Pariser, E. (2011). *The filter bubble: How the new personalized web is changing what we read and how we think.* Penguin Books.

Rhodes, M. (1961). An Analysis of Creativity. *Phi Delta Kappan, 42*(7), 305–310. https://www.jstor.org/stable/20342603

Rogoff, B. (2003). *The cultural nature of human development. Oxford University Press.*. https://global.oup.com/academic/product/the-cultural-nature-of-human-development-9780195131338?cc=no&lang=en&

Sando, O. J., Kleppe, R., & Sandseter, E. B. H. (2021). Risky play and children's well-being, involvement and physical activity. *Child Indicators Research, 14*(4), 1435–1451. https://doi.org/10.1007/s12187-021-09804-5

Shengjergji, S., Myrendal, J., & Pramling, N. (2024). Responding to children's semiotic repertoires in collaborative digital storytelling. *Early Childhood Education Journal, 1–12.* https://doi.org/10.1007/s10643-024-01761-2

Sica, L. S., Kapoor, H., & Ragozini, G. (2022). Grasping creative valences: A person-centered study on creativity as a resource for young people's optimal identity formation. *Identity (Mahwah, N.J.),* 1–15. https://doi.org/10.1080/15283488.2022.2050727

Sicari, S., J. F. Cevallos, M., Rizzardi, A., & Coen-Porisini, A. (2024). Open-ethical AI: Advancements in open-source human-centric neural language models. *ACM Computing Surveys.* https://doi.org/10.1145/3703454

Strubell, E., Ganesh, A., & McCallum, A. (2020). Energy and Policy Considerations for Modern Deep Learning Research. *Proceedings of the AAAI Conference on Artificial Intelligence, 34*(9), 13693–13696. https://doi.org/10.1609/aaai.v34i09.7123

Taussig, H., & Weiler, L. (2019). Innovative approaches to improving outcomes for children involved with child welfare: Youth mentoring. In *Child Maltreatment* (pp. 315–326). Springer International Publishing. https://doi.org/10.1007/978-3-030-05858-6_19

Undheim, M. (2022). Children and teachers engaging together with digital technology in early childhood education and care institutions: A literature review. *European Early Childhood Education Research Journal, 30*(3), 472–489. https://doi.org/10.1080/1350293X.2021.1971730

van der Vlist, F., Helmond, A., & Ferrari, F. (2024). Big AI: Cloud infrastructure dependence and the industrialisation of artificial intelligence. *Big Data & Society, 11*(1). https://doi.org/10.1177/20539517241232630

Vervaeke, J., & Coyne, S. (2024). Mentoring the Machines: Origins—Part 2: Surviving the Deep Impact of the Artificially Intelligent Tomorrow: Vervaeke, John, Coyne, Shawn: 9781645010845: Amazon.com: Books.

Vretudaki, H. (2022). 'Tell me the whole story': moving from narrative comprehension to narrative production skills. *European Early Childhood Education Research Journal, 30*(6), 949–960. https://doi.org/10.1080/1350293x.2022.2098991

Vygotsky, L. S. (1978). In M. Cole, V. John-Steiner, S. Scribner, & E. Souberman (Eds.), *Mind in society: The development of higher psychological processes*. Harvard University Press. https://doi.org/10.2307/j.ctvjf9vz4

Wang, S., Tang, H., Wang, M., Zhang, H., Liu, X., Li, W., Hu, X., & Zhang, L. (2024). Gnothi seauton: Empowering faithful self-interpretability in black-box models. *arXiv [cs.LG]. arXiv.* http://arxiv.org/abs/2410.21815

Holmes, W., & Porayska-Pomsta, K. (Eds.). (2023). *The ethics of artificial intelligence in education: Practices, challenges, and debates*. Routledge. https://doi.org/10.4324/9780429329067

Xie, J., Jia, Q., & Lu, F. (2024). An energy-efficient intelligence sharing scheme in intelligence networking-empowered edge computing. *IEEE Access: Practical Innovations, Open Solutions, 12*, 90940–90951. https://doi.org/10.1109/access.2024.3421652

Xu, Y., Harms, M. B., Green, C. S., Wilson, R. C., & Pollak, S. D. (2023). Childhood unpredictability and the development of exploration. *Proceedings of the National Academy of Sciences of the United States of America, 120*(49), e2303869120. https://doi.org/10.1073/pnas.2303869120

Yalçin, V. (2022). Design Thinking model in early childhood education. *International Journal of Psychology and Educational Studies, 9*(1), 196–210. https://doi.org/10.52380/ijpcs.2022.9.1.715

Yogman, M., Garner, A., Hutchinson, J., Hirsh-Pasek, K., & Golinkoff, R. M. (2018). The power of play: A pediatric role in enhancing development in young children. *Pediatrics, 142*(3), e20182058. https://doi.org/10.1542/peds.2018-2058

Zhang, Y., Zeng, D., Luo, J., Fu, X., Chen, G., Xu, Z., & King, I. (2024). A survey of trustworthy federated learning: Issues, solutions, and challenges. *ACM Transactions on Intelligent Systems and Technology, 15*(6), 1–47. https://doi.org/10.1145/3678181

Zhou, E., & Lee, D. (2024). Generative artificial intelligence, human creativity, and art. *PNAS Nexus, 3*(3), gae052. https://doi.org/10.1093/pnasnexus/pgae052

Part V
Ethics, Policy and AI-Driven Assessment

Chapter 15
AI-Supported Pedagogy in Irish Primary Schools: Opportunities and Challenges

Ann Marcus-Quinn

Abstract Artificial Intelligence (AI) is increasingly shaping the pedagogical landscape of Irish primary education, offering new avenues for enhancing teaching and learning across the curriculum. This chapter explores how primary school teachers in Ireland are incorporating AI tools, particularly large language models like ChatGPT, into classroom practice. Some teachers are integrating AI across all subjects taught at primary level, using it to support lesson planning, resource creation, and pupil engagement. ChatGPT is also being exploited in specific subjects with the mainstream media reporting on teachers using AI to help them to design interactive historical narratives, simulate dialogues with historical figures, and generate differentiated reading materials and quizzes, thereby supporting inclusive and personalised learning. AI is also being used to facilitate project-based learning by helping pupils brainstorm research ideas, structure presentations, and make cross-curricular connections, particularly in subjects such as history, geography, and art. This chapter examines these applications, considering both the opportunities AI presents for pedagogical innovation and the challenges it raises, including issues of teacher preparedness, ethical use, and classroom integration. The analysis highlights evolving teacher roles and the broader implications of AI-supported pedagogy in Irish primary schools.

Keywords Artificial intelligence · AI classroom practice · Primary Education · Education

Introduction

AI is has the potential to rapidly transform primary education in Ireland, offering new possibilities for personalised learning, inclusive pedagogy, and administrative efficiency. This chapter investigates how Irish primary school teachers are currently integrating AI tools, particularly large language models like ChatGPT, into classroom

A. Marcus-Quinn (✉)
School of English, Irish, and Communication, Faculty of Arts, Humanities and Social Sciences, University of Limerick, Dublin, Ireland
e-mail: Ann.Marcus.Quinn@ul.ie

S. Papadakis (ed.), *AI Applications in Preschool and Primary Education*, Advances in Artificial Intelligence in Education 5, https://doi.org/10.1007/978-3-032-17190-0_15

practice to support lesson planning, resource creation, and pupil engagement. It situates these developments within the broader context of national and EU-level policy, including the AI Literacy Framework and the Artificial Intelligence Act. The chapter also explores departmental supports, teacher-led initiatives, and emerging communities of practice that are shaping AI adoption in schools. By examining both the opportunities and challenges of AI-supported pedagogy, this contribution provides a timely analysis of how technology is reshaping teaching roles and learning environments in Irish primary education.

In recent years, an increasing number of governments have implemented restrictive policies to curb young people's use of smartphones and social media, citing concerns related to mental health, distraction, and online safety (McCoy and Marcus-Quinn, 2025). Against this backdrop, this chapter explores how primary school teachers in Ireland are incorporating AI tools, particularly large language models like ChatGPT, into classroom practice. The increasing prevalence of generative AI tools presents both opportunities and challenges across all sectors of education (Ali et al., 2024). While such technologies can enhance learning and innovation, their misuse raises significant concerns regarding academic integrity (Selwyn, 2019). It is imperative that all stakeholders receive clear guidance on the ethical application of AI, ensuring that assessments evaluate genuine comprehension rather than reliance on automated outputs. As an EU member state Ireland has core compliance obligations within the EU Artificial Intelligence Act that are relevant to schools: the requirement for AI literacy training among staff, and the mandated processes of risk assessment and classification (Office of the European Union L- & Luxembourg, 2024). From February 2025, schools are expected to implement compulsory AI literacy programmes for both teaching and administrative personnel. These initiatives aim to equip staff with a foundational understanding of how AI systems function, their ethical implications, and the relevant regulatory standards under the Act. However, the implementation of such training is likely to pose significant challenges. Constraints related to funding, time, and staff digital competencies may hinder schools' ability to deliver consistent and meaningful training. Moreover, ensuring ongoing engagement, accessibility, and monitoring of participation adds layers of complexity that may necessitate external support and targeted investment to enable equitable compliance across schools. In addition, the requirement to assess and classify AI tools according to risk levels, ranging from minimal to unacceptable, presents further difficulties. School leaders may lack oversight of the full range of AI tools being employed by staff, complicating efforts to evaluate their compliance status. Given the technical expertise and time required, schools may need to engage external consultants to conduct these assessments, placing additional pressure on already limited financial resources.

Guidelines on the Use of AI in the Education Sector

All educational institutions must establish explicit policies governing AI usage, integrate AI literacy into curricula, and implement strategies for detecting and mitigating unauthorised AI-generated content. The Department of Education and Youth (2025) published "Guidance on Artificial Intelligence in Schools" in October 2025. This is designed to help teachers and school leaders plan for the use of AI in teaching and learning, emphasising safe, ethical, and appropriate use. At second and third level, to uphold the validity of assessments, educators may require students to engage in live discussions about their work or submit drafts at various stages, thereby ensuring that their submissions reflect independent thought rather than AI-assisted production. Additionally, assessment design should prioritise critical engagement and the learning process over mere final outputs, fostering deeper intellectual development and reducing the risk of academic dishonesty. While there is mention of primary education in the broader scope, much of the public discussion has focused on post-primary/assessment settings, rather than detailed rules for younger (primary) pupils. The opportunities and challenges presented by AI in the primary education sector differ from those at the secondary and tertiary levels (Girdham, 2024; Wieczorek and Costello, 2024). However, addressing these issues remains equally critical to ensuring the responsible and effective integration of AI in learning environments (Jackson et al., 2025; Marcus-Quinn & McCoy, 2025).

While AI presents significant opportunities for improving lesson planning, personalising learning, and reducing teacher workload, it also raises important ethical considerations, including data privacy and academic integrity (Schiff, 2022; Murphy et al., 2021). The European Commission has released ethical guidelines regarding the use of AI and data in educational settings. These guidelines aim to assist educators in recognising the benefits that AI applications and data usage can bring to education while also highlighting the potential risks involved. The goal is to empower educators to interact with AI systems in a positive, critical, and ethical manner, thereby maximising the potential advantages of these technologies (European Commission: Directorate-General for Education, 2022). The EU Education Hub also established a squad to look specifically at the use of AI in education settings. The output from the squad includes a report which offers important insights into the balance between the potential benefits and risks of using AI in education, emphasising that risk levels are shaped more by context than by the technology itself. The report highlights how AI can effectively support teaching through feedback, lesson planning, and learning analytics, while warning against overreliance in high-stakes decision-making without sufficient human oversight. Its focus on Explainable AI and ethical considerations makes it particularly valuable for guiding the responsible integration of AI in primary education settings (Le Borgne Y. et al., 2023).

In May 2025 the European Commission, OECD, and Code.org collaboratively released a draft of the *Empowering Learners for the Age of AI: An AI Literacy Framework for Primary and Secondary Education* (AILit Framework). The framework is currently in a six-month consultation phase, during which feedback is actively being sought from stakeholders. Designed to be clear, accessible, and practically oriented, the framework builds on existing models while aiming to offer a unified, globally relevant structure for AI literacy (EU Commission and OECD, 2025). Key features include alignment with the upcoming 2029 PISA Media and AI Literacy Assessment, classroom-based exemplars for both primary and secondary levels, and guidance for curriculum, assessment, and teacher professional development. Developed through an international, community-driven process, the framework outlines a core set of knowledge, skills, and attitudes needed to navigate AI effectively in educational contexts. The Department of Education and Youth "Guidance on Artificial Intelligence in Schools" document also makes reference to this framework.

Departmental Supports for AI Use in Irish Primary Schools

Oide is Ireland's national support service for teachers and school leaders, established on September 1, 2023. It was formed by integrating four key educational support services: the Centre for School Leadership (CSL), Junior Cycle for Teachers (JCT), the National Induction Programme for Teachers (NIPT), and the Professional Development Service for Teachers (PDST). Funded by the Department of Education, Oide provides high-quality, evidence-informed professional learning supports and services aimed at empowering educators to create dynamic and impactful learning experiences for all students. Within Oide, the Technology in Education division focuses on promoting and supporting the integration of digital technology in teaching, learning, and assessment in primary and post-primary schools. This includes offering professional learning opportunities through online courses, webinars, and face-to-face workshops, as well as providing guidance on digital infrastructure and internet safety. Oide Technology in Education also manages key initiatives such as Scoilnet, the Department of Education's official portal for Irish education, and Webwise, the internet safety awareness centre.

Oide Technology in Education offers a comprehensive suite of supports to assist Irish teachers and school leaders in integrating AI into their classrooms. Central to these offerings is the "AI for Schools" online course, which launched in May 2024. This introductory course provides educators with a foundational understanding of AI, exploring its potential benefits, limitations, and ethical considerations within the educational context. It aligns with the Digital Strategy for Schools to 2027 (DES, 2022) and includes insights from the Adapt Centre and the AI4T project, ensuring that participants are informed about current policies and best practices related to AI in education.[1] Complementing the course is the AI for Schools Video Series, which features interviews with experts discussing the role of AI in Irish and European education. These videos provide practical insights into how AI is currently being used in schools and offer guidance on effective implementation strategies. Additionally, Oide has also developed resources such as the "Five Considerations for Teacher

[1] https://www.ai4t.eu/about/.

Use of AI" infographic and the RASE Prompt Framework, which support educators in responsibly and effectively incorporating AI tools into their teaching practices. For those concerned with online safety, the Webwise AI Hub offers articles and resources addressing the challenges and considerations of AI use in schools. Together, these resources provide a robust support system for educators aiming to navigate the evolving landscape of AI in education.

In response to increasing foresight and horizon-scanning research highlighting the growing impact of AI on education, Oide joined the European 'Artificial Intelligence for and by Teachers' (AI4T) project in 2021. Led by the French Ministry for Education and funded through Erasmus+, this three-year initiative explores how AI can be integrated into teaching and learning across both primary and post-primary education. A significant outcome of the project has been the development of a textbook specifically designed for educators, addressing the evolving role of the teacher in an AI-enhanced learning environment. The textbook covers a range of essential topics, including the importance of understanding AI as an educator, the dynamics of the information ecosystem, the use of data and learning management systems to support teaching, the potential for personalised learning, and the implications of AI for language-related skills such as listening, speaking, and writing.

Communities of Practice

In Ireland, Communities of Practice have long played a central role in the education sector, spanning all levels from early childhood to higher education (Marcus-Quinn, 2013). These collaborative networks of educators, researchers, and practitioners have traditionally facilitated the sharing of expertise, reflection on practice, and the co-construction of knowledge within and across schools and institutions. In the current context of rapid technological change, particularly with the emergence of large language models (LLMs) such as ChatGPT, these communities are becoming increasingly important. They are now serving as vital spaces for peer-led exploration, professional learning, and the exchange of strategies for integrating AI tools into pedagogical and administrative practices. By providing educators with a forum for critical discussion and collective problem-solving, Communities of Practice continue to offer meaningful support as the sector navigates the opportunities and challenges presented by generative AI. One example of this activity is the Dublin West Education Centre, which provides insights into practical applications of AI in the classroom, highlighting initiatives where educators are leveraging AI to create personalised learning experiences.

The Computers in Education Society of Ireland (CESI) is solution-focussed and serves as a valuable support network for primary school teachers (Marcus-Quinn et al., 2024). Members support those seeking to integrate AI into their classroom practice at both primary and second level. Through practical workshops such as *AI in Action: Practical AI Education for the Classroom*, CESI provides hands-on strategies that teachers can implement directly in their teaching (Computer Education

Society Ireland CESI, 2025). The society also fosters a collaborative community of educators across all levels, encouraging the sharing of best practices and innovations in educational technology. CESI's annual conferences offer professional development opportunities focused on real-world applications of emerging technologies, including AI, within the Irish educational context. Furthermore, CESI actively advocates for clear, system-wide guidance and adequate resourcing to ensure the ethical and effective use of AI in schools, making it a key enabler of responsible digital innovation in primary education.

This peer-led knowledge-sharing is also evident in the work of school leaders who are actively contributing to sector-wide learning. Many school principals and teachers are independently exploring the educational potential of artificial intelligence. Overall, the media's coverage of this community activity provides a nuanced understanding of AI's role in schools, balancing its promising benefits with the potential risks that require careful consideration. For example, the mainstream Irish media has given coverage to school leaders and teachers' use of AI. One such example of this is newspaper and radio coverage featuring the principal of the Educate Together primary school in Carlow who has been engaged in disseminating AI-related resources and practical guidance to support fellow educators in navigating emerging technologies (Lewis, 2024). These include Mash.plus, a subsidiary of Ireland's largest teacher resource-sharing platform, Mash.ie, designed as a collaborative space for investigating how AI can enhance teaching and learning in primary education. In light of the advancements in generative AI, the platform has developed various experimental resources. For instance, teachers can enter any address in Ireland, and the site generates a comprehensive unit of work related to that location, incorporating historical and geographical activities formatted as a school textbook. Additionally, Mash.plus offers a service known as Scoirr, which features AI-generated, swipeable interactive activities for whiteboards. The platform has also created a series of courses aimed at assisting educators in developing their own AI-generated resources, titled Code Without Coding. Lewis also publishes a regular podcast where he shares reflections such as what he would do if he were Minister for Education offering valuable insights informed by his dual perspective as both a school leader and former classroom teacher. This type of engagement by principals and teachers with emerging technologies is driven by professional curiosity and a commitment to pedagogical innovation, much of which is pursued in their own time and without formal resourcing. These efforts form a critical, practice-based layer of knowledge that complements academic research and supports other educators navigating this evolving field.

Understanding how AI can be integrated effectively and responsibly is crucial for maximising its potential while ensuring high-quality education (Selwyn, 2023). One of the key benefits of AI in primary education is its ability to streamline lesson planning and resource creation. Teachers can use AI to generate tailored lesson plans, quizzes, and worksheets, saving valuable time and allowing for a more differentiated approach to student learning. Additionally, AI supports personalised learning by adapting content to meet individual student needs, offering real-time feedback, and enabling teachers to monitor progress more efficiently. Beyond the classroom,

AI assists with administrative tasks such as grading and report writing, freeing up teachers to focus on engaging with their students and refining their teaching strategies.

Primary school teachers in Ireland are increasingly integrating AI tools such as ChatGPT, Gemini, Perplexity, Deepseek and Claude into their classrooms to enhance teaching and streamline administrative tasks. These applications range from lesson planning and resource creation to personalised student assessments. AI tools can offer valuable applications for teaching subjects like history in primary schools by enabling teachers to create interactive narratives and simulate conversations with historical figures, which enhances student engagement. Additionally, it facilitates the generation of customised learning materials and supports scenario-based discussions that promote critical thinking, while also allowing for cross-curricular connections with subjects like geography and art, making history a more dynamic and integrative learning experience. Educators are also using AI to design differentiated lesson plans, generate customised worksheets and quizzes, and create materials tailored to their students' needs. This significantly reduces preparation time, allowing teachers to focus more on interactive and engaging teaching methods. To support this transition, organisations like the Dublin West Education Centre (DWEC) have begun offering webinars and training sessions on effectively using AI in the classroom. These initiatives aim to equip teachers with the skills to create personalised learning experiences, making education more adaptable to individual student needs. AI is also being used to develop and grade quizzes, providing instant feedback to students and helping teachers track progress more efficiently. However, the adoption of AI in primary education also presents challenges, particularly concerning plagiarism, data privacy, and ethical considerations. Many educators are calling for clearer guidelines and training to ensure AI is used responsibly in the classroom (Jackson et al., 2025). Despite these concerns, Irish primary school teachers are embracing AI's potential to enrich learning while remaining mindful of the need for appropriate safeguards and support.

Challenges for Schools

Despite the advantages lauded by many the integration of AI also presents challenges (Bozkurt et al., 2024). Plagiarism and academic integrity are growing concerns, as students may use AI to generate assignments without demonstrating their own understanding. Educators must develop strategies to ensure original work while fostering digital literacy and responsible AI usage. Data privacy and security are also significant issues, as AI tools often collect and process student information. Schools must navigate regulations and implement safeguarding measures to protect sensitive data. Furthermore, teacher readiness and training are essential, as not all educators have the same level of digital literacy. Professional development programmes and AI-focused training are needed to ensure teachers can confidently incorporate AI into their classrooms.

As AI transforms the educational landscape, the role of teachers is also evolving. Without doubt, collaboration is key to success across all education sectors, particularly in addressing challenges posed by disruptions such as the COVID-19 pandemic and the emergence of new generative AI tools (Huijser et al., 2024). Rather than being the primary source of information, teachers are increasingly becoming facilitators of learning, guiding students in critical thinking and ethical AI usage. AI can support blended learning approaches, where traditional teaching methods are combined with AI-driven tools to create a more dynamic and engaging classroom experience. However, it is crucial to view AI as a supportive tool rather than a replacement for human educators. Teachers will continue to play an essential role in fostering creativity, social development, and problem-solving skills. These are all areas where AI still falls short.

Teacher Training and Readiness

The role of teachers in the classroom is evolving as AI becomes more integrated into education. Rather than simply serving as providers of information, educators are increasingly taking on the role of learning facilitators. AI has the potential to shift teachers' responsibilities from delivering content to mentoring students, encouraging critical thinking, and fostering problem-solving skills. This transformation allows teachers to focus more on personalised support and guidance, ensuring that students develop a deeper understanding of concepts rather than passively absorbing information. Blended learning approaches are also emerging as a key aspect of AI integration in education. By combining AI-driven tools with traditional teaching methods, educators can create more dynamic and adaptive learning environments. AI can assist in tailoring lessons to individual student needs, providing instant feedback, and automating routine tasks such as grading. However, this does not mean AI replaces traditional instruction; rather, it complements teachers' expertise by allowing them to dedicate more time to interactive and student-centred learning experiences.

Crucially, AI should be viewed as a supportive tool rather than a replacement for teachers. While AI can enhance efficiency and provide valuable insights, human educators remain essential in fostering creativity, emotional intelligence, and social development; areas where AI still lacks depth. A balanced teacher-AI partnership ensures that technology enhances learning while maintaining the irreplaceable human element of education. Educators are actively exploring AI tools while simultaneously addressing significant concerns related to plagiarism, privacy, data security, and regulatory compliance. These issues are particularly pressing when AI applications collect data from children under the age of 16, necessitating parental consent. To enhance their AI literacy, many teachers engage with high-quality yet time-intensive online training, webinars, and podcasts. However, as schools strive to adopt AI technologies that prioritise child welfare, the absence of officially sanctioned tools and clear regulatory frameworks forces educators to navigate this evolving landscape with limited guidance.

From February 2025, primary schools in Ireland are required to introduce compulsory AI literacy training for teachers and administrative staff. This training aims to equip all personnel with a comprehensive understanding of how AI tools function, their ethical considerations, and the regulatory compliance standards outlined in the Act. However, implementing these mandatory training programmes may prove challenging due to financial constraints, time limitations, and varying levels of digital literacy among staff. Ensuring consistent access to training, maintaining staff engagement, and effectively monitoring progress further complicates the process. To address these challenges and ensure fair and widespread implementation, schools may require external funding and support. Additionally, the EU AI Act's requirement for risk assessment and classification presents another layer of difficulty for schools in Ireland. Many school managers lack visibility into the specific AI tools being used by teachers, making it difficult to categorise them as minimal, low, high, or unacceptable risks. Without the necessary expertise and resources, schools may need to engage external consultants to carry out these assessments, placing additional financial pressure on already stretched budgets.

Research rooted in socio-cultural frameworks demonstrates that children's perceptions of digital skills development are significantly shaped by their social and school environments. In particular, children from lower socio-economic backgrounds and households with fewer technological resources tend to rely more heavily on schools for ICT learning (Griffin et al., 2025). This finding has direct implications for the equitable integration of AI tools in Irish primary schools: without deliberate support structures and targeted interventions, AI-supported pedagogy risks deepening existing digital divides. As Irish primary schools begin incorporating AI into learning environments, policymakers must prioritise resource allocation, teacher training, and infrastructure investment in socio-economically disadvantaged schools to ensure that all students have equal opportunities to develop essential AI literacy skills. To ensure equitable access to AI, children must be supported in developing AI competencies through inclusive, age-appropriate, and accessible education. Without such support, disparities will grow between those who can afford advanced AI tools and those who cannot. Preparing children to become critical, creative, and responsible citizens in the AI era requires proactive measures, including the integration of AI literacy and tools into the curriculum to equip them for the challenges and opportunities of the future.

Media Coverage of Best Practices

The integration of AI in primary education is a relatively recent development, resulting in a limited body of academic literature on the subject. Consequently, much of the available information is sourced from media outlets and broadsheet newspapers, which provide valuable insights and case studies that help illuminate current practices and perspectives within this emerging field. The media coverage of ChatGPT in educational settings, both in Ireland and internationally, reflects a diverse range of perspectives on its implications for teaching and learning. Many reports highlight the benefits of integrating AI tools (including ChatGPT) into schools, emphasising its potential to enhance student engagement, improve accessibility to learning resources, and facilitate dynamic learning experiences (McGuire, 2024; O'Brien C & Malone E, 2023). These positive narratives underscore how AI tools can personalise education and cater to diverse learning needs, making them valuable assets in contemporary classrooms. Conversely, the media also addresses significant challenges associated with the use of ChatGPT in educational contexts. Concerns regarding the reliability of information generated by AI, ethical dilemmas surrounding data privacy, and the potential for misuse by students are frequently discussed. These challenges raise critical questions about the appropriate implementation of AI in education and the need for guidelines to ensure responsible usage. Overall, the media's coverage provides a nuanced understanding of ChatGPT's role in schools, balancing its promising benefits with the potential risks that require careful consideration.

Irish media coverage has highlighted a growing number of examples demonstrating how primary schools across the country are beginning to integrate AI into both teaching and administrative practices. The use of AI is increasingly being framed not merely as a technological shift but as an opportunity to support more personalised and responsive approaches to learning. In some schools, AI tools are being used to assist with routine administrative tasks such as budgeting, as well as to develop individualised lesson plans aligned with pupils' strengths and interests. Teachers are also experimenting with AI-supported assessment, including auto-grading and the provision of tailored feedback. Rather than viewing AI solely through a lens of risk or restriction, a growing number of school leaders advocate for its role in developing pupils as capable and critically engaged digital citizens. A report from 2025 details how a principal of a primary school in County Wexford sees the integration of AI in primary education as presenting significant opportunities for transformative learning. This principal is advocating for the development of students as competent digital citizens rather than adopting a protective stance against technological advancements. Many principals are using AI for various administrative functions, including budgeting and the formulation of personalised lesson plans that cater to individual student strengths and interests. Some primary schools are using AI such as Google Gemini, a to explore AI applications for auto-grade assessments and provide tailored feedback (McGuire, 2024; O'Brien C & Malone E, 2023). The Education correspondent for RTE News has covered AI activities in schools for the last couple of years including an innovative history lesson at Boherbue Comprehensive School in North Cork, featuring an AI-generated "ghost" of a medieval peasant, offered students an immersive insight into medieval life and demonstrated the educational potential of artificial intelligence (O'Kelly, 2023). The lesson, created by a post-primary teacher using ChatGPT, captivated students and became a focal point in a record-breaking webinar attended by nearly 900 teachers. The webinar, titled

"Join the revolution! How ChatGPT is transforming education," showcased how AI can enhance teaching, particularly through reducing administrative workload and enabling creative classroom engagement.

Despite concerns about potential misuse, particularly in relation to student cheating in coursework, Hickey and others advocate for embracing the technology while promoting responsible and critical use. He emphasized that AI cannot replace good teaching, but teachers who adopt it may gain a significant advantage. Hickey, supported by Education Support Centres and echoed by figures such as Bill Gates, views AI as a transformative force in education. Nonetheless, he acknowledges its limitations, inaccuracies, and the urgent need for clear ethical guidelines and assessment safeguards. The State Examinations Commission has warned students against AI-assisted cheating, indicating serious consequences. As AI adoption grows, its implications for teaching and assessment are expected to feature prominently in national education policy and practice.

During the annual teacher conference in 2024, the Minister for Education announced the initiation of research to evaluate the benefits and risks associated with AI in educational contexts. Despite the increasing integration of AI as a learning tool, there are notable concerns regarding its potential misuse by students, particularly as educational reforms transition from traditional examinations to project-based assessments. Researchers such as Wieczorek (Irish Research Council Fellow) have acknowledged both the significant potential and the complex challenges associated with the integration of AI in primary and secondary education. Key concerns identified include the financial burden of acquiring commercial AI tools, the urgent need for comprehensive teacher training, and the risk of cultivating an overreliance on technological solutions. In addition, Wieczorek draws attention to the transparency of many AI systems, which may encode biases reflective of their developers and risk perpetuating inequalities, particularly among marginalised student groups. Nonetheless, he maintains that AI can positively contribute to educational practice, particularly in areas such as lesson planning and student assessment, by expanding the range and adaptability of available resources to better support diverse learner needs (Wieczorek, 2025; Wieczorek et al., 2024). Interviews with educators reveal a predominantly optimistic perspective on the potential of AI with many teachers emphasising the utility of AI in developing inclusive pedagogical strategies and generating comprehensive feedback for students. In May 2025, it was reported that the Irish Government was reportedly exploring the possibility of introducing ChatGPT into school classrooms, following a model already underway in Estonia, where tens of thousands of students and teachers are participating in a nationwide AI rollout (Weckler, 2025). This initiative comes amid growing usage of generative AI tools among Irish secondary school students, with recent survey data by Studyclix indicating that over 70% have already engaged with platforms like ChatGPT for schoolwork (Studyclix, 2025). While OpenAI representatives, including CFO Sarah Friar, have met with senior Irish officials to discuss a controlled "enterprise" deployment managed by schools, education stakeholders stress the need for thorough preparation and meaningful engagement with teachers before implementing such technologies. Meanwhile, some school leaders have also expressed caution about the rise of AI-generated student work and called for more robust policy and oversight to balance innovation with integrity in education. Given the increasing integration of AI in secondary education and the emphasis on early digital literacy in EU policy, it is plausible that similar deployments of tools like ChatGPT could be extended to primary schools, particularly to support foundational skills in personalised learning, creativity, and critical thinking from an early age.

National Strategies

Ireland's national AI strategy, "Here for Good," published in 2021 before the arrival of the tools such as Chat GPT is still relevant and underscores the necessity for deliberate consideration of AI's role in education (Department of Enterprise, 2021). The national strategy recognises AI is a rapidly evolving field, necessitating ongoing updates to educational curricula to equip students with the competencies required to engage with AI confidently and effectively in the future. The strategy also notes that educators must develop a clear understanding of AI's capabilities and limitations, recognising both its potential to enhance teaching and learning and the associated ethical implications and risks. AI-driven educational technologies offer notable advantages, including personalised learning experiences, adaptive feedback, support for remote education, and tools tailored to the needs of non-traditional learners and students with diverse requirements. Critically, as future generations will be most affected by AI advancements, integrating AI into the classroom can help foster early familiarity and comfort with these technologies. The Department of Education is actively conducting research to assess the implications of AI on teaching and learning practices, with a commitment to equipping educators with the requisite resources and skills. The ongoing curriculum reforms reflect a concerted effort to thoughtfully integrate AI into educational frameworks, balancing the numerous opportunities it presents with the challenges it entails.

As AI becomes increasingly integrated into primary education, several challenges and ethical considerations emerge, particularly concerning academic integrity and data privacy. These issues need to be addressed to ensure a responsible and effective implementation of AI tools in the classroom. One of the foremost challenges related to AI in education is the risk of academic dishonesty, particularly through plagiarism. With AI tools capable of generating essays, reports, and other assignments, students may be tempted to submit AI-generated content as their own work. This poses a significant threat to the principles of originality and personal accountability that are essential in educational settings. To combat this issue, educators can implement strategies that promote originality in student work. For instance, teachers can encourage the use of AI as a supplementary tool rather than a replacement for critical thinking and creativity. Assignments can be designed to require personal reflection, unique perspectives, or specific contextual knowledge that AI cannot replicate. Moreover, incorporating technology such as plagiarism detection software can help educators identify instances of dishonesty and reinforce the importance of academic integrity.

Another critical consideration in the use of AI in primary education is the collection and processing of student data. AI tools often require access to sensitive information to function effectively, raising concerns about data privacy and security. Schools must be vigilant in understanding how these tools collect, store, and use student data, as breaches could have severe implications for student privacy and safety. To address these concerns, it is essential for educational institutions to establish robust safeguarding policies that comply with regulations such as the General Data Protection Regulation (GDPR). This includes ensuring that data collection practices are transparent and that parents are informed about how their children's data will be used. Additionally, schools should prioritise the selection of AI tools that are designed with privacy in mind, opting for those that minimise data usage and employ encryption methods to protect sensitive information. While AI has the potential to enhance learning experiences in primary education, it is imperative to navigate the associated challenges and ethical considerations thoughtfully. By addressing issues of academic integrity and prioritising data privacy and security, educators can harness the benefits of AI while safeguarding the interests of students and maintaining the integrity of the educational process.

Recommendations and Best Practices

As AI continues to evolve, its integration into primary education is poised to expand significantly. Emerging AI technologies are set to transform classroom dynamics, with innovations aimed at enhancing the learning experience. These advancements may include more sophisticated educational platforms that adapt to individual student needs, offering personalised content and real-time feedback, ultimately fostering a more engaging and effective learning environment. However, it is crucial to strike a balance between the use of AI and the promotion of human-centred learning. While AI can provide valuable resources and support, it should not overshadow the development of essential skills such as creativity, social interaction, and emotional intelligence. Educators must ensure that AI tools are designed to complement traditional teaching methods rather than replace the vital human elements of education. In light of these developments, there is an urgent need for policy and regulation surrounding AI use in educational settings. Establishing guidelines and best practices will be essential to mitigate potential risks associated with AI, such as data privacy concerns and ethical considerations. By implementing comprehensive policies, schools can harness the benefits of AI while ensuring a safe and supportive learning environment for all students.

Conclusion

When examining the use of artificial intelligence in primary school classrooms, it is important to acknowledge that academic literature will invariably lag behind real-time developments in educational practice. The rapid pace of technological change, coupled with the time required for rigorous peer review and publication, means that scholarly research often reflects a retrospective view. Consequently, to gain a more immediate and nuanced understanding of how AI is currently being implemented in classrooms, it is essential to engage with media reports, practitioner accounts, and broader public discourse. These sources offer timely insights into emerging practices, teacher innovation, and the evolving challenges and opportunities that may not yet be captured in formal academic studies. AI presents exciting possibilities for Irish primary education, offering new ways to personalise learning, enhance efficiency, and support teachers. However, its successful integration requires careful consideration of ethical challenges, professional training, and the evolving role of educators. By balancing the benefits of AI with responsible implementation, schools can harness its potential to create a more effective and engaging learning environment. Looking ahead, AI is likely to continue shaping education, making it vital for educators, policymakers, and parents to work together in navigating its future impact.

Implications for Practice and Ethics

Educators and policymakers can draw on this chapter to guide the responsible integration of AI tools that enhance teaching and learning while supporting inclusive and personalised education. Ethical considerations include safeguarding student data, ensuring transparency in AI-generated content, and addressing equity in access to AI resources. Crucially, Departments and Ministries of Education must actively engage with teachers when shaping AI policy, recognising the nuanced blend of innovation and caution already evident in classrooms. Teachers are demonstrating thoughtful practice-based leadership in navigating AI's potential, balancing creativity with ethical responsibility, to ensure meaningful and safe learning experiences.

References

Ali, O., Murray, P. A., Momin, M., Dwivedi, Y. K., & Malik, T. (2024). The effects of artificial intelligence applications in educational settings: Challenges and strategies. *Technological Forecasting and Social Change, 199*, 123076. https://doi.org/10.1016/j.techfore.2023.123076

Bozkurt, A., Xiao, J., Farrow, R., Bai, J. Y. H., Nerantzi, C., Moore, S., Dron, J., Stracke, C. M., Singh, L., Crompton, H., Koutropoulos, A., Terentev, E., Pazurek, A., Nichols, M., Sidorkin, A. M., Costello, E., Watson, S., Mulligan, D., Honeychurch, S., et al. (2024). The manifesto for teaching and learning in a time of generative AI: A critical collective stance to better navigate the future. *Open Praxis, 16*(4), 487–513. https://doi.org/10.55982/openpraxis.16.4.777

Computer Education Society Ireland CESI. (2025). *AI in action*. https://www.cesi.ie/pw/ai-in-action-practical-ai-education-for-the-classroom/. Accessed June 2025

Department of Education. (2022). Digital strategy for schools to 2027. *Government of Ireland.*. https://www.gov.ie/en/department-of-education/publications/digital-strategy-for-schools-to-2027/. Accessed June 2025

Department of Education and Youth. (2025). *Guidance on Artificial Intelligence in Schools 2025* (Version 1). https://assets.gov.ie/static/documents/dee23cad/Guidance_on_Artificial_Intelligence_in_Schools_2025.pdf. Accessed 4 Nov 2025

Department of Enterprise, Trade and Employment. (2021, July 8). *AI—here for good: National artificial intelligence strategy for Ireland. Government of Ireland*. https://enterprise.gov.ie/en/publications/national-ai-strategy.html. Accessed June 2025

EU Commission and OECD. (2025). *Empowering Learners for the Age of AI An AI Literacy Framework for Primary and Secondary Education With Support from Open for use within the restrictions granted by Creative* Commons Attribution-ShareAlike 4.0 (CC BY-SA 4.0): https://creativecommons.org/licenses/by-sa/4.0. https://ailiteracyframework.org. Accessed June 2025.

European commission: Directorate-general for Education, youth, sport and culture, ethical guidelines on the use of artificial intelligence (AI) and data in teaching and learning for educators, Publications Office of the European Union. (2022). https://data.europa.eu/doi/10.2766/153756. Accessed June 2025

Girdham, J. (2024). A super-charged technology threatens to destroy the integrity of the leaving cert. *The Irish Times*. https://www.irishtimes.com/ireland/education/2024/10/27/a-super-charged-technology-threatens-to-destroy-the-integrity-of-the-leaving-cert/. Accessed June 2025

Griffin, M., Mohan, G., McCoy, S., & Lyons, S. (2025). Who says school provides computer skills? Early ICT exposure and later skill perceptions—Evidence from school and home environments in Ireland. *Technology, Pedagogy and Education, 1–26*. https://doi.org/10.1080/1475939X.2025.2505130

Huijser, H., Ames, K., Bozkurt, A., Corrin, L., Costello, E., Cowling, M., Czerniewicz, L., Deneen, C., Han, F., Littlejohn, A., Wise, A., Wright, M., & Zou, T. (2024). Collaboration or competition? The value of sector-wide collaboration in educational technology research. *Australasian Journal of Educational Technology, 40*(3), 1–8. https://doi.org/10.14742/ajet.10077

Jackson, L., Sidorkin, A. M., Jandrić, P., Costello, E., Heybach, J. A., Greenhalgh-Spencer, H., Hytten, K., Gourlay, L., Buchanan, R., & Tesar, M. (2025). The voice of artificial intelligence: Philosophical and educational reflections. *Educational Philosophy and Theory, 1–12*. https://doi.org/10.1080/00131857.2025.2481588

Le Borgne Y. et al. (2023). *Education hub's squad on artificial intelligence in education.*

Marcus-Quinn, A. (2013). *Digital repositories and their associated services: From capacity building to digital repositories and their associated services*. https://hdl.handle.net/10344/4128

Marcus-Quinn, A., Fotiadis, T., Yeratziotis, A., & Papadopoulos, G. A. (2024). Accessibility of e-books for secondary school students in Ireland and Cyprus. In *Transforming media accessibility in Europe* (pp. 229–245). Springer Nature Switzerland. https://doi.org/10.1007/978-3-031-60049-4_13

Marcus-Quinn, A., & McCoy, S. (2025). *Future proofing schools: Bringing school policies into the AI era*.

McCoy, S., & Marcus-Quinn, A. (2025). Navigating youth, smartphones, and policy: A balanced perspective on digital wellbeing. *Pediaticr Research*. https://doi.org/10.1038/s41390-025-04288-3

McGuire. (2024). It's revolutionising the classroom': Meet the teachers embracing AI. *The Irish Times*. https://www.irishtimes.com/ireland/education/2024/05/07/its-revolutionising-the-classroom-meet-the-teachers-embracing-ai/. Accessed May 2025

Murphy, C., Marcus-Quinn, A., & Hourigan, T. (2021). Exploring the ripple effect of 'always on' digital work culture in secondary Education settings. In *Handbook for online learning contexts: Digital, Mobile and open*. Springer. https://doi.org/10.1007/978-3-030-67349-9_23

O'Brien, C., & Malone, E. (2023). Teachers' views on AI: Is artificial intelligence to be embraced or feared. *The Irish Times*. https://www.irishtimes.com/ireland/education/2023/04/12/teachers-views-on-ai-is-artificial-intelligence-to-be-embraced-or-feared/. Accessed May 2025

O'Kelly, E. (2023). ChatGPT: Revolutionising education with AI, but at what cost? https://www.rte.ie/news/2023/0325/1366189-chatgpt-education/. Accessed May 2025

Office of the European Union L-, P., & Luxembourg, L. (2024). *Regulation (EU) 2024/1689 of the European Parliament and of the Council of 13 June 2024 laying down harmonised rules on artificial intelligence and amending Regulations (EC) No 300/2008, (EU) No 167/2013, (EU) No 168/2013, (EU) 2018/858, (EU) 2018/1139 and (EU) 2019/2144 and Directives 2014/90/EU, (EU) 2016/797 and (EU) 2020/1828 (Artificial Intelligence Act)Text with EEA relevance*. http://data.europa.eu/eli/reg/2024/1689/oj

Schiff, D. (2022). Education for AI, not AI for Education: The role of Education and ethics in national AI policy strategies. *International Journal of Artificial Intelligence in Education, 32*(3), 527–563. https://doi.org/10.1007/s40593-021-00270-2

Selwyn, N. (2019). *Should robots replace teachers? AI and the future of Education*. Policy Press.

Selwyn, N. (2023). The critique of digital education. In *Rethinking sociological critique in contemporary Education* (pp. 48–62). Routledge. https://doi.org/10.4324/9781003279457-5

Lewis Simon. (2024). *https://simonmlewis.medium.com/my-irish-primary-education-review-2024-july-to-december-05d12cd518ce*. Accessed June 2025.

Studyclix. (2025). *Studyclix student opinion survey 2025: AI, social media, misinformation & LC holidays*. https://www.Studyclix.Ie/Blog/Studyclix-Student-Opinion-Survey-2025-Ai-Social-Media-Misinformation-Lc-Holidays. Accessed May 2025

Weckler, A. (2025). Its about competitiveness. Government considering chatgpt rollout to schools. *Irish Independent*. https://www.independent.ie/irish-news/its-about-competitiveness-government-considering-chatgpt-rollout-to-schools/a1548139771.html. Accessed May 2025

Wieczorek and Costello. (2024). AI tools could revolutionise education but leave Gaelscoileanna behind. *The Irish Times*. https://www.irishtimes.com/ireland/education/2024/09/02/ai-tools-could-revolutionise-education-but-leave-gaelscoileanna-behind/. Accessed June 2025

Wieczorek, M. (2025). Why AI will not democratize Education: A critical pragmatist perspective. *Philosophy & Technology, 38*(2), 53. https://doi.org/10.1007/s13347-025-00883-8

Wieczorek, M., Hosseini, M., & Gordijn, B. (2024). *Unpacking the ethics of using AI in primary and secondary education: A systematic literature review*. https://doi.org/10.31219/osf.io/3txme

Chapter 16
Enhancing Sustainability Education through AI-Powered Experiential Learning

Hen Friman

Abstract This chapter investigates the integration of artificial intelligence (AI) tools into sustainability education within higher education, utilizing the Green Ambassadors in the Community program at Holon Institute of Technology (HIT) as a case study. The program employs AI technologies to create immersive and interactive learning experiences that enhance students' comprehension of sustainability concepts. Through virtual simulations and data-driven scenarios, students can examine complex environmental challenges and devise innovative solutions in a risk-free environment. This AI-enhanced methodology not only augments knowledge retention but also cultivates critical thinking and problem-solving skills essential for addressing real-world sustainability issues. The AI-powered Green Ambassadors program promotes collaborative learning and interdisciplinary problem-solving through real-time data analysis and predictive modeling. Students participate in dynamic scenario planning and decision-making exercises, reflecting real-world sustainability challenges. This hands-on approach enhances adaptability and fosters innovative, data-driven solutions. The program's AI technologies facilitate personalized learning experiences, with adaptive algorithms modifying virtual simulations according to individual progress. This tailored approach improves learning outcomes and strengthens students' connection to sustainability issues, potentially inspiring lifelong environmental advocacy. Within this program, students design and deliver experiential lessons on sustainability, renewable energy, and environmental awareness. Throughout their work, they utilize AI tools to assist with lesson planning, content creation, and the simulation of real-world environmental scenarios, enriching both their own learning experience and the quality of the educational materials they develop. The chapter examines various AI applications, including virtual assistants, interactive simulations, and AI-driven data analysis, which support students in crafting more engaging and effective lessons. By incorporating AI technologies, students can personalize their teaching, simulate environmental processes, and analyze data to make informed decisions regarding lesson content and teaching strategies. At the conclusion of the program, an evaluation was conducted to assess

H. Friman (✉)
Electrical and Electronics Engineering, H.I.T—Holon Institute of Technology, Holon, Israel
e-mail: henf@hit.ac.il

S. Papadakis (ed.), *AI Applications in Preschool and Primary Education*, Advances in Artificial Intelligence in Education 5, https://doi.org/10.1007/978-3-032-17190-0_16

the impact of AI-enhanced teaching on elementary school students' understanding of sustainability concepts. The results indicated increased engagement and improved learning outcomes, underscoring AI's potential as a transformative tool in experiential education. The chapter emphasizes the importance of integrating AI into future educational programs to promote sustainability awareness and inspire the next generation of environmentally conscious citizens.

Keywords Sustainability education · AI-supported experiential learning · Adaptive simulations · Environmental awareness

Introduction

This chapter examines how AI-supported experiential learning in higher education can inform and meaningfully connect to AI integration in early and primary education. Drawing on HIT's "Green Ambassadors in the Community" program, we show how adaptive simulations, data-driven activities, and virtual assistants translate complex sustainability ideas into concrete, age-appropriate experiences.

Incorporating sustainability education into higher education is essential for preparing future generations to address the intricate environmental, economic, and social issues of the twenty-first century (Mustafa et al., 2024). As climate change intensifies, natural resources become scarcer, and pollution increases, it is imperative for universities to equip students with the knowledge, skills, and critical thinking needed to devise innovative and sustainable solutions (Friman, 2024). Higher education institutions are pivotal in driving transformative change by promoting interdisciplinary learning that combines environmental science, engineering, policy, and social responsibility (Janakiraman, 2020). By integrating sustainability principles into their curricula, universities do more than just raise awareness—they empower students to become proactive agents of change in their respective fields (Friman, 2024).

However, sustainability education must extend beyond theoretical knowledge. To effectively prepare students for real-world challenges, learning should be experiential, and problem based (Friman, 2024; Topping et al., 2024). Traditional lectures alone are insufficient to develop the comprehensive understanding required to tackle sustainability issues. Instead, hands-on projects, community engagement, and advanced technologies—such as artificial intelligence (AI), data analytics, and virtual simulations—can enhance learning and deepen student engagement (Topping et al., 2024). These methods enable students to address real environmental problems, collaborate across disciplines, and apply cutting-edge technologies to create practical solutions (Hajj-Hassan et al., 2024; Strielkowski et al., 2025).

Programs like the Green Ambassadors in the Community demonstrate how experiential sustainability education can have a significant impact both within academic institutions and in society at large (Friman, 2024). Furthermore, integrating sustainability education into higher learning aligns with global initiatives such as the United

Nations Sustainable Development Goals (SDGs), particularly Goal 4 (Quality Education) and Goal 13 (Climate Action). Universities have a duty to nurture environmentally conscious professionals who will influence policies, technologies, and industries toward a more sustainable future (Lee, 2025). Given the urgency of the climate crisis, sustainability education should be regarded as a core, interdisciplinary component across all academic fields, rather than an optional subject. By leveraging AI-powered tools and experiential learning methods, universities can enhance sustainability literacy, foster innovation, and inspire the next generation of leaders to tackle today's critical environmental challenges (Liu, 2025; Memarian & Doleck, 2023).

The Role of Experiential Learning in Fostering Environmental Awareness

Experiential learning is a powerful way to build environmental awareness by immersing students in real-world sustainability challenges (Mustafa et al., 2024). Unlike traditional classroom learning, which focuses on theory, experiential learning engages students through hands-on activities like fieldwork, lab experiments, and project-based learning (Friman, 2024). These experiences help them understand environmental processes, recognize the impact of unsustainable practices, and develop practical solutions for sustainability (Janakiraman, 2020). By working directly with environmental issues, students gain a deeper sense of responsibility for conservation and sustainable development. A key advantage of experiential learning is the strong connection it fosters between students and their communities (Yim & Su, 2024). When students take part in sustainability initiatives—such as waste reduction campaigns, renewable energy projects, or ecosystem restoration—they not only gain technical skills but also develop a sense of environmental responsibility (Friman, 2024). Collaborating with peers, educators, and community members enhances their critical thinking and teamwork, essential for addressing global environmental challenges (Topping et al., 2024). Programs like Green Ambassadors in the Community demonstrate how experiential learning empowers students to become active participants in environmental education and advocacy (Friman, 2024). Additionally, integrating advanced technologies—such as AI-driven simulations, virtual reality, and real-time environmental monitoring—further enriches experiential learning (Topping et al., 2024). These tools help students visualize and analyze environmental data, model climate scenarios, and assess sustainability strategies (Liu, 2025; García-López & Trujillo-Liñán, 2025). By using AI and digital tools, students can make data-driven decisions and test solutions in interactive, controlled environments before applying them in real-world settings (Yim & Su, 2024). This combination of hands-on learning and technology not only enhances engagement but also equips students with the skills needed to tackle future sustainability challenges (Strielkowski et al., 2025; Hajj-Hassan et al., 2024) (Fig. 16.1).

Fig. 16.1 Students sorting waste using a magnet during the "Green Ambassadors" activity. *Source* Author, 2025

The Emergence of AI in Education: Opportunities and Challenges

The integration of artificial intelligence (AI) into education has brought about a profound shift in pedagogical approaches, offering new avenues for both personalized and scalable learning (Lee, 2025; Strielkowski et al., 2025). Adaptive platforms, virtual tutors, and automated feedback systems enable instructors to tailor instruction based on individual student needs, allowing learners to progress at their own pace and reinforcing comprehension through customized learning paths (Topping et al., 2024; García-López & Trujillo-Liñán, 2025). In the context of sustainability education, these technologies are particularly valuable: AI-driven simulations help visualize the outcomes of different climate policies or energy strategies, promoting systems thinking and environmental literacy (Janakiraman, 2020).

In addition to personalization, AI significantly enhances instructional efficiency. For example, automated assessment platforms like Grades cope reduce educators' administrative burden, allowing more time for mentoring and curriculum development (Yim & Su, 2024). Moreover, AI-powered tools such as chatbots and virtual assistants—e.g., IBM Watson—facilitate real-time interaction, guiding students through complex topics and offering immediate clarification or supplemental resources (Memarian & Doleck, 2023; Liu, 2025).

Despite its potential, the widespread adoption of AI in education introduces ethical and practical concerns. Data privacy, algorithmic bias, and unequal access remain major barriers (Topping et al., 2024). AI systems that rely on biased training data can perpetuate inequalities, unintentionally disadvantaging underrepresented student groups (Mustafa et al., 2024). Likewise, the digital divide limits access to AI-enhanced tools, especially in underserved communities—raising concerns about equity in learning outcomes (Yim & Su, 2024).

To address these challenges, initiatives such as UNESCO's AI for Good and collaborations between public institutions and tech companies seek to democratize access to advanced educational technologies (Liu, 2025). These efforts must be paired with comprehensive educator training programs to build AI literacy and ensure that AI augments rather than replaces human-centered teaching (Friman, 2024; Hajj-Hassan et al., 2024).

In summary, when deployed ethically and equitably, AI can empower educators and learners alike—particularly in sustainability-focused programs like Green Ambassadors in the Community—by enhancing engagement, improving access, and fostering the development of critical thinking and data-driven decision-making skills (Friman, 2024; Lee, 2025).

Overview of the "Green Ambassadors in the Community" Program

The Green Ambassadors in the Community initiative at the Holon Institute of Technology (HIT) is a pioneering program that bridges academic knowledge with hands-on sustainability education (Friman, 2024; Mustafa et al., 2024). For over seven years, it has empowered engineering and science students to design and deliver experiential lessons on environmental responsibility, renewable energy, and sustainable living to elementary school children (Lee, 2025). These students take on the role of environmental advocates, promoting awareness through engaging activities that help young learners understand complex sustainability concepts (Janakiraman, 2020; Yim & Su, 2024).

The program is administered by HIT's Social Engagement Unit and receives academic support from the Faculty of Engineering and the Center of Excellence for Alternative Energies and the Smart Grid. Its foundation lies in experiential learning—students not only acquire theoretical knowledge but also apply it directly within the community (Topping et al., 2024). A flagship initiative of the program is the mobile laboratory, a flexible educational unit that brings sustainability tools and demonstrations into the classroom setting (Yim & Su, 2024; Strielkowski et al., 2025).

Hands-on experiments featured in the mobile lab illustrate concepts such as energy efficiency, pollution, and technological innovation. Children explore the differences between incandescent and LED bulbs, engage with hydrogen-powered model vehicles, and examine the effects of contaminated versus fertile soil on plant growth (Hajj-Hassan et al., 2024; Friman, 2024). These activities not only reinforce classroom learning but also encourage long-term environmental stewardship among participants (Liu, 2025; Memarian & Doleck, 2023) Fig. 16.2 and Fig. 16.3.

Fig. 16.2 Comparing contaminated and fertile soil; demonstration of a car model powered by a hydrogen fuel cell. *Source* Author, 2025

In recent years, the Green Ambassadors in the Community program has expanded its pedagogical toolkit by incorporating artificial intelligence (AI) to boost its impact and reach (Friman, 2024; Hajj-Hassan et al., 2024). AI tools now support a range of instructional activities, from lesson planning and adaptive simulations to data-driven decision-making in teaching strategies (Strielkowski et al., 2025). By integrating AI-powered virtual tutors and environmental data modeling tools, the program has succeeded in delivering more personalized, immersive, and effective learning experiences for both university students and the schoolchildren they mentor (Lee, 2025; Topping et al., 2024).

This integration not only enhances educational outcomes but also prepares students for future roles in sustainability and technology-driven industries by building digital fluency and analytical thinking skills (Friman, 2024; Liu, 2025). Beyond academics, the program emphasizes civic engagement and leadership development. Through public speaking, collaborative lesson design, and active participation in school and community-based projects, students cultivate essential soft skills such as communication, teamwork, and project management (Mustafa et al., 2024; Yim & Su, 2024).

These real-world experiences reinforce students' understanding of sustainability while positioning them for influential roles in academia, industry, and environmental advocacy (Topping et al., 2024). As a model for merging experiential learning, AI innovation, and environmental education, the Green Ambassadors program demonstrates how higher education institutions can shape socially responsible, digitally literate professionals (Janakiraman, 2020; Memarian & Doleck, 2023). With ongoing advancements in AI technologies, the program is well positioned to expand its educational scope and societal impact in the years ahead (Liu, 2025; Yim & Su, 2024).

AI as a Tool for Enhancing Educational Content Creation

AI is transforming education by making learning materials more personalized, interactive, and accessible. AI-powered tools assist educators in designing adaptive lessons, interactive simulations, and real-time feedback mechanisms that enhance both engagement and instructional efficiency (Liu, 2025; Friman, 2024). Technologies such as natural language processing (NLP) now automate content generation—producing summaries, quizzes, and explanations that support differentiated instruction (García-López & Trujillo-Liñán, 2025; Liu, 2025). Furthermore, AI systems generate multimodal content (text, images, video, and immersive environments), making lessons more accessible and appealing to diverse learners (Yim & Su, 2024).

One of the most impactful applications of AI is in adaptive learning. AI-driven platforms adjust content in real time based on student performance, ensuring that learners receive instruction suited to their current skill level (Strielkowski et al., 2025). In sustainability education, this allows students to explore environmental issues—such as carbon reduction strategies or renewable energy optimization—through personalized simulations and scenarios (Janakiraman, 2020; Hajj-Hassan et al., 2024).

AI also supports collaborative content development by facilitating co-creation between educators and students. Tools that aid in brainstorming, automated structuring, and multilingual translation expand the reach of sustainability education and make it more culturally responsive (Friman, 2024). This is especially relevant in programs like Green Ambassadors in the Community, where students work with diverse groups and benefit from tailored digital tools (Memarian & Doleck, 2023; Yim & Su, 2024).

However, as AI becomes more prevalent, ethical considerations become increasingly important. Biases in training data, the opacity of algorithmic decision-making, and unequal access to technology all pose significant challenges (Mustafa et al., 2024; Topping et al., 2024). Educators must remain central to the learning process—validating AI-generated content, fostering critical thinking, and ensuring educational equity (Liu, 2025; Janakiraman, 2020). Establishing clear standards for transparency, data privacy, and inclusive design is essential to harnessing the benefits of AI while minimizing risks (Topping et al., 2024; Liu, 2025).

As AI technology evolves, its role in sustainability-focused programs like Green Ambassadors is expected to grow. Thoughtful integration of these tools can foster deeper engagement and prepare learners to tackle global environmental challenges through innovation and collaboration (Friman, 2024; Hajj-Hassan et al., 2024).

AI as Personalized Learning through AI-Driven Platforms

One of the most promising applications of artificial intelligence (AI) in education is its capacity to personalize learning. AI-powered platforms monitor students' learning styles, pace, and performance to adapt content in real time. These systems offer customized assignments and feedback, helping students stay engaged while progressing at their own level. This is especially valuable in sustainability education, where learners arrive with varying levels of prior knowledge and motivation. AI can identify individual learning gaps, suggest interactive simulations, and provide problem-solving tasks to reinforce difficult concepts. Within the Green Ambassadors program, personalized AI tools enable students to explore environmental issues independently and receive tailored guidance throughout their learning journey (Topping et al., 2024; Lee, 2025; Strielkowski et al., 2025; García-López & Trujillo-Liñán, 2025; Friman, 2024).

Simulating Real-World Environmental Scenarios with AI

AI plays a key role in simulating real-world environmental situations, allowing students to explore complex systems in a controlled virtual space. AI-powered simulations can model various sustainability challenges, such as climate change and resource management (Janakiraman, 2020). These tools let students experiment with different solutions to global issues, helping them understand cause and effect without the ethical or logistical challenges of real-life experiments. For example, AI models can show how different energy production methods might impact ecosystems or predict the effects of climate policies on carbon emissions. AI tools, like machine learning algorithms, enhance these simulations by analyzing large datasets to predict future environmental outcomes more accurately. They help students assess the effectiveness of initiatives like solar power or electric vehicle infrastructure systems (Hajj-Hassan et al., 2024; Friman, 2024). Programs like Green Ambassadors incorporate these simulations into their lessons, allowing students to design and test sustainable solutions in virtual settings before applying them in real life. Through AI-assisted simulations, students gain a deeper understanding of environmental systems and are empowered to make informed, sustainable decisions (Friman, 2024; Yim & Su, 2024; Yim & Su, 2024).

AI-Powered Data Analysis for Sustainable Decision-Making

AI plays a crucial role in sustainability education by enabling data-driven decision-making through advanced data analysis tools. In environmental science, AI can process large datasets from sensors, satellites, and monitoring systems to detect patterns that might otherwise go unnoticed (García-López & Trujillo-Liñán, 2025; Topping et al., 2024). For instance, AI can analyze air and water quality data, predict pollution levels, and pinpoint environmental damage sources, offering valuable insights for policymakers, businesses, and educators. These tools are especially useful in sustainable resource management, helping decision-makers find the best strategies for managing resources like water or land. By using AI to address sustainability challenges, students in the Green Ambassadors program can work with real-world data, understand the consequences of their decisions, and test the outcomes of various policies (Friman, 2024; Strielkowski et al., 2025). AI also helps them identify trends and make recommendations based on data predictions, improving their ability to make informed, sustainable choices. AI-driven data analysis tools are vital for informed, sustainable decision-making, turning raw data into actionable insights. As AI advances, its ability to handle complex data will become even more important in sustainability education, helping students develop essential skills to tackle environmental challenges (Janakiraman, 2020; Friman, 2024; Memarian & Doleck, 2023).

AI Integration in the "Green Ambassadors" Program

The Green Ambassadors in the Community program, launched at the Holon Institute of Technology (HIT), is an educational initiative that aims to promote environmental awareness and sustainability. The program allows students to design and run hands-on activities for local communities, especially focusing on sustainability and renewable energy. It combines environmental science, engineering, and community involvement to create engaging learning experiences, including for elementary school children (Friman, 2024). Through these activities, students develop practical skills in teaching, communication, and leadership while addressing environmental challenges. A key development in the program was the integration of artificial intelligence (AI), which enhanced the effectiveness of the educational activities. AI tools were introduced to help students with lesson planning, content creation, and simulating real-world environmental scenarios. The goal was to give students advanced resources to develop innovative teaching materials, simulate environmental conditions, and use data analysis to assess sustainability projects. AI technologies, including virtual assistants, interactive simulations, and AI-powered data analytics, made the learning environment more dynamic and allowed students to explore environmental issues in real time. This chapter will examine how AI was used in the program, its impact on learning, and the potential for expanding AI-based education in sustainability (Lee, 2025; Yim & Su, 2024).

Engaging Students in Experiential Sustainability Education

Engaging students in sustainability education goes beyond theory; it involves active participation in real-world problem-solving and hands-on activities that connect with their personal experiences. Programs like Green Ambassadors in the Community allow students to work with local communities, bridging classroom learning with real-world impact (Friman, 2024). This approach helps students apply sustainability concepts to practical scenarios, deepening their understanding of environmental issues. For example, when students design projects on renewable energy or waste management, they gain technical knowledge and develop important skills like leadership and teamwork. Integrating AI tools can further enhance engagement by offering personalized learning experiences, where students simulate environmental impacts or analyze data on sustainability outcomes. This student-centered approach nurtures a strong sense of responsibility, empowering students to take action on sustainability (Friman, 2024; Hajj-Hassan et al., 2024; Liu, 2025).

Fig. 16.3 Converting motion to electricity: a classroom wind-energy demonstration. *Source* Author, 2025

The Role of AI in Lesson Planning and Delivery

AI is revolutionizing education by improving lesson planning and delivery. In sustainability education, AI tools help instructors transform theoretical content into engaging lessons. AI platforms can suggest relevant activities and resources aligned with learning goals, creating a curriculum that covers key sustainability topics like renewable energy and conservation, tailored to students' cognitive levels. AI streamlines the process, allowing educators to focus on personalizing content rather than administrative tasks. Once the lesson plan is set, AI can suggest experiments or simulations to bring the lesson to life. For example, in the Green Ambassadors program, AI could recommend virtual experiments on solar energy or wind turbines, providing students with practical experiences before they apply concepts in the field. Additionally, AI can adjust lesson plans based on student performance and provide real-time feedback, offering personalized learning experiences (Janakiraman, 2020; Liu, 2025).

AI also helps with logistical tasks like purchasing and organizing materials for experiments. By predicting the resources needed, AI can compare prices, track inventory, and ensure that supplies are always available. This reduces administrative workload, allowing educators to focus more on teaching and student engagement. Moreover, AI can generate interactive educational content like quizzes, presentations, and assessments, which adapt to individual learning styles and speeds. These tools make lessons more engaging, helping students better understand complex topics like the environmental impact of energy sources. By incorporating AI, educators can create more effective, personalized, and interactive learning experiences (Topping et al., 2024; Friman, 2024; Yim & Su, 2024; Mustafa et al., 2024).

AI-Driven Interactive Simulations for Environmental Education

AI-driven interactive simulations are a powerful tool in sustainability education, allowing students to engage with dynamic models that mimic real-world environmental issues like climate change and resource management. These simulations help students understand how factors such as energy use, emissions, and natural resource consumption affect ecosystems, energy systems, and communities. For instance, an AI simulation might show the long-term impacts of adopting renewable energy, enabling students to see the effects on both the environment and local populations. By adjusting variables and interacting with these models, students gain a deeper understanding of environmental processes and sustainability challenges. AI-powered simulations also provide instant feedback, guiding students and helping them develop critical thinking and problem-solving skills as they analyze outcomes, form hypotheses, and modify their strategies. They also offer the chance to explore environmental processes that are hard to replicate in a traditional classroom, like simulating the effects of natural disasters or pollution. These AI-driven tools make sustainability education more engaging, personalized, and immersive, offering students an interactive way to explore the environmental issues shaping our world today. Virtual laboratories and ecosystem simulations are transforming environmental education through AI technology (Friman, 2024; Hajj-Hassan et al., 2024; Strielkowski et al., 2025). These platforms offer students the chance to conduct experiments and explore environmental systems in a virtual space, without the limitations of traditional labs. AI-powered simulations allow students to observe the effects of factors like pollution, climate change, or plant growth in different conditions, providing real-time data and feedback. This hands-on experience is hard to replicate in a typical classroom. A major benefit of AI-driven virtual labs is their ability to adapt to each student's learning pace and style. Adaptive algorithms can adjust difficulty levels, offer hints, and guide students toward areas of further interest, helping them understand ecological concepts more deeply. These labs also enable the simulation of rare or hazardous scenarios, such as chemical spills or wildfires, which would be difficult to recreate in real life. This allows students to appreciate the complexity of ecosystems and the need for sustainable practices (Mustafa et al., 2024; Topping et al., 2024).

AI in Modeling Renewable Energy Systems

AI applications have greatly improved the way renewable energy systems are modeled, offering students a hands-on, data-driven way to understand these systems. AI algorithms can process large amounts of data from sources like wind, solar, and hydro power, enabling accurate simulations of energy production. In the classroom, AI models allow students to experiment with different energy setups, assess new technologies, and predict system performance under various conditions. This helps them grasp the challenges and potential of integrating renewable energy into modern grids (Li & Wang, 2023). AI also plays a key role in optimizing energy production by analyzing both historical and real-time data. Through predictive modeling, it can forecast energy output from solar panels or wind turbines based on weather, helping students understand issues like variability and intermittency. Students can also explore how different systems interact in smart grids, how energy storage works, and how policies like subsidies impact renewable energy projects. These AI-driven simulations create a deeper learning experience, bridging theory and real-world application (Topping et al., 2024; Friman, 2024; Lee, 2025; Mustafa et al., 2024; García-López & Trujillo-Liñán, 2025; Liu, 2025).

Enhancing Student Engagement through Gamification

Gamification, boosted by AI, is a powerful tool for education. By adding game elements like rewards, challenges, and progression levels, teachers can make sustainability education more engaging (Lee, 2025; Liu, 2025). AI personalizes the experience for each student, adapting challenges based on their performance. For example, students can work on solving environmental issues, like reducing carbon emissions, through a gamified setup. AI ensures the tasks are appropriate for each student, offering continuous feedback that helps them improve and stay engaged. Gamification also encourages collaboration, allowing students to work together on projects like designing sustainable cities. This fosters teamwork, problem-solving, and critical thinking, while deepening students' passion for sustainability (Liu, 2025; Yim & Su, 2024).

Assessment Methods and Criteria in AI-Enhanced Sustainability Education

AI opens new ways to assess student progress in sustainability education. Traditional assessments may not capture the skills students gain from interactive AI simulations or virtual labs. Performance-based assessments, where students tackle complex environmental challenges, offer better insights into their problem-solving and decision-making abilities. AI tracks their progress, providing a more accurate view of their understanding. AI can also create personalized assessments that adjust difficulty based on a student's past performance, ensuring fairness and challenge. Additionally, AI analyzes response patterns to identify struggling areas and provide tailored support. This helps educators assess whether students are mastering sustainability concepts. AI also tracks student engagement through data on participation and task completion, giving insight into their motivation and commitment to sustainability. This, combined with traditional assessments, provides a comprehensive evaluation. Over time, AI can help measure how well students retain and apply sustainability knowledge in real-world scenarios, ensuring they not only learn but can also apply their knowledge in practical ways (Topping et al., 2024).

The chapter highlight the significant role that technologies like AI-driven gamification play in enhancing student engagement and motivation in sustainability education. By integrating game mechanics into learning, students become actively involved in solving environmental challenges, gaining not only theoretical knowledge but also practical skills such as teamwork, problem-solving, and critical thinking. The continuous feedback provided by these systems helps students improve their performance and encourages them to continue exploring and learning about sustainability. The Green Ambassadors project, which aims to raise environmental awareness and teach renewable energy and sustainability to diverse groups of young students, these concepts can add great value. By incorporating AI-powered gamification tools, the Green Ambassadors can guide elementary school students using interactive and innovative methods. Additionally, AI-based assessment systems can help track student engagement, measure their understanding of sustainability concepts, and offer personalized feedback, ensuring that the students stay engaged and deepen their commitment to environmental issues.

The integration of AI in the "Green Ambassadors in the Community" program enhances interactive and personalized learning experiences in sustainability education. By leveraging virtual simulations, real-time data analysis, and adaptive algorithms, students develop critical thinking, problem-solving, and collaborative learning skills. AI also supports lesson planning, content creation, and real-world environmental scenario simulations, enriching both teaching methods and student engagement. AI not only improves the program's effectiveness but also helps tailor teaching strategies and strengthen participants' digital skills. Through data-driven learning, decision-making exercises, and virtual environmental modeling, students gain a deeper understanding of sustainability challenges. Ultimately, AI serves as a key tool for fostering community engagement, educational innovation, and the development of sustainable solutions (Friman, 2024; Yim & Su, 2024; Hajj-Hassan et al., 2024).

Conclusion and Recommendations

Recent studies exploring the integration of digital games, AI-powered storytelling, computer-assisted instruction (CAI), and virtual reality (VR) into sustainability education consistently demonstrate positive learning outcomes. Among the reviewed interventions, digital games such as Undercities, Sustain, Minecraft, and other educational platforms. The studies reported statistically significant improvements in students' knowledge, attitudes, or behaviors related to sustainability. Furthermore, engagement levels were notably high learners exhibited increased motivation, enjoyment, and active participation, especially when collaborative play and interactive feedback were present. Thematic analysis indicates that digital and AI-enhanced tools effectively fostered curiosity, systems thinking, and emotional connection with sustainability concepts. Structured storytelling in early childhood, particularly when AI-generated, was found to be especially effective in boosting comprehension and narrative understanding. These findings underscore the transformative potential of technology in sustainability education and further validate the pedagogical strategies employed in the Green Ambassadors program.

This chapter demonstrated how AI can enhance sustainability education through personalized, interactive, and experiential approaches, exemplified by the Green Ambassadors program at HIT. For broader educational impact, these insights should be adapted to younger age groups using tools such as storytelling, simulations, and gamification. Educators should prioritize ethical use of AI, ensure inclusivity, and maintain human-centered guidance. By leveraging AI responsibly, we can inspire environmental awareness from early childhood and empower future generations to act for a sustainable planet.

Generative AI Acknowledgment Part of the language editing was assisted by generative AI tools. The authors reviewed and verified all content and bear responsibility for the final version (Springer policy, 2025).

Ethics Statement This school-based study complied with the ethical procedures of the Israeli Ministry of Education for research conducted in schools. Prior to participation, written informed consent was obtained from the parents/guardians of all participating students; consent covered participation in the learning activities, the collection and analysis of research data, and permission to publish photographs from the activities. School leadership and teachers granted permission, and student assent was obtained where appropriate.

References

Friman, H. (2024). Shaping the engineers of tomorrow: Integrating renewable energies and advanced technologies in electrical and electronics engineering education. *Energies, 17*, 4146. https://doi.org/10.3390/en17164146

García-López, I. M., & Trujillo-Liñán, L. (2025). Generative AI use in K–12 education: A systematic review. *Frontiers in Education, 10*, 1647573. https://doi.org/10.3389/feduc.2025.1647573

Hajj-Hassan, M., Chaker, R., & Cederqvist, A.-M. (2024). Environmental education: A systematic review on the use of digital tools for fostering sustainability awareness. *Sustainability, 16*(9), 3733. https://doi.org/10.3390/su16093733

Janakiraman, S. (2020). Digital games for environmental sustainability education: Implications for educators. In *proceedings of the eighth international conference on technological ecosystems for enhancing Multiculturality* (TEEM'20). https://doi.org/10.1145/3434780.3436649

Lee, Y. (2025). Developing a computer-based tutor utilizing generative AI and retrieval-augmented generation. *Education and Information Technologies, 30*, 7841–7862. https://doi.org/10.1007/s10639-024-13129-5

Li, X., & Wang, Y. (2023). The role of artificial intelligence in the procurement process: State of the art and research agenda. *Journal of Purchasing and Supply Management, 29*(3), 100823. https://doi.org/10.1016/j.pursup.2023.100823

Liu, L. (2025). Impact of AI gamification on EFL learning outcomes and nonlinear dynamic motivation: Comparing adaptive learning paths, conversational agents, and storytelling. *Education and Information Technologies, 30*, 11299–11338. https://doi.org/10.1007/s10639-024-13296-5

Memarian, B., & Doleck, T. (2023). Fairness, accountability, transparency, and ethics (FATE) in AI and higher education: A systematic review. *Computers & Education: Artificial Intelligence, 4*, 100152. https://doi.org/10.1016/j.caeai.2023.100152

Mustafa, M. Y., Tlili, A., Lampropoulos, G., Huang, R., Jandrić, P., Zhao, J., Salha, S., Xu, L., Panda, S., López-Pernas, S., & Saqr, M. (2024). A systematic review of literature reviews on artificial intelligence in education (AIED): A roadmap to a future research agenda. *Smart Learning Environments, 11*, 59. https://doi.org/10.1186/s40561-024-00350-5

Strielkowski, W., Grebennikova, V., Lisovskiy, A., Rakhimova, G., & Vasileva, T. (2025). AI-driven adaptive learning for sustainable educational transformation. *Sustainable Development, 33*(2), 1921–1947. https://doi.org/10.1002/sd.3221

Topping, K. J., Gehringer, E., Khosravi, H., Gudipati, S., Jadhav, K., & Susarla, S. (2024). Enhancing peer assessment with artificial intelligence. *International Journal of Educational Technology in Higher Education*. https://doi.org/10.1186/s41239-024-00501-1

Yim, I. H. Y., & Su, J. (2024). Artificial intelligence (AI) learning tools in K–12 education: A scoping review. *Journal of Computers in Education*. https://doi.org/10.1007/s40692-023-00304-9

Chapter 17
AI-Driven Assessment in Early and Primary Education: Tools, Strategies, and Ethical Considerations

Elena Even-Simkin

Abstract Artificial Intelligence (AI) is becoming an integral part of the industrial world, medicine and education. Recent studies have shown a growing interest among educators in AI-powered educational tools and AI-driven assessments. AI-driven tools in education, in general, and in student assessment, in particular, propose many benefits in various areas, including: (a). offering personalized learning monitoring that addresses the student's strengths as well as weaknesses and individual learning pace; (b). allowing test development targeting specific areas requiring improvement; (c). offering continuous evaluation to foster real-time and customized feedback for facilitating tailored intervention programs. In addition to providing a more comprehensive view of students' progress, AI-powered assessment can help educators focus on more creative aspects of teaching to ensure that students receive consistent data-driven support that can capture the nuances of individual learning progress. However, besides these evident benefits, ethical considerations concerning overreliance on AI-driven solutions and data privacy pose crucial challenges. Nonetheless, despite these challenges and limitations, AI offers evident potential for enhancing teaching and learning experiences as well as leading to improved educational outcomes. This chapter explores future directions and key innovative approaches to AI-driven educational assessment.

Keywords AI-Driven Assessment · Education Tools · Ethical Considerations · Advanced Learning Technologies · Personalized Learning and Feedback

E. Even-Simkin (✉)
SCE Sami Shamoon College of Engineering, Beer Sheva, Israel
e-mail: elenaev@sce.ac.il

S. Papadakis (ed.), *AI Applications in Preschool and Primary Education*, Advances in Artificial Intelligence in Education 5, https://doi.org/10.1007/978-3-032-17190-0_17

Introduction

This chapter provides a critical analysis of how artificial intelligence can enhance assessment practices, support personalized learning and improve pedagogical efficiency in early education. Situated within the broader discourse on technology-mediated learning, it examines the dual role of AI as both a pedagogical aid and an ethical challenge in child-centered educational environments. Drawing on recent empirical studies and theoretical insights, the chapter underscores AI's potential to deliver adaptive feedback, enable individualized instruction and promote inclusive learning opportunities. At the same time, it foregrounds the ethical, methodological and sociocultural complexities inherent in applying AI to young learners, emphasizing the necessity of maintaining transparency and human-centered integration of AI in early and primary education, as well as in all educational applications.

The field of Artificial Intelligence (AI) has evolved as a transformative technology for data interpretation, learning and then data adaptation in various fields for reaching significant implications in medicine, industry and education (Haenlein & Kaplan, 2019), demonstrating human-like abilities such as learning and problem-solving (Nagendraswamy & Salis, 2021). As Toosi et al. (2021, p. 2) note, "AI technology is sweeping the globe, leading to bold statements by notable figures: '[AI] is going to change the world more than anything in the history of mankind (Clifford, 2019)'". As AI continues to advance, it gains far-reaching impacts on organizational structures (Benbya et al., 2020; Haenlein & Kaplan, 2019) and education, necessitating ongoing research and adaptation to harness its potential effectiveness (Ogunsakin, 2024; Rane, 2023).

While its adoption in large enterprises is still in the early stages (Benbya et al., 2020), AI is revolutionizing education, offering opportunities for personalized learning, automated assessment and enhanced teaching practices (Ogunsakin, 2024; Rane, 2023). AI technologies generate diverse educational content, saving time for educators while providing customized assignments (Rane, 2023). However, this technology presents challenges and opportunities, requiring careful consideration of its implications. On the one hand, AI-powered tools offer numerous benefits, including improved educational assessment, thus offering more dynamic, efficient and personalized feedback (Owan et al., 2023). Furthermore, besides the ability of these systems to provide adaptive and real-time assessment methods, they can evaluate higher-order competencies like critical thinking (Saputra et al., 2024). On the other hand, integrating AI into education also faces many challenges, such as data privacy concerns, potential biases and ethical considerations (Elam, 2024; Pop et al., 2024). Addressing these challenges requires an interdisciplinary collaboration between researchers, policymakers, and industry stakeholders for the effective integration of Big Data and AI in education (Elam, 2024) and leveraging the potential of AI to improve operational outcomes, particularly in assessment and personalized learning.

It is also worth noting that AI has a significant benefit in the educational sector, i.e., the ability to enhance earlier predictions of academic failure and improve the teaching-learning process (Duarte et al., 2023). However, the integration of AI into education requires a balanced approach that complements human expertise in various fields for maintaining educational core values and supporting dynamic, inclusive and personalized learning experiences (Miller, 2024). Therefore, despite the promising improvement in student engagement and learning outcomes through the integration of AI in online learning environments, challenges persist, including concerns about academic integrity, data privacy and algorithmic bias (Ogunsakin, 2024; Rane, 2023) and, most importantly, ethical considerations still have to be addressed (Lyanda et al., 2024). Thus, developing ethical guidelines, advancing adaptive learning technologies, creating more inclusive AI systems (Elam, 2024) as well as establishing transparent and accountable practices are crucial to harnessing AI's full potential in education.

Recent studies have shown that AI in education offers significant potential for enhancing teaching and learning experiences, improving administrative efficiency and advanced analytics (Eden et al., 2024; Ray & Ray, 2024) by adapting instructions to individual learning styles, automating administrative tasks and also creating immersive learning environments (Eden et al., 2024). Nevertheless, this rapid digital advancement also brings additional educational obstacles, such as the need for teacher training to adapt to such innovations (Elam, 2024). Furthermore, as AI adoption grows, besides comprehensive teacher training, there is a need for robust ethical guidelines and ongoing research to ensure effective and responsible implementation of AI-based tools in the educational sector (Luan et al., 2020; Ogunsakin, 2024). Accordingly, evaluation of the efficiency, reliability and validity of the integration of AI in learning environments in higher education and, particularly, in elementary school and preschool education plays a crucial role in navigating these challenges, mastering new technologies in education and ensuring AI's ethical use (Miller, 2024). Indeed, AI-based assessment has significant potential to transform educational assessment and improve learning outcomes (Owan et al., 2023; Saputra et al., 2024) by offering adaptive, personalized feedback to promote pupils' engagement and foster individualized learning paths. This chapter contributes to the broader aim of this volume by critically exploring how AI-driven assessment can enhance personalized learning and teacher agency while addressing essential ethical and pedagogical challenges in early and primary education.

Background and Ethical Aspects in the Integration of AI Tools in Early Education

The ongoing development of Generative AI has significantly influenced education, forwarding the study of its implications for cognitive development, learning outcomes and educational interventions. Recent studies have revealed a controversial impact of AI on its integration in education. Deng et al.'s (2025) outcomes of the meta-analysis of AI's impact on student learning indicate that AI, particularly the ChatGPT interventions, are predominantly implemented in language learning and most often at the university level. They report a significantly positive effect of the AI intervention, ranging from a ten-minute session to an academic semester of 16 weeks, on academic performance and higher-order thinking skills. However, their analysis highlights a critical limitation of the reviewed studies regarding the adequacy of the sample sizes, pointing out that only 8.01% of the reviewed studies conducted a power analysis, thus raising concerns regarding the validity of the reported findings. On the other hand, the effect sizes in international education interventions are larger in small-scale studies (Evans & Yuan, 2022), which can help situate new findings within current knowledge and design novel studies for the identification of the statistically sufficient effect, further underscoring Deng et al.'s (2025) concerns about the methodological rigor of AI intervention studies. Interestingly, in the study of AI's role in enhancing students' essay writing and English learning as a Second Language (ESL), it was found a significantly higher students' performance in writing guided by AI compared to the performance of those students who received guidance from human experts (Fan et al., 2025). Nevertheless, there has been no significant difference in ESL knowledge gain between human-guided and AI-assisted groups. These findings suggest that while AI can improve short-term task performance, there is no substantial advancement in the ESL skills of AI-assisted learners. Moreover, learners may become overly reliant on AI, potentially causing "metacognitive laziness" that can hinder the students' self-regulated learning abilities and deep cognitive engagement. Similarly, Gerlich's (2025) study of AI impact on the learners' critical thinking skills development by applying Braun and Clarke's (2006) six-phase framework for identifying recurring themes, such as "AI Dependence", "Cognitive Engagement" and "Ethical Concerns", strengthens this kind of concern, suggesting that although AI tools facilitate learning, they also can reduce students' intrinsic motivation towards the study's objectives, further raising ethical concerns about their long-term impacts on education.

Interestingly, Lee et al. (2025) in their investigation of the impact of AI tools on the critical thinking skills of knowledge workers (following Drucker (1959) and Kidd's (1994) conceptualization), also found that while AI can enhance efficiency and quality of work, AI-generated content must be critically evaluated as far as the AI responses need verification due to potential inaccuracies. Lee et al. (2025) study aligns with Fan et al. (2025) findings on AI over-reliance as well as with Imundo et al.'s study (2024) on the different impact of the generative AI that takes on to support thinking depending on the knowledge of a user, thus suggesting that critical thinking remains essential for effective integration of AI tools in education. For example, Mollick and Mollick (2023) propose the following seven approaches for using AI in classrooms: AI mentor providing feedback, AI tutor providing direct instruction, AI coach increasing metacognition, AI teammate increasing collaborative intelligence, AI teaching as a more powerful learning technique, AI simulator creating opportunities for practice and AI tool for a wide variety of purposes. In this practical framework for integrating AI in the educational process, they present AI as a supportive tool in the learning process rather than a replacement for the human mentor, teacher, and/or an educator. Due to the above-mentioned benefits of AI, it is not surprising that AI has been recently integrated into the education process not only as an assistant tool for generating content but also as revolutionizing assessment methods in the learning experience for providing personalized feedback, adaptive learning tailored to individual needs and real-time monitoring of the learning process.

Current studies explore the challenges and benefits of emerging AI assessment in preschool and early childhood education. For example, Le Courtois et al. (2025) present ambivalent parents' perception of automated AI assessment in childhood developmental screening for detecting motor and cognitive skill delays, suggesting that AI-based assessment, on the one hand, can enhance the identification of developmental delays. On the other hand, besides the potential benefits of AI assessment, they emphasized the importance of the ethical implementation of AI-based methods and the requirement of parental involvement as well as transparency concerning the potential risks and benefits of AI methods. Another study on predicting early childhood readiness for school reports a successful application of AI assessment methods in preschool education (Puspitorini et al., 2024). This study presents significantly high accuracy rates in predicting children's school readiness by using an AI algorithm based on the Naïve Bayes (Wickramasinghe & Kalutarage, 2021) method, thus demonstrating a high efficiency of the AI algorithm in predicting school readiness further (a). enabling early intervention strategies for children who might need additional support; and (b). helping educators personalize learning approaches based on preschool behavioral data.

Most recently, AI-driven methods have also been integrated into speech and language assessment to detect pronunciation errors and speech delays in addition to measuring the cognitive and psychological readiness to school, which play a crucial role in early childhood language development. For example, Dutta et al. (2025) developed privacy-preserving AI tools for assessing preschoolers' communication and language acquisition skills. Their findings showed a very accurate assessment of speech development in preschoolers using AI-driven tools. However, in their research, they also pay particular attention to enhancing strict regulations concerning children's data privacy and emphasize the necessity for establishing solutions that could allow the generation of reliable child-centered AI technologies. That is, they highlight the importance of the security enforcement of children's data protection in AI-driven assessment. Similar to Dutta et al.'s (2025) study, Nishio et al. (2024) propose the efficiency of the AI-based diagnostic tool for detecting language disorders in non-English-speaking children in special and early education, also suggesting that AI can be successfully applied for diagnosing language developmental disorders by identifying speech irregularities. These studies present further benefits of applying AI-assisted speech screening methods for multilingual children in early education, similar to monolingual children. Likewise, AI has also been used in the assessment of special needs for identifying and supporting children with ADHD, learning and other developmental disabilities. The most recent study by Singh et al. (2024) of ADHD detection in preschool education has shown high accuracy rates of the AI-based predictive model for early identification of children at risk for ADHD by analyzing their emotional responses, behavioral patterns and activity levels. The outcomes of these studies present promising benefits of AI assessment tools in measuring developmental deficits and emotional state, thus helping not only in detecting early learning disabilities and ADHD but also in further enhancing the earlier implementation of personalized AI intervention programs in special education and early childhood. A more holistic AI-based nutritional assessment for tracking child growth is proposed by Ma'ruf et al. (2024). Their study shows the benefits of integrating AI in monitoring potential risks of malnutrition and nutritional deficiencies in children, thus allowing a more holistic child assessment that encompasses emotional, cognitive and physical developmental aspects.

Despite the multiple advantages of AI in education, ethical challenges concerning data privacy and algorithmic biases must be addressed. Bush and Alibakhshi (2025) propose that in order to ensure the creation of truly engaging scientific content using AI for preschool children, as well as to ensure its ethical application in early education, it is necessary to generate an age-appropriate context using the established pedagogical criteria and to ensure that AI-generated content is developmentally tailored to the users. In addition, it is necessary to supplement the AI-generated content with other interactive learning elements. However, along with providing solutions for the reliable and ethical development and implementation of child-centered AI-generated assessment tools, it is critical to raise further attention to the ongoing requirement to develop special AI training programs for teachers. As O'Dea and Ng (2024) claim, AI literacy among educators can ensure proper implementation of AI-generated tools, minimize biases and improve the effectiveness of AI-based assessments.

The Main Benefits and Challenges of AI-based Tools Integration in Educational Settings

Recent studies have indicated a growing interest in using AI technologies in early childhood education to enhance the teaching and assessment processes, as well as learning efficiency, since AI offers opportunities such as fast data analysis and personalized learning. However, as AI-driven technologies grow, their ethical implementation in education must be ensured for children's safety by relevant institutions, such as the Children's Online Privacy Protection Act (COPPA) rule for the US online services and websites, the European Union General Data Protection Regulations (EU GDPR) providing guidelines for academic research and industry as well as government policy on AI regulations and ethics. Considering the legislative actions and ethical regulations on AI applications in education and possible challenges, it is necessary to note the subsequent benefits of this human-level performance technology expected to efficiently and effectively complement humans in various tasks (Eloundou et al., 2024).

AI-based Tools Benefits

The following are the main benefits of AI-based tools in education once they are ethically regulated:

1. *Skill Development*—AI-generated tools mediated to children by educators can help to develop necessary technological and essential cognitive and social skills for functioning as independent adults, promote the development of creativity, problem-solving and critical thinking, as well as to develop digital literacy. For example, AI tools can (1) promote imagination and creativity by generating images; (2) facilitate natural voice conversations, thus helping children express their thoughts clearly; (3) enhance understanding and creation of stories and poems by using digital books; (4) develop critical-thinking skills and problem-solving skills by asking open-ended questions and encouraging children to think about different interpretations of events using activities involving AI.
2. *Engaging Learning*—AI-based tools can make the learning process more enjoyable and interactive by raising curiosity and, consequently, motivation for the learning process. For example, AI-generated educational tools can encourage understanding scientific ideas via AI-based visualized presentations and expand children's linguistic world, thus promoting interdisciplinary knowledge.
3. *Personalized Learning Experience*—AI-based technologies can enable educators to adapt teaching methods to the individualized needs of children via ongoing personalized feedback. For example, AI tools can customize teaching to different learning styles, potentially improving learning outcomes.
4. *Aiding Educators*—the use of AI tools in administrative tasks and assessments can be time-efficient, allowing educators to focus on teaching and personalized interaction with children.
5. *Promoting Digital Literacy*—Introducing AI-based tools in earlier stages can help children prepare for their future since AI-based technology is becoming an integral part of daily life in the twenty-first century. Early exposure of children to advanced technology can equip them with the skills necessary for the effective use of digital devices. Besides, teaching children about the potential risks can help them become more informed and critical customers of AI-based tools as adults.

Ethical Considerations

By considering the benefits of the integration of AI-based tools in education, it is important to recognize and emphasize ethical challenges, considerations and recommendations for the use of AI-generated tools in early education:

1. *The Importance of Human Interaction*—direct interaction with educators, peers and real, non-virtual sources is crucial for children's psychologically healthy

development. Thus, a balanced integration of AI-generated activities with traditional teaching methods, including indoor and outdoor games, social interactions and books in the curriculum, is required to allow the use of AI-based tools in conjunction with in-person social activities for the balanced growth.
2. *Social and Cultural Issues*—it is important to adapt AI-generated tools to various cultural and social contexts, fitting various communities' linguistic aspects and values.
3. *Ensuring Appropriate Use*—since most learning at a young age occurs in an active and collaborative way, it is important to consider the child's developmental stage in choosing AI-based tools. It is also significant to provide a supervised and gradual exposure to the advanced technologies with the educator's mentoring of the children's application of the AI-based tools and contexts. That is, adjusting AI-generated activities to the child's age is essential. In addition, it is crucial to explain its use and ensure that the AI tool's implementation is under the educational staff's control and with their persistent guidance.
4. *Privacy and Security*—it is vital to follow strict regulations on anonymizing children's data and to protect the privacy and security of the data collected by AI systems.
5. *Educator's Training*—the teaching staff needs ongoing training and support on the rapidly developing AI tools to gain adequate knowledge of advanced AI-based technology. Furthermore, it is important to ensure an appropriate and effective implementation of these tools in the educational process.

Practical Methods for Integration of AI-based Tools in Education

AI-based Assessment Tools

Despite the unlimited opportunities of AI-generated tools that can enhance the learning process in education, including preschool, elementary school and special education, it is crucial to ensure the ethical and carefully balanced implementation of these tools for children's well-being and development. An integral step of the children's development in preschool and early education is an accurate and real-time assessment for the earlier identification of the pupils' strengths and weaknesses to enhance individually tailored intervention programs. While further research is necessary, initial findings suggest promising outcomes of AI-based assessment tools in the educational process. Several tools have shown promising results in areas, such as early childhood development, literacy assessment and special education interventions (see Table 17.1).

1. *Language Environment Analysis* (LENA) System—a speech and language development tool that can assess the language of a young neurotypically developing child. This AI-based tool identifies the auditory environment a child is exposed

to and participates in during the day rather than providing a direct child test. Analysis of LENA's ability to assess early language environments using the recordings collected during a day shows the system's notable accuracy and reliability in its application on infants to four-years-old children (Gilkerson et al., 2017). Furthermore, this assessment tool can give insight into the child's speaking frequency and linguistic environment, which are vital factors in language acquisition (Wang et al., 2025). For example, this tool can be used by speech-language pathologists to screen for language delays and to aid educators in providing feedback to caregivers/parents on improving language simulation. It is worth pointing out that Wang et al.'s (2025) findings align with the earlier study by Weisleder and Fernald (2013) in showing that children who were exposed more to adult conversations and consequently experienced more verbal interaction, had better vocabulary growth and stronger language-processing skills. Thus, the automated analysis of the AI-based tool LENA can be applied to assessing and enriching the early language environment, further improving children's speech skills and language development. Alongside that, Jones et al.'s (2019) findings regarding this tool suggest a less reliable detection of speech vocalizations in older children and adolescents with Autism Spectrum Disorder (ASD), thus highlighting the necessity for the development of a more reliable method for older children, in general, and for adolescents with ASD, in particular.

2. Eye-Tracking Reading Assessment—*Lexplore*—is an AI-driven eye-tracking technology designed to detect reading difficulties, including dyslexia, during a short reading task. Nilsson Benfatto et al.'s (2016) study of this screening tool reported significantly high accuracy rates in identifying struggling readers in the first to eighth grades. Using machine learning, this quick assessment could provide educators with insights into the children's reading level and detect potential problems related to reading fluency and decoding difficulties. Following Nilsson Benfatto et al. (2016) study, this AI-based assessment tool could effectively help in the accurate differentiation between readers with and without dyslexia, thus enabling significantly earlier implementation of the intervention programs.
3. *Assessment and Learning in Knowledge Spaces* (*ALEKS*) for generating an individualized learning program and mathematics assessment tools, such as *DreamBox Learning*.
4. The applied educational studies of the AI-based tool *ALEKS* reported a prominent efficiency of an AI-based tutoring system based on Knowledge Space Theory in assessing a child's knowledge of the subject and in predicting readiness for a new material in real-time for mathematics in elementary to higher education (Craig et al., 2013; Huang et al., 2024; Kumor et al., 2024; Sabo et al., 2013). These studies note a particular improvement in mathematical problem-solving skills and material retention performance, as this assessment tool could accurately identify the pupils' gaps and reinforce personalized learning in conjunction with standard teaching.

5. Another adaptive mathematical AI-based assessment tool, i.e., *DreamBox Learning*, was also found to be efficient as a supplement to teacher-led learning, particularly in mastering the numerical competencies of pupils in preschool and elementary school education from diverse socioeconomic backgrounds (Foster, 2024). Notably, children showed measurable improvement in mathematical achievements through interactive AI-based lessons, the content and difficulty level of which was adjusted by the AI algorithm of *DreamBox*, thus tailoring each pupil's skill level and personalizing the curriculum in real-time. However, it is worth noting that in contrast to the *ALEKS* assessment tool, no significant effect on mastering mathematical problem-solving skills was found (Wang & Woodworth, 2011).

Though much research is needed to study the effectiveness of these tools in education, current encouraging results show that these AI-based methods can provide teachers with real-time analytics on pupils' progress, further enhancing personalized teaching in classrooms.

In addition to the above-discussed AI-based learning assessment tools, there is ongoing research on designing accurate AI-driven ASD diagnostic tools. For example, Wall et al. (2012) studied a shortened observation-based screening using 16 different machine learning algorithms based on the analysis of Autism Diagnostic Observation Schedule (ADOS) Module 1. Their findings suggest a notable specificity and sensitivity of the *ADTree* machine-learning classifier for ASD diagnosis accuracy, based on eight items out of twenty-nine used in the complete version of ADOS in the previously received records. Similarly, another study by Tariq et al. (2018) on mobile detection of ASD in young children, using machine learning on home video, reported high effectiveness in providing a quantified and quickly accessed indicator of autism online. However, it is worth noting that these machine-learning models are built on the records from the earlier provided diagnosis and, thus, further studies are required for the evaluation of the efficiency of this method in prospective undiagnosed cases. The first machine-learning ASD diagnostic aid that showed promising accuracy rates for earlier, more accurate and practical ASD diagnosing in children 18 to 72 months old is reported in Megerian et al.'s (2022) study of AI-based software designed as a medical device, which was approved by the USA Food and Drug Administration (FDA). This AI-based tool that was designed to aid healthcare providers (HCP) could enable performing a timely and efficient assessment in the primary care setting in conjunction with clinical judgment by the specialist, following the DSM-5 criteria for ASD diagnosis, thus helping in promoting the timely intervention programs, which are particularly significant at the earlier developmental stages.

Following this ongoing technological development, integrating AI curriculum into early childhood education gains particular importance. The above-presented studies indicate that AI-based assessment tools are increasingly being integrated into clinical settings to support diverse children's needs and provide timely feedback in special education as well as in preschool and elementary school settings. Furthermore, there is an increasing interest in enhancing learning experiences and outcomes, especially in early childhood education, by implementing AI-based tools

Table 17.1 AI Assessment Tools with Promising Results in Early Education

Tool	Subject	Target	Target Age Group	Effectiveness Evidence	Practical Application of the Tool	Limitations
Language Environment Analysis (LENA)	Speech and Language Development	For assessing early language environments using the recordings collected during a day	0–4 years old	It can provide a child's speaking frequency and linguistic environment (Wang et al., 2025)	This tool can be used by speech-language pathologists to screen for language delays and to aid educators in providing feedback to caregivers/parents on improving language simulation	This tool is less reliable in the detection of speech vocalizations in older children and adolescents with ASD (Jones et al., 2019)
Lexplore	Eye-Tracking Reading Assessment	An eye-tracking technology for detecting reading difficulties, including dyslexia, during a short reading task	The first to eighth grades	Significantly high accuracy rates in identifying struggling readers (Nilsson Benfatto et al., 2016)	Educators can use this quick assessment for detecting children's reading level and potential problems related to reading fluency and decoding difficulties	Specific challenges were reported with the organizational logistics around implementing assessments and log-in difficulties, which can reduce user engagement (Davies et al., 2021)

(continued)

Table 17.1 (continued)

Tool	Subject	Target	Target Age Group	Effectiveness Evidence	Practical Application of the Tool	Limitations
Assessment and Learning in Knowledge Spaces (ALEKS)	An AI-based tutoring system based on Knowledge Space Theory	Generating an individualized learning program	Elementary to higher education pupils	Prominent efficiency in assessing a child's knowledge of the subject and predicting readiness for new material in real-time for mathematics (Craig et al., 2013; Sabo et al., 2013; Huang et al., 2024; Kumor et al., 2024)	This tool can help educators identify the pupils' gaps and reinforce personalized learning in conjunction with standard teaching	First, this tool has some limits in marking the students' correct answers if they are written in the incorrect form and, second, some written explanations could be challenging for the students (Kumor et al., 2024)
DreamBox Learning	Adaptive Mathematics Assessment Tools	For tailoring pupils' skill level and personalizing the curriculum in real-time	Preschool and elementary school children	This tool is efficient as a supplement to teacher-led learning, particularly in mastering the numerical competencies (Foster, 2024)	This tool can provide teachers with real-time analytics on pupils' progress	No significant effect on mastering mathematical problem-solving skills was found (Wang & Woodworth, 2011)

in the education curriculum to generate more adaptive and personalized learning content. For example, problem-based learning is reported to be the most influential teaching method in AI-based education (Su & Zhong, 2022). Su and Zhong (2022) propose a framework comprising four main components: aims, content, methods and assessment, for achieving AI literacy by equipping preschool children with the following main AI competencies: (1) AI knowledge about the basic ideas of AI; (2) AI skills for using AI tools; and (3) AI attitude that includes collaborating with AI. This framework underscores the importance of introducing the conceptual understanding as well as responsible engagement with AI tools and suggests the significant role of age-appropriate pedagogical strategies for the implementation of AI-based methods in fostering children's critical thinking and ethical awareness, along with curiosity in relation to AI-based technologies.

Implementation of AI-based Methods in the Classroom

However, studies exploring educators' perception of AI tools in kindergarten and elementary education suggest that for adopting new technologies in classroom teaching and assessment, it is crucial to provide educators with the necessary infrastructure and sufficient training (Arnone et al., 2023). As Arnone et al. (2023) propose in their study, this type of economic investment in education can have potentially significant benefits, including improved learning outcomes resulting from personalized AI-based mentoring, interactive assessment and engaging education. Similarly, Kölemen & Yildirim (2025) highlight the benefits of integrating AI-based tools in education. They report on educators' willingness to implement AI-based technology in early education, claiming that the application of AI-driven methods in teaching can improve children's computational skills and AI literacy. They also raise concerns about implementing AI in classrooms due to the lack of appropriate infrastructure and address the security concerns related to protecting children's personal data.

Focusing on the essential elements for implementing AI tools in elementary schools, it should be mentioned that the central purpose of integrating AI-based tools into the curriculum is to support students and to assist teachers (Arriola-Mendoza & Valerio-Ureña, 2024). For example, the AI-generated tools, such as conversational language AI-generated models, digital storytelling, text and image-generating AI, PBL and practical exercises using AI, were identified as the most prevalent in education for enhancing pedagogical practices (Arriola-Mendoza & Valerio-Ureña, 2024). Yet, it is worth noting the supplementary educational character of the AI-based tools in the above-discussed pedagogical approaches. As Bush and Alibakhshi (2025) conclude in their study concerning the evaluation of AI tools for early education, there are significant differences in performance within various scientific disciplines. Their findings suggest, for example, stronger AI performance in converting biological rather than chemistry topics to AI-generated children-appropriate content, thus highlighting the significance of human expertise in child education for tailoring appropriate pedagogical methods to content generation. In addition, Bush and Alibakhshi

(2025) similar to Bhandari & Brennan (2023), who studied the trustworthiness of LLMs-based generated children's stories, note a less engaging nature of the AI-generated content for preschool children, further emphasizing the crucial role of the human expert in early education in developing and application of a child-appropriate content and educational standards. Integrating AI-based tools in early education can be efficient if their use is balanced with teacher/educator-managed direct individual guidance. Likewise, adding AI-interfaced robotic toys in early childhood educational practices can foster a child's inquiry literacy development (Kewalramani et al., 2021), further suggesting the potential benefits of integrating technology into children's play for supporting cognitive development and enhancing the learning process.

Recommendations for Practice

Therefore, it is unsurprising that a range of AI-generated tools are increasingly present in today's classrooms, fostering personally paced educational programs by advancing timely feedback and objective evaluation of the individualized pupils' progress. As a result, recent studies have proposed several ways that AI-based assessment tools can be efficiently applied in early education:

1. *Incorporation of AI-generated context into the teacher training programs for improving computational and problem-solving skills of future educators, as well as practicing an effective procedure for evaluating pupils' computational thinking skills in their classrooms:*

   Hijón-Neira et al. (2024) reported a potential efficiency of integrating the AI-generated context in teaching computational skills, robotics and implementing computational assessment tools for developmentally appropriate measurement of critical thinking skills in young learners. Their findings suggest a necessary step in upgrading teaching practices by integrating AI into teacher-training programs to enhance the students' computational skills and cultivate early childhood computational education.
2. *Creative tools for easing administrative burden and supporting teaching in education:*

   Kanders et al. (2024) identified 35 possible AI-based use cases in teaching, daily operations, content generation and family support in early education. For example, AI-assisted administrative tasks and teaching materials, such as lesson planning, designing games and activities, writing stories, helping in record-keeping, drafting teacher observations, various enrollment forms and assisting in assessments or surveys (Boyd, 2013; Thorpe et al., 2018; Waldman, 2023), could bolster early childhood educators in creating learning materials and assessment tools that provide an objective and instant feedback tailored to the individual child's developmental level and background (Baskara, 2023).

3. *Utilizing Large Language Models (LLMs), such as GPT series (Open AI), Gemini (Google DeepMind), Claude (Anthropic) and LlaMa (Meta) for generating AI literacy assessment:*

   AI assessments generated by using LLMs showed promising results (Stamper et al., 2024) in language learning (Caines et al., 2023), programming (Doughty et al., 2024), medicine (Indran et al., 2024) and in enriching AI literacy materials in K-12 education (Wang et al., 2025). For example, the LLM-powered *Multi-Agent* multiple-question generation framework that has been developed by Wang et al. (2025) for preparing AI-literacy resources and reliable AI assessment, following Bloom's Taxonomy and grade levels, demonstrated future potential for the application of the pedagogically scalable AI-based assessment tools in educational settings.
4. *Virtual assessment of algorithmic thinking in preschool and elementary school education:*

   Algorithmic Thinking (AT) is a cognitive process that involves executive functioning and logical reasoning and is essential for everyday problem-solving in the rapidly developing digital era. Adorni and Piatti's (2024) study proposes a scalable digital solution for simultaneous and automatic assessment—the virtual Cross Array Task (CAT) for evaluating algorithmic skills across various developmental stages for children, four to twelve years old, spanning kindergarten children to lower secondary school levels.
5. *AI-based interactive tools for improving communication skills through engaging collaborative activities and for stimulating imagination through digital writing and storytelling in early childhood education:*

   Scoping reviews (Su & Yang, 2022; Su et al., 2023) on AI integration in early childhood education show an ongoing interest in including AI-based tools in the curriculum. These studies report that using AI devices in early education, such as AI social robots and chatbots, AI drawing and writing tools, as well as AI-based games (Kewalramani et al., 2021; McStay & Rosner, 2021; Ng et al., 2023; Tazume et al., 2020), enhances digital literacy skills, problem-solving, collaborative skills and other skills, which are essential for children's intellectual development, thus advising to include AI-based tools in the early education curriculum. Henceforth, the government's support in equipping preschool education and schools with AI technology is necessary for its efficient integration and application in educational settings (Jeon et al., 2024; Su et al., 2023).

Conclusion

AI-based tools have a significant potential for enhancing assessment methods in preschool and elementary education by offering personalized learning experiences and immediate objective feedback, as well as creating efficient learning materials and activities, thereby supporting both children and educators in the learning process.

Considering the aforementioned studies, it is important to highlight the following key benefits of AI-based assessment technology in education:

a) Automated and instant feedback to improve the learning process;
b) Adaptive evaluation that can modify testing for personalized learning, based on children's responses and individual pupils' needs;
c) Evaluating pupils' progress through tracking learning advancement and gaps;
d) Linguistic and behavioral analysis through interactive activities and games;
e) Digital assistance and monitoring in administrative tasks and educators' work.

In light of these prominent advantages of AI-based assessment tools, it is unsurprising that AI-driven tools might become increasingly effective in preschool and elementary school education. However, further studies should examine educators' challenges in implementing AI-based assessment technology and address ethical concerns to ensure AI's responsible use and children's personal data protection. Moreover, although AI-generated tools have substantial potential to enhance the learning process, detect developmental difficulties and personalize educational practices, concerns about over-dependence on AI-generated tools, metacognitive over-reliance and methodological rigor still remain. Thus, balancing AI-based technology with the teacher's guidance and hands-on activities is particularly important to mitigate over-reliance on AI-based tools and allow diverse learning experiences. Even so, to successfully implement AI strategies into the early and elementary school education curriculum, educators should get adequate training and be digitally equipped to use AI tools to address AI biases effectively. At the same time, integrating human-proficient pedagogical oversight into AI assessment models could proficiently refine and potentially enhance the accuracy and efficiency of AI-based assessment tools.

Implications for Practice and Ethics

For educators and policymakers, the discussion presented in this chapter emphasizes the need for intentional and ethically grounded integration of AI into preschool and primary education, since AI tools hold substantial potential to enhance assessment accuracy, pedagogical differentiation and administrative efficiency when implemented under rigorous ethical and pedagogical frameworks. At the same time, institutions should establish transparent instructions to protect children's privacy and ensure unbiassed and developmentally appropriate use. Ultimately, AI should serve as a complement to, rather than a substitute for human pedagogy, preserving the relational, creative and socio-emotional dimensions that are foundational to early learning.

References

Adorni, G., & Piatti, A. (2024). The virtual CAT: A tool for algorithmic thinking assessment in Swiss compulsory education. *arXiv preprint arXiv:2408.01263.*

Alison Kidd. (1994). The marks are on the knowledge worker. In *Proceedings of the SIGCHI conference on Human factors in computing systems.* 186–191.

Arnone, K., Hutson, J., & Woodruff, K. (2023). Demystifying artificial intelligence (AI) for early childhood and elementary education: A case study of perceptions of ai of state of Missouri educators. *Journal of Innovation and Technology, 2023*(18), 1–18.

Arriola-Mendoza, J., & Valerio-Ureña, G. (2024). Essential elements for implementing AI tools in elementary school: A systematic literature review. *Education Sciences, 14*(12), 1292.

Baskara, F. R. (2023, July). Fostering culturally grounded learning: Generative ai, digital storytelling, and early childhood education. In *International Conference of Early Childhood Education in Multiperspectives* (pp. 351–361).

Benbya, H., Davenport, T. H., & Pachidi, S. (2020). Artificial Intelligence in Organizations: Current State and Future Opportunities (December 3, 2020). MIS Quarterly Executive: Vol. 19: Iss. 4, Article 4, Available at SSRN: https://doi.org/10.2139/ssrn.3741983

Bhandari, P., & Brennan, H. (2023). Trustworthiness of children stories generated by large language models. In *Proceedings of the 16th International Natural Language Generation Conference* (pp. 352–361). Association for Computational Linguistics.

Braun, V., & Clarke, V. (2006). Using thematic analysis in psychology. *Qualitative research in psychology, 3*(2), 77–101.

Boyd, M. (2013). "I Love My Work But..." The professionalization of early childhood education. *Qualitative Report, 18*, 71.

Bush, A., & Alibakhshi, A. (2025, April). Bridging the early science gap with artificial intelligence: Evaluating large language models as tools for early childhood science education. In *Proceedings of the Extended Abstracts of the CHI Conference on Human Factors in Computing Systems* (pp. 1–6).

Caines, A., Benedetto, L., Taslimipoor, S., Davis, C., Gao, Y., Andersen, O., Yuan, Z., Elliott, M., Moore, R., Bryant, C., Rei, M., Yannakoudakis, H., Mullooly, A., Nickolls, D., & Buttery, P. (2023). On the application of large language models for language teaching and assessment technology. arXiv preprint arXiv:2307.08393.

Catherine Clifford. The 'oracle of a.i.': These 4 kinds of jobs won't be replaced by robots. https://www.cnbc.com/2019/01/14/the-oracle-of-ai-these-kinds-of-jobs-will-not-be-replaced-by-robots-.html, January 2019.

Craig, S. D., Hu, X., Graesser, A. C., Bargagliotti, A. E., Sterbinsky, A., Cheney, K. R., & Okwumabua, T. (2013). The impact of a technology-based mathematics after-school program using ALEKS on student's knowledge and behaviors. *Computers & Education, 68*, 495–504.

Davies, S. M., Jardine, J., Gutridge, K., Bernard, Z., Park, S., Dawson, T., Abel, K. M., & Whelan, P. (2021). Preventive digital mental health for children in primary schools: acceptability and feasibility study. *JMIR Formative Research, 5*(12), e30668.

Deng, R., Jiang, M., Yu, X., Lu, Y., & Liu, S. (2025). Does ChatGPT enhance student learning? A systematic review and meta-analysis of experimental studies. *Computers & Education, 227*, 105224.

Doughty, J., Wan, Z., Bompelli, A., Qayum, J., Wang, T., Zhang, J., Zheng, Y., Doyle, A., Sridhar, P., Aqarwal, A., Bogart, C., Keylor, E., Kültür, C., Šgvelka, J., & Sakr, M. (2024, January). A comparative study of AI-generated (GPT-4) and human-crafted MCQs in programming education. In *Proceedings of the 26th Australasian Computing Education Conference* (pp. 114–123).

Drucker, P. F. (1959). *Landmarks of tomorrow*. Harper.

Duarte, N., Pérez, Y. M., Beltrán, A., & García, M. B. (2023). Use of artificial intelligence in education: A systematic review. In *Proceedings of the 4th South American International Industrial*

Engineering and Operations Management Conference. IEOM Society International, Lima, Peru, May 9–11, 2023.

Dutta, S., Irvin, D., & Hansen, J. H. (2025). Exploring discrete speech units for privacy-preserving and efficient speech recognition for school-aged and preschool children. *International Journal of Human-Computer Studies, 199*, 103460.

Eden, C. A., Chisom, O. N., & Adeniyi, I. S. (2024). Integrating AI in education: Opportunities, challenges, and ethical considerations. *Magna Scientia Advanced Research and Reviews, 10*(2), 6–13.

Elam, K. M. (2024). Exploring the challenges and future directions of big data and AI in education. *Journal of Artificial Intelligence General science (JAIGS) ISSN: 3006–4023, 5*(1), 81–93.

Eloundou, T., Manning, S., Mishkin, P., & Rock, D. (2024). GPTs are GPTs: Labor market impact potential of LLMs. *Science, 384*(6702), 1306–1308.

Evans, D. K., & Yuan, F. (2022). How big are effect sizes in international education studies? *Educational Evaluation and Policy Analysis, 44*(3), 532–540.

Fan, Y., Tang, L., Le, H., Shen, K., Tan, S., Zhao, Y., Shen, Y., Li, X., & Gašević, D. (2025). Beware of metacognitive laziness: Effects of generative artificial intelligence on learning motivation, processes, and performance. *British Journal of Educational Technology, 56*(2), 489–530.

Foster, M. E. (2024). Evaluating the impact of supplemental computer-assisted math instruction in elementary school: A conceptual replication. *Journal of Research on Educational Effectiveness, 17*(1), 94–118.

Gerlich, M. (2025). AI tools in society: Impacts on cognitive offloading and the future of critical thinking. *Societies, 15*(1), 6.

Gilkerson, J., Richards, J. A., Warren, S. F., Montgomery, J. K., Greenwood, C. R., Oller, D. K., Hansen, J. H. L., & Paul, T. D. (2017). Mapping the early language environment using all-day recordings and automated analysis. *American Journal of Speech-Language Pathology, 26*(2), 248–265.

Haenlein, M., & Kaplan, A. (2019). A brief history of artificial intelligence: On the past, present, and future of artificial intelligence. *California management review, 61*(4), 5–14.

Hijón-Neira, R., Pizarro, C., Borrás-Gené, O., & Cavero, S. (2024). AI-generated context for teaching robotics to improve computational thinking in early childhood education. *Education Sciences, 14*(12), 1401.

Huang, R., Bao, Y., Wang, Y., & Wei, J. (2024). *Exploring AI tools in early childhood education: Usage patterns, functions, and developmental outcomes*. https://doi.org/10.5772/intechopen.1007116

Imundo, M. N., Watanabe, M., Potter, A. H., Gong, J., Arner, T., & McNamara, D. S. (2024). Expert thinking with generative chatbots. *Journal of Applied Research in Memory and Cognition, 13*(4), 465–484.

Indran, I. R., Paranthaman, P., Gupta, N., & Mustafa, N. (2024). Twelve tips to leverage AI for efficient and effective medical question generation: A guide for educators using Chat GPT. *Medical Teacher, 46*(8), 1021–1026.

Jeon, I. S., Kim, S. Y., & Kang, S. J. (2024). Developing standards for educational datasets by school level: A framework for sustainable K-12 education. *Sustainability, 16*(12), 4954.

Jones, R. M., Plesa Skwerer, D., Pawar, R., Hamo, A., Carberry, C., Ajodan, E. L., Caulley, D., Silverman, M. R., McAdoo, S., Meyer, S., & Tager-Flusberg, H. (2019). How effective is LENA in detecting speech vocalizations and language produced by children and adolescents with ASD in different contexts? *Autism Research, 12*(4), 628–635.

Kanders, K., Stupple-Harris, L., Smith, L., & Gibson, J. L. (2024). Perspectives on the impact of generative AI on early-childhood development and education. *Infant and Child Development, 33*, e2514.

Kewalramani, S., Palaiologou, I., Dardanou, M., Allen, K. A., & Phillipson, S. (2021). Using robotic toys in early childhood education to support children's social and emotional competencies. *Australasian Journal of Early Childhood, 46*(4), 355–369.

Kölemen, E. B., & Yıldırım, B. (2025). A new era in early childhood education (ECE): Teachers' opinions on the application of artificial intelligence. *Education and Information Technologies*, 1–42.

Kumor, T., Uribe-Flórez, L., Trespalacios, J., & Yang, D. (2024). ALEKS in high school mathematics classrooms: Exploring teachers' perceptions and use of this tool. *TechTrends, 68*(3), 506–519.

Le Courtois, S., Barnes, M., & Gibson, J. L. (2025, January 25). "It depends on the choices that are made now." Parental perspectives on the use of automated methods in early childhood developmental checks. https://doi.org/10.31234/osf.io/6wg5r

Lee, H. P., Sarkar, A., Tankelevitch, L., Drosos, I., Rintel, S., Banks, R., & Wilson, N. (2025, April). The impact of generative AI on critical thinking: Self-reported reductions in cognitive effort and confidence effects from a survey of knowledge workers. In *Proceedings of the 2025 CHI Conference on Human Factors in Computing Systems* (pp. 1–22).

Luan, H., Geczy, P., Lai, H., Gobert, J., Yang, S. J. H., Ogata, H., Baltes, J., Guerra, R., Li, P., & Tsai, C. C. (2020). Challenges and future directions of big data and artificial intelligence in education. *Frontiers in Psychology, 11*, 580820.

Lyanda, J. N., Owidi, S. O., & Simiyu, A. M. (2024). Rethinking higher education teaching and assessment in-line with AI innovations: A systematic review and meta-analysis. *African Journal of Empirical Research, 5*(3), 325–335.

Ma'ruf, K., Setiawan, R. J., Saputra, A. A., Belani, A. Q., Tsani, L. M., & Azizah, N. (2024, December). Development of integrated nutritional monitoring application utilizing machine learning and artificial intelligence for child growth assessment. In *2024 International Conference on Decision Aid Sciences and Applications (DASA)* (pp. 1–5). IEEE.

McStay, A., & Rosner, G. (2021). Emotional artificial intelligence in children's toys and devices: Ethics, governance and practical remedies. *Big Data & Society, 8*(1). https://doi.org/10.1177/2053951721994877 (Original work published 2021).

Megerian, J. T., Dey, S., Melmed, R. D., Coury, D. L., Lerner, M., Nicholls, C. J., et al. (2022). Evaluation of an artificial intelligence-based medical device for diagnosis of autism spectrum disorder. *NPJ digital medicine, 5*(1), 57.

Miller, W. (2024). Adapting to AI: Reimagining the role of assessment professionals. *Intersection: A Journal at the Intersection of Assessment and Learning, 5*(4), 99–113.

Mollick, E., & Mollick, L. (2023). *Assigning AI: Seven approaches for students, with prompts*. arXiv preprint arXiv:2306.10052.

Nagendraswamy, C., & Salis, A. (2021). A review article on artificial intelligence. *Annals of Biomedical Science and Engineering, 5*, 13–14.

Ng, D. T. K., Lee, M., Tan, R. J. Y., Hu, X., Downie, J. S., & Chu, S. K. W. (2023). A review of AI teaching and learning from 2000 to 2020. *Education and Information Technologies, 28*(7), 8445–8501.

Nilsson Benfatto, M., Öqvist Seimyr, G., Ygge, J., Pansell, T., Rydberg, A., & Jacobson, C. (2016). Screening for dyslexia using eye tracking during reading. *PLOS ONE, 11*(12), e0165508.

Nishio, M., Koyanagi, A., Takamori, A., Hasuike, K., Shimoura, Y., Yakura, H., & Shi, S. (2024, November). Automatic assessment of language developmental disorders in non-english contexts. In *2024 IEEE International Conference on E-health Networking, Application & Services (HealthCom)* (pp. 1–6). IEEE.

O'Dea, X., & Ng, D. T. K. (Eds.). (2024). *Effective practices in AI literacy education: Case studies and reflections*. Emerald Publishing Limited.

Ogunsakin, I. B., & Babatimehin, T. (2024). Unlocking the potential of artificial intelligence: A new paradigm for assessment in twenty-first-century education. *International Journal of Research in STEM Education, 6*(2), 37–49.

Owan, V. J., Abang, K. B., Idika, D. O., Etta, E. O., & Bassey, B. A. (2023). Exploring the potential of artificial intelligence tools in educational measurement and assessment. *EURASIA Journal of Mathematics, Science and Technology Education, 19*(8), em2307.

Pop, A-M., Sim, M-A., Sturza, A., & Caciora, S-V. (2024). A Perspective Into The Future Of Teaching And Learning In The Context Of The Rising Interest In Artificial Intelligence In

Education. Opportunities and Ethical Challenges. iTHE ANNALS OF THE UNIVERSITY OF ORADEA/i, i33/i(1), 434–441.

Puspitorini, S., Kahar, N., & Kartika, I. (2024). Predicting early childhood readiness to enter elementary school using the naive bayes classification. *Arcitech: Journal of Computer Science and Artificial Intelligence, 4*(2), 84–99.

Rane, N. (2023). Enhancing the quality of teaching and learning through ChatGPT and similar large language models: Challenges, future prospects, and ethical considerations in education. *Future Prospects, and Ethical Considerations in Education* (September 15, 2023).

Ray, S., & Ray, D. P. (2024). Artificial intelligence in education: Navigating the nexus of innovation and ethics for future learning landscapes. *International Journal of Research-GRANTHAALAYAH, 11*(12), 163–174.

Sabo, K. E., Atkinson, R. K., Barrus, A. L., Joseph, S. S., & Perez, R. S. (2013). Searching for the two sigma advantage: Evaluating algebra intelligent tutors. *Computers in Human Behavior, 29*(5), 1833–1840.

Saputra, I., Kurniawan, A., Yanita, M., Putri, E. Y., & Mahniza, M. (2024). The evolution of educational assessment: How artificial intelligence is shaping the trends and future of learning evaluation. *The Indonesian Journal of Computer Science, 13*(6), 9056–9058.

Singh, T., Dutta, S., Vyas, S., & Rocha, Á. (Eds.). (2024). *Explainable AI for Education: Recent Trends and Challenges*. Springer.

Stamper, J., Xiao, R., & Hou, X. (2024, July). Enhancing llm-based feedback: Insights from intelligent tutoring systems and the learning sciences. In *International Conference on Artificial Intelligence in Education* (pp. 32–43). Springer Nature Switzerland.

Su, J., Ng, D. T. K., & Chu, S. K. W. (2023). Artificial intelligence (AI) literacy in early childhood education: The challenges and opportunities. *Computers and Education: Artificial Intelligence, 4*, 100124.

Su, J., & Yang, W. (2022). Artificial intelligence in early childhood education: A scoping review. *Computers and Education: Artificial Intelligence, 3*, 100049.

Su, J., & Zhong, Y. (2022). Artificial intelligence (AI) in early childhood education: Curriculum design and future directions. *Computers and Education: Artificial Intelligence, 3*, 100072.

Tariq, Q., Daniels, J., Schwartz, J. N., Washington, P., Kalantarian, H., & Wall, D. P. (2018). Mobile detection of autism through machine learning on home video: A development and prospective validation study. *PLOS Medicine, 15*(11), e1002705.

Tazume, H., Morita, T., & Hotta, H. (2020, June). Young children's literacy and cognition to interactive AI robots: A multifaceted study of potential enhancement to early childhood education. In *EdMedia+ innovate learning* (pp. 323–328). Association for the Advancement of Computing in Education (AACE).

Thorpe, K., Irvine, S., Pattinson, C., & Staton, S. (2018). Insider perspectives: The 'tricky business' of providing for children's sleep and rest needs in the context of early childhood education and care. *Early Years, 40*(2), 221–236.

Toosi, A., Bottino, A. G., Saboury, B., Siegel, E., & Rahmim, A. (2021). A brief history of AI: How to prevent another winter (a critical review). *PET clinics, 16*(4), 449–469.

Wall, D. P., Kosmicki, J., Deluca, T. F., Harstad, E., & Fusaro, V. A. (2012). Use of machine learning to shorten observation-based screening and diagnosis of autism. *Translational psychiatry, 2*(4), e100–e100.

Waldman, J. (2023). Streamlining preschool administration with ChatGPT: Your AI-powered assistant - playground|the modern childcare management app. https://www.tryplayground.com/blog/streamlining-preschool-administration-with-chatgpt-your-ai-powered-assistant

Wang, H., & Woodworth, K. (2011). Evaluation of Rocketship Education's use of DreamBox Learning's online mathematics program. *Center for Education Policy*.

Wang, J., Xiao, R., & Tseng, Y. J. (2025, February). Generating AI Literacy MCQs: A Multi-Agent LLM Approach. In *Proceedings of the 56th ACM Technical Symposium on Computer Science Education V. 2* (pp. 1651–1652).

Weisleder, A., & Fernald, A. (2013). Talking to children matters: Early language experience strengthens processing and builds vocabulary. *Psychological Science, 24*(11), 2143–2152.
Wickramasinghe, I., & Kalutarage, H. (2021). Naive Bayes: Applications, variations and vulnerabilities: a review of literature with code snippets for implementation. *Soft Computing, 25*(3), 2277–2293.

Chapter 18
Artificial Intelligence in Preschool Education and Primary Education

Georgios Lampropoulos and Stamatios Papadakis

Abstract With artificial intelligence being increasingly used in educational settings, artificial intelligence literacy has become an integral component of all educational levels for all education stakeholders. Therefore, this chapter aims to provide an overview of the use of artificial intelligence in preschool education and primary education. Based on the results, artificial intelligence constitutes a valuable and meaningful educational tool that can support both teachers and students. Due to the ability of artificial intelligence tools to function as both tutors and peer learners, delivering personalized, collaborative, and adaptive learning experiences while offering individualized feedback, support, guidance, and recommendations, improved learning outcomes and performance were observed. Although students and pre-service teachers expressed mostly positive attitudes toward the use of artificial intelligence in education, teachers expressed mixed opinions which were mostly related to their characteristics, including gender, age, background, digital literacy, and prior experiences. Since the integration of artificial intelligence in education is likely to increase the digital divide, the need to ensure that its implementation is inclusive, accessible, responsible, ethical, and equitable is highlighted. Other key challenges identified included concerns about ethical issues, privacy, security, misinformation, bias, and lack of infrastructure and of teachers' artificial intelligence literacy. The chapter also points out the need to further examine the impact of artificial intelligence on teachers' practices and on young students' development, well-being, and learning and to also consider its societal, technological, and economical implications. Finally, the importance of developing young students' artificial intelligence literacy, reasoning, critical thinking, and computational thinking is highlighted.

Keywords Artificial Intelligence · AI · Early Childhood Education · ECE · Preschool Education · Primary Education · Education · Review · Implications · Benefits · Challenges

G. Lampropoulos (✉) · S. Papadakis
Department of Preschool Education, University of Crete, Crete, Greece
e-mail: lamprop.geo@gmail.com

S. Papadakis
e-mail: stpapadakis@uoc.gr

S. Papadakis (ed.), *AI Applications in Preschool and Primary Education*, Advances in Artificial Intelligence in Education 5, https://doi.org/10.1007/978-3-032-17190-0_18

Introduction

Despite the existing challenges and due to the educational benefits it can yield and its potential to transform the educational domain, artificial intelligence is being used in educational settings and as a result, the interest and research into this field is increasing (Chen et al., 2020; Chiu et al., 2023). Artificial intelligence refers to intelligent, sophisticated systems that mimic the way humans learn, reason, communicate, and act as they are inspired by the human nervous system (Brynjolfsson & Mcafee, 2017; Ertel, 2018; Li & Du, 2017). These adaptive systems can make decisions, interact, and response to their environment in a rational, intelligent, and autonomous manner (Duan et al., 2019; Haenlein & Kaplan, 2019; Stone et al., 2016).

As artificial intelligence is becoming an important aspect of our daily lives, it is important to educate citizens and teach students even from a young age what artificial intelligence is and how they can use it (Ottenbreit-Leftwich et al., 2023). Recent studies have highlighted the educational value that artificial intelligence holds (Lampropoulos & Papadakis, 2025) and its ability to enrich and transform existing teaching and learning approaches and practices (Holmes et al., 2020; Hwang et al., 2020). Additionally, studies have highlighted the merits of applying adaptive learning (Gligorea et al., 2023; Wang et al., 2023), personalized learning (Bernacki et al., 2021; Zhang et al., 2020), advanced learning analytics and educational data mining (Lampropoulos, 2023b; Viberg et al., 2018), and recommendation systems (Rivera et al., 2018; Urdaneta-Ponte et al., 2021) in education, elements that are essential in twenty-first century education (González-Pérez & Ramírez-Montoya, 2022) and that are supported and enriched by artificial intelligence.

Furthermore, the integration of artificial intelligence into education involves the combination of several technologies and approaches including machine learning, deep learning, computer vision, big data analytics, and natural language processing (Jin, 2019; Yi et al., 2024). In this context, particular interest is shown in the use of generative artificial intelligence (Baidoo-Anu & Ansah, 2023; Bozkurt et al., 2023), chatbots (Deng & Yu, 2023; Okonkwo & Ade-Ibijola, 2021), social robots (Belpaeme & Tanaka, 2021; Lampropoulos, 2025c), intelligent tutoring systems (Lampropoulos, 2025a; Mousavinasab et al., 2021), immersive technologies (Kovács et al., 2015; Lampropoulos, 2025b), and virtual tutors (Hemachandran et al., 2022; Ward et al., 2011). Due to the benefits that artificial intelligence can bring in the educational domain, there has been an increase in the global interest surrounding the use of artificial intelligence in early childhood education (Latorre-Medina & Abdelmaula-Mesaud, 2025; Yi et al., 2024). Recent scoping studies mapping the global landscape of AI affordances in early childhood confirm this trend, while also identifying significant research gaps regarding how these tools are practically implemented across different cultural contexts (Chen, 2024). However, in contrast to other educational levels, the use of artificial intelligence in early childhood education, including preschool education and early primary education is explored to a lesser extent (Mustafa et al., 2024; Prentzas, 2013). Therefore, this chapter aims to provide an overview regarding the adoption and integration of artificial intelligence into preschool education and primary school education.

Artificial Intelligence in Preschool Education

Although still in its infancy, artificial intelligence, and more recently generative artificial intelligence, show great potential to effectively support teaching and learning activities and to reform early childhood education (Crescenzi-Lanna, 2023; Kanders et al., 2024; Nan, 2020). When used in combination with intelligent agents and educational robots, artificial intelligence can create embodied learning opportunities and offer personalized and interactive learning (Lampropoulos, 2025c; Yang et al., 2024).

Artificial intelligence can be used to create immersive, multi-modal, and collaborative learning activities which students find interesting and are fond of (Aslan et al., 2024), thus resulting in students' demonstrating increased learning outcomes, learning motivation, and learning engagement (Aslan et al., 2024; Prentzas, 2013). Through the personalized learning experiences offered, students achieve higher academic performance (Zhang et al., 2025), improved concept comprehension (Villegas-Ch. et al., 2022), enhanced cognitive and attitudinal facets (Zhang & Chen, 2022), and increased interest in and enthusiasm for learning (Nan, 2020). Additionally, artificial intelligence can support students with special needs (Prentzas, 2013), promote students' inquiry literacy, as it increases their collaborative inquiry, creative inquiry, and emotional inquiry development, (Kewalramani et al., 2021), and enable them to familiarize themselves with artificial intelligence concepts and devices that are increasingly being used in everyday life (Williams et al., 2019).

Furthermore, to effectively develop artificial intelligence-based educational tools, such as smart devices, tools, toys, and robots, it is important to consider both teachers' and students' needs and perspectives and follow participatory design processes (Akdeniz & Özdinç, 2021). In addition to students, teachers were also favorable toward the use of artificial intelligence in education and recognized the merits it can yield; however, they expressed concerns regarding privacy and security, misinformation issues, and lack of infrastructure (Kölemen & Yıldırım, 2025; Lamanauskas & Makarskaitė-Petkevičienė, 2025). Additional issues are related to the empathy gaps of artificial intelligence systems which render them unable to adequately respond to students' emotional needs (Kurian, 2025). Teachers and preservice teachers that are more familiar with artificial intelligence express more positive attitudes and viewpoints regarding its use in education than those with less experience and familiarity; however, both agree that artificial intelligence systems cannot replace teachers (Lamanauskas & Makarskaitė-Petkevičienė, 2025). Given the role of teachers in planning and implementing artificial intelligence in education, their insights are vital for the effective development, adoption, and integration of artificial intelligence in education (Lim, 2024). However, a lack of teachers' knowledge and skills regarding the introduction of artificial intelligence and its use in their classrooms is observed (Köken & Dagal, 2024). This inconsistency in usage is evident across different cultural contexts; for example, studies regarding Hong Kong educators highlight that while teachers may hold positive attitudes toward generative AI, they often struggle to navigate the digital shift required to integrate these emerging technologies effectively into their daily practice (Wong et al., 2025). Additionally, there is a lack of artificial intelligence-related teaching guidelines and curriculum design (Su et al., 2023). Hence, it is important to develop programs to strengthen teachers' and pre-service teachers' digital skills, self-efficacy, and artificial intelligence literacy (Lim, 2023).

Moreover, artificial intelligence design should be children-centered, be in line with their development level, and comply with strict ethical guidelines (Jin, 2019; Kurian, 2025) to create ethical and equitable learning environments (Berson et al., 2025), as there are several ethical concerns that should be taken into consideration while accounting for young learners' needs (Berson et al., 2025). Chief among these is the risk of algorithmic bias. Commercial classification systems have been shown to exhibit significant accuracy disparities based on gender and skin type (Buolamwini & Gebru, 2018), raising critical questions about equity when deploying such systems in diverse early childhood classrooms. Additionally, in both physical and virtual learning artificial intelligence-enriched environments, ensuring students' digital security and privacy is imperative; hence, effective cybersecurity protocols should be developed and implemented to safeguard young students' digital identity (Zhang, 2023). As a result, among the challenges associated with the integration of artificial intelligence into early childhood education, data protection and data privacy policies remain significant concerns, as they require strict regulatory adherence and raise ethical questions about the collection, storage, processing, and use of sensitive information related to young students (Crescenzi-Lanna, 2023). Other key concerns are related to the influence of artificial intelligence on young students' development and learning (El Zaatari et al., 2024).

Nonetheless, carefully designed, artificial intelligence interventions can improve young students' artificial intelligence literacy, concept understanding, creativity, critical thinking, and computational thinking (Su & Yang, 2022, 2024; Williams et al., 2019). Additionally, when adopting suitable approaches, such as problem-based learning, and focusing on cultivating students' artificial intelligence knowledge, skills, and attitudes, their artificial intelligence literacy can be improved (Su & Zhong, 2022). Hence, to cultivate students' artificial intelligence literacy, it is important to develop appropriate strategies, curricula, and education resources that are culturally sensitive, adhere to diverse students' learning needs, and are student-centered (El Zaatari et al., 2024).

Artificial Intelligence in Primary Education

When examining the use of artificial intelligence in primary education, studies utilize mixed methods, focus on human-agent interaction, computational thinking, adopting constructivist methodologies, and project-based learning, adopt computer science perspectives, Bloom's taxonomy, and the constructivist theoretical framework, and mostly report positive learning outcomes in terms of academic, behavioral, and affective outcomes (Yim, 2024a; Yim & Su, 2025). Although artificial intelligence can effectively support different courses within the curriculum (Lampropoulos & Papadakis, 2025), it is being more widely adopted and examined in science and mathematics courses (Topkaya et al., 2025).

In the context of twenty-first century education cultivating students' computational thinking, digital literacy, and artificial intelligence literacy using new technologies and approaches is imperative (Hong & Kim, 2025; Lampropoulos, 2023a). Hence, pedagogical approaches that aim at enhancing students' artificial intelligence literacy should be adopted as they can increase students' performance, intrinsic motivation, and confidence while reducing their learning anxiety (Dai, 2024). Additionally, artificial intelligence tools and applications can improve young students' learning performance through continuous learning support, collaborative learning environments, and personalized learning experiences which tend to students' needs and learning preferences (Pardamean et al., 2022). Artificial intelligence can also promote collaborative learning and provide automatic feedback, evaluation, and recommendation systems which can enrich primary students' learning (Wen et al., 2025).

Having user-centric features, artificial intelligence tools, such as chatbots, can support both students and teachers, enhance instruction quality, and offer adaptive learning experiences (Yuan, 2024). However, it is important to adopt interdisciplinary approaches that promote students' learning engagement and motivation to effectively implement artificial intelligence in educational settings (Yeter et al., 2024). In this context, students' behavioral intention of using artificial intelligence to support their learning is significant. Students' intention of learning using artificial intelligence can be influenced by their artificial intelligence self-efficacy, readiness, literacy, and perception as well as their overall behavioral intention (Chai et al., 2021). Specifically, students' behavioral intention to learn using artificial intelligence is significantly influenced by their social influence, performance expectancy, and effort expectancy while facilitating conditions have a more drastic effect on their actual use behavior (Du & Lv, 2024). Their behavioral intention to use artificial intelligence is also heavily influenced by their programming skills and indirectly related to their artificial intelligence literacy and artificial intelligence ethic knowledge and perspectives (Luo et al., 2025). Students' motivation to learn in artificial intelligence curriculum is mostly influenced by their intrinsic motivation but factors such as relevance, confidence, and attention also affect it (Lin et al., 2021).

Using suitable approaches that focus on cultivating students' artificial intelligence literacy and problem-solving skills can significantly increase students' artificial intelligence knowledge, attitudes, and ethics (Yue et al., 2025). Additionally, the application of pedagogical approaches based on human–artificial intelligence comparison has also revealed significant benefits as students who learnt through them demonstrate increased skill mastery and comprehension of the subject matter, improved attitudes, performance, and critical thinking, as well as enhanced learning engagement (Dai et al., 2024a, 2024b). Other student-centered approaches, such as arts-based learning and digital storytelling and writing, can also promote students' artificial intelligence competencies and literacy in using and applying their artificial intelligence knowledge to solve real-life problems (Ng et al., 2022a, 2022b; Yim, 2024a, 2024b). Hence, when designing and creating artificial intelligence curriculum and intervention, it is important to adopt co-design approaches involving both teachers and students throughout the development process so that meaningful learning can occur (Ottenbreit-Leftwich et al., 2023). Finally, when designing artificial intelligence educational interventions, there are several ethical considerations that should be taken into account, including inclusivity, security, privacy, and bias (Alawneh et al., 2024).

The development of effective artificial intelligence curriculum requires a collaborative effort among education stakeholders (Dai et al., 2023) who might not share the same viewpoints regarding the use of artificial intelligence. Students perceive artificial intelligence as both a concept with or without human characteristics as well as a machine and as a result, their affective perceptions toward artificial intelligence are mixed (Walan, 2025). Additionally, students express positive attitudes toward the use of artificial intelligence tools in education and do not perceive them as threats to or as deteriorating factors of the educational system (Lozano & Blanco Fontao, 2023). Specifically, they view artificial intelligence as a guiding tool, a source of information, and a service tool with human-like characteristics (Kalemkuş & Kalemkuş, 2025). However, teachers express mixed attitudes toward the use of artificial intelligence in educational settings with their perspectives being significantly dependent on their digital literacy, gender, age, and use of artificial intelligence tools (Mazı, 2024).

Conclusions

The adoption and integration of artificial intelligence into preschool education and primary education is increasing. The outcomes of this study highlight the educational benefits that artificial intelligence can bring about as well as the fact that digital literacy and artificial intelligence literacy have become integral parts of all educational levels.

Since artificial intelligence tools can act both as tutors and as peer learners offering personalized, collaborative, and adaptive learning and providing individualized feedback, support, guidance, and recommendations, increased learning outcomes and performance were observed. Artificial intelligence can support both students and teachers. Students and pre-service teachers express mostly positive attitudes toward the use of artificial intelligence in education while there are mixed opinions expressed by teachers which are mostly affected by their characteristics (e.g., gender, age, digital literacy, etc.). This fact indicated that students' and teachers' perspectives and behavioral intention should be further examined.

Despite the benefits of artificial intelligence, several challenges and limitations were identified. Given that a lack of teachers' artificial intelligence literacy was observed, it is important to examine how to best improve their skills to more effectively integrate artificial intelligence in their classrooms. Similarly, it is important to create artificial intelligence-related teaching guidelines, curriculum and material design methods, as well as development programs for improving teachers' artificial intelligence self-efficacy and digital literacy.

Furthermore, if and how artificial intelligence impacts young students' development, well-being, and learning should be further examined. As there is a significant emphasis on the examination of artificial intelligence into science-related courses, future studies should focus on exploring its impact on other courses as well. The need to develop effective co-design approaches and involve both teachers and students when creating artificial intelligence tools, material, and activities is highlighted.

As the introduction of artificial intelligence in education is likely to increase the digital divide, it is important to ensure that its implementation is inclusive, accessible, responsible, ethical, and equitable. Other important challenges include concerns about security, privacy, lack of infrastructure, bias, and misinformation. As there are ethical considerations, it is important to examine the ethical implications of using artificial intelligence in education and to develop strict and robust ethical guidelines and policies.

Finally, the need to develop young students' artificial intelligence literacy, reasoning, critical thinking, and computational thinking is highlighted. However, besides the educational implications, it is equally important to evaluate the societal, technological, and economical implications that the use of artificial intelligence in education can bring.

References

Akdeniz, M., & Özdinç, F. (2021). Maya: An artificial intelligence based smart toy for pre-school children. *International Journal of Child-Computer Interaction, 29*, 100347. https://doi.org/10.1016/j.ijcci.2021.100347

Alawneh, Y. J. J., Radwan, E. N. Z., Salman, F. N., Makhlouf, S. I., Makhamreh, K., & Alawneh, M. S. (2024). Ethical considerations in the use of AI in primary education: Privacy, bias, and inclusivity. *International Conference on Knowledge Engineering and Communication Systems (ICKECS), 2024*, 1–6. https://doi.org/10.1109/ickecs61492.2024.10616986

Aslan, S., Durham, L. M., Alyuz, N., Okur, E., Sharma, S., Savur, C., & Nachman, L. (2024). Immersive multi-modal pedagogical conversational artificial intelligence for early childhood education: An exploratory case study in the wild. *Computers and Education: Artificial Intelligence, 6*, 100220. https://doi.org/10.1016/j.caeai.2024.100220

Baidoo-Anu, D., & Ansah, L. O. (2023). Education in the era of generative artificial intelligence (AI): Understanding the potential benefits of ChatGPT in promoting teaching and learning. *Journal of AI, 7*(1), 52–62. https://doi.org/10.61969/jai.1337500

Belpaeme, T., & Tanaka, F. (2021). Social robots as educators. In OECD digital education outlook 2021 pushing the frontiers with artificial intelligence, blockchain and robots: Pushing the frontiers with artificial intelligence, blockchain and robots (p. 143). OECD Publishing Paris.

Bernacki, M. L., Greene, M. J., & Lobczowski, N. G. (2021). A systematic review of research on personalized learning: Personalized by whom, to what, how, and for what purpose(s)? *Educational Psychology Review, 33*(4), 1675–1715. https://doi.org/10.1007/s10648-021-09615-8

Berson, I. R., Berson, M. J., & Luo, W. (2025). Innovating responsibly: Ethical considerations for AI in early childhood education. *AI, Brain and Child, 1*(1). https://doi.org/10.1007/s44436-025-00003-5

Bozkurt, A., Junhong, X., Lambert, S., Pazurek, A., Crompton, H., Koseoglu, S., Farrow, R., Bond, M., Nerantzi, C., Honeychurch, S., et al. (2023). Speculative futures on ChatGPT and generative artificial intelligence (AI): A collective reflection from the educational landscape. *Asian Journal of Distance Education, 18*(1), 53–130.

Brynjolfsson, E., & Mcafee, A. (2017). Artificial intelligence, for real. *Harvard Business Review, 1*, 1–31.

Buolamwini, J., & Gebru, T. (2018). Gender shades: Intersectional accuracy disparities in commercial gender classification. In S. A. Friedler & C. Wilson (Eds.), *Proceedings of Machine Learning Research, 81*, 1–15. https://proceedings.mlr.press/v81/buolamwini18a/buolamwini18a.pdf

Chai, C. S., Lin, P.-Y., Jong, M. S.-Y., Dai, Y., Chiu, T. K., & Qin, J. (2021). Perceptions of and behavioral intentions towards learning artificial intelligence in primary school students. *Educational Technology & Society, 24*(3), 89–101.

Chen, J. (2024). A scoping study on AI affordances in early childhood education: Mapping the global landscape, identifying research gaps, and charting future research directions. *Journal of Artificial Intelligence Research, 81*, 701–740. https://doi.org/10.1613/jair.1.16882

Chen, L., Chen, P., & Lin, Z. (2020). Artificial intelligence in education: A review. *IEEE Access, 8*, 75264–75278. https://doi.org/10.1109/access.2020.2988510

Chiu, T. K. F., Xia, Q., Zhou, X., Chai, C. S., & Cheng, M. (2023). Systematic literature review on opportunities, challenges, and future research recommendations of artificial intelligence in education. *Computers and Education: Artificial Intelligence, 4*, 100118. https://doi.org/10.1016/j.caeai.2022.100118

Crescenzi-Lanna, L. (2023). Literature review of the reciprocal value of artificial and human intelligence in early childhood education. *Journal of Research on Technology in Education, 55*(1), 21–33. https://doi.org/10.1080/15391523.2022.2128480

Dai, Y., Liu, A., Qin, J., Guo, Y., Jong, M. S.-Y., Chai, C.-S., & Lin, Z. (2023). Collaborative construction of artificial intelligence curriculum in primary schools. *Journal of Engineering Education, 112*(1), 23–42. https://doi.org/10.1002/jee.20503

Dai, Y. (2024). Dual-contrast pedagogy for AI literacy in upper elementary schools. *Learning and Instruction, 91*, 101899. https://doi.org/10.1016/j.learninstruc.2024.101899

Dai, Y., Lin, Z., Liu, A., Dai, D., & Wang, W. (2024a). Effect of an Analogy-Based approach of artificial intelligence pedagogy in upper primary schools. *Journal of Educational Computing Research, 61*(8), 1695–1722. https://doi.org/10.1177/07356331231201342

Dai, Y., Lin, Z., Liu, A., & Wang, W. (2024b). An embodied, analogical and disruptive approach of AI pedagogy in upper elementary education: An experimental study. *British Journal of Educational Technology, 55*(1), 417–434. https://doi.org/10.1111/bjet.13371

Dai, Y., Lin, Z., Liu, A., Dai, D., & Wang, W. (2024c). Effect of an Analogy-Based approach of artificial intelligence pedagogy in upper primary schools. *Journal of Educational Computing Research, 61*(8), 1695–1722. https://doi.org/10.1177/07356331231201342

Deng, X., & Yu, Z. (2023). A Meta-Analysis and systematic review of the effect of chatbot technology use in sustainable education. *Sustainability, 15*(4), 2940. https://doi.org/10.3390/su15042940

Du, L., & Lv, B. (2024). Factors influencing students' acceptance and use generative artificial intelligence in elementary education: An expansion of the UTAUT model. *Education and Information Technologies, 29*(18), 24715–24734. https://doi.org/10.1007/s10639-024-12835-4

Duan, Y., Edwards, J. S., & Dwivedi, Y. K. (2019). Artificial intelligence for decision making in the era of big data—evolution, challenges and research agenda. *International Journal of Information Management, 48*, 63–71. https://doi.org/10.1016/j.ijinfomgt.2019.01.021

El Zaatari, W., Alsereidi, M., & Alamassi, S. (2024). An insight into uses, benefits and challenges of integrating AI in early childhood education. *Global Congress on Emerging Technologies, GCET-2024*, 71–78. https://doi.org/10.1109/gcet64327.2024.10934465

Ertel, W. (2018). *Introduction to artificial intelligence*. Springer.

Gligorea, I., Cioca, M., Oancea, R., Gorski, A.-T., Gorski, H., & Tudorache, P. (2023). Adaptive learning using artificial intelligence in e-learning: A literature review. *Education Sciences, 13*(12), 1216. https://doi.org/10.3390/educsci13121216

González-Pérez, L. I., & Ramírez-Montoya, M. S. (2022). Components of education 4.0 in twenty-first century skills frameworks: Systematic review. *Sustainability, 14*(3), 1493. https://doi.org/10.3390/su14031493

Haenlein, M., & Kaplan, A. (2019). A brief history of artificial intelligence: On the past, present, and future of artificial intelligence. *California Management Review, 61*(4), 5–14. https://doi.org/10.1177/0008125619864925

Hemachandran, K., Verma, P., Pareek, P., Arora, N., Rajesh Kumar, K. V., Ahanger, T. A., Pise, A. A., & Ratna, R. (2022). Artificial intelligence: A universal virtual tool to augment tutoring in higher education. *Computational Intelligence and Neuroscience, 2022*, 1–8. https://doi.org/10.1155/2022/1410448

Holmes, W., Bialik, M., & Fadel, C. (2020). *Artificial intelligence in education: Promises and implications for teaching and learning*. Center for Curriculum Redesign.

Hong, J., & Kim, K. (2025). Impact of AIoT education program on digital and AI literacy of elementary school students. *Education and Information Technologies, 30*(1), 107–130. https://doi.org/10.1007/s10639-024-12,758-0

Hwang, G.-J., Xie, H., Wah, B. W., & Gašević, D. (2020). Vision, challenges, roles and research issues of artificial intelligence in education. *Computers and Education: Artificial Intelligence, 1*, 100001. https://doi.org/10.1016/j.caeai.2020.100001

Jin, L. (2019). Investigation on potential application of artificial intelligence in preschool children's education. *Journal of Physics: Conference Series, 1288*(1), 012072. https://doi.org/10.1088/1742-6596/1288/1/012072

Kalemkuş, J., & Kalemkuş, F. (2025). Primary school students' perceptions of artificial intelligence: Metaphor and drawing analysis. *European Journal of Education, 60*(1). https://doi.org/10.1111/ejed.70007

Kanders, K., Stupple-Harris, L., Smith, L., & Gibson, J. L. (2024). Perspectives on the impact of generative AI on early-childhood development and education. *Infant and Child Development, 33*(4). https://doi.org/10.1002/icd.2514

Kewalramani, S., Kidman, G., & Palaiologou, I. (2021). Using artificial intelligence (AI)-interfaced robotic toys in early childhood settings: A case for children's inquiry literacy. *European Early Childhood Education Research Journal, 29*(5), 652–668. https://doi.org/10.1080/1350293x.2021.1968458

Köken, C., & Dagal, A. B. (2024). Investigation of preschool education teachers, preschool children and mothers' opinions on artificial intelligence. *International Technology and Education Journal, 8*(1), 24–35.

Kölemen, E. B., & Yıldırım, B. (2025). A new era in early childhood education (ECE): Teachers' opinions on the application of artificial intelligence. *Education and Information Technologies*. https://doi.org/10.1007/s10639-025-13478-9

Kovács, P. T., Murray, N., Rozinaj, G., Sulema, Y., & Rybárová, R. (2015). Application of immersive technologies for education: State of the art. *2015 International Conference on Interactive Mobile Communication Technologies and Learning (IMCL)*, 283–288. https://doi.org/10.1109/IMCTL.2015.7359604

Kurian, N. (2025). AI's empathy gap: The risks of conversational artificial intelligence for young children's well-being and key ethical considerations for early childhood education and care. *Contemporary Issues in Early Childhood, 26*(1), 132–139. https://doi.org/10.1177/14639491231206004

Lamanauskas, V., & Makarskaitė-Petkevičienė, R. (2025). Pre-service preschool and primary school teachers' position on artificial intelligence. In *EAI/Springer innovations in communication and computing* (pp. 183–197). https://doi.org/10.1007/978-3-031-81261-3_14

Lampropoulos, G. (2023a). Augmented reality and artificial intelligence in education: Toward immersive intelligent tutoring systems. In *Augmented reality and artificial intelligence* (pp. 137–146). https://doi.org/10.1007/978-3-031-27166-3_8

Lampropoulos, G. (2023b). Educational data mining and learning analytics in the twenty-first century. In *Encyclopedia of data science and machine learning* (pp. 1642–1651). https://doi.org/10.4018/978-1-7998-9220-5.ch098

Lampropoulos, G. (2025a). Augmented reality, virtual reality, and intelligent tutoring systems in education and training: A systematic literature review. *Applied Sciences, 15*(6), 3223. https://doi.org/10.3390/app15063223

Lampropoulos, G. (2025b). Combining artificial intelligence with augmented reality and virtual reality in education: Current trends and future perspectives. *Multimodal Technologies and Interaction, 9*(2), 11. https://doi.org/10.3390/mti9020011

Lampropoulos, G. (2025c). Social robots in education: Current trends and future perspectives. *Information, 16*(1), 29. https://doi.org/10.3390/info16010029

Lampropoulos, G., & Papadakis, S. (2025). The educational value of artificial intelligence and social robots. In *Studies in computational intelligence* (pp. 3–15). https://doi.org/10.1007/978-3-031-82915-4_1

Latorre-Medina, M. J., & Abdelmaula-Mesaud, S. (2025). Artificial intelligence applied to early childhood education: A focus for educational research? *Contemporary Issues in Early Childhood, 26*(1), 140–153. https://doi.org/10.1177/14639491241303746

Li, D., & Du, Y. (2017). *Artificial intelligence with uncertainty*. CRC press. https://doi.org/10.1201/9781315366951

Lim, E. M. (2023). The effects of pre-service early childhood teachers' digital literacy and self-efficacy on their perception of AI education for young children. *Education and Information Technologies, 28*(10), 12969–12995. https://doi.org/10.1007/s10639-023-11724-6

Lim, E. M. (2024). Metaphor analysis on pre-service early childhood teachers' conception of AI (artificial intelligence) education for young children. *Thinking Skills and Creativity, 51*, 101455. https://doi.org/10.1016/j.tsc.2023.101455

Lin, P.-Y., Chai, C.-S., Jong, M. S.-Y., Dai, Y., Guo, Y., & Qin, J. (2021). Modeling the structural relationship among primary students' motivation to learn artificial intelligence. *Computers and Education: Artificial Intelligence, 2*, 100006. https://doi.org/10.1016/j.caeai.2020.100006

Lozano, A., & Blanco Fontao, C. (2023). Is the education system prepared for the irruption of artificial intelligence? A study on the perceptions of students of primary education degree from a dual perspective: Current pupils and future teachers. *Education Sciences, 13*(7), 733. https://doi.org/10.3390/educsci13070733

Luo, J., Cao, J., & Chen, J. (2025). Towards a model for primary students' behavioral intention to learn AI: Programming ability, AI literacy and ethics as three fundamental pillars. *Interactive Learning Environments, 1–15*. https://doi.org/10.1080/10494820.2025.2450658

Mazı, A. (2024). Investigation of primary school teacher's attitudes towards artificial intelligence. In *Advances in educational technologies and instructional design* (pp. 27–58). https://doi.org/10.4018/979-8-3693-3944-2.ch002

Mousavinasab, E., Zarifsanaiey, N., R. Niakan Kalhori, S., Rakhshan, M., Keikha, L., & Ghazi Saeedi, M. (2021). Intelligent tutoring systems: A systematic review of characteristics, applications, and evaluation methods. *Interactive Learning Environments, 29*(1), 142–163. https://doi.org/10.1080/10494820.2018.1558257

Mustafa, M. Y., Tlili, A., Lampropoulos, G., Huang, R., Jandrić, P., Zhao, J., Salha, S., Xu, L., Panda, S., Kinshuk, L.-P., & S., & Saqr, M. (2024). A systematic review of literature reviews on artificial intelligence in education (AIED): A roadmap to a future research agenda. *Smart Learning. Environments, 11*(1). https://doi.org/10.1186/s40561-024-00350-5

Nan, J. (2020). Research of application of artificial intelligence in preschool education. *Journal of Physics: Conference Series, 1607*(1), 012119. https://doi.org/10.1088/1742-6596/1607/1/012119

Ng, D. T. K., Luo, W., Chan, H. M. Y., & Chu, S. K. W. (2022a). Using digital story writing as a pedagogy to develop AI literacy among primary students. *Computers and Education: Artificial Intelligence, 3*, 100054. https://doi.org/10.1016/j.caeai.2022.100054

Ng, D. T. K., Luo, W., Chan, H., & Chu, S. (2022b). An examination on primary students' development in AI literacy through digital story writing. *Computers & Education. Artificial Intelligence, 100054*(3), 100054.

Okonkwo, C. W., & Ade-Ibijola, A. (2021). Chatbots applications in education: A systematic review. *Computers and Education: Artificial Intelligence, 2*, 100033. https://doi.org/10.1016/j.caeai.2021.100033

Ottenbreit-Leftwich, A., Glazewski, K., Jeon, M., Jantaraweragul, K., Hmelo-Silver, C. E., Scribner, A., Lee, S., Mott, B., & Lester, J. (2023). Lessons learned for AI education with elementary students and teachers. *International Journal of Artificial Intelligence in Education, 33*(2), 267–289. https://doi.org/10.1007/s40593-022-00304-3

Pardamean, B., Suparyanto, T., Cenggoro, T. W., Sudigyo, D., & Anugrahana, A. (2022). AI-Based learning style prediction in online learning for primary education. *IEEE Access, 10*, 35725–35735. https://doi.org/10.1109/access.2022.3160177

Prentzas, J. (2013). Artificial intelligence methods in early childhood education. In *Studies in computational intelligence* (pp. 169–199). https://doi.org/10.1007/978-3-642-29694-9_8

Rivera, A. C., Tapia-Leon, M., & Lujan-Mora, S. (2018). Recommendation systems in education: A systematic mapping study. In *Proceedings of the international conference on information technology & systems (ICITS 2018)* (pp. 937–947). https://doi.org/10.1007/978-3-319-73450-7_89

Stone, P., Brooks, R., Brynjolfsson, E., Calo, R., Etzioni, O., Hager, G., Hirschberg, J., Kalyanakrishnan, S., Kamar, E., Kraus, S., Leyton-Brown, K., Parkes, D., Press, W., Saxenian, A., Shah, J., Tambe, M., & Teller, A. (2016). *Artificial intelligence and life in 2030: The one hundred year study on artificial intelligence*. https://doi.org/10.48550/ARXIV.2211.06318

Su, J., & Yang, W. (2022). Artificial intelligence in early childhood education: A scoping review. *Computers and Education: Artificial Intelligence, 3*, 100049. https://doi.org/10.1016/j.caeai.2022.100049

Su, J., & Yang, W. (2024). Artificial intelligence (AI) literacy in early childhood education: An intervention study in Hong Kong. *Interactive Learning Environments, 32*(9), 5494–5508. https://doi.org/10.1080/10494820.2023.2217864

Su, J., & Zhong, Y. (2022). Artificial intelligence (AI) in early childhood education: Curriculum design and future directions. *Computers and Education: Artificial Intelligence, 3*, 100072. https://doi.org/10.1016/j.caeai.2022.100072

Su, J., Ng, D. T. K., & Chu, S. K. W. (2023). Artificial intelligence (AI) literacy in early childhood education: The challenges and opportunities. *Computers and Education: Artificial Intelligence, 4*, 100124. https://doi.org/10.1016/j.caeai.2023.100124

Topkaya, Y., Doğan, Y., Batdı, V., & Aydın, S. (2025). Artificial intelligence applications in primary education: A quantitatively complemented mixed-meta-method study. *Sustainability, 17*(7), 3015. https://doi.org/10.3390/su17073015

Urdaneta-Ponte, M. C., Mendez-Zorrilla, A., & Oleagordia-Ruiz, I. (2021). Recommendation systems for education: Systematic review. *Electronics, 10*(14), 1611. https://doi.org/10.3390/electronics10141611

Viberg, O., Hatakka, M., Bälter, O., & Mavroudi, A. (2018). The current landscape of learning analytics in higher education. *Computers in Human Behavior, 89*, 98–110. https://doi.org/10.1016/j.chb.2018.07.027

Villegas-Ch., W., Jaramillo-Alcázar, A., & Mera-Navarrete, A. (2022). Assistance system for the teaching of natural numbers to preschool children with the use of artificial intelligence algorithms. *Future Internet, 14*(9), 266. https://doi.org/10.3390/fi14090266

Walan, S. (2025). Primary school students' perceptions of artificial intelligence—for good or bad. *International Journal of Technology and Design Education, 35*(1), 25–40. https://doi.org/10.1007/s10798-024-09898-2

Wang, S., Christensen, C., Cui, W., Tong, R., Yarnall, L., Shear, L., & Feng, M. (2023). When adaptive learning is effective learning: Comparison of an adaptive learning system to teacher-led instruction. *Interactive Learning Environments, 31*(2), 793–803. https://doi.org/10.1080/10494820.2020.1808794

Ward, W., Cole, R., Bolaños, D., Buchenroth-Martin, C., Svirsky, E., Vuuren, S. V., Weston, T., Zheng, J., & Becker, L. (2011). My science tutor. *ACM Transactions on Speech and Language Processing, 7*(4), 1–29. https://doi.org/10.1145/1998384.1998392

Wen, Y., Chiu, M., Guo, X., & Wang, Z. (2025). AI-powered vocabulary learning for lower primary school students. *British Journal of Educational Technology, 56*(2), 734–754. https://doi.org/10.1111/bjet.13537

Williams, R., Park, H. W., & Breazeal, C. (2019). A is for artificial intelligence: The impact of artificial intelligence activities on young children's perceptions of robots. *Proceedings of the 2019 CHI Conference on Human Factors in Computing Systems*, 1–11. https://doi.org/10.1145/3290605.3300677

Williams, R., Park, H. W., Oh, L., & Breazeal, C. (2019). PopBots: Designing an artificial intelligence curriculum for early childhood education. *Proceedings of the AAAI Conference on Artificial Intelligence, 33*(1), 9729–9736. https://doi.org/10.1609/aaai.v33i01.33019729

Wong, J. M. S., Liu, P. H. C., & Yip, C. W. H. (2025). Navigating the digital shift: Early childhood educators' attitudes towards generative artificial intelligence and emerging technologies. In E. C. K. Cheng (Ed.), *Innovating education with AI* (pp. 87–97). Springer Nature. https://doi.org/10.1007/978-981-96-4952-5_6

Yang, W., Hu, X., Yeter, I. H., Su, J., Yang, Y., & Lee, J. C.-K. (2024). Artificial intelligence education for young children: A case study of technology-enhanced embodied learning. *Journal of Computer Assisted Learning, 40*(2), 465–477. https://doi.org/10.1111/jcal.12892

Yeter, I. H., Yang, W., & Sturgess, J. B. (2024). Global initiatives and challenges in integrating artificial intelligence literacy in elementary education: Mapping policies and empirical literature. *Future in Educational Research, 2*(4), 382–402. https://doi.org/10.1002/fer3.59

Yi, H., Liu, T., & Lan, G. (2024). The key artificial intelligence technologies in early childhood education: A review. *Artificial Intelligence Review, 57*(1). https://doi.org/10.1007/s10462-023-10637-7

Yim, I. H. Y. (2024a). A critical review of teaching and learning artificial intelligence (AI) literacy: Developing an intelligence-based AI literacy framework for primary school education. *Computers and Education: Artificial Intelligence, 7*, 100319. https://doi.org/10.1016/j.caeai.2024.100319

Yim, I. H. Y. (2024b). Artificial intelligence literacy in primary education: An arts-based approach to overcoming age and gender barriers. *Computers and Education: Artificial Intelligence, 7*, 100321. https://doi.org/10.1016/j.caeai.2024.100321

Yim, I. H. Y., & Su, J. (2025). Artificial intelligence literacy education in primary schools: A review. *International Journal of Technology and Design Education*. https://doi.org/10.1007/s10798-025-09979-w

Yuan, Y. (2024). An empirical study of the efficacy of AI chatbots for English as a foreign language learning in primary education. *Interactive Learning Environments, 32*(10), 6774–6789. https://doi.org/10.1080/10494820.2023.2282112

Yue, M., Jong, M. S.-Y., Dai, Y., & Lau, W. W.-F. (2025). Students as AI literate designers: A pedagogical framework for learning and teaching AI literacy in elementary education. *Journal of Research on Technology in Education, 1–22*. https://doi.org/10.1080/15391523.2025.2449942

Zhang, L., Basham, J. D., & Yang, S. (2020). Understanding the implementation of personalized learning: A research synthesis. *Educational Research Review, 31*, 100339. https://doi.org/10.1016/j.edurev.2020.100339

Zhang, Q. (2023). Secure preschool education using machine learning and metaverse technologies. *Applied Artificial Intelligence, 37*(1). https://doi.org/10.1080/08839514.2023.2222496

Zhang, S., & Chen, X. (2022). Applying artificial intelligence into early childhood math education: Lesson design and course effect. In *2022 IEEE International Conference on Teaching, Assessment and Learning for Engineering (TALE)* (pp. 635–638). https://doi.org/10.1109/tale54877.2022.00109

Zhang, Z., Zhang, X., & Liu, X. (2025). A novel algorithm for personalized learning in preschool education using artificial intelligence. *Journal of Computational Methods in Sciences and Engineering, 25*(3), 2562–2576. https://doi.org/10.1177/14727978251314562

Appendix
Conclusion: Rethinking teaching with AI in the classroom

1. Synthesis: The "Human-in-the-Loop" imperative

This volume started from a simple observation: AI tools are now shaping what happens in early childhood and primary classrooms every day, from the way teachers prepare materials to how children search, write, and play. Across seventeen chapters, the contributors have shown that Artificial Intelligence (AI) is not merely a technical novelty but a "cultural artifact" that reshapes how young children play, learn, and construct meaning. Yet, a unifying thread runs through every contribution: the necessity of the "Human-in-the-Loop."

Whether we are discussing the use of chatbots to differentiate tasks (Chapter 6), the generation of resources for primary mathematics (Chapter 9), or the design of "AI Personas" to scaffold creativity (Chapter 13), the evidence presented in this book confirms the stance of the UNESCO (2025) guidance: AI must remain a tool for augmentation, not automation. The teacher's role has not been diminished; it has been elevated. In an era of "Agentic AI", systems capable of autonomous action, the educator becomes the essential arbiter of pedagogical value, emotional safety, and ethical integrity.

As an editor collaborating with contributors from different systems and cultures, I have repeatedly seen how the same AI tool can either deepen children's engagement or quietly undermine it, depending on how the teacher frames its use.

2. Bridging the global gap: Context matters

The chapters show that AI integration is never uniform. It depends on where the school is, how its curriculum has developed over time, and what resources teachers actually have. So far, most of the debate about AI in education has been shaped by Western voices, with a strong emphasis on tailoring learning to each individual learner and much less attention to the shared good of the group.

This volume challenges that hegemony by highlighting the divergence in global implementation. In Western contexts, AI adoption is often driven by a narrative of "novelty" and efficiency. However, as Chen (2024) shows in her global scoping review, the landscape in East Asia is driven by different pedagogical philosophies.

S. Papadakis (ed.), *AI Applications in Preschool and Primary Education*, Advances in Artificial Intelligence in Education 5, https://doi.org/10.1007/978-3-032-17190-0

Wong et al. (2025) provide a crucial counterpoint in their study of Hong Kong educators, noting that the "digital shift" in Eastern contexts is often accompanied by significant cultural hesitation about the displacement of traditional teacher authority.

This difference really matters for how the field develops. Going forward, we should be cautious about treating AI integration as if there were a single right model. A "Playmate" role that fits well in a Scandinavian, constructivist classroom may need to look quite different in a tightly structured primary school in Singapore or in a low-resource classroom in the Global South. Future studies need to pay closer attention to these cross-cultural comparisons so that AI tools support local educational aims instead of quietly exporting a Silicon Valley view of what good teaching looks like.

3. Ethics in practice: Who owns the data and who is protected?

Multiple chapters grappled with the "Black Box" problem, the opacity of algorithmic decision-making. This concern was raised as early as Chapter 1 on biases in speech recognition and revisited extensively throughout Part V. We must take seriously the warnings of Buolamwini and Gebru (2018) regarding "gender shades" and intersectional accuracy disparities. When we deploy facial recognition or predictive analytics in a primary classroom, we are not just deploying code; we are deploying the biases of the data on which that code was trained.

For early years educators, this means moving from simply using whatever data-driven tools are available to asking who controls the data and how it is used. As the French Ministry of National Education (2025) notes, schools need to give preference to tools that keep pupil data under public control and out of commercial data markets. We cannot allow the playful interactions of a 5-year-old to become fuel for surveillance capitalism. The "critical resistance" advocated in our Introduction is not just a theoretical stance; it is a safeguarding obligation. For instance, several contributors mentioned school leaders who refused to adopt tools that exported children's data outside the EU, even when these tools were free and popular.

4. Policy implications for the next decade

Based on the findings of this volume, future policy and practice must rest on three foundational shifts. First, we need to redefine literacy, moving beyond the "learn to code" mantra. As the Raspberry Pi Foundation (2025) argues, the primary goal must be AI Literacy equipping children with the agency to understand the intent, mechanisms, and limitations of the systems they interact with.

Second, this requires a sovereign infrastructure. Policymakers must invest in "Public AI" models trained on vetted educational data rather than the open internet. This safeguarding step is essential to reduce the risk of hallucinations and exposure to age-inappropriate content, as flagged by the JRC (2025) outlook.

Finally, we must prioritize teacher agency. Professional development cannot remain a one-off workshop. As Chapter 5 shows, helping teachers move from anxiety to confidence requires ongoing support. Only then can we reach the kind of "co-creAItivity" described in Chapter 13, where teachers have the protected time to explore these tools before modeling them for children.

5. Looking ahead

The choices we make now will figure out whether AI in our schools becomes a tool for standardization or liberation. Allowing these systems to replace teacher judgment risks creating classrooms that are more automated but less human. Conversely, if we deploy AI strictly to reduce routine burdens, we can build learning environments where children's curiosity and empathy remain central.

In that future, AI manages the paperwork, while the educator focuses on listening, guiding, and opening the questions that truly matter. The chapters in this volume prove that AI does not have to weaken early childhood education.

References

Buolamwini, J., & Gebru, T. (2018). Gender shades: Intersectional accuracy disparities in commercial gender classification. *Proceedings of Machine Learning Research, 81*, 1–15. http://proceedings.mlr.press/v81/buolamwini18a.html

Chen, J. (2024). A scoping study on AI affordances in early childhood education: Mapping the global landscape. *Journal of Artificial Intelligence Research, 81*, 701–740. https://doi.org/10.1613/jair.1.16882

European Commission, Joint Research Centre. (2025). *Generative AI outlook report 2025*. Publications Office of the European Union. https://publications.jrc.ec.europa.eu/repository/handle/JRC142598

French Ministry of National Education. (2025). *Framework for using AI in education* [Report]. https://edunumrech.hypotheses.org/15271

Raspberry Pi Foundation. (2025). *Why kids still need to learn to code in the age of AI* [Position paper]. https://static.raspberrypi.org/files/about/Why-kids-still-need-to-learn-to-code-in-the-age-of-AI-2025-Raspberry-Pi-Foundation-position-paper.pdf

UNESCO. (2025). *Guidance on generative AI in education and research (Revised orientations)*. UNESCO Publishing. https://www.unesco.org/en/articles/guidance-generative-ai-education-and-research

Wong, J. M. S., Liu, P. H. C., & Yip, C. W. H. (2025). Navigating the digital shift: Early childhood educators' attitudes towards generative artificial intelligence. In E. C. K. Cheng (Ed.), *Innovating education with AI* (pp. 87–97). Springer Nature. https://doi.org/10.1007/978-981-96-4952-5_6

Index

S. Papadakis (ed.), *AI Applications in Preschool and Primary Education*, Advances in Artificial Intelligence in Education 5, https://doi.org/10.1007/978-3-032-17190-0

The manufacturer's authorised representative in the EU is Springer Nature Customer Service Centre GmbH, Europaplatz 3, 69115 Heidelberg, Germany. If you have any concerns regarding our products, please contact ProductSafety@springernature.com

Printed and bound by CPI Group (UK) Ltd, Croydon, CR0 4YY
21/09/2026
02219988-0008